A VICTORIAN
SURGEON

James Fitzjames Fraser West, surgeon, LSA, MRCS, FRCS (1833–83) in the 1860s. Source: JFF West Archive.

A VICTORIAN SURGEON

A Biography of

JAMES FITZJAMES FRASER WEST 1833–83

BIRMINGHAM SURGEON

GERALDINE M GOODMAN

BREWIN BOOKS

WES

First published by
Brewin Books Ltd, 56 Alcester Road,
Studley, Warwickshire B80 7LG in 2007
www.brewinbooks.com

ISBN: 978-1-85858-412-6 (Paperback)
ISBN: 978-1-85858-413-3 (Hardback)

A Cataloguing in Publication Record
for this title is available from the British Library

Typeset in Baskerville
Printed in Great Britain by
Cromwell Press Ltd.

CONTENTS

DEDICATION   ix
ACKNOWLEDGEMENTS   x
PREFACE   xi
LIST OF ILLUSTRATIONS   xii
SIMPLIFIED FAMILY TREE   xvi

CHAPTER ONE   1
Roots – 'Aromatic Bermondsey'   1
Fraser family   6
'Mr Fraser requests'   8
Schooling   10
James Fraser – 'a slight man, of small stature'   12

CHAPTER TWO   15
Education and Training   16
John Flint South – 'easily roused to wrath'   18
Medical student – 'an unexploded torpedo cast loose from its moorings'   21
*Astley Cooper's accounts – 'two male and two female from
    Murphy 50/8/0'*   27
'The art of surgery'   30
St Thomas' Hospital nurse, 1853 – 'a sizzie for a nurse'   33
Aspiring doctors – 'for many, dreams of success failed to materialise'   35
'By examination'   37
The right sort of background   41

CHAPTER THREE   43
Birmingham – from town to second city   43
Medical institutions in Birmingham   45
'The insidious intrusion of malignant dissenters'   46
The duties of residential medical officers   48
'Queen's Hospital Scandal'   52
'One of those disasters which annihilate hope'   56
'Your professional attainments everything I could wish for'   59

'Null and void'	61
'Fustian and inconsequential nonsense'	65
Resolution in compromise	67
'Birmingham Duelling Pistols; Out twelve times but, as yet, unfired'	71
Recovery of Queen's College	72
Queen's Hospital	75
Hospital conditions	79
Attitudes towards patients	83
Bedside manner	84
'Persons of dissolute character'	87
Broth and beef tea	90
'Gun shot case doing fairly well'	93
Listerism – 'Only fools would ignore it'	95
CHAPTER FOUR	103
The fragility of life	103
Emily Brontë – 'no poisoning doctor'	104
Preventing disease	106
'Such is the history of this poor girl'	107
Bleeding	108
Medicinal use of coffee and tobacco	112
Blisters	113
Acupressure	114
Homœopathy	115
Developing expertise	117
Contributions to the Surgical History of Syphilis	119
'Copious notes'	123
Female practitioners	124
Vivisection and experimentation	126
DISSEMINATING KNOWLEDGE	130
Midland Medical Society	130
Embracing risk: Ovariotomy – the 'bête noir' of surgical procedures	138
Other abdominal procedures	143
Pathological specimens and cases of special pathological interest	145
Saving limbs	148
CANCER	156
Oral cancer – 'a capital new lip'	160
Identifying and defining cancer	165

CHAPTER FIVE   170
Marriage   170
Incomes   173
Yorkshire land and property   177
Sarah – 'free from control of husband'   180
Income from rents and coal   181
Social standing   186
Servants and other living expenses   190
Transport   192
Civic Gospel   194
Clubs and Societies   199
Birmingham Medical Benevolent Society   200
British Medical Association   205
International Medical Congress, London, 1881   207
West and his circle   214
Professional circles   214
Birmingham Medical Institute   218
Non-medical societies and festivals   223
THE ARTS   224
Music   224
Visual arts   228
Languages, ancient and modern   231
Literature   232
Birmingham Dramatic Club   235
"By medicine life may be prolonged"   241
The last four months   247
Son, husband and father   253
Walter Sellers West   254
Friends   257
Displeasure   259
Sarah – wife   262

EPILOGUE   264
Executors   264
Other friends and family   266
Bereavement   267
Issue   275
Amy Valentine   276

John Frederick   277
Gertrude   278
Conrad Kershaw   281
Constance Margery   283

DIARY OF JAMES FITZJAMES FRASER WEST,   288
    JANUARY, 1883 – APRIL, 1883

APPENDIX   314
William Sands Cox   314
John Birt Davies   314
Joseph Sampson Gamgee   316
Thomas Pretious Heslop   316
Oliver Pemberton   317
George Jordan Lloyd   318
Robert Lawson Tait   318

BIBLIOGRAPHY   321

DEDICATION

*Charlotte A Goodman, Penelope J Goodman, daughters,
and Patricia P Style, sister-in-law.*

ACKNOWLEDGEMENTS

The private archive of James Fitzjames Fraser West excepted, the fruition of my work has been made possible thanks to the generosity of family, friends and professionals employed in numerous libraries, archives and medical institutions. Special thanks are due to Robert Arnott, Director of the Centre for the History of Medicine at the University of Birmingham, for the support and encouragement he has given me in the realisation of this book. Janet Barson, librarian, Elaine Simpson and the rest of the team at the Birmingham Medical Institute allowed me free access to their extensive archive and extended a warm welcome to me on every occasion. I am also grateful to staff in the Departments of Local Studies and Science and Medicine in Birmingham Central Library as well as to City Archivists who have helped me in my endeavours.

My greatest debt, though, is to family and friends who encouraged me in this enterprise. Four – my daughter, Charlotte Anne Goodman; sister-in-law, Patricia Pauline Style; and friends, Mary Jean Riordan and Eva Hannah Wishart – willingly gave their time as proof-readers. My daughter, Penelope Goodman, university lecturer in Roman History by profession, rapidly developed expertise in deciphering West's handwriting while helping me make sense of diary entries written in Italy. This, in turn, enabled her to unlock other words hitherto abandoned as undecipherable from elsewhere in the diary. She has been a patient IT coach whenever I have needed one and has been responsible for setting up the JFF West diary online project. Patricia Style's mastery of genealogy has been at my service whenever I have asked for it. She has spent days with me in the libraries, archives and graveyards of Yorkshire as well as some without me. I am particularly grateful to my husband, Colin, who has rescued me from numerous IT crises and has tutored me on scanning and other IT mysteries.

Advice on medical matters has been generously given by Christopher Gardner-Thorpe MD FRCP FACP, Harold Ellis CBE DM MCh FRCS, John Kirkup MD MA FRCS Dip. Hist. Med. and Leon D Abrams MS ChB FRCS. For advice on Victorian pharmaceutical issues I have been assisted by Peter Homan FR Pharm S.

PREFACE

In 1991, following the death of my step-mother, Constance Margery West, I found a number of deed boxes containing family archive. It came as no surprise. Numerous stories about my step-mother's family had filtered down to me over the years. I had been proudly told that James Fitzjames Fraser West (1833–83), grandfather of Constance, was the illegitimate son of James Fraser, the publisher. On the Yorkshire side of the family, documents dating back to the reign of Queen Elizabeth I had survived. My father's scholarly efforts in deciphering some of these texts had not gone unnoticed.

The removal of the archive to my own house sparked a renewed interest in James West and his family. He soon became one of thirty-three Birmingham hospital doctors I studied in the mid-1990s for an MA in English Local History at the University of Birmingham. From the start, I believed his life was sufficiently interesting in its own right to justify writing a biographical account of it. This is the result. I have set West's life in the context of Birmingham's medical professionals and that of his family and personal friends. In many ways, West was a typical hospital surgeon and it is hoped that the reconstruction of his life, patchy though it is, will shed light on the life-styles and interests of other Birmingham professionals and of those from elsewhere.

LIST OF ILLUSTRATIONS

James Fitzjames Fraser West, surgeon, LSA, MRCS, FRCS (1833–83)   ii
   in the 1860s. Source: JFF West Archive.

Mary West (1811–87), mother of James Fitzjames Fraser West, ca.1880.   2
   Source: JFF West Archive.

St George's Road, Southwark, London in 1819. Mary West's house,   3
   number 50, was situated on the southern side of the road. It can be seen
   on the corner of Ely Place and Prospect Place. Source: Fourth edition
   Richard Horwood's map of London. Scale 26 inches to the mile.

Terraced housing on St George's Road, Southwark in 2002.   4
   Author's photograph.

The Fraserians. Clockwise from centre back: William Maginn, Mahony, Gleig,   8
   Sir E Brydges, Carlyle, Cunningham, D'Orsey, Mair, Brewster, Theo. Hook,
   Lockhart, Grafton, Croker, James Fraser (centre front), Jerdan, Dunlop, Galt,
   Hogg, Coleridge, Ainsworth, Macnish, Serg. Murphy, Churchill, Thackery,
   Percival Banks, Southey, Barry Cornwall. Source: By kind permission
   University of Birmingham Library.

The invitations sent by James Fraser in 1835. Source: JFF West Archive.   9

Davidge Terrace, Kennington, London in 2002. One or more of these   11
   houses was used by Dr Pinches for his 'celebrated' school.
   Author's photograph.

Old operating theatre, St Thomas' Hospital, London. By kind permission   19
   The Old Operating Theatre Museum and Herb Garret.

John Flint South (1707–1882) MRCS; FRCS. Surgeon to St Thomas'   20
   Hospital, London. Source: Wellcome Library, London.

St Thomas' Hospital. 1840. Source: Wellcome Library, London.   20

George Jordan Lloyd (1854–1913) MRCS; LSA; FRCS; MD.ChB; MSc   36
   West's successor at Queen's Hospital. Source: History of the Birmingham
   School of Medicine.

Sword-stick engraved with the words JAMES F WEST MRCS. The stick dates   36
   from between 1854 and 1867 – after West had gained the Membership,
   and before he achieved the Fellowship, of the Royal College of Surgeons.'

Queen's College, Paradise Street, Birmingham, 1873. Source: By kind   43
   permission Birmingham Central Library.

Thomas Pretious Heslop (1823–85) FRCP; MD ca.1865. Source: By kind permission Special Collections, University of Birmingham. — 49

William Sands Cox FRCS, FRS (1801–75) and John Birt Davies MD (1799–1878). Source: William Sands Cox & the Birmingham Medical School. — 53

James Fitzjames Fraser West (1833–83) LSA, MRCS, FRCS & Joseph Sampson Gamgee (1828–86) MRCS, FRS Ed. – West's rival in the election dispute. Sources: JFF West Archive & by kind permission Special Collections, University of Birmingham. — 54

Silver Inkstand inscribed with the words, 'presented to James F West Esq. by the students of Queens' College Hospital as a mark of their appreciation of his valuable services to that Institution. October, 1857.' In private ownership. — 63

Marble Clock (H:35, W:27, D:15cms). engraved with the words, 'presented to JF West Esq. by the students of Queen's College Hospital 1857.' In private ownership. — 63

Staff of Queen's Hospital, Birmingham, 1861. Back row from left to right: Joseph Sampson Gamgee, David Malins, James Fitzjames Fraser West, Balthazar Walter Foster, Thomas Furneaux Jordan, John St Swithin Wilders and front Willoughby Francis Wade, William Sands Cox, John Manle Sutton, Rev WH Poulten. Source: By kind permission Birmingham Central Library. — 75

Queen's Hospital, Bath Row, Birmingham in 1873 after the new detached fever wing was opened. Source: The History of the Birmingham School of Medicine. — 76

Robert Lawson Tait (1845–99) MRCS; FRCS; LRCP; LRCS Edin. Source: By kind permission Special Collections, University of Birmingham. — 86

James Fitzjames Fraser West ca.1864, the year of his marriage. Source: JFF West Archive. — 89

Diagrams to illustrate West's first paper in the Birmingham Medical Review, 1872. Source: By kind permission of the General Committee of the Birmingham Medical Institute. — 122

Dissecting Room, Queen's College ca.1880. Source: By kind permission Special Collections, University of Birmingham. — 143

Men's ward, Queen's Hospital in 1899. Source: By kind permission of the University of Birmingham Library. — 150

The Operating Theatre at Queen's Hospital in 1899. Source: By kind permission of the University of Birmingham Library. — 150

Oliver Pemberton (1825–97) FRCS England & Edin. Source: By kind   152
    permission Special Collections, University of Birmingham.

Sarah Hammond West (née Sellers), 1844–1910, wife of James Fitzjames   171
    Fraser West ca.1864, the year of her marriage. Source: JFF West Archive.

House of James Fitzjames Fraser West & his wife, Sarah, on the Hagley   187
    Road, Edgbaston, Birmingham. It was numbered 117 in his lifetime
    but was re-numbered 247 shortly after he died in 1883.
    Source: JFF West Archive.

Sarah Hammond West with three of her children ca.1881.   188
    Source: JFF West Archive.

The marker shows the location of West's house on the Hagley Road,   189
    Edgbaston in 1923. Source: By kind permission Birmingham
    Central Library.

Surgeon-Major George Yates (1824–1907). Friend and colleague of   204
    JFF West. Source: By kind permission Special Collections, University
    of Birmingham.

Statue of William Harvey, Folkstone. Author's photograph 2005.   211

A group photograph taken at the International Medical Congress, London,   212
    1881. West's head is encircled. Source: Wellcome Library, London.

The survival of this ticket for the George Dawson Public Memorial   216
    Ceremony in 1881 strongly suggests that the Wests were amongst
    those gathered to remember this remarkable man.
    Source: JFF West Archive.

The Birmingham Medical Institute in the 1960s. Reproduced by the kind   222
    permission of the General Committee of the Birmingham
    Medical Institute.

Programme for the concert attended by West on 6 March, 1883.   227
    Source: By kind permission Birmingham Central Library.

Page from the diary of James Fitzjames Fraser West, April, 1883.   230
    Source: JFF West Archive.

Jump Farm. Source: By kind permission Barnsley Archives.   235
    Copyright of Arthur Clayton.

The solicitor, Samuel Dinsdale Balden (b.1865) photographed in 1895   236
    during his time in office as a councillor. Born in Acock's Green
    in the same year as West's firstborn son, he was later prosecuted for
    fraud. Source: By kind permission Birmingham Central Library.

Charles Green (1844–1906), manufacturer of jewellery, friend and executor   238
    of JFF West. Source: JFF West Archive.

James Fitzjames Fraser West ca.1880. Source: By kind permission Special   241
    Collections, University of Birmingham.

Walter Newton Fisher, (b.1844), friend and executor of James Fitzjames   242
    Fraser West. Source: By kind permission University of Birmingham Library.

Roseneath, Reservoir Road, Ladywood, home of Mary West and   257
    Fanny de la Hunt. Photographed by the author in 2002.

Mrs Katarina Green in 1886. Source: JFF West Archive.   260

Elizabeth (Lizzie) Silverwood Lorraine. Source: JFF West Archive.   266

The West family help out with hay-making in Yorkshire, ca.1900.   267
    Source: JFF West Archive.

The West family in the company of friends and relatives in the eighteen   268
    nineties. Sarah, widow of James Fitzjames Fraser West is seated just
    to the left of centre with most of her own family to her right.
    Source: JFF West Archive.

Bertram Evelyn West (1881–95), son of James Fitzjames Fraser West.   271
    Source: JFF West Archive.

Amy Valentine Redfern (née West); 1877–1937 in 1906.   276
    Source: JFF West Archive.

Barbara Joyce Redfern (seated) and Constance Margery West with their   277
    grandmother's maid in 1907. Source: JFF West Archive.

John Frederick West with Conrad Kershaw West's widow Ellen, in the 1930s.   278
    Source: JFF West Archive.

Gertrude West (1872–1951) ca.1918. Source: JFF West Archive.   279

Conrad Kershaw West ca.1900. Source: JFF West Archive.   282

Constance Margery with her father, Conrad Kershaw West in 1911.   283
    Source: JFF West Archive.

Constance Margery West, affectionately known as 'Margery' all of her life   284
    in the 1940s. Source: JFF West Archive.

Church of the Ascension, Hall Green, Birmingham – burial place of   285
    James Fitzjames Fraser West and most of his family. Photographed
    by the author in 1999.

SIMPLIFIED FAMILY TREE

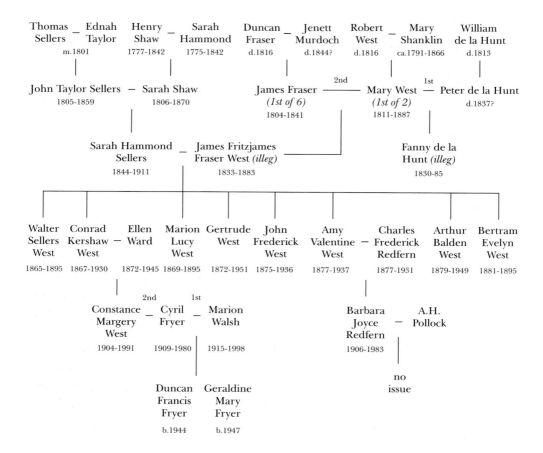

CHAPTER ONE

James Fitzjames Fraser West died an affluent and successful man in 1883. He was forty-nine and lived in Birmingham's most salubrious suburb, Edgbaston. By the time he died, he had been Professor of Anatomy and of Clinical Surgery at Birmingham's medical college, Senior Surgeon at one of the town's two general hospitals, Consulting Surgeon to Birmingham's Dental Hospital and a General Practitioner. He had also occupied prominent positions in a variety of local medical clubs and societies. West's success was not exceptional amongst his circle, but his background was.

Roots – 'Aromatic Bermondsey'

Life began for James West in London, south of the river Thames. Like his half-sister Fanny de la Hunt, who was some three years his senior, he was an illegitimate child. West predeceased Fanny by two years and his mother by four, but he remained physically and emotionally close to them both throughout his life. Fanny was christened at St George the Martyr in Southwark on 15 February, 1837 and James at St Mary Magdalene on 25 June of the same year. James was four at the time of his christening and his sister seven. Christening children as opposed to babies was not uncommon in the first half of the nineteenth century although the choice of 1837 was probably taken to secure an official record of birth before Civil Registration commenced on 1 July of that year. The latter phenomenon has been observed across the country by present-day genealogists. The demand for christenings on 25 June was so great that the address given on the parish register is simply 'St George.' For the earliest record of James' full address, we must look instead, to the 1841 census, where it appears as 50, Prospect Place, St George's Road, Southwark.

Census reports reveal that neither Mary West, mother of Fanny and James, nor her offspring were consistent in their response to enumerators' questions about their places of birth. In the census of 1851, for instance, Mary West told the enumerator the birthplace of her son, James, was Camberwell. In the 1861 census, James West himself says he was born in Peckham, Surrey, and his sister, Fanny, who was living with him at the time, is described by her half-brother as having been born in Southwark. Mary

Mary West (1811–87), mother of James Fitzjames Fraser West, ca.1880.
Source: JFF West Archive.

West's own baptismal record has survived but, like that of her son, lacks an address. The ceremony took place at St George the Martyr in Southwark in 1811 and she is described on the certificate as daughter of Robert and Mary West. The only other known child born to Robert and Mary West was a girl, Harriet. The paucity of clues that shed light on Robert West and his wife means we can only surmise as to their social standing. Robert West was described as a Leather Dresser at the time of Harriet's baptism in 1816 and the family are recorded in Parish Registers as living in Bermondsey New Road – a road which was to be modified and re-named Tower Bridge Road in 1902.

Born, the second illegitimate child of a woman whose own father was a Leather Dresser, it is tempting to think James West must have been a boy of humble origins. That little is known of Mary West's parents is itself enough to lend credence to the theory. Robert West's name certainly does not appear in contemporary trade directories although directories, particular early ones, do not provide definitive lists of all who practised a particular trade or profession. Far from it.

Nineteenth century accounts of Bermondsey and Southwark describe the area in which the West family resided as the most foul-smelling of any in London. The stench emanating from the district's leather industry, reached its zenith during the nineteenth century. Butchers in the City of London had first established the right to dump hides in Bermondsey in the year 1392, and the development of a tanning industry had been a natural consequence. The juxtaposition of oak trees and a plentiful supply of water allowed the tanning industry to flourish. The quality of the air in this part of London was described by a reporter writing for *The People* in 1906 in the following uncomplimentary terms. 'In aromatic Bermondsey, within a stone's throw of London Bridge, there is an old-world market-place.[1] It is' he goes on 'without exception the smelliest place in the county of London.'

Edgbaston, the Birmingham suburb developed by the Lords Calthorpe for the town's elite, and home of Robert West's grandson James in the last eleven years of his life, was in marked contrast to 'aromatic Bermondsey.' Referred to by some as Birmingham's 'Belgravia,' Edgbaston was located not only on high ground, up-wind of the town's evil smelling industrial heartland, but was expensive and exclusively residential. Even if Robert West were self employed, a man who supported himself from, and who lived in close proximity to, London's leather industry was unlikely to have commanded the recognition his grandson acquired through an Edgbaston address, professional status and the affluence that came with it.

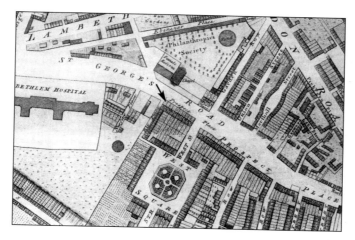

St George's Road, Southwark, London in 1819. Mary West's house, number 50, was situated on the southern side of the road. It can be seen on the corner of Ely Place and Prospect Place. Source: Fourth edition Richard Horwood's map of London. Scale 26 inches to the mile.

---

[1] The market referred to was the Leather and Skin Market built in 1833, the year of JFF West's birth, at a cost of £50,000.

Nevertheless, the surviving Georgian terraces along St George's Road in the vicinity of Prospect Place are elegant as are the equally genteel squares behind them. To brand the road and its properties as inferior would defy the evidence. Indeed, the Descriptive Map of London Poverty published in 1889 by Charles Booth (1840–1916), marks both Prospect Place and St George's Road as 'well to do, middle class.'

Why James West's mother, Mary, bore two illegitimate children sired by two different fathers remains a mystery. Fanny's father was Peter de la Hunt who was described on her death certificate in 1885 as a deceased half-pay army officer. The latter was a fabrication [2] but there is nothing to suggest his name was fabricated. Attempts to trace him on army lists have not borne fruit, but he has appeared in another source. Peter de la Hunt's name is listed in contemporary London directories between 1813 and 1820 as a timber merchant at a business address on the river's south bank at 85 Shad Thames. Given that the nineteenth century tanning industry depended on regular supplies of tree bark it may not be fanciful to suggest that his trade brought him business from individuals like Robert West or, if he was not self-employed, his employer.

In 1813, Peter de la Hunt's name is directly above that of William de la Hunt who was also described as a timber merchant. William could have

Terraced housing on St George's Road, Southwark in 2002.
Author's photograph.

---

[2]   A father who, by the nature of his occupation, would be sent overseas or even perish in some
       far distant land would have been an attractive proposition to anyone hoping to keep a father's
       identity hidden.

been uncle, brother or father of Peter de la Hunt but his disappearance from the directory for good after 1813 makes father seem the most likely. De la Hunt emerges from the shadows again in France in the late 1830s when a bachelor, of that name, died intestate in Paris. Fortunately, he left a brief written account of how he wished his estate to be dispersed after his death. It was accepted as being in his hand by the courts thanks to an affidavit signed by his friend, Frederick Bestley.[3] De la Hunt made no mention of Mary West or her child, Fanny, in his self-styled will, but the document does provide a clue which supports the theory that he was the father of Mary West's first-born child. He is described in the document as a former resident of Bermondsey New Road, London, which, as we have seen, is the address which appears on the baptismal record of Mary's sister, Harriet. It is fair to assume that there was unlikely to have been more than one individual of that name living in Bermondsey New Road at the same time as Mary West and her family.

Mary West's decision to use de la Hunt as the surname of her first-born suggests she was content, or even proud, to allow the identity of the child's father to be known. The same is true of her second-born, James Fitzjames Fraser West. It was known from the beginning of this investigation into the life of West that his natural father was James Fraser (1804–41), the London publisher and bookseller. His name appeared in London trade directories for the first time in 1830 and stayed there until his death in 1841. Fraser undoubtedly did have close links with those who supplied leather although who those individuals were is not known.

One document, kept by the family, shows that James Fraser left money in trust for his son.[4] There is no way of knowing if the provision made in it constitutes the only contribution made by Fraser towards the upkeep of his son, or whether it was a part. The document in question is an itemised bill drawn up by Mr WW Burton, the solicitor acting for the Fraser family, and is dated 1854, the year of James FF West's majority. It indicates that James Fitzjames was the beneficiary of investments set up by his father. A sum of £20 was to be advanced immediately to cover some of the costs incurred by James FF West for his medical training, but apart from a further reference to dividends, the document leaves the reader guessing as to the exact value of the provision. Mr Burton's account covers a period of just over a month and is for a total of £11/15/–, a sizeable sum if charged to administer a paltry Trust fund.

---

[3]   Last Will and Testament of Peter de la Hunt. Probate 11/1896.
[4]   James Fitzjames Fraser West private archive, referred to as JFF West Archive in future.

Whether or not James West knew the identity of his father is not known for certain. A number of clues suggest he did. The deliberate use, by his mother, of James Fitzjames Fraser in her son's name, hardly comprises a cover up. The prefix 'Fitz' had, in any case, been in use as an indication of illegitimate status for some time. Co-authors of *Family Fortunes, Men and Women of the English Middle Class 1750–1850*, Leonore Davidoff and Catherine Hall [5] found that children born out of wedlock in the early decades of the nineteenth century were accepted more readily than was the norm in Victorian England. Even so, the situation Mary West found herself in cannot have been an easy one. Family, friends and neighbours would all have been aware of her marital status. Her move to Birmingham in the mid-1850s, would have provided her with the perfect opportunity to put her past behind her. She seized that chance. Known in Birmingham as Mrs West, widow, she appears to have kept up the pretence with perfect success during her own lifetime and beyond it. When her son, James, died in 1883, Sarah, James' widow and daughter in law of Mary West was oblivious of his illegitimate status. She remained ignorant of the fact for a further seven years.

Fraser family

James Fraser, father of James Fitzjames Fraser West, was well known. His family originated from Inverness in the Scottish Highlands. Duncan Fraser, father of James Fraser, was highly successful. He is listed in early nineteenth century London Trade Directories as a 'taylor.' The entries show, not only that he was self-employed, but they provide us with an address – 7 Titchfield Street. Situated in the parish of St Marylebone, Titchfield Street was in a prosperous part of London. The property served as the family's business premises and their home.[6] Exactly why they chose to reside on the premises is not known but it was unlikely to have been for reasons of economy. Duncan Fraser's last will and testament reveals that, by the time he died in 1816, he owned no less than twenty-seven London houses in addition to the Titchfield Road property.[7]

Parish records show that Duncan Fraser married twice. His second marriage, to Jenett Murdoch, took place in 1803, and James Fraser, born in 1804, was the first-born of that union. Over the course of the next ten years a further five children were born to the Frasers. The census of 1841

---

[5]   Davidoff Leonore & Catherine Hall, *Family Fortunes. Men and Women of the English Middle Class 1750–1850* (London: Routledge, 1987).

[6]   The addresses which appear on the birth certificates of Duncan Fraser's children are the same as that given as his business address in the trade directories.

[7]   Last Will and Testament of Duncan Fraser, Probate 1816, 11/2031.

shows, not only that Duncan's widow and family were living an affluent lifestyle, but that all six children had survived into adult life. At a time when annual mortality rates in the most impoverished areas of big towns and cities stood at around 26 per 1,000, the high survival rate of the Frasers' offspring alone would have signified a life free of want.

Their son, James Fraser, was the first to die. He wrote his last will and testament on 17 August, 1841, as he lay dying at his mother's house in Argyll Street, St James, Westminster. The house was one of four situated in Argyll Street that had been owned by his father in his lifetime. James Fraser normally lived at his business premises in 215, Regent St, Westminster, but he appears to have inherited two of the Argyll Street properties in his own right. According to his will he owned numbers twenty-three and twenty-four Argyll Street. One, he states at the time of writing, was leased to a Mrs Allen and the other was occupied by Dr Forbes.

Drawn up only a matter of two months before he died in October, 1841, the will is more detailed than many. It contains interesting clues about the family, as well as giving an indication of their wealth. Money bequeathed by James Fraser to his mother and siblings suggests, for instance, that the family were close. None of the Fraser 'children' had married by 1841, and both census and will show that, with the exception of James Fraser, none had dispersed. This is surprising since the youngest, Duncan, was already twenty-seven years of age.

The chief beneficiaries of James Fraser's will were his siblings, and what he bequeathed to them was to be shared equally among them. He left all five equal use of, or the proceeds from, the two houses owned by him in Argyll Street. He also bequeathed them what he describes as the share and interest to which he was entitled in reversion or remainder expectant on the decease of his mother in the sum of ten thousand pounds 3% bank annuities. Fraser also left £415 in specified sums to a number of different individuals – his mother, his assistant, George William Nickisson,[8] and various servants among them. There is no mention of Mary West or her son James in the will but we know, of course, that this does not reflect a failure to provide for them on his part.

As editor and publisher of the magazine founded by his namesake, Hugh Fraser,[9] James Fraser was a familiar and respected figure in literary circles. The magazine, officially named *Town and Country*, soon became

---

[8] GW Nickisson succeeded James Fraser as publisher of Fraser's Magazine.
[9] Hugh Fraser has been described variously as 'the notorious socialite,' a 'bohemian,' 'barrister' and 'merchant.'

The Fraserians. Clockwise from centre back: William Maginn, Mahony, Gleig, Sir E Brydges, Carlyle, Cunningham, D'Orsey, Mair, Brewster, Theo. Hook, Lockhart, Grafton, Croker, James Fraser (centre front), Jerdan, Dunlop, Galt, Hogg, Coleridge, Ainsworth, Macnish, Serg. Murphy, Churchill, Thackery, Percival Banks, Southey, Barry Cornwall. Source: By kind permission University of Birmingham Library.

known simply as '*Fraser's Magazine*.' James Fraser was also the figurehead of the illustrious circle of intellectuals known as *The Fraserians* [10] and can be seen in the foreground of the well-known cartoon of the group. Fraser's face is seen in profile. The artist, Daniel Maclise (1806–70), sketched Fraser seated with his back to the observer so that a book which bears the artist's name on its cover, though partially concealed inside the tails of his coat, is nevertheless clearly visible.

'Mr Fraser requests'

It is impossible to say how much involvement there was between James Fraser and Mary West after the arrival of their son, James Fitzjames, but the chance survival of one item proves that there was some contact between the two families. The writer has been fortunate enough to inherit a selection of family documents and memorabilia from her late step-mother, Constance Margery Fryer (née West), the last descendant of James West. Two invitation cards sent out by James Fraser are among them. Both concern an invitation to Harriet, the sister of Mary West. One is addressed to Harriet in her own right, and the

---

10   More will be said about the group in the final chapter.

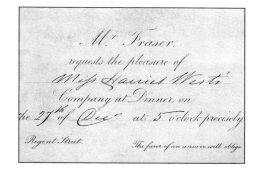

The invitations sent by James Fraser in 1835. Source: JFF West Archive.

other is an indirect invitation to Harriet via her mother and says 'Mr Fraser requests the pleasure of *Mrs West's Junior*'s Company at Dinner on *Sunday* the *27th*, of *Dec r.* at 5 o'clock precisely'. The year of the invitation was not stated, but a look at the years in which Sunday fell on 27 December suggests that it was probably 1835. Harriet West was nineteen years of age in 1835, an age during which time she would have been both a 'junior' and eligible for an invitation of this sort in her own right. Another item the author discovered in the *JFF West Archive* was a bound copy of Fraser's Magazine dating from January, 1837 to the time of James Fraser's death in October, 1841. It does not prove that Mary West maintained contact with James Fraser, but it does imply she remained interested in him and his affairs.

Mary West's father may have been a Bermondsey leather dresser and her children illegitimate but the census of both 1841 and of 1851 reveal that her circumstances were comfortable. Her house, 50, Prospect Place, St George's Road, Southwark was, as we have seen, spacious and was set in a fine Georgian terrace. The twenty-five year old Mary West described herself as living on 'independent means' in the 1841 census. By 1851, the twenty one year old Fanny De La Hunt was also describing herself as being of 'independent means.' James Fitzjames, recorded as we might expect, as a medical student in 1851, enjoyed the luxury of consuming the family's income rather than contributing towards it.

Nothing is known about the educational background of Mary West and little about that of Fanny. A sampler worked by Fanny in 1837, during the eighth year of her life survives, but there is no way of knowing whether it was worked at home or in school. Fanny was certainly at home on the night of the census of 1841 as were the rest of the family – her mother Mary West, her aunt Harriet, and half-brother, James. The census also reveals that two other individuals were in residence. One was Caroline Cunnington whose occupation is not recorded, and the other was Sophia Woodruff, a governess. Whether Fanny, then thirteen years of age, and James, who was seven, were both receiving lessons at home in 1841 is unknown.

At the very least, Mary, Harriet and their mother, Mary Anna West before them, were literate. James Fraser sent written invitations to their home, after all, and he is unlikely to have formed close relationships with ignorant and ill-educated women. Mary may even have forged a relationship with James Fraser through having been a member of one of London's literary circles herself. If she was an educated woman, there is no reason to suppose she would have denied her daughter an education when she had the means to procure it. As a young, single and independent woman she may even have considered her daughter's education more important than many of her contemporaries did.

Lack of educational options and opportunities were the most likely obstacles to have been faced by those who sought an education for daughters in the 1830s and 40s. Educational establishments would have been plentiful for James, but schools for girls were virtually non-existent in the first half of the nineteenth century. It is known for certain that James attended at least two schools and, if his education was placed in the hands of a governess at all, it was almost certainly restricted to the early years. Fanny, on the other hand, may have depended for her education on Miss Woodruff entirely. Whatever form her education took, the two sources [11] which shed light on Fanny De La Hunt in adult life show that she not only enjoyed the cultural interests and pursuits of middle class life, but that she mixed on equal terms with educated people.

Schooling

One of the bonuses of researching the lives of professionals is that source material is more plentiful than for many other groups. Educational institutions – schools, medical colleges and universities alike – kept records. In some cases, their archives have survived when the institutions themselves have ceased to exist. Many doctors worked in institutions themselves as well as belonging to societies and clubs. They published professional papers and were the subject of obituaries. It is also possible to find material which provides information about the medical training and

---

[11] The Will of Fanny De La Hunt, Birmingham City Archives, and the last diary of James Fitzjames Fraser West. (JFF West Archive).

Davidge Terrace, Kennington, London in 2002. One or more of these houses was used by Dr Pinches for his 'celebrated' school. Author's photograph.

schooling of individuals in other sources. The magazine *Edgbastonia*,[12] for instance, provides us with an account, albeit somewhat flawed, of JFF West's schooling and his medical training.

According to *Edgbastonia*, the first school West attended was Hadleigh School in Essex.[13] Corroboration of this can not be found and it is assumed to be in error. There was an established and well known preparatory school in the neighbouring town of Rayleigh though. It was described as a 'classical and commercial school' and boasted a good reputation. Its staff, with the Reverend Pilkington at its head, consisted of a school master and eight other teachers in 1851. The 1851 census lists thirty-six boarders, although the school had day pupils too. If this was, indeed, the school West attended, he is likely to have been a boarder. We do not know when James West first started school, but his presence at the family home on the day of the 1841 census intimates that his school-days commenced after his seventh birthday.

Edgbastonia describes West's second school as 'the celebrated school of Dr Pincher, of Kennington.'[14] Again, the source is not entirely reliable.

---

[12] *Edgbastonia* was a magazine devoted to the lives and interests of Edgbaston society. The obituary is to be found in the July issue of 1883; iii: pp.98–99. (Birmingham Central Library, hereafter BCL).

[13] *Edgbastonia* states that JFF West spent most of his school days at Hadleigh in Essex. 'Hadleigh' is almost certainly an error. The Local Studies Dept. of Southend-on-Sea Central Library could find no trace of a school which could have provided the right sort of education in Hadleigh, but they did trace a likely school in the nearby town of Rayleigh.

[14] Ibid., p.98.

Efforts to corroborate these details revealed that it was Dr Conrad Pinches rather than Pincher who ran a school in Kennington, and other sources [15] have confirmed that this was, indeed, the school attended by James FF West. One is an inventory compiled by West's granddaughter, Constance, a women who had inherited the worthy head master's first name at one step removed. A portrait of the 'celebrated' Dr Pinches had been passed onto her by her father, Conrad Kershaw West. She described him as the head of her grandfather's school and added that he had been a founder member of the College of Preceptors – the first institution to provide training and set examinations for teachers. Pinches' interest in, and membership of, an institution of this sort tends to indicate that he was a forward-looking educationist. Constance went on to explain that her grandfather had named his second-born son, Conrad, after Conrad Pinches. Another source, a book prize won by West, provides us with the name of the school or, at least, one of its houses – Clarendon House.

Various sources, obituaries included, reveal that West was a well-read all rounder. His medical training, qualifications and achievements will be discussed in a later chapter, but he was also accomplished in other quite diverse fields. *Edgbastonia* states that West acquired, 'a complete mastership of Latin and several modern languages' at the school he attended in Essex. The prize awarded to West at Dr Pinches' school was for Greek. The magazine and other sources refer to West's interest in the theatre and to Shakespeare in particular. He was, as *Edgbastonia* correctly informs us 'a leading member of the Shakespeare Dramatic Club.'[16]

James Fraser – 'a slight man, of small stature'

As we have seen, James Fraser, the father of James Fitzjames was well-known in literary circles, and a number of obituaries were printed in journals around the country on the occasion of his death in 1841. All testify, if a little too effusively, to his distinguished literary skills. James Fraser may have taken an active interest in the education of his son and fostered in him a taste for literature, but it seems unlikely. Fraser was in poor health for the last five years of his life and was dead well before his son reached his ninth birthday.

James Fraser's death at the age of thirty-seven in 1841 was hastened, some believed, by the effects of head injuries he suffered in 1836 when he

---

[15] A description of a portrait of Pinches which is in an inventory belonging to the JFF West Archive, contemporary Directories and an inscription in a book West was given as a prize while at the school of Dr Pinches.

[16] *Edgbastonia*; 1883; iii: p.97. (BCL).

was assaulted by the Berkeley brothers. The perpetrators of the attack, the Honourable George Charles Grantley Fitzhardinge Berkeley and the Honourable Craven Fitzhardinge Berkeley, inflicted injuries which may have led to chronic health problems. Some obituaries written on the occasion of James Fraser's death certainly claim that this was the case. James Fraser and the Berkeley brothers fought a cross action for libel on the one hand, and for assault on the other, in the Exchequer Court at Westminster on Saturday 3 December, 1836. Space does not allow for anything other than a brief account of the incident here.

Fraser had published a highly unfavourable review of a book written by Grantley Berkeley about his ancestral home, Berkeley Castle. The book was savagely criticised by its reviewer. He was quoted by the defence as having said, *'Berkeley Castle* in conception is the most impertinent, as in execution it is about the stupidest, it has ever been our misfortune to read', but that was not all. Mr Thessiger, acting for the defence, tried to excuse his clients' behaviour on the grounds that the reviewer, (believed by most to have been Dr William Maginn) had written a personal attack about the Berkeleys. He quoted the reviewer as having said that 'Mr Grantley Berkeley's mother lived with Mr Grantley Berkeley's father as his mistress, and that she had at least one child before she could induce the old and very stupid lord to marry her.'

Thanks to the court case,[17] what happened on the day of the attack and its consequences are well documented. On 3 August, 1836, the two brothers, together with a hired hit-man, assaulted Fraser, first of all with their fists, and after with a horse whip. The assailants struck during the lunch hour, a time when Fraser could be expected to be alone. James Fraser was described in the court case as 'a slight man, of small stature.' Craven Berkeley was stationed at the door of the premises to ensure that Fraser's escape route was blocked and also to prevent any passer-by from coming to the victim's assistance. Fraser suffered injuries to the hands and head as a result of the blows which rained down on him that day and, but for the intervention of a passer-by who managed to force his way past the brother posted at the doorway, may have perished.

From the account given, the attack was a ferocious one. The whip used was described as the sort used by 'rough-riders in the army, for the purpose of taming unruly horses.' Fraser was hit with both lash and butt-end of the

---

[17] Article on 'Fraser v. Berkeley and Another, and Berkeley v. Fraser' in which details of the case heard at the Exchequer Court at Westminster on Saturday 3 December, 1836 were recalled. *Fraser's Magazine*; January, 1837; pp.100–137.

whip. The extent of the attack and Fraser's injuries were verified by a number of individuals, and an account of the immediate aftermath was given by Fraser's servant, Mary Lane. Lane declared that her employer had suffered a convulsive fit after the attack. She recalled that Fraser had been confined to his room for several days as a result of his injuries and when she was asked if her employer had continued to suffer ill-health she is quoted as saying 'Yes; he is not well now, nor never has been since.' When asked how long the disfigurement caused by the injuries had lasted, Mary Lane had replied 'They were visible for a month.'

Mary West cannot have been ignorant of this incident. The case was widely reported in newspaper articles as far afield as the Fraser's old homeland, Inverness, and it was not the only episode related to the review that attracted the attention of the press. Maginn, with Hugh Fraser acting as his second, even went as far as to fight a duel with Grantley Berkeley on Friday 5 August, 1836. No-one was harmed, but three shots were fired before Hugh Fraser intervened and withdrew his principle. Maginn wrote his own account of the duel in an article in *Fraser's Magazine* [18] itself, but it was also reported elsewhere. *The Times*, for instance, had printed two articles on the event by the time it went to press on the morning of 6 August.[19] If James Fraser was providing a steady income for Mary West and her son she may well have feared for it in August, 1836.

Any support James Fraser gave Mary West during his lifetime would have been vulnerable to a number of forces but would, in any case, have ended abruptly in 1841 on his death. Mary West's continued prosperity can only have been maintained if it had been secured by James Fraser before he died or if it had emanated from another, but unknown, source. But, whatever the source, Mary West possessed the means to enable her to put her son through an educational system which was capable of preparing young men to enter the professions.

[18] William Maginn's account can be found in his article 'Defence of Fraser's Magazine in the Berkeley Affair.' *Fraser's Magazine*; January, 1837; pp.137–143.
[19] *The Times*, 'Assault on Mr Fraser,' Saturday 6 August, 1836, p 3.

CHAPTER TWO

Those entering the medical profession in the middle of the nineteenth century did so at a time when changes, which would transform medical practitioners into serious professionals, were beginning to take hold. Before this process began, the medical elites of London had both imposed, and maintained, a hierarchical tripartite system in which physicians occupied top place, surgeons the middle and apothecaries the bottom. The inherent inequalities of the tripartite system had fuelled jealousies and resentment. In the first half of the nineteenth century, training was often inadequate and examinations set by the medical bodies inappropriate. For the sick and injured, it was a time when medical intervention often did more harm than good. By the end of the nineteenth century, medical practitioners had been transformed into a group of unified professionals, who possessed expertise, and who could expect a high success rate in their endeavours to relieve and cure the sick.

James West qualified just four years before one of the most significant landmarks in the history of the medical profession – the Medical Act of 1858. The Act was the result of prolonged and bitter struggles between reformers and the London elites. The stormy, eighteen-year-long history, and sixteen abortive bills which lay behind the Act reflect the strength of opposition to reform. London elites – accustomed to the restrictive practices and monopolies which maintained their own status in the old tripartite system – proved themselves tough adversaries.

Significant though it was, most historians agree that the 1858 Act was a disappointment to the majority of medical professionals. For many, the greatest disappointment was the failure of government to make it an offence to practise without qualifications. Many practitioners believed that the reforms ascribed to the Act were already underway. Its chief outcome was, without doubt, the foundation of the General Medical Council (GMC). The GMC was given overall responsibility for the minimum entry requirements of new recruits, and was empowered with the authority to strike off practitioners found guilty of incompetence and misconduct. It was also responsible for the introduction of the medical register, which, for the first time, required all qualified medical practitioners to be registered on equal terms.

Historians are divided in their opinions about how significant these developments really were. M J Peterson [1] and Philip Elliot [2] believe that the effects of the Act made little difference. Ivan Waddington [3] on the other hand, believes that the GMC became the focus of the modern system of professional self-regulation and self-government, and that by identifying the qualified as a separate group from the unqualified, the Act helped to create medical professionalism in the United Kingdom.

On the face of it, later landmarks, like the establishment of the Conjoint Examining Board in 1884, which was given responsibility for examining students in all branches of the profession, and the Medical Act Amendment Act of 1886, which finally prohibited unqualified practice came too late to affect James West. But, like the 1858 Act, they too implemented improvements which were already underway irrespective of legislation.

Education and Training

In the first half of the nineteenth century educational establishments did little to equip boys with knowledge in subjects other than the Arts and it was a situation which was slow to change. [4] Even the most enlightened schools failed to provide any formal education in the sciences and the chances are that James West received no instruction in these subjects before he embarked on his medical training. In this respect, he would have been entirely typical. How much of a handicap this was during the days when West did his training is hard to say, but a lack of scientific knowledge was no obstacle to the examinations set by either of the Royal Colleges in the first half of the century. At that time, the examinations set by the Royal Colleges were farcical, and the qualifications they awarded, of dubious benefit. Oral examinations, conducted entirely in Latin, were the norm, and their content had little, or nothing, to do with medicine or even science.

The Society of Apothecaries, traditionally considered the most lowly of the three branches of medicine, was the first to tackle the deficiencies in its provision for new recruits to the medical profession. In 1815 it won parliamentary backing for the introduction of a number of important changes. The Apothecaries Act of that year, made it an offence to practise

[1]   MJ Peterson, *The Medical Profession in Mid-Victorian London* (Berkeley: California, 1978).
[2]   Philip Elliot, *The Sociology of the Professions* (London: Macmillan, 1972).
[3]   Ivan Waddington, *The Medical Profession in the Industrial Revolution* (Dublin: Gill and Macmillian, 1984).
[4]   Edwin Rickards, West's young colleague, bemoaned the fact that the teaching of science was still being neglected in schools in an introductory address he gave to the students of Queen's College, Birmingham in 1882. He inclined to the belief that the 'dead languages' could be sacrificed in order to make room for the sciences. Introductory Address, October, 1882. pp.6–8. (BCL).

as an apothecary without licence, and introduced a five year compulsory apprenticeship. Syllabuses were revised, and the standard required in their examinations was raised. The qualification awarded by the Society of Apothecaries – the Licentiateship – (LSA), became the first medical qualification which could be described as relevant. James West's first interest was in surgery, but like many of his contemporaries, he opted for a dual qualification – the LSA and the Royal College of Surgeons' own qualification, the Membership of the Royal College of Surgeons (MRCS). A lack of confidence in the qualifications offered by the Royal College of Physicians coupled with an obligation imposed by the College which restricted physicians to working within fifty miles radius of London, meant that most would-be surgeons preferred to acquire their knowledge of medicine from the Society of Apothecaries.

In order to satisfy the requirements demanded by the Royal College of Surgeons for membership status in the middle of the nineteenth century, medical students were required to attend a series of lectures, serve an apprenticeship with a qualified practitioner in private practice or in a hospital and pass the necessary examinations. In medical schools associated with hospitals, the best students were awarded a dressership or clerkship in the second or third year and some, like West, won both. In these roles, students learnt the art of surgery and medicine under the direction of a maestro in the operating theatres and on the wards of the country's hospitals.

Serving an apprenticeship under a relative or a family friend was a well established and popular way of gaining experience. West himself was an articled pupil of John Wilcocks Wakem (d.1865) and Dr Hooper, presumed to be Dr Robert Hooper, both of whom are listed in directories at 6, London Road, Southwark in 1854. It was probably the address of their practice. Dr Hooper worked as a general practitioner and was remembered as a resident, not of Southwark, but of Kennington, in *Edgbastonia* in West's obituary. There is nothing to suggest that either was a blood relative. The connection could have been made through Conrad Pinces, the head of West's school in Kennington, but they might just as easily have been the family's medical practitioners or their friends or both.

The reference to West's time as a pupil of Hooper appears just once, in *Edgbastonia*, but Wakem wrote a testimonial for West in 1854 [5] which has survived intact. Wakem described himself as surgeon to the Queen's Bench Prison in 1854 and gave 6, London Road as his address, but he can also be found in residence in West Square, an elegant Georgian Square, a few

---

[5] Queen's Hospital, Birmingham D/1 Part 2, L46.11 Testimonials to Mr JF West. (BCL).

metres from West's own family home in St George's Road, Southwark. He says he has known West for several years rather than all his life. Exactly when West became Wakem's pupil is not known. He used the past tense in referring to West's apprenticeship, but added that West had continued to assist him right up to the time when the testimonial was written.

West trained at St Thomas' Hospital in London. Only one of the two procedures which would transform surgery in the middle of the nineteenth century had been discovered at the time. Anæsthesia, used for the first time in Boston, USA, in 1846, caught on quickly, and was well established by the time West was in practice, but the use of antiseptic procedures during and after surgery was a thing of the future. Surgery, even straightforward or superficial surgery, was a high risk undertaking in the mid-nineteenth century. In the 1850s, infection of wounds during surgery and in the post-operative period could, and frequently did, result in death.

Statistics on post-operative mortality by John Flint South of St Thomas', illustrate the hazards of hospitalisation in the middle of the nineteenth century. The report, [6] which covers the period 1835–40 inclusive, shows that of fifty-four cases of amputation, only twenty-eight were performed for primary amputation. The remaining thirty-six were undertaken because of disease which had set in after admission to hospital. Of the patients admitted for the primary purpose of amputation, seven were of the arm, with no deaths; nine were for part of the leg, with two deaths and five were for amputation of the leg at the thigh, all of whom died. While these statistics make grim reading, it is only fair to point out that the figures recorded by South are in accordance with those reported by hospitals elsewhere.

John Flint South – 'easily roused to wrath'

West spent his years as a dresser working under the direction of John Flint South (1797–1882) a man, who, like many in his profession, had medical connections. He was born the son of an affluent Southwark druggist. His half-brother – who in later life became Sir James South, President of the Royal Astronomical Society – was also a qualified medical man. South qualified for membership of the Royal College of Surgeons in 1819, and by the time West began his training the 'maestro' was already in his mid-fifties.

---

[6] Report on *St Thomas' Hospital for the Charity Commissioners, 17 June, 1864*, p.112, HI/ST/A44/2, STHA – cited in Lindsay Patricia Granshaw's PhD thesis, *St Thomas' Hospital, London. 1850–1900* (USA: University Microfilms International, Ann Arbor, Michigan, 1981) (Wellcome Library). LP Granshaw became Baroness Northover of Cissbury in the County of West Sussex in the year 2000.

Old operating theatre, St Thomas' Hospital, London. By kind permission The Old Operating Theatre Museum and Herb Garret.

Sources which shed light on JF South, suggest that he was a conservative man, who enjoyed a leisurely lifestyle. Indeed, he was chastised more than once by the hospital authorities for dereliction of duty. Accusations made by the Treasurer of the hospital over 'irregularities' in the days and hours of his lectures are quoted in Lindsay Patricia Granshaw's thesis,[7] and there is also a contemporary diary [8] which hints at South's cavalier attitude towards his hospital duties. For South, even medical emergencies did not seem to generate a sense of urgency. The 'maestro,' who lived in Blackheath, seven miles from the hospital, insisted on awaiting the arrival of a cab sent out by the hospital to collect him from home when there was an emergency. This time-wasting practice was criticised by a hospital committee in the 1850s, but their words fell on deaf ears. South was not the only practitioner whose commitment to St Thomas' fell short of what was expected. His old friend and colleague, Joseph Henry Green (1791–1863), was much the same. An investigation of 1853 [9] showed that he too, neglected his hospital patients.

South was described as a man who was 'old-fashioned in dress, wearing a black cut-away coat with large pockets, and a high white stock around his neck.' His appearance was described as 'puritanical,' and his manners as

---

[7] Ibid., p.327.

[8] Diary, 'S not there', 'S late' and 'S late' can all be found in the entries for 1851, and presumably refer to John Flint South. HI/ST/73/1. (London Metropolitan Archives, hereafter LMA).

[9] Editorial, The Disingenuous Conduct of the Authorities at St Thomas'; *The Lancet*; 1853; ii: pp 60–61.

Left: John Flint South (1707–1882) MRCS; FRCS. Surgeon to St Thomas'
Hospital, London. Source: Wellcome Library, London. Right: St Thomas'
Hospital. 1840. Source: Wellcome Library, London.

'punctilious.' When challenged, he was apparently 'easily roused to wrath,'
and, on such occasions, 'did not measure his language.'[10] A conservative,
arrogant and cantankerous man, South was opposed to many of the
reforms in medicine which were then gathering pace.

His own progress in the medical profession was unremarkable. It is true
he earned a two-page entry in Plarr's *Lives of the Surgeons*, but an inspection
of it reveals nothing out of the ordinary. By the age of twenty-three, South
had attained the post of Assistant Demonstrator of Anatomy at St Thomas'
on an annual salary of £100, but it took him a further five years to rise to
the position of Lecturer. There was nothing exceptional about his progress
through the ranks as surgeon either. He had to wait until the age of thirty-
seven for a post as Assistant Surgeon and a further six years before he was
promoted to the position of full Surgeon.

South's progression up through the ranks of his profession was, if
anything, below average for a London surgeon of his day.[11] It is hardly
surprising. His attitude and unwillingness to embrace change was a
frequent cause of concern and frustration to the hospital authorities. In

---

10 Plarr, *Lives of the Fellows of the Royal College of Surgeons of England. Plarr's Lives* – revised by Sir
    D'Arcy Power (England: Royal College of Surgeons – 2 Volumes, 1930), pp.330–332.

11 In the 1840s the average age by which a surgeon reached 'assistant' status was 31 years, whilst that
    of 'surgeon' was attained at the age of 41. By the 1870s the average age for promotion to that of
    surgeon was up to 44 years. Peterson, *The Medical Profession in Mid-Victorian London*, p.156.

1841, for instance, he was forced to resign his post as an Anatomy lecturer on account of an illness which was described in *The Lives* as an illness 'largely of a neurotic character.' Granshaw has revealed that a resolution of 1858,[12] which decreed that physicians and surgeons should retire at sixty or practise for no more than twenty years, was made to limit the tenure of the uncooperative South and others like him.

Peterson [13] and other historians have described South as one of the fiercest opponents of Florence Nightingale's proposal to found her school for nurses at St Thomas' in 1860. South was a man of sixty-three at the time. With a reckless disregard for the consequences, he decided the only solution was to procure a position elsewhere. Joseph Henry Green was South's long-standing friend, and it was Green's intervention that probably saved South from a humiliating rejection for a more prestigious post in another hospital. He felt compelled to dissuade his friend from making the application for fear that he would not compare favourably with younger and more able members of the profession. A letter in the South archive at the Royal College of Surgeons Library of Medicine,[14] reveals that Green urged his friend to think twice before jeopardising what he already had.

Medical student – 'an unexploded torpedo cast loose from its moorings'
James West probably received a satisfactory training from South in spite of his failings. Contemporary criticisms of John Flint South focused on his personality rather than on his competence, and he did hold prestigious positions in various medical institutions during his lifetime. He may have been conservative and disagreeable, but he was the product of the distinguished Sir Astley Cooper (1768–1841) who, in turn, was a protégé of Henry Cline (1750–1827) – another surgical giant. Cooper enjoyed great prestige in his day and beyond the grave, but South held his mentor in contempt. If his own testament [15] is anything to go by, we learn that Astley Cooper 'had read little and therefore knew little….. He was no orator, had not any large choice of words…. and he continued throughout his life to talk of the prostrate gland.' South may have been unfair in his criticisms of Cooper, but it must be admitted that on the question of the prostate gland at least, the pupil's knowledge was superior to that of the master.

[12] The new rule – put into effect in 1863, trapped South into retiring that year. Cited, Granshaw, *St Thomas' Hospital, London 1850–1900;* p.335.
[13] Peterson, *The Medical Profession in Mid-Victorian London*, p.177.
[14] Letters to John Flint South and notes on his family 1817–71. MS0232/9 (Royal College of Surgeons Library)
[15] JF South, *Memorials*, (London, Centaur Press Ltd. Edited by Gitting Litt.D 1884), p.84.

The historian, Lindsay Granshaw [16] tells us that students at St Thomas' paid £90 to attend all classes and practise in the hospital throughout their training in 1860. The cost was, on average, between £10 and £20 more than elsewhere, although it was more than double the fee charged by Anderson's University in Glasgow.[17] Fortunately, an account of the training received at St Thomas' by a near contemporary of West has survived.[18] The identity of the individual is not known for certain, on account of the fact that the article written by him has only the initials, WHS at its close.[19]

According to his account,[20] students could enter upon the course of training at any time, though he does say that it was preferable to join at the beginning of a session in either the winter or the summer. He says that a certificate of preliminary examination or of registration was required before a student could commence. In order to qualify, students were obliged to remain at the hospital three years. In that time they were expected to attend lectures and acquire the certificates of attendance which were demanded by the licensing bodies. A fourth year of study within the hospital, though not compulsory, was regarded by WHS as indispensable. With the obligation to attend lectures over, students had the opportunity, he explains, to spend their entire time in the study of disease in the wards of the hospital. Those students who chose to leave the hospital after the minimum three years were, in any case, expected to engage themselves in the acquisition of professional knowledge elsewhere.

WHS's account outlines the content of the course at St Thomas' in the 1850s. The recommended order of attendance of lectures was as follows:

FIRST YEAR (Winter) – Anatomy, Dissections, Physiology, Chemistry.
(Summer) – Materia Medica, Botany, Practical Physiology,
Practical Chemistry.
SECOND YEAR (Winter) – Anatomy, Physiology, Dissections, Clinical
Medicine, Clinical Surgery. (Summer) – Midwifery, Comparative
Anatomy, Practical Surgery, Clinical Medicine, Clinical Surgery.

---

[16] Granshaw, *St Thomas' Hospital, London 1850–1900*. p.315.

[17] A little over £40, according to Granshaw. A table of the comparative cost of medical education at the various hospitals and medical schools in the UK can be found in the July issue of *The Lancet*; 1860; ii: p.302.

[18] *St Thomas' Hospital Gazette*; 1985; summer: pp 76–83.

[19] One possibility is WH Sissons, although the dates of his studentship do not correspond to the dates given in the article. If the list of prize winners in the *St Thomas' Hospital Reports* for 1894 is to be trusted, Sissons began his training in 1858, not 1854.

[20] A reprint of an article, 'Medical Students at Work. Sketches of St Thomas' Hospital', from the GLC Archives published in the 1985 summer edition of *the St Thomas' Hospital Gazette;* pp 76–83.

THIRD YEAR (Winter) – Medicine, Surgery, Practical Surgery, Clinical Medicine, Pathological Anatomy, Clinical Medicine, Clinical Surgery.

Whether the presence of Clinical Medicine and Clinical Surgery twice within a single year represents courses of different levels or repetitions is unclear, although our source does say that students had to satisfy the Examining Board in their examinations at the end of the second year before they could continue into the third year. Other courses were available to the enthusiast, and WHS says that students were well advised to attend them. In their first Winter Session students could attend courses on Physics and Natural Philosophy, while in their third or fourth Summer Session there were courses on Practical and Manipulative Surgery as well as courses on Mental Disease and Public Health. For students in their third or fourth winter there was a practical course in Pathological Anatomy and there were opportunities to attend Obstetric Demonstrations. These students could also attend courses on Diseases of the eye.

As well as spending as much time as possible in the wards during the course of a fourth year of study, WHS tells us that students were encouraged to 'devote, during the whole of their attendance at the hospital, as much time as they (could) spare from their other engagements to clinical study in the wards and in the out-patients room.' Time spent by students on the hospital wards was known somewhat quaintly as 'walking the wards.'

The certificates gained by James West have survived, so it is possible to chart his achievements as a student. In addition to the courses completed at The Medical School of St Thomas', he was also working for a degree from the University of London. The certificates issued by St Thomas' date from 1853 and 1854 respectively, and consist of Certificates of Honour in Midwifery, Forensic Science and Pathology. Hospital records also reveal that he was given a prize for his Ophthalmic Reports at the prize giving ceremony of 1855.[21] He competed for, and won, positions as both Clinical Clerk and Dresser during his time at St Thomas'. West was awarded a Certificate of Honour in the latter role, and a reference written for him in 1854 [22] indicates that he was also awarded first prize as Physician's Clinical Clerk. Some of West's London University certificates also date from 1854. In that year he was awarded a First in the First Examination in Medicine at the Pass Examination set

---

[21] *St Thomas' Hospital Reports*; 1894: p.72.

[22] Testimonials to Mr JF West, p.35. Testimonial written by TA Barker, senior physician to St Thomas' Hospital. *Queen's Hospital Birmingham*, D/1, Part Two, L46.11. (BCL).

by the university,[23] and was sixth in the list of candidates who obtained Honours in Anatomy and Physiology in the First Examination in Medicine. The qualifications gained by West in 1854 – namely, the LSA and MRCS – enabled him to take up his first professional post at Queen's Hospital in Birmingham.

The certificates he gained in 1856 and 1857 were a requirement of the University of London and consist of a schedule of Medical Certificates which testify that West attended courses and received supervision during dissection and labour. The requirements demanded for this, the Second Examination for the degree of Bachelor of Medicine, also included an examination and the presentation of a Certificate of Moral Character. The schedule shows that West attended forty lectures on each of the following topics – Comparative Anatomy, Clinical Surgery and Clinical Medicine as well as a further seventy-five lectures on the Principles of Practical Medicine. He also performed one dissection and conducted twelve labours under supervision. For all that, West never did acquire a university degree. An incident in West's life during the course of 1857 could well account for the cessation of study for a degree at that stage, but more will be said about that later.

It has been suggested that the educational background of would-be medical students would have had very little in it which could, even loosely, be described as science. The entrance examinations for the various examination bodies reflect this. A list, found in the West archive and dated 8 November, 1849, gives details of the requirements for the matriculation and BA examinations of London University for the years 1850 and 1851 reads as follows:

CLASSICAL SUBJECTS FOR THE MATRICULATION AND B.A. EXAMINATIONS IN 1850 AND 1851

MATRICULATION

1850   HOMER – Odyssey, Book XXII
       CAESAR – Civil War

1851   XENOPHON – Anabasis, Book II
       VIRGIL – Georgics, Book I

---

[23] Details of the regulations for the MB and MD degrees of the University of London for 1851 can be found in Appendix B of *By Candlelight. The Life of Dr Arthur Hill Hassall, 1817–94* by Ernest A Gray (London: Robert Hale, 1983); pp.171–181.

BACHELOR OF ARTS

1850 XENOPHON – Anabasis, Books II and III
      HORACE – Odes, Satires and Ars Poetica

1851 SOPHOCLES – The Electra
      TACITUS – The Agricola; Germania; and Annals, Book II

The Preliminary Examination, taken by West in 1851 in order to qualify for his studentship with the Society of Apothecaries, was much the same. In this case, the list of texts consists of Virgil's Aeneid, Book 1; the Gospel of St Luke, in Greek; Cicero, Oratio pro Milone; Euclid, Book 1; and Xenophon's Anabasis. The one and only concession made towards the inclusion of subjects non-classical by the Society of Apothecaries, was the addition of Algebra. As we have seen, there is reason to believe that James West was an able student of the classics. We have seen already that *Edgbastonia* has claimed that West had 'acquired a complete mastership of Latin,' during his school days. John Flint South was also renowned as a Latin scholar. The account of his life in *Plarr's Lives*, says that South's mastery of Latin was such that he was selected to examine the articled pupils in Latin before they were apprenticed at the Royal College of Surgeons. A shared interest and ability in Latin may even have encouraged South to take on the young West as his protégé. We do not know whether West was as accomplished at Greek as he was in Latin, but he must have been good enough to pass the various qualifying examinations and, of course, there is the book-prize for progress in Greek mentioned earlier.

Apart from the account given by WHS, other sources exist which reflect on what life was like for medical students at St Thomas'. We know, for instance, that the number of students at the medical school during the 1850s ranged from 60 to 120.[24] We also have a good idea what sort of men these students were. Medical historians agree that would-be doctors generally came from professional families, most of whom were affluent.

According to Granshaw, students at St Thomas' came from middle or even upper class backgrounds. She found that approximately a quarter were the sons of medical men, while another quarter were sons of merchants who enjoyed similar status to that of the hospital governors. The remaining 50%

---

[24] Granshaw, *St Thomas' Hospital, London. 1850–1900*, p.319.

were, for the most part, sons of other professionals – clergymen, military men, educators or architects.[25] When West began his training at St Thomas' in 1850 there were few entrance scholarships, and those that did exist were seldom awarded to the needy. One striking exception was the case of a black American, who was given a free place at St Thomas' in the 1850s.[26] The student – barred entrance to American medical schools on account of his colour – was considered a special case by the Committee of Lecturers in 1852.

Medical historians agree that the quality which young men entering medical schools in the middle of the nineteenth century should aspire to above all else was gentlemanly conduct. A classical education was considered the best way of reinforcing gentlemanly qualities and, as Granshaw says, to have such an education would give students the elements of conversation and provide them with a similar background to the highest social groups in the country.[27] All the evidence suggests that West was well possessed of the necessary accomplishments.

Gentlemanly status could even serve as a shield against rebuke when boisterous students found themselves on the wrong side of the law. WHS believed that disorderly conduct was becoming unacceptable by the time he was a student at St Thomas', but he could recall incidents when students evaded justice purely on account of their status as medical students. Their positions as medical students at one of the prestigious medical schools could, he tells us be 'turned to considerable advantage by the rollicking and roistering section of our youth' when 'even the worthy magistrate (could not) be hard upon the contrite and repentant victim of some midnight encounter with members of the Force if he gives his name as "Jones of Guy's."'[28]

James West was fortunate in being able to live at home during his student years and, on top of that, he would have been provided with rooms and commons, free of charge, during the time he spent as clinical clerk and dresser in the hospital.[29] WHS speaks of inflated rents in houses around the hospital which, he says, were suddenly increased to 75/– pa from 25/–. He does not give dates, so it is impossible to know the real extent of exploitation by landlords. Lodging-house keepers were also quick to take advantage of the need for student accommodation around St Thomas' according to our source. Students, too, were guilty of exploitation. In their case, it involved the exploitation of their new found freedom from parental

25 Granshaw, *St Thomas' Hospital, London. 1850–1900*, p.515.

26 Minutes of the Committee of Lecturers, 15 May, 1852, STHMSL. (LMA).

27 Granshaw, *St Thomas' Hospital, London. 1850–1900*, p.317.

28 Article from *The Graphic*, 2 October, 1886 – published in *St Thomas' Gazette*; 1985; summer: p.76.

29 Article entitled, St Thomas' Hospital. Scholarships and Appointments, *The Lancet*; 1854; ii: p.238.

control. WHS believed that the patience of landlords was sometimes 'sorely taxed by arrears of rent, and even losses (caused by the) carelessness and extravagance of their youthful inexperienced tenants.'[30] Like others who have written on the subject, WHS was aware of the temptations the big city presented to the young students. 'A young man coming up to town for the first time with a cheque of 50/– or more in his pocket' he tells us 'is a loaded shell, an unexploded torpedo cast loose from its moorings.'[31] WHS also speaks of the bonds which held students together in the medical schools and hospitals of his day – there was a sense of 'clansmanship which' he says 'is strong in all the better schools.'[32] The bond of family connections has already been alluded to. Some medical families, he tells us, were sufficiently well known at St Thomas' to be referred to affectionately as 'big B and little B, tenor G and two treble G's, Omega and the two Omicrons.'[33]

WHS singled out Anatomy as the single most important subject taught at medical school. Anatomy, he says 'stands at the threshold of all sound knowledge.' The subject was close to the hearts of both James West and his mentor, John Flint South. West was to go on to hold a post as professor of Anatomy at Queen's Hospital, Birmingham, when a supply of bodies for college dissection came courtesy of Her Majesty's executioner, but South began his career as demonstrator of Anatomy at St Thomas' in the days of the infamous resurrectionists, or body-snatchers.

Astley Cooper's accounts – 'two male and two female from Murphy – 50/8/0'

Astley Cooper,[34] maestro of John Flint South, left a record of some of the fees he paid to resurrectionists. They reveal that he even paid bail costs and helped to support some families when the 'breadwinner' was incarcerated. Cooper may not have stopped there. Sarah Wise [35] has shown that some surgeons paid the legal fees of body-snatchers and provided luxuries to those imprisoned for their activities. South's use of 'subjects' was alluded to in relation to the trial for murder of the infamous London body-snatchers-turned-murderers, John Bishop, Thomas Head (alias

---

[30] Article from *The Graphic* published in *St Thomas' Gazette*; 1985; summer: p.80.

[31] Ibid..

[32] Ibid., p.79.

[33] Ibid..

[34] Evidence in the case of body-snatchers, John Bishop, Thomas Williams and James May, who were convicted of murder in the early 1830s, proves that South used the services of resurrectionists while Cooper gave evidence to the Select Committee on Anatomy which supplied the necessary data to William Warburton MP – the man behind the Anatomy Act of 1832.

[35] Sarah Wise, *The Italian Boy. Murder and Grave-Robbery in 1830s London* (London: Jonathan Cape, 2004), p.168.

Williams).[36] Bishop's post-trial confession reveals that he offered the body of at least one victim to Mr South's footman at St Thomas'. South was busy at the time and told his footman to ask Bishop to return with the body the next day. The 'subject' went instead to Mr Richard Grainger's private anatomical school in Webb Street, and from there to King's College, where it was seen by anatomist, Richard Partridge. The demand for cadavers in the medical schools was great. Resurrectionists and other opportunists (a boatman or fisherman who wanted to supplement his income, perhaps) found the river Thames a useful source of bodies and some were known to have snatched bodies from both workhouses and private houses. And, in cases where the state of decomposition was considered unacceptable,[37] body parts were harvested.

In the years following the building by William House of the Enon Chapel in Clement's Lane in the Strand in 1822, the source must have been more plentiful than ever. On the face of it, House 'interred' 12,000 bodies in a six foot deep vault measuring sixty feet by twenty-nine.[38] He managed this extraordinary feat partly in hastening decomposition by dousing bodies in quicklime, but he also sent cart loads of decomposing corpses to the Thames for disposal, and deposited bodies directly in an open sewer which conveniently ran under the chapel. Indeed, the existence of the sewer enabled the infamous House to flush bodies away as fast as they arrived. From the sewer, it was but a short 'ride' to the Thames and the opportunists.

A legitimate supply of cadavers only became available after the Anatomy Act of 1832, although Richard Partridge, the man who had been behind the arrests of the notorious pair of London 'burkers,' [39] had the satisfaction of dissecting John Bishop following his execution on 5 December, 1831. The Act had been necessary because public outcry over the activities of grave-robbers had reached unprecedented proportions when it was discovered that some had turned murderers. A resurrectionist's trade had been a lucrative one. Sarah Wise [40] says that the London body-snatchers, could command between twelve and fourteen guineas from the city's medical schools. It is hardly surprising that the more unscrupulous of that unscrupulous band of men turned to murder.

---

[36] A third man, James May, was also on trial for murder, but was shown to have no knowledge of how the bodies in question had been procured. He was reprieved following the confession of John Bishop. Sarah Wise, *The Italian Boy. Murder and Grave-Robbery in 1830s London.*

[37] Thomas Wharton, FRCP, 'Sir Astley Cooper and the Resurrectionists', *St Thomas' Hospital Gazette*; 1986; winter: p.39.

[38] Lee Jackson and Eric Nathan, *The Victorian Dictionary. The Social History of Victorian London* (London: New Holland, 2004) pp 96–7.

[39] So-called after their Scottish counterparts, William Burke and William Hare.

[40] Sarah Wise, *The Italian Boy. Murder and Grave-Robbery in 1830s London.*

A dearth of bodies for dissection was a perennial problem for teachers of Anatomy in the medical schools both before and after the Act of 1832. If anything, the supply diminished after the fall of the resurrectionists. Once murder was deemed acceptable by resurrectionists, it had been possible to supply corpses at a rate which matched demand.

The hospital itself provided a steady supply of corpses, of course, and any unclaimed bodies automatically went to the dissecting room for post-mortem. Interest in conducting post-mortems varied. A Dr Barker, for instance, performed a mere four post-mortems.[41] In the 1850s post-mortems and dissections were performed by the curator of the museum or an assistant who was selected from among the most able students.

The St Thomas' Hospital Dead Book [42] reveals that, of the 353 deaths in 1853, 224 were examined in post-mortem.[43] In 1854, one hundred and eighty-nine deceased were examined post-mortem as against 212 who were not. The book also confirms that unclaimed dead were dispatched to the dissecting room. In James West's day, the greatest number of deaths per surgeon were to be found in those under the care of his maestro, John Flint South. There is no evidence to suggest that this was due to incompetence on South's part. As an experienced practitioner, he may well have been dealing with the more complicated cases, or the figures may simply reflect the man-hours spent dealing with hospital patients as opposed to time devoted to private practice. They may also reflect the fact that there were changes in personnel around that time.[44] South's colleague, Green, resigned on 14 June, 1852 and was replaced by Mr Samuel Solly (d.1871) on the 28th of that month. Two more surgeons – Frederick Le Gros Clark (1811–92) and John Simon (1816–1904) were elected less than a month later on the 20th, July. In any case, difficult cases were unlikely to have been entrusted to the new young and inexperienced surgeons.

We know from the *'Minutes of the Committee of Lecturers'* entry for 17 July, 1852 [45] that a request was made for more bodies for the dissecting room at St Thomas' at that time. James FF West would have benefited from this directly, since it was a request designed to give the clinical clerks and dressers responsible for cases the opportunity to attend the mortuary in order to 'furnish whatever information may be required as to the previous

---

[41] Cited by Granshaw in, *St Thomas' Hospital, London. 1850–1900*, p.285 from the source, *Our Hospitals: St Thomas' Lloyd's Weekly Pager*, 12 March, 1897.

[42] HI/ST/B18/5. (LMA).

[43] There were fifty-two inquests for the same period.

[44] Diary HI/ST/73/1. (LMA).

[45] Cited by Granshaw in, *St Thomas' Hospital, London. 1850–1900*, p.286. STHMSL.

history of the case.'[46] It reflects the growing importance that was attached to post-mortems in this period, and its timing probably accounts for the fact that the young West became one of its devotees.[47]

'The art of surgery'

James West and his contemporaries were thrown into practical involvement with patients with, what would seem to us today, horrifying haste. Theoretically, clerkships and dresserships provided young medical students with opportunities to practise their skills under supervision. Our source WHS [48] suggests that positions as clinical clerk and dresser followed on, one to the other. The former, he suggests, being a second year appointment and the latter a third year one. Practice, no doubt, varied from one medical school to another. Some medical historians state that, in their second year, aspiring physicians sought the position of clinical clerk, and would-be surgeons a dressership.

West's experience followed the pattern outlined by WHS. As we have seen, he won a place as both clinical clerk and dresser during his years at St Thomas'. The obituaries written for West say that he was dresser to JF South, and although there is no reason to suppose that he was not, John Simon also claimed that West worked as his dresser for a year at St Thomas'. In references they wrote for West at the time he sought an appointment as House Surgeon at Queen's Hospital, Birmingham, several St Thomas' men refer to West's role as clinical clerk during his time as a student. One, Dr Thomas A Baker, stated that West had been given first prize as Physician's Clinical Clerk.

It is clear from a number of sources that a dresser could be called on to undertake all sorts of surgical tasks. Dressing wounds which were the result of surgical procedures or injury was seen as the principle role of the

---

[46] Granshaw, *St Thomas' Hospital, London. 1850–1900*, p.286.

[47] West began his professional career at Queen's Hospital, Birmingham, an institution in which the town's first coroner, John Birt Davies worked. In common with his other juniors, West was required to assist Davies in autopsies from time to time. This probably accounted for the fact that, in future years, West was sometimes required to perform post-mortems in cases where practitioners were accused of incompetence. In early July, 1876, for instance, a post-mortem was ordered on Mrs Brown of Malvern, who died shortly after childbirth. There had been no post-mortem initially, but Richard Brown, husband of the deceased, accused Alexander Cooksey, surgeon, of causing his wife's death as a result of incompetence. The autopsy, performed in this case by Mssrs West, Walshe and Parnell, showed that Cooksey had lacerated the bowel in his attempts to assist the birth. Cooksey incriminated himself further by asking those who conducted the post-mortem to cover up for him but, it seems he had nothing to fear. Worcester Assizes, in their wisdom, acquitted him. *Birmingham Daily Post*, 8 July, 1876. (BCL).

[48] 'Medical Students at Work', *St Thomas' Hospital Gazette*; 1985; summer: p.82.

dresser, but in reality, he was often expected to deputise for his superiors. West's years as an articled pupil to Hooper and Wakem probably meant he was well acquainted with some of the practical tasks which fell to medical men. When the surgeon, JH Green, stood accused of neglecting his duties at St Thomas' in 1853, the chief criticism was of the way in which responsibility for, and treatment of, patients fell to the least qualified. The editor is quoted as saying 'JH Green was so preoccupied with his private practice that he left his tasks to the assistant surgeon. The latter therefore left his proper area, the outpatients, to the house surgeons who in turn were so busy that they enlisted substantial help from the dressers or other pupils who had no specific positions.'[49]

In part two of an article written by Dr Charles Pither, a present day consultant in the department of Anæsthetics at St Thomas' Hospital, entitled 'Anæsthesia at St Thomas'. *The Early Days 1848–1878*' [50] we discover that dressers also administered anæsthetics. Pither cites correspondence between the surgeon John Simon and the Association Journal (later to become the *British Medical Journal*) on the occasion of the death of a patient whilst under the effects of chloroform in 1856. This was not the first death from anæsthetic at St Thomas',[51] and there is nothing to suggest that the dresser who administered the anæsthetic was considered in any way culpable. There seems to have been no question of abandoning the use of dressers in the administration of anæsthetics because of the tragedy, and since anæsthesia clearly was a task performed by dressers in 1856, there is every reason to suppose that West will have learnt the art of anæsthesia during his days as a dresser. It would have been a skill which he would have practised throughout his life as a surgeon in Birmingham. There was nothing unusual about this. House surgeons at St Thomas' continued to administer anæsthetics right up until the time a full time specialist in anæsthetics was appointed in 1878. In those days – before the 'birth' of the specialist – house surgeons had significant influence over medical practice at St Thomas'. Most tasks in the hospital fell to them, according to Granshaw.[52]

Anæsthesia was in its infancy in 1856, and it was recognised even then that there was much to learn, but a death at the hands of a dresser was not always overlooked. In 1857 the death of an injured man, who had been

---

[49] From the editorial, *The Disingenuous Conduct of the Authorities at St Thomas'*, *The Lancet:* 1856; ii: pp.60–61.

[50] *St Thomas' Hospital Gazette*; 1987; summer: p.60.

[51] The first being on 9 October, 1849.

[52] Granshaw, *St Thomas' Hospital, London. 1850–1900*; p.307.

treated and sent home by a dresser, led the Committee to examine why the case had been dealt with by a dresser in the first place. The resulting enquiry revealed, not only a complete absence of qualified personnel on the day in question, but that only one member of the surgical staff lived in London anyway, and his house was not located near the hospital.[53]

The opportunity afforded to medical students to observe and assist in operations in the early 1850s was limited on account of the small number of operations that were performed at the time. With the danger of death on the operating table unacceptably high, and post-operative mortality rates at terrifyingly high levels, it was not a procedure undertaken lightly. In James West's time at St Thomas', six surgeons shared a single operating theatre and operations took place once a week – on Saturdays.[54] The chances of one's own maestro being able to provide adequate opportunity for passing on the art of surgery were, at best, limited.

At the time when West trained, few would have questioned the use of the phrase 'the art of anæsthesia' or 'the art of surgery.' The scientific approach – in its infancy in the mid-nineteenth century – was embraced and advanced by the men of West's generation. In 1854, the year West qualified, St Thomas' appointed a lecturer in chemistry for the first time. One of the first tasks he undertook was that of analysing the urine of patients who had been admitted to the physician's ward. By the end of that year he had analysed a total of 1,330 samples.[55] Chemistry was well established by the 1860s, and the medical school had its own laboratory and pharmacy soon after.

Eighteen fifty-four was also the year in which nineteen St Thomas' medical school students wrote to the Committee complaining of the difficulties they had in gaining access to the one and only microscope. The Committee of Lecturers responded favourably, and an extra microscope was made available. This was not the case six years later, when the governors petitioned for a third microscope. They met with a refusal. A failure to appreciate the potential of the microscope must have played a part in the lack of provision in the early 1850s. But this was soon to change. Dr Bristowe, the demonstrator of morbid anatomy, is reported to have examined an ulcerated tumour which had been removed from the heel of a patient under the microscope in 1852.[56] His description of what he found

53 Granshaw, *St Thomas' Hospital, London. 1850–1900*; p.337.
54 Ibid., p.253.
55 Ibid., p.290.
56 Ibid., p.288.

there, concentrated on the arrangement of malignant cells. Eighteen fifty-two was also the year in which the Dixon Prize was introduced. It was a prize for the best report on malignant disease, and it was the first award which called explicitly for the use of the microscope.

St Thomas' Hospital nurse, 1853 – 'a sizzie for a nurse'

Many of the advances that took place in medicine in the second half of the nineteenth century were thanks to a growing awareness of hospital hygiene and the determination to improve upon it. Without a remedy for the problems caused by lack of hygiene and the failure to use antiseptic methods, advances in surgery could not have materialised. James West was fortunate to have gone into surgery at a time when the causes of hospital diseases were being understood and remedied for the first time. Later on he would reap the benefits of Joseph Lister's (1827–1912) revolutionary ideas on antisepsis.

Lister was not the first person to concern himself with the prevention of infection. The Hungarian doctor, Ignaz Philipp Semmelweis (1818–65) for instance, had brought about major reductions in the incidence of Puerperal Fever in Vienna through the employment of rigorous hygiene measures in the late 1840s. The nursing profession too was about to undergo radical reform. Florence Nightingale is well known, and it easy to attribute the revolution in nursing entirely to her. This would be to deny other worthy women the credit they deserve. One came to St Thomas' in 1853, when West was a student. The lady in question, Mrs Sarah Wardroper, brought about improvements in nursing long before Miss Nightingale's school of nurses was established there in 1860.[57] The changes made by Mrs Wardroper won the approval of Miss Nightingale, and it was precisely because the latter recognised one of like mind, that the Nightingale Training School of Nurses was installed at St Thomas' in the first place.

If the recollections of Miss ME Fowler [58] are anything to go by, the changes brought about by Mrs Wardroper were long overdue. Miss Fowler went to visit a patient at St Thomas' in the year of Sarah Wardroper's appointment. The patient was the husband of her friend, and her account of it conjures up a scene in keeping with Dickensian Southwark. She begins

[57] One thing for which Mrs Wardroper was renowned, was the eradication of drunkenness in the nurses of St Thomas'. Article 'Florence Nightingale', in *St Thomas' Hospital Gazette*; 1991; summer: p.4.
[58] Recollections of Miss ME Fowler, *A Hospital Nurse, 1853*. H1/ST/1/4. (LMA).

by saying that the building itself was situated in a dirty neighbourhood, but it was what went on inside it that makes sickening reading. She describes how they were met at the door by a dirty old woman.[59] The lady in question, she says, was 'wearing a dirty old net cap...It looked as if it had been picked out of the dustbin.' She goes on to say that her dress – 'green and brown from wear' – had once been black. Her face was no better. Fowler writes 'I wondered when she had washed her face.' Fowler's description of the ward itself is not intended as a complimentary piece of writing, but it does suggest that some effort had been made to make it agreeable. While the nurse stood talking to her friend and her husband, Miss Fowler took the opportunity to take a look at her surroundings.

'I has (sic) usual took stock with my eyes. Iron bedsteads with tall uprights to hold blue and white check curtains – ditto bed covers. A long room with a number of beds each side – I had heard people say they would sooner die at home than go to be nursed at a hospital and I think I thought the same.'

At some point during Miss Fowler's visit, the nurse was summoned by a patient further down the ward. Fowler describes the incident as follows:

'My eyes followed her. She went to a man looking terribly ill – lent over to hear what he said, pulled him upright, shook him hard, smacked his head soundly – and pushed him down on his pillow and threw the sheet over him.'

Miss Fowler and her friend were warned, before leaving the hospital, that the nurse was likely to pursue them in the hope of extracting some money from them. She did indeed, and was rewarded by Miss Fowler's friend, Milly, with a sixpenny piece. The memory of that experience remained with Miss Fowler, as the following extract shows:

'and the way she wrinkled up her dirty old face as she said – "A sizzie, a sizzie for a nurse." I have never forgotten.'

Although improvements in the state of hospital wards in St Thomas' at the time when West did his training have to be acknowledged, it would be wrong to suppose that all was well. There was much to learn at St Thomas' and elsewhere. The diary [60] states that both water closets and gas lighting were installed in a number of wards in 1849 and 1854 and while everyone would agree that gas lighting was preferable to candles, the advantages of the new water closets as we know them may not have been attainable. A water closet is, after all, only as good as the sewers that service it, and since

---

[59] The central character of the narrative; namely, the nurse.
[60] Diary; HI/ST/73/1. (LMA).

the great Victorian sewer building projects had barely begun in the mid-century, we must keep our approbation in check to some extent. Granshaw says that, at St Thomas', there was fierce opposition to remedies which were designed to combat infection, and hospital infection was a continuing threat to the sick who entered its wards as late as 1880. The eradication of hospital infection was a challenge which still lay ahead when West qualified in 1854, and it was one which was embraced first and foremost by doctors in the provinces.

Aspiring doctors – 'for many, dreams of success failed to materialise'

The proliferation of medical schools in London and the provinces at around about the time West and his contemporaries were training, imbued students not only with a pride in their institutions but gave them a sense of corporate identity which had hitherto been unknown. Even so, for men of James West's generation, there was little uniformity in the path to a medical career. Not all aspiring medics attended medical school. The apprenticeship system, used by would-be apothecaries and surgeons in the earlier part of the nineteenth century, continued up until the 1870s. Many worked out their apprenticeships under the watchful eye of a father or other close relation already in the profession, and like medical courses, they were not regulated in the 1850s. Some, like West himself, availed themselves of both routes to professional status – apprenticeship and a medical course in a leading medical school. Degree courses in medicine were few and far between.

There was no guarantee of an appointment let alone a successful career for medical students who qualified in Victorian England either. A survey conducted by James Paget (1809–92) in 1869 [61] showed that for many, dreams of success failed to materialise. He investigated a total of 1,000 individuals who had attended the medical school of St Bartholomew's between the years 1839 and 1859. Of the 1,000 studied, only twenty-three had distinguished careers – defined by Paget, as holding a post in one of the universities or large hospitals. Sixty-six achieved what he described as 'considerable success,' with posts in leading practices or high positions in the public services. Five hundred and seven had 'fair success,' having a reasonably successful practice or holding a steady public position. One hundred and twenty-four had 'limited success,' with a meagre living, while fifty-six failed entirely. Failure was put down to a number of factors and included ill health, intemperance and laziness. Of the rest, ninety-six had

---

[61] MJ Peterson, *The Medical Profession in Mid-Victorian London*, p.133.

 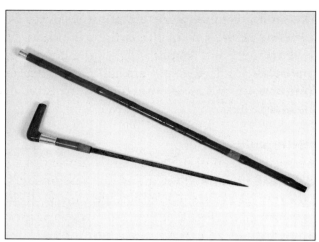

*Left: George Jordan Lloyd (1854–1913) MRCS; LSA; FRCS; MD.ChB; MSc
West's successor at Queen's Hospital. Source: History of the Birmingham School of
Medicine. Right: Sword-stick engraved with the words JAMES F WEST MRCS. The
stick dates from between 1854 and 1867 – after West had gained the Membership,
and before he achieved the Fellowship, of the Royal College of Surgeons.'*

abandoned medicine and had taken up another profession, eighty-seven
had died within twelve years of commencing practice, and a further forty-
one died during pupilage.

Whilst the majority of men who left the profession are unknown to us
today, some went on to excel in other fields and enjoyed considerable
success. One 'failure' Sir Arthur Conan Doyle (1859–1930), became famous
as a writer of detective stories after he abandoned his career as a doctor.
Francis Brett Young (1884–1954), born a generation later, was another
doctor who, after some years in service as a doctor, elected to earn his living
as a writer. Young studied at the Birmingham Medical School after it had
been incorporated into the new University. Five of his books, *My Brother
Jonathan*, *Dr Bradley Remembers*, *Cold Harbour*, *Portrait of Claire* and *The Young
Physician*, rely heavily on his own experience as both medical student and
doctor and include thinly disguised characterisations of well known
Birmingham medical personnel. According to those who knew West's
successor at Queen's Hospital, George Jordan Lloyd (1854–1913), Brett
Young's fictional character, Lloyd Moore, was an accurate portrayal of this
most colourful of Birmingham surgeons.

James West was fortunate in securing a post as house surgeon at Queen's Hospital in Birmingham when he qualified in 1854. Not everything went smoothly for him there, but by the time he died in 1883, he had enjoyed considerable success as a doctor and held a position of status in the society of Edgbaston – Birmingham's most desirable suburb.

'By examination'

In the first half of the nineteenth century, the best British medical degrees were to be obtained from Dublin, Glasgow or Edinburgh. Aberdeen and St Andrews also awarded medical degrees but these were 'bought degrees.' To procure a degree from one or other of those universities, all that was required was the written backing of two medical professionals and the payment of a fee. It was not even necessary to attend a degree ceremony. The degree certificate could be, and frequently was, dispatched by post. The appeal of an Edinburgh degree persisted beyond the time when degrees could be obtained from London,[62] but London degrees became more common in the second half of the century, and it was even possible to obtain degrees from Manchester and Birmingham by the dawn of the twentieth century.

A degree from continental Europe held attractions for some. Female practitioners like Louise Catherine Fanny Atkins and Annie Elizabeth Clarke (1845–1924) of Birmingham, both of whom qualified in 1877, had had no choice but to study abroad. Louise Atkins spent most of her working life in London although, strangely, her name is recorded in the list of medical officers at the newly founded Women's Hospital, Birmingham in 1872 some five years before she qualified. Annie Clarke was one of just three female practitioners working in Birmingham in 1900, and in common with other British women of her generation, commenced her studies at a time when entry to medical school was barred to women in England. She qualified instead, with an MD from Berne in 1877. Of those who could train in England, many who could afford to do so, chose to supplement their studies by spending a period of time in one of the medical schools or hospitals on the continent.

James West was one man who found the lure of continental Europe irresistible, though in his case, the trips began after he had qualified and continued right up to the time of his death. Obituaries written on the

---

[62] The University Colleges of London were founded in 1828 (University College) and 1834 (King's College) respectively.

occasion of West's death, describe him as a man who made regular trips abroad to study continental practices. His habit of writing copious notes for the benefit of his students and colleagues on the observations he made during these visits, was well known. In her study of the medical profession of mid-Victorian London,[63] MJ Peterson found that Paris was the favourite venue selected by medical students during the 1850s but that it had been virtually abandoned in favour of Vienna and the German cities by the 1880s. No such shift in popularity is evident among Birmingham hospital doctors. For them, a preference for Paris prevailed, but Vienna, Berlin and other European centres also proved attractive throughout.

The predilection of those who became doctors in the second half of the nineteenth century for obtaining a number of different medical qualifications has already been mentioned. Out of a group of thirty-three Birmingham hospital doctors [64] who practised in the second half of the nineteenth century, and which includes James West, the most striking thing about their qualifications is their diversity. No-one possessed the somewhat discredited MRCP which, as we have seen, was of little use outside London, but the MB, the MD, the LSA and the MRCS were all popular. The medical degree, which incorporated both medicine and surgery, had obvious attractions, but just as the combination of LSA and MRCS was popular with surgeons, some physicians chose to supplement their knowledge by taking the MRCS. Twenty-two members of the Birmingham group held the MRCS altogether, and of these, nine were physicians.

Entrenched prejudices towards the low status of apothecaries persisted though, and although men could obtain first appointments in hospitals with the dual qualification or even the LSA on its own, it became increasingly difficult to attain senior positions without additional qualifications.[65] In the Birmingham group those who held qualifications over and above the basic essentials fell into two distinct categories, with physicians holding a medical degree (an MB, MD, or both) and a Fellowship of the Royal College of Physicians (FRCP) and surgeons holding a Fellowship of the Royal College of Surgeons (FRCS). Few were content with anything less. If we exclude one young doctor, who held the joint

---

[63] Peterson, *The Medical Profession in Mid-Victorian London.* (Berkeley: California, 1978). P179.

[64] The author's MA dissertation was based on a study of these thirty-three Birmingham Hospital Doctors. All practised between 1850 and 1900. (BCL).

[65] Even so, the LSA had not been ruled out as a starting point even as late as 1884. In that year Ernest J Eliot LSA was appointed Obstetric and Ophthalmic House Surgeon at Queen's on condition that he obtained a membership or fellowship of the Royal College of Surgeons within a year. (*General Committee Book, May 1880 – February 1886*). (Birmingham City Archives, hereafter BCA).

qualification introduced by the Conjoint Board in 1884,[66] fifteen out of the sixteen physicians possessed a medical degree and all held the FRCP, while eleven out of the sixteen surgeons possessed the FRCS.

James West gained the Fellowship of the Royal College of surgeons (FRCS) in the year 1867. An FRCS was almost always acquired mid-career and West was no exception. Fellowship examinations, introduced in the second half of the nineteenth century, superseded the old practice of election to the title. The Royal College of Surgeons had not always shown wisdom in its selection of Fellows in the past, and the election of the undeserving had earned the College the contempt of many of the earlier generation. By the time men of West's day sought extra credentials, many thought the status of a Fellowship could only be guaranteed if the letters FRCS were qualified by the assurance that it had been gained through examination. West himself left nothing to chance, and insisted that the words 'by examination' appeared in parenthesis after the title in the years immediately following his acquisition of the title.

The acquisition of qualifications was taken seriously by both West and his colleagues in Birmingham. Of the Birmingham group of thirty-three, there were some who possessed qualifications well over and above those considered strictly necessary. Not all were medical or even scientific, but of those that were, there were four Masters of Science, two Masters of Surgery and two Fellows of the Royal Society. Added together, four out of the thirty-three possessed five separate medical or medically related qualifications.

An examination of successful hospital doctors can give a false impression of how easy it was to succeed as a medical practitioner in the nineteenth century. The Birmingham hospital group had, by definition, been successful and among those who were the most distinguished were men who had gained awards as students. Twelve of the thirty-three Birmingham hospital doctors had been awarded prizes during their days as students.[67] A few of them were multiple prize winners,[68] and two of the twelve had also received scholarships. The scholarship won by Charles J Bracey (1838–87) during his time as a student in London amounted to £100 – a prize considered equal to the highest award for surgery – the Gold Medal.[69]

---

[66] LRCP/MRCS.

[67] JFF West was one. It will be remembered that he was given a prize for his Ophthalmic Report.

[68] *Edgbastonia* describes John St Swithin Wilders (1837–1907) as having won many prizes during his days at Queen's College and Alfred Carter (1849–1918) as having gained three gold and two silver medals whilst a student at University College, London. *Edgbastonia*, 1892; XII: p.162 (BCL).

[69] *Edgbastonia*; 1887; VII: p.66. (BCL).

Peterson [70] is inclined to think that the connection between winning prizes and a prestigious career was exaggerated by contemporaries, but it is clear from the Birmingham sample that prize winners did fare well in competing for hospital posts and that, for them, a prize from one of the Birmingham Medical Schools was best of all.[71] Of the eleven prize-winners, six were holders of prizes which had been awarded during their days as students in Birmingham. Appointing a distinguished candidate who was well known personally to hospital staff made good sense. Doing so would act as an incentive to students with ambition, and as something of a guarantee of quality to those supplying the posts.

By the end of the century, attitudes were changing. As Birmingham doctor, Felix Coulson Vinrace (1858–1927), proved, the best opportunities were afforded to those who had studied elsewhere. When he analysed the number of Birmingham students who went on to secure Birmingham hospital appointments in 1898, he found that local students were more successful if they supplemented their training at medical school outside Birmingham.[72]

Birmingham Medical Students & Hospital Appointments

Name of Hospital	Officers educ. at Birmingham Medical Sch. only	Officers educ. at Birmingham & other medical schools	Officers educ. at other medical schools & not in Birmingham	Total no. of medical & surgical officers on acting staff
The General	1	2	11	14
Queen's	2	4	6	12
Women's	1	2	2	5
Eye	0	0	3	3
Children's	3	1	5	9
Ear & Throat	1	1	3	5
Orthopædic	2	1	1	4
Skin & Urinary	2	2	0	4
Total	12	13	31	56

---

70   Peterson, *Medical Profession*; p.83.
71   This was especially true of Queen's Hospital.
72   Letter sent by Felix Vinrace to *The Daily Post* 26 August, 1898. (BCL).

The right sort of background

Historians agree that another factor which predisposed an aspiring medic to a successful career was having the right sort of background. A man with an advantageous background, particularly if it was a medical one, could expect to do better than one less privileged. As far as we know, James West had no relatives who were medically qualified and it is quite possible that he had no other connections which would have been advantageous either. Parental occupations are not available for the whole of the Birmingham hospital group mentioned earlier, but out of the twenty-seven known, ten were sons of medical men and there were others who had some other close relative who was medically qualified.

Medical historian, Irvine Loudon, says that to find successive members of the same family practising medicine for at least a century is not uncommon. He cites numerous examples in *Medical Care and the General Practitioner 1750–1850*. Goldwyen of Bristol, he says, produced thirteen surgeons and two physicians in five generations, while the Maurice family of Marlborough, produced six generations of medical practitioners from 1792 to the present day.[73] The Maurice clan had its rivals across the Irish Sea in the shape of the Moore family.[74] The youngest generation of that family have, by choosing careers in medicine, taken the family tradition into the eighth generation. All descend from William Moore, apothecary, who began work in 1740.

Birmingham, too, had its share of medical families. A few of West's contemporaries came from medical families that stretched back to include grandfathers and several went on to sire future generations of medical practitioners. The Underhill [75] and Chavasse families spawned numerous medical practitioners between them, but there were other legendary examples. Edward Johnstone (1757–1851), one of the original members of staff at Queen's Hospital, was the son of the celebrated Worcester physician, James Johnstone.[76] Edward was not the only son to enter medicine. An older brother, James, became a physician but died young,

---

[73] Irvine Loudon. *Medical Care and the General Practitioner 1750–1850*. (England: Oxford University Press, 1986), p 34.

[74] Richard Moore FRCGP. *Leeches to Lasers. Sketches of a Medical Family*. (Ireland: Morrigan, 2002). Richard Moore practised for most of his working life in Shrewsbury. Not content to have written a book on his distinguished family, has just completed a PhD at the University of Birmingham's Centre for the History of Medicine.

[75] One member of that family, William Lees Underhill (1814–94) of Tipton, alone is to be credited with supplying the medical profession with sizeable injection of manpower. Of his eight sons, six became doctors.

[76] James Johnson of Worcester discovered how hydrochloric acid could be used in arresting contagion and wrote on Ganglions of the Nerves.

while a younger sibling, John (1768–1836), occupied a post in Birmingham General Hospital for more than thirty years. Francis Brett Young, doctor turned novelist, was the son of a GP from Halesowen, near Birmingham, and was also the grandson of another doctor on the maternal side.

The numbers of Birmingham doctors who were sons of medical men or fathered medical offspring in the second half of the nineteenth century are too numerous to list. They include Joseph Sampson Gamgee (1828–86), George Jordan Lloyd (1854–1913), James Russell (1818–85), Thomas Furneaux Jordan (1830–1911), Oliver Pemberton (1825–97) and William Sands Cox (1802–75). West himself fathered eight children by the time he died, but none followed him in taking up a career in medicine or surgery. John Frederick (b.1875) came close. He matriculated as a student of the University of London in January, 1892 and was placed in the first division. He also took and passed the preliminary scientific examinations for the degree of Bachelor of Medicine in 1894, but that was as far as he went. At that point, John Frederick West abandoned medicine and turned his attention instead to law.

Money too, was crucial. The cost of training was not the only expense incurred by the families of aspiring doctors. The opportunity to embark on a course of training would only have been available to those who could pass the necessary entrance examinations to medical school. Whether this came by virtue of a school or a private governor, the family would have paid out some considerable sum for a son's education long before his medical training commenced. Added to that, the newly qualified doctor had to look the part. As Loudon and others have shown, newly qualified medical practitioners needed to demonstrate their fitness for the position first by attiring themselves in appropriate dress, but also by riding in a type of carriage which reflected their status and by belonging to the best social circles. If a practitioner failed to convince those he served – patients and hospital governors alike – that his social status was in keeping with his aspirations to work as a medical professional, he could lose all.

CHAPTER THREE

Birmingham – from town to second city

When James West came to Birmingham to take up his appointment at Queen's Hospital, he was given accommodation on the premises. The hospital, situated in Bath Row, just to the south west of the centre of the town, was an elegant building which had been built in 1841 as a teaching hospital for Queen's College.

We know nothing of what West thought of the town when he first arrived, but it must have struck him as quite unlike the city he had left behind. London was the largest city in the world in 1851, and it was a position it held on to right up until the end of West's life. Its population, of around 2,363,000 in 1851, dwarfed that of Birmingham, which stood at the 265,000 mark for the same year. The census reveals that in 1851, Birmingham was the fifth largest town in the United Kingdom. Liverpool lay in second place, whilst Glasgow and Manchester occupied third and

Queen's College, Paradise Street, Birmingham, 1873. Source: By kind permission Birmingham Central Library.

fourth positions respectively.[1] Birmingham was set to grow rapidly during West's years in the town. The town was destined to become not just a city [2] in Queen Victoria's lifetime but second city.

Occupational diversity characterised the town's workforce by 1849,[3] according to a contemporary Board of Health Commissioner cited by Asa Briggs in his book, *Victorian Cities*. Recent archaeological finds have confirmed the fact that Birmingham has been a thriving industrial centre since the middle-ages, but in the nineteenth century, the town was renowned, above all, for its metal working tradition. The close proximity of abundant supplies of coal and iron in the nearby Black Country, and the easy, cheap transportation of them facilitated by the new canals, allowed the metal working trade in Birmingham to flourish. Every 'Brummie' knows that Birmingham has more miles of canal than Venice, and the rapid growth in the town's population coincided with the heyday of the canal. According to Catherine Hall,[4] Birmingham's population grew from 35,000 in 1780 to a quarter of a million by 1850. Population growth continued to gather pace in the latter half of the century. Victor Skipp writes that Birmingham's population rose threefold during the reign of Queen Victoria alone – from about 170,000 in 1837 to 522,204 in 1901.[5]

Birmingham's old centre, around St Martin's church, was one of the most impoverished areas of the town by the time West arrived, but there were other areas in which houses, built in Georgian times, graced pleasant squares and wide tree-lined streets. Edgbaston has been mentioned already, but there were also fine houses around the town's two baroque churches of St Paul's and St Philip's, as well as those in Old Square and on the estates developed by the Colmore family of New Hall. The houses built on the Colmore estates had large gardens, as did those of Edgbaston, but the town had been surrounded by a belt of gardens and orchards in the late eighteenth century and many of these remained well into Victoria's reign.

The social structure of Birmingham's population was different from most other industrial towns of the period and this may even have been obvious to the newly arrived recruit. Birmingham's labouring workforce

---

1   Geoffrey Best, *Mid-Victorian Britain*. (London: Fontana Press, 1979), p.29.

2   1889.

3   Asa Briggs in *Victorian Cities*. (London: Penguin Books, 1968) p.186. The Commissioner believed the diversity he spoke of gave Birmingham trades 'exceptional elasticity.'

4   RJ Morris and Richard Rodger (eds), *The Victorian City, A Reader in British Urban History 1820–1914* (UK: Longman, 1993), p.311.

5   Victor Skipp, *The Making of Victorian Birmingham*. (Birmingham: Published by the author from 5, Clay Lane, Yardley, B26 1DU), p.7.

worked in small workshops rather than factories. Their masters were 'small men,' and Asa Briggs [6] is not the only historian to talk of the mutual interests and interdependence of both parties. Another way in which Birmingham differed from many other industrial towns, was in its long standing tolerance of religious dissenters. Skipp [7] says that the municipal borough of Birmingham had fifty-four nonconformist chapels as against twenty-five Anglican churches in 1851, and that by 1872 the figures had risen to ninety and forty-six respectively. A few of these non-conformist churches and chapels acted as 'pulpits' for a number of extraordinary men, and it was those men and others like them who proclaimed what was known at the time and afterwards as 'the civic gospel.'

It is evident from West's diary that he was a committed churchgoer. His faith – Anglicanism – was, as we have seen, the minority faith in Birmingham, but as far as his career went, membership of the Church of England was essential. West would not even have qualified for an appointment at Queen's had he subscribed to any other faith. Membership of the Church of England was a pre-requisite for a post holder at Queen's. He will not have encountered much of the spirit of the 'civic gospel' amongst his employers in his new post. In spite of the efforts of Birmingham's radical reformers and others like them elsewhere, there was some considerable way to go before social justice and equality could be achieved. The old social order of hierarchy and deference was alive and well at Queen's, as it was in society in general. West was of the generation of medical men who would help to sweep away the old habits and attitudes which had been responsible for holding up reform and the process of professionalisation. There was, however, trouble ahead for both West and the hospital when he arrived in 1854 and it was not long in coming.

Medical institutions in Birmingham

There were two general hospitals in Birmingham when West arrived in 1854. One, The General Hospital, founded in 1779, was in Summer Lane, a site which was at the time, just in the countryside on the north east edge of the town. From the time of its foundation, its medical staff involved themselves in the education of would-be medical practitioners through the training of apprentices. Sydenham College, The General Hospital's own medical school, opened in 1851, but it was to last only seventeen years.

---

[6] A Briggs, *Victorian Cities*. p.186.
[7] Skip, *The Making of Victorian Birmingham*, p.116.

Queen's College and its hospital came into existence thanks to the efforts of William Sands Cox (1802–75) and his supporters. Cox – himself the son of a surgeon – started a series of lectures on anatomy at his father's house in Temple Row, Birmingham, in the year 1825. The venture proved popular, and it soon became necessary to transfer the developing medical school to larger and better equipped premises at Snow Hill. It was not long before the Snow Hill site also proved inadequate, and the school moved again. The new premises, which Cox acquired in 1834, were in Paradise Street, and they remained in use until medical courses were transferred to Mason Science College in 1896. The premises in Paradise Street still exist, and the inscription, *Queen's College*, can be seen clearly over its door to this day.

To begin with, the medical school flourished. Cox had nineteen students when he started in 1825, and by 1834 the number had risen to ninety.[8] Historians agree that the status of an institution was enhanced if it was given royal recognition, and Cox saw to it that he sought out and obtained royal patronage. His medical school was honoured, not once, but twice, in less than ten years. The school first became known as, *The Royal School of Medicine and Surgery*, under the patronage of William IV in 1836, and then, *Queen's College*, when it was granted a Royal Charter by Queen Victoria seven years later.

'The insidious intrusion of malignant dissenters'

William Sands Cox received financial assistance from a number of sources, his father included. Parental support was the young William Sands Cox's only source of funding initially, but by the early 1830s he was actively seeking funding elsewhere. In those early days, aid and donations amounting to £900 [9] enabled him to set up a museum and library. The biggest benefactor by far was the Reverend Dr Warneford (1762–1855), Rector of Bourton on the Water, Gloucestershire. Warneford's contributions towards the institution amounted to some £27,000 [10] over the course of fourteen years, and its founder fondly assumed that more would be forthcoming in a handsome legacy on the death of the great benefactor. It was not to be. By the time Warneford died in 1855, the institution was already a troubled one. The goodwill of Warneford towards

---

[8] Joint Committee of The Medical Faculty of the University of Birmingham and The Medical Review, *The History of the Birmingham Medical School 1825–1925*, (Birmingham: Cornish Brothers Ltd, 1925), pp.26 &28.

[9] Ibid., p.27

[10] Ibid., p.29

Queen's had evaporated, and the institution was left to solve its problems without his assistance.[11]

Dr Warneford's involvement in Queen's had, in any case, come at a price. Warneford's views on religious matters were severe, if not extreme. Letters written to Cox are littered with sentiments which are, by present day standards, paranoid. After reminding Cox that the donations he had given were given on the understanding that 'sound religious principles' were 'inculcated' into the students, Warneford says that while he is confident in the current supporters of the College, he warns that 'great deliberation is surely required to guard against future Satanic subtlety.' He goes on to state that it is necessary to 'guard against the subtle designs of the Jesuits and the insidious intrusion of malignant dissenters.'[12] Both students and staff alike, were required to demonstrate their allegiance to the Anglican church, and what started out as a medical school, had already branched out into other disciplines by the mid 1840s. A department of Theology, funded by Dr Warneford, was opened in 1851, but even before that, the range of courses offered had grown to include Law, Civil Engineering and Architecture, Arts and General Literature and Theology. There was also a separate junior department. Cox may not have shared the staunch views of Warneford for all we know, but was presumably obliged to acquiesce with his benefactor in order to avoid alienating him.

Fortunately, Queen's Hospital, designed as a teaching hospital, was built before the institution got into serious difficulties in the 1850s and 60s. The hospital, which opened in 1841, had the distinction of being among the first provincial teaching hospitals in the country. Like other hospitals of its day, it was a charitable institution, funded by voluntary donations, subscriptions, fund raising and legacies. Its patients were the sick and injured poor of the town. Apart from its most junior medical officers, who received a modest stipend in addition to their board and lodging, its medical staff held honorary positions. When the hospital first opened, its medical staff were even expected to surrender the apprenticeship fees which were customarily paid directly to the surgeons and physicians who worked in such institutions. Surrender of fees over the course of the ten years between 1842 and 1852, brought the institution just over £4,186. Staff may have started off by foregoing all of their fees to the institution, but this seems not to have persisted. The text [13] which refers to the figure of

---

[11] Ibid., p.29.

[12] Ibid., p.29.

[13] Ibid., p.37.

1852, states that the medical staff had given a large proportion of the fees paid to them by students to Queen's.

The duties of residential medical officers

In 1853, the year before West took up his first appointment at Queen's, the duties of residential medical officers were amended. The list of twenty-one duties covers everything from the minimum qualification requirements to suspension and removal. There is no mention of a requirement to belong to the Anglican Church in the list dating from 1853, but it is present in the Rules and Regulations printed in 1857. Salaries are mentioned in the 1853 document, although the figure is not specified. The Annual report of 1856 [14] lumps the salaries of the House Surgeon, the Chaplain, the Dispenser, the Matron and the House Steward together at £250. Of the documents which still exist from around the time of West's appointment to a position as medical officer, the first one which gives a definitive figure for a surgeon's salary is to be found in the House Committee Report Book dated 30 January, 1869, where a salary of £50 plus board and lodging is given.

Records suggest that Queen's employed three medical officers at the time when West started his career. The Report from 1856 begins, as was customary, with a list of personnel. The report lists medical staff in order of seniority, and in it, West is placed immediately above two unqualified Junior Medical Officers, JT Smith and JH Wright. West's position is described as, Resident Medical Officer. The 1856 report also lists two honorary physicians, JK Booth, MD (d.1859) and Edward Townsend Cox (1769–1863) though the latter, like his son, was a surgeon. Directly below Booth and Cox are the hospital's three physicians, John Birt Davies, MD (1799–1878); Thomas Pretious Heslop, MD (1823–85) and George Fife, MD (d.1857). The three corresponding surgical positions were held by William Sands Cox, FRS, FRCS; GB Knowles FLS, FRCS (1790–1866), and Langston Parker, FRCS (1803–71). The only other medical man who appears on the list is Samuel Berry, FRCS (1808–87), the Superintendent of The Lying-In Department. The old prejudices seem to have persisted in the minds of those who designed the reports, for in them, physicians are placed above surgeons and the man responsible for midwifery (a speciality, like ophthalmic surgery, considered of low status) occupies a place at the bottom.

Medical personnel listed in the 1856 report as honorary post-holders often became consultants later on. The two who held those positions in 1856 were unlikely to have been consulted very often, however. Edward

---

[14] *Queen's Hospital, Birmingham Annual Report.* (BCL).

Thomas Pretious Heslop (1823–85) FRCP; MD ca.1875.
Source: By kind permission Special Collections, University of Birmingham.

Townsend Cox was a man of eighty-seven in 1856, and Booth was old enough to have taught the young William Sands Cox during his late teenage years in the early eighteen twenties. John Birt Davies was to hold office at Queen's for just another two years in 1856. He would eventually retire from active involvement in medicine in 1873 at the age of 75, after having worked as the town's coroner for thirty-five years. Thomas Pretious Heslop was elected to a position as physician in 1852. He was ten years older than West, and apart from a brief period when relations must have been strained at the end of 1857 and the beginning of 1858, a friendship developed between the two men which remained sound right up to the time of West's death, twenty-seven years later.

George Fife, physician, spent just four years at Queen's. He was elected the year before West qualified in 1854, but died in 1857. WS Cox was in his mid-fifties in 1856, while the surgeon George Beauchamp Knowles, retired the following year. Samuel Berry, as we have seen, specialised in obstetric surgery. His medical career had taken off in 1838 when he joined forces with one of Birmingham's most eminent medical men, Dr Ingleby, lecturing on the diseases of women and midwifery at the medical school. When Ingleby died in 1845, Berry took over as professor of Midwifery at the College – a position he would hold for more than twenty years. What West thought of Berry is not known, but he was described as courteous, genial, kind and sympathetic in the magazine, *Edgbastonia*.[15]

---

[15] *Edgbastonia*; 1881; i: p.58. (BCL).

Life as a medical officer at Queen's must have been busy for West. Practical surgery, administrative duties and further study all had to be squeezed in. We know already that he attended forty lectures in each of the three subjects – Comparative Anatomy, Clinical Surgery and Clinical Medicine and we know of the seventy-five lectures he went to on Principles of Practical Medicine. We may also remember that there were twelve supervised labours and a dissection on top of that. An inscription on a silver ink-stand and an ornamental time-piece presented to West on his resignation in 1857 by the students, junior residential medical officers and clinical clerks of Queen's suggest that he was also responsible for teaching his juniors.

As far as his official duties were concerned, West will have performed the daily routines which were outlined in the *Amended Duties of Residential Medical Officer* document of 1853. Administrative responsibilities out-number surgical tasks in the document, but this probably reflects the fact that surgical needs are to a large extent unpredictable and cannot be defined in advance.

A Residential Medical Officer was obliged to place the patient's name, time of admission and the names of the surgeon/physician and the dresser/clinical clerk as appropriate on the beds of any patients admitted by him. He was to place the books and papers of the medical staff on the tables with written reports of any important amendments made each morning. He was also responsible for the accuracy with which drugs were made up and administered and had to ensure that nurses performed their duties properly and report any shortcomings. Wines, spirits and beer were all used medicinally in West's day, and it was the duty of the Residential Medical Officer to enter the orders for wines, spirits and malt liquor requested by the surgeons and physicians. He had to record quantities, dates and changes in such a way that they could be checked against the diet book.

Surgical instruments and appliances had to be in perfect condition and always ready for use and responsibility for this lay with the Residential Medical Officer. He was also expected to provide the Weekly Board with a list of the patients who had been admitted each week, give the names of those who had been inpatients for two months and inform them of which patients were to be discharged. He was obliged to prepare the daily diet list and give it to the matron before eleven each morning. He was responsible for the drug stock book, signing orders made by the dispenser and providing the Pharmaceutical Committee with a list of the drug and appliance requirements for the forthcoming quarter. It was his duty to place notices of all the operations, post-mortems and clinical lectures in the physicians' and surgeons' rooms and forward them to the Medical Tutor at the College. He was also required to take a role call of all the clinical clerks and dressers at nine o'clock each morning. And if there was bad news which had to be imparted to the patient's friends, the luckless residential medical officer was the man who was obliged to pass it on.

In reality, Residential Medical Officers must have undertaken a great many more surgical tasks than the document would suggest. Queen's Hospital is unlikely to have been appreciatively different from St Thomas' in London, and we have already seen how practical surgery was frequently undertaken by those less well qualified than Medical Officers in that institution. In documents dated 1857, West himself claims that while at Queen's he has had 'valuable opportunities for the study and treatment of every form of disease.' He also states that with the permission of his superior, Mr Knowles, he has had 'the peculiar advantage of making (himself) practically conversant with operative surgery.'[16] In another document West says that by 1857 he had been 'for the last eighteen months actually performing the majority of the more important duties of Surgeon...'[17]

The regulations do, in any case, specify certain surgical responsibilities which were to be undertaken by the Residential Medical Officer. He was responsible, for instance, for admitting accidents and acute medical cases, notifying the physician or surgeon of the week and if it was deemed necessary, he was to adopt intermediate measures. The document states that the Residential Medical Officer was to perform bleedings, cuppings and any other minor operations, when directed to do so. He had to visit the wards between eight and nine in the morning and again in the evening between six and eight. He was to prescribe, if directed, and provide a written account of every important case which he was to forward to the appropriate medical man. He had to accompany his superiors on their ward rounds and prescribe for patients in their absence. In the absence of the physician or surgeon, he was responsible for admitting patients in the case of an emergency.

Queen's hospital, like other mid-nineteen century hospitals, was governed primarily by lay personnel, and it was customary to list its patron, presidents, honorary governors, trustees and councillors first on Annual Reports. Any hospital anxious to attract status and generous funding would have had lay personnel from among the rich and powerful on its board,

[16] Letter of application for the post of Surgeon, 28 September, 1857. JFF West Archive.
[17] Document in support of his election to the post of Surgeon, 13 November, 1857. JFF West Archive.

and Queen's was no exception. In the 1840s, the honorary governors consisted of forty-six men, so powerful, that the list reads like a Who's Who of the country's grandees. Under the Honorary Governors, there were other Governors with powers and privileges directly related to the donations they had made and below them, there were members. When it came to decision making, doctors themselves – even those who had been responsible for the founding of hospitals – were subordinate to the lay powers. It was a situation much resented by the medical profession and it could lead to some very bitter disputes.

James Fitzjames Fraser West himself became the centre of one of the most damaging disputes in the history of Queen's in the second half of the nineteenth century, and it was all to do with an application he made for the post of Surgeon in 1857. The episode must have had a profound affect on West, and the unpleasantness of it persisted in the minds of the family he would go on to father. The writer's late step-mother who, it will be remembered was the granddaughter of West, had an envelope containing documents relating to the incident upon which she had written 'Grandfather's Papers. Queen's Hospital Scandal,' amongst her possessions when she died in 1991. She was not alone in describing the incident as a 'scandal.' *The Birmingham Journal* used this term and others like it in the numerous articles they published on the disputed election.

'Queen's Hospital Scandal'
The terms 'House Surgeon,' 'Medical Officer' and 'Assistant Surgeon' were not as tightly defined in 1857 as they are now. Some documents relating to those times and to West, in particular, use the terms, House Surgeon and Residential Medical Officer as synonymous, as well as using the term Medical Officer to refer to any medical professional who worked for an institution of one sort or another. In other cases, they denote hierarchical positions. It is hoped the context will make the meanings clear.

The 'scandal' which broke out in 1857 was triggered by West's successful application for a post as surgeon at Queen's Hospital. The appointment, like all posts at the hospital, involved teaching medical students at the College, and, in accordance with the constitution all such appointees were known as 'Professors.' Most of the existing professors – the hospital's founder William Sands Cox and John Birt Davies, in particular – favoured another candidate, Joseph Sampson Gamgee. To their dismay and astonishment, the Council chose to disregard their preference and elect West instead.

*William Sands Cox FRCS, FRS (1801–75) and John Birt Davies MD
(1799–1878). Source: William Sands Cox & the Birmingham Medical School.*

The concept of medical ethics was in its infancy in the 1850s, and when it
was conceived, it more often than not concerned the behaviour of medical
men towards each other. There is a well known cartoon [18] in the *Wellcome
Library for the History and Understanding of Medicine* which shows rival medical
men in dispute while to their right a patient sinks and dies. Animosity
between medical professionals was what had kept the old hierarchical
tripartite system in place in the first half of the nineteenth century, and there
were episodes in Birmingham, and elsewhere, which show there was still a
long way to go before unprofessional behaviour was eradicated. In the same
way, the concepts of patronage and the old-boy network were only just
being seriously questioned in mid-nineteenth century England. Lindsay
Granshaw [19] says that at St Thomas' Hospital in London, posts almost always
went to insiders and that this persisted beyond the 1850s.

James West made an unsuccessful application to join the medical staff
at the Liverpool Infirmary in 1856, but when Mr GB Knowles announced
his decision to retire from Queen's in the summer of 1857, West decided to
try his luck once more. He was, of course, known at the hospital, but he
must have been aware his age and relative lack of experience counted
against him. His maestro, John Flint South, had, after all, been obliged to
wait until the age of forty-three before he was promoted to the post of
Surgeon at St Thomas' Hospital, London.

---

[18] Doctors Differ and their Patients Die. Wellcome Institute for the History of Medicine Library.
Ref: V0011049C00.

[19] *St Thomas' Hospital, London, 1850–1900*, p.360.

There were six applicants for the position of Surgeon at Queen's in 1857, and of those who did apply, there were some strong candidates. In accordance with custom, the professors considered the merits of the candidates, discussed their preferences and submitted a list of those considered eligible to the Council. William Sands Cox and John Birt Davies expressed a clear preference for Joseph Sampson Gamgee, and as medical experts, they fully expected their lay colleagues to act on their recommendations. The Council's decision to elect West, the story behind how this happened, what those opposed to the decision did to try and reverse the decision, and how the various parties behaved, is a long and unhappy one.

The official report on the suitability of the candidates, which the Professors submitted to the Council can be seen below:

Mr JOSEPH SAMPSON GAMGEE, Staff Surgeon of the First Class, Principal Medical-Officer of the British-Italian Legion during the late War; late Assistant Surgeon to the Royal Free Hospital, London, House Surgeon and Ophthalmic Surgeon's Assistant at University College Hospital.

Mr BENJAMIN HUNT, late House Surgeon of University College Hospital; late Resident Physician's Clinical Assistant at the Hospital for

James Fitzjames Fraser West (1833–83) LSA, MRCS, FRCS & Joseph Sampson Gamgee (1828–86) MRCS, FRS Ed. – West's rival in the election dispute. Sources: JFF West Archive & by kind permission Special Collections, University of Birmingham.

Consumption at Brompton; late House Surgeon to the Kent County Hospital for Diseases of the Eye and Ear; and late Medical Officer of the Queen's Hospital.

Mr FURNEAUX JORDAN, late Resident Surgeon of the Warneford Hospital and Bathing Institution, Leamington, and Junior Anatomical Demonstrator at Queen's College.

Mr HENRY LAKIN, Surgeon to the General Dispensary; late Assistant-Surgeon Dreadnought Hospital Ship, Greenwich; late Assistant-Surgeon Smyrna Hospital and General Hospital before Sebastopol.

Mr JAMES WILLIAM MOORE, Surgeon in the Bombay Army, Honourable East India Company's Service; late Resident Medical Officer of the Queen's Hospital.

Mr JAMES F WEST, late Resident Medical Officer of the Queen's Hospital.

West's position at the bottom of the list is coincidental – the list was arranged alphabetically – but the words which describe his eligibility are sparse and imply that he was considered the weakest candidate. The professors' doubts about West's suitability for the post were not unreasonable. He was the youngest of the competitors by several years, and compared to the other candidates, lacked experience. West had gained three Honorary Certificates and a prize for his Ophthalmic Report during his time as a student at St Thomas', as well as honours in Anatomy in the first examination for an MB as we have already seen. Gamgee, on the other hand, had won five gold medals while he was a student at University College, London.

Young men looking for hospital posts in the 1850s had the best chance of attaining a position in the hospitals where they were known, and this is reflected by the fact that four – West, Benjamin Hunt (1827–83), James William Moore and Furneaux Jordan – had connections with Queen's. The professors at Queen's were certainly not opposed to the practice of appointing old boys either. In the statement they made to the public [20] in response to the election of West, they state that with regard to the election of old pupils. 'Some (that is, professors) leaned to old pupils of the College, as offering a stimulus and a reward to the highest class of students...' The professors were well pleased with the calibre of the candidates who applied. In their statement they say 'The Professors could not but feel gratified that so many candidates of repute, and many of such standing, should offer themselves for this honourable post.'

---

[20] *Statement of the Professors and Other Documents. Queen's Hospital Birmingham* D/1 Part Two, (BCL).

The vacancy was advertised in the local press and the medical journals in August, 1857. There was no clause to the effect that canvassing for votes was considered unsporting never mind, prohibited. It was an attention to detail that the professors would come to regret. Canvassing – considered normal practice up to, and beyond, the middle of the nineteenth century – would have been taken for granted unless specifically outlawed at the time. The professors had been careful to warn that no canvassing was permitted in an advertisement they placed in the press only a few months earlier. Canvassing was not the only aid which candidates used to influence those who might appoint them. Those aspiring to posts also armed themselves with a quantity of testimonials written for them by the great and the good. There were no interviews. The professors even used the fact that they had not met Gamgee at the time of the election as proof that they could not have been biased in their choice. In their various protestations, the professors frequently pointed out that Gamgee only appeared in the town for the first time ever, a few days after West had been elected.

'One of those disasters which annihilate hope'
Gamgee too made much of his claim to have stayed away from Birmingham until after the election, but this is contradicted in a biography written by one of his descendants.[21] She says that Gamgee went to Birmingham in anticipation of the vacancy, found a house and sent to London for his sister, Emma. He even put up a plate outside stating his credentials. The survival of a letter Emma sent to her father, a prominent veterinary surgeon, shows the extent to which Gamgee's sister shared his grievance over West's election. 'Not only Joseph [Sampson Gamgee] but the other competitors have been injured by the unexpected election of Mr West; the latter is considered wholly incompetent to fill the post, for above his lack of ability, he is unfortunately short-sighted.'[22]

West and his supporters denied that he had resorted to canvassing, and the attempts made by his opponents to prove that he had done so, failed. The popularity he enjoyed amongst students, patients and members of the Council may have made canvassing unnecessary, in any case. One supporter of the professors claimed that West had 'so far ingratiated himself with many of the Council by his amiability and praiseworthy attention to the patients, that they have, out of kind feelings towards him,

---

[21] Ruth D'Arcy Thompson. *The Remarkable Gamgees. A Story of Achievement*, (Edinburgh: Ramsey Head Press, 1974).
[22] Ibid., p.88.

disregarded the pledge given in the invitation of candidates, that testimonials of qualification would, as required by the laws of the College, alone determine the choice.'[23]

A team of Hospital Visitors, chosen from among the subscribers, inspected the hospital once a week in order to ensure that patients were satisfied and conditions up to scratch. When West sought election to a post as full surgeon at Queen's in 1857, he first had to resign his position as House Surgeon. West turned to these men for appraisal and was not disappointed. A document,[24] signed by twenty-four hospital Visitors – many of whom can be found listed in the report by Queen's Hospital Visitors dated 1857/8 – testifies to West's competence and diligence whilst performing his duties as a House Surgeon and still exists today. The confidence they expressed in West's abilities was based on their observations of the young House Surgeon at work within the hospital. They had signed a testimony to that effect and, for the most part, they were prepared to stand by what they had said.

When the Council voted for West they may have been motivated by spite. Cox's incompetence as an administrator and his quick temper had already harmed relations between the professors and the hospital governors by the time that West was elected to the office of Surgeon in 1857. KD Wilkenson, the editor of, *The History of the Birmingham Medical School,* describes the situation with masterly understatement when he says 'at the time Mr Sands Cox was not on very good terms with the majority of the Council.'[25] An alienated Council may well have enjoyed the power it could wield in refusing the recommendations of the hospital's headstrong founder. The election of West would have provided the perfect opportunity to remind Cox of his station in life.

West was elected by a majority of one on 14 October, winning eight votes against Gamgee's seven. Gamgee's sister, Emma, told her father that 'the election of West came upon them all like a thunderbolt. Sands Cox' she said 'cried like a child on account of it.'[26] The professors openly described the result as 'one of those disasters which annihilate hope'[27] and they did everything in their power to overturn it. If Emma Gamgee

[23] Letter written to the Council and Supporters of Queen's Hospital 5 December, 1857 by JP Wilmot. Appendix D Queen's Hospital Birmingham, D/1 Part Two, (BCL).

[24] (JFF West Archive).

[25] *The History of the Birmingham Medical School. 1815–1925* A Special number of the *Birmingham Medical Review,* hereafter called *BMR* (Birmingham: Cornish Brothers Ltd., 1925) p.54.

[26] R Thompson, *The Remarkable Gamgees.* p.88.

[27] *Queen's Hospital. Statement of the Professors.* p.15. D/1 Part Two. (BCL).

had had her way, Cox would have prevented this 'disaster' by a pre-emptive stroke of cunning. Remarks she made at the time of the election dispute indicate that she herself would have been prepared to turn a blind eye to corrupt practice if it had served her brother's ambition to become Honorary Surgeon at Queen's Hospital. Her words imply that she was sure that Sands Cox would not have hesitated in doing so either. She wrote to her father after the election of West saying 'Had Professor Sands Cox had the slightest suspicion of this fact (West's short-sightedness) he would have prevented it (West's election) by adding an additional number of persons to vote for Joseph.'[28] Emma Gamgee was clearly confident in her belief that, but for an oversight, Cox could have engineered a different outcome. She may well have been right, but why she thought that a man who had been in almost daily contact with James West for three years was ignorant of the fact that West was short-sighted is more of a puzzle. Sisterly love is, perhaps, blind.

The statement produced by the professors in response to the wrong they believed they had suffered, extends to twenty-two sides of small print with appendices of a further five and a half sides. For his part, Gamgee addressed Lord Brougham in a document of some twenty-two sides. Furious letters to the press and between individuals were exchanged over a period of more than six months. Those involved were educated men, and they could articulate their feelings and argue with skill.

The idea of appointing a medical man on account of merit alone was something of a novelty in 1857. The General Medical Council (GMC) which implemented the registration of qualified personnel on equal terms, was established as a result of the Medical Act of 1858, but even after that, regulations prohibiting the unqualified from practising were inadequate. Discrepancies in the law meant that surgeons, in particular, could practise without any type of qualification up until the eighteen eighties. A surgeon who prescribed drugs without a LSA qualification could be prosecuted, while an apothecary who practised surgery was not breaking the law. Waddington [29] states that lack of medical knowledge did little to detract from a practitioner's status and that status was not based on any criteria we would recognise today. Peterson [30] says that in mid-Victorian London, hospital appointments were often made on the basis of a candidate's looks and manner. As science

[28] R Thompson, *The Remarkable Gamgees*. p.88.
[29] Ivan Waddington, *The Medical Profession in the Industrial Revolution*, (Dublin: Gill and Macmillian, 1984), p.19.
[30] MJ Peterson, *The Medical Profession in Mid-Victorian London*, (Berkeley: California, 1978), p.128.

advanced and expertise grew, attitudes changed, and it was the men who qualified around the 1850s who would see those changes implemented.

At the end of the address he made to Lord Brougham, Gamgee attached thirty testimonials written in support of James West as well as fifty-two of his own. It is clear that both candidates had taken responsibility for approaching referees themselves. The references do not even all date from the same time. Among West's, there are testimonials from 1854, 1856 and 1857 respectively. They represent the time he first sought a post at Queen's in 1854, his application for a position at Liverpool Infirmary some two years later and the most recent post for Surgeon at Queen's. Gamgee's testimonials also refer to different appointments, and there were others which he must have collected routinely on his departure from the various Continental hospitals and medical schools that he had visited during the two years he spent studying abroad. Gamgee had even sent copies of the various works he had published to complete strangers for appraisal. Lay governors – many of whom remembered the days when dubious medical qualifications provided little indication of a medical man's suitability – still had little to guide them in the 1850s. Without recourse to interviews, and without the benefit of confidential testimonials, lay appointees could only seek the advice of medical professionals and follow their own instincts. If a lack of trust between lay governors and their professional colleagues existed there could be, and frequently was, trouble.

'Your professional attainments everything I could wish for'

West's testimonials differ in tone from those Gamgee submitted. References to industriousness and sheer brilliance crop up over and over again in the testimonials written for Gamgee, whereas West won great acclaim for his gentlemanly conduct and bedside manner. The thirty testimonials of West have ten references to gentlemanly behaviour between them and there are a further ten to his unblemished character. Gamgee, on the other hand, has only two references to his gentlemanly conduct, and five which testify to his good character among the fifty-two testimonials written for him. Gamgee's diagnostic and technical genius at the bedside is alluded to in several of his references, but West is praised for qualities held in much higher esteem in mid-nineteenth century, namely: kindness and sympathy at the bedside. Professional abilities were not neglected by the referees, with both men winning praise for the distinction they showed at medical school and beyond, but here, Gamgee does score significantly over West.

The majority of West's references are from medical professionals who knew him during his days as a student in London, but there were seven from among his connections at Queen's. One was written by the Reverend W Hunt, but all the others were written by medical colleagues. Embarrassingly for them, there are good references from the very men who later sought to overturn the election.

William Sands Cox, his father Edward Townsend Cox and John Birt Davies all wrote references for James West when he applied for the post at Liverpool Infirmary in 1856. Phrases like 'your professional attainments everything I could wish for' (ET Cox); 'I have had an opportunity of witnessing the zeal with which he has discharged the duties of a similar office at the Queen's Hospital, and also the gentlemanly kindness and attention which both patients and pupils have experienced at his hands' (WS Cox) and 'Mr West's general conduct, his attention to his duties, and his professional ability and discretion, have been deserving of the highest praise that I can give them' (JB Davies) can be found in their testimonials. Mr GB Knowles for his part wrote, 'West has been Resident House Surgeon at Queen's Hospital upwards of one year and seven months and has fulfilled the duties of that situation to my entire satisfaction.' Langston Parker, surgeon, says in his testimonial that he has, 'every reason to be satisfied with Mr West's skill and attention to his patients' and that written by Thomas Heslop, physician, was complimentary too. In his testimonial, Heslop says 'I have had the opportunity of knowing and admiring the zeal and ability with which he has prosecuted Medical and Surgical Science, as well as the diligent attention which has characterised him both in reference to the comfort of patients, and to the directions of Medical Officers.' The references written by West's teachers at St Thomas' are written in a similar vein.

How Gamgee got hold of West's testimonials is not known. There is no way of knowing if the thirty constitute all of the references written for West either, but the absence of protest by West or his supporters to that effect suggest that Gamgee had not omitted any. While the testimonials written for West speak of a creditable and honourable ability, Gamgee's tell of exemplary, if not, brilliant talent. His contain a plethora of flattering commendation. For the most part, the references were written by his old teachers and medical colleagues, but there are seven amongst them which were written by individuals who were not even personally acquainted with him. Three were written by fellow-students.[31]

---

[31] One was written by the, as yet unknown, Joseph Lister.

Words like 'zeal,' 'energy' and 'promise' crop up again and again in Gamgee's references, but there is greater accolade to be found. One, written by John Erichsen FRCS of University College, London, says he has no hesitation 'in deliberately stating that (he) knows *no one* in the profession, not already holding such an appointment, who is in every way so highly qualified as Mr Gamgee...' He goes on to say that he has noticed 'the very extraordinary and unfaltering zeal with which he has devoted himself to the study of the profession' and also that Gamgee has 'much independence and originality of thought.' Erichsen concludes that he considers Gamgee *eminently* qualified for the post...' Comments like 'original thinker;' 'bold and accurate observer' (Edward Ballard); as well as references to his 'remarkable faculties,' (Francesco Rizzoli) and 'striking abilities' (Francis C Webb) can be found time and again among Gamgee's testimonials. Several referees believe any hospital that employs Gamgee should congratulate itself, and some of his Continental referees say that Gamgee will bring credit to both his country and his profession.

Walter Hayle Walshe (1812–92) said that Gamgee's mental attributes could not be better signified than with the words of Pascal, which, he tells us Gamgee chose as the epigraph to his recent work on Clinical Surgery. They were the words of a man "qui ne trouve le repos que dans la recherche sincère de la vérité."[32] Andrew Clark's [33] high opinion of Gamgee is reflected in his testimonial. He writes that Gamgee is 'endowed with great natural abilities which he has carefully cultivated and rigorously disciplined; that he is eager, resolute, and untiring in his search for truth; that he is an acute observer; a deep, clear, fresh, and fertile thinker; a close, methodical reasoner; and a ready and fearless speaker and writer.' Joseph Lister, wrote the longest reference written by a fellow-student. All three of the 'student' referees had admired Gamgee when they were students and had continued to do so, but we get an indication of Gamgee's competitive nature in the testimonial written by fellow-student, Thomas Hillier. He states that when Gamgee was in competition with others he 'always succeeded,' and had 'a resolution to be first in everything that he undertook.'

'Null and void'

Gamgee's resolution to be the first in everything he undertook is evident in the attempts he made to persuade the public that the election of James West should be overturned. William Sands Cox and John Birt Davies were

---

[32] (a man) 'who finds rest only when searching for the truth.'
[33] Later Sir Andrew Clark, 1826–93.

equally determined. The row which followed the election of West provided the town's newspapers with material for more than six months. It is hard to imagine an episode of this sort being given the same amount of coverage in the press today, but the behaviour of the professors and Gamgee caused an outrage at the time. West had, after all, been elected quite legitimately. Yet within days, and in a meeting which was unconstitutional, he stood accused of canvassing, his election was declared 'null and void' and Gamgee was appointed in his place. Gamgee, for his part, lost no time in calling on West personally and asking him to stand down in favour of himself.

As tempers became more frayed, furious letters and articles started to appear in the local press and the medical journals. *The Lancet*, the *British Medical Journal* (*BMJ*) and the *Medical Times and Gazette* all covered the dispute, but the local newspapers entered into the fray with a vengeance. Accusations and outpourings can be found in virtually every issue of the Birmingham weekly newspaper, *Aris's Gazette*, from the middle of October to the end of March, 1858. *The Birmingham Journal*, a bi-weekly newspaper, totalled some thirty-one articles altogether, with two, three and even four articles in some issues. *The Birmingham Daily Post* published three editions with two articles each in its twenty-seven features on the dispute, as well as including one on Christmas Day itself. Many of the articles which appeared in the press were lengthy, but the longest was published in *The Birmingham Daily Post* on 10 December, 1857, and consisted of some 670 lines.

Interestingly, the first instinct of *The Lancet*, a journal known at the time for its support of the rank and file, championed the cause of the professors. The press was not universal in its support for West either. *Aris's Gazette* backed the professors initially – an act which provided the other newspapers with plenty of ammunition when it began to temper its attitude at the beginning of 1858. The other newspapers gave West their backing from the start. It was not long before the papers discovered that Davies' own son, John Redfern Davies (1835–67),[34] had been one of the candidates in the early rounds. On 4 November, *The Birmingham Journal* voiced its suspicions that the attempt to appoint Gamgee had been largely a convenient means of avoiding offence to Dr Davies. In electing an outsider, they could dodge the issue of appointing a local rival instead of the young Davies. Even more of an embarrassment was the exposure by the press that John Birt Davies had himself canvassed members of the Council in the

---

[34] Redfern Davies did not remain idle for long. He was appointed surgeon to the Birmingham Workhouse on 9 June, 1858. His life was cut short as a result of serious injury sustained in a riding accident eighteen months before he died (*The Lancet*; 1867; i: p 319).

Left: Silver Inkstand inscribed with the words 'presented to James F West Esq. by the students of Queens' College Hospital as a mark of their appreciation of his valuable services to that Institution. October, 1857.' Right: Marble Clock (H:35, W:27, D:15cms) engraved with the words, 'presented to JF West Esq. by the students of Queen's College Hospital 1857.' Both in private ownership.

hope that they would look favourably on his son. In a report of one of the many Meetings of Subscribers it is stated 'so little did the Professors consider canvassing a disqualification, when it suited their own purpose, that one of them, Dr Birt Davies, solicited the votes of Members of the Council in favour of his own son...'[35]

It will be remembered that the students from the College together with a number of junior residential medical officers and clinical clerks presented West with a silver inkstand and an ornamental time-piece when he resigned his post in order to apply for the surgeonship in 1857. In the address given by them on that occasion, they are quoted as saying 'We cannot allow you to resign the post... without testifying our appreciation of the manner in which you have discharged the duties of that office during the three years you have been with us. We have ever found you zealous in the discharge of the responsible duties that necessarily devolve on you in a large clinical hospital, and we feel sure that it will be a source of the highest gratification to you to know that the duties you have performed so sedulously and efficiently have met with the warm approbation of the students.'

It is hardly surprising then that the students of the college joined in the controversy by expressing their dismay over West's treatment in letters to

---

[35] *'The Management of the Queen's Hospital,'* from the meeting held on Wednesday 3 March, 1858. (JFF West Archive).

the press and medical journals. Their letters supported West's claim and protested at the injustice he had suffered. They were considered impertinent by *The Lancet* and *Aris's Gazette* but were reported with sympathy by *The Birmingham Journal*. In an article dated 18 November, 1857, which commences with the words 'The plot thickens, and new actors come on the stage' the newspaper states 'The third act opened on Saturday morning' and it details the particular incident which provoked the students into putting pen to paper. Mr West, who the paper says was 'surrounded by a score of students' was attending to out-patients when the door opened and Sands Cox entered together with Drs Davies, Heslop, Fleming, Mr Knowles, Mr Gamgee and two others whom the paper describes as 'minor performers.' Mr Knowles was then asked whether he was to hand his patients over to Mr Gamgee. He said that he was. The article goes on 'and amid ominous silence possession is taken of the remaining out-patient, poor devil, and he is "treated" by the opposition Surgeon. Mr West protests, the students are requested to follow Mr Gamgee, to a man they decline to stir a step; no invitation to breakfast, dinner, and et ceteras – no mean attractions to students "in residence" – will tempt them to recognise Mr Gamgee.'

The professors tried to persuade West to accept a position as assistant surgeon in the early days of the dispute, but West's supporters and his solicitor, Mr Slaney, urged him to refuse the offer. West had discovered early on that he had plenty of support, and much of it was from among Birmingham's elite. He was to remind newspaper readers of the fact in an address he made to the Birmingham papers in November when he said, 'as the Editor of the Birmingham Daily Press observed at the time, it is impossible that such men as the Mayor (John Ratcliff), Rev Dr Miller (1814–80),[36] Mr Thomas Bagnall, Mr Edward Armfield, Mr F.I. Welch, or Mr Samuel Haines, could vote for me from any other motive than that of public duty, and a firm conviction that in so doing they were promoting the best interests of the College and Hospital.'[37]

The Reverend Dr Miller, Rector of St Martins, was a key player in the dispute, and it was Miller and others of like-mind, who orchestrated the foundation of a Committee of Subscribers which almost brought about the

---

[36] The Reverend Dr John Cale Miller deserves to be remembered for his contribution to hospital funding in Birmingham through "Hospital Sunday," a scheme he devised for collecting donations from the town's churches on specified Sundays. It proved so successful that the idea spread to other parts of the country and even to America.

[37] Address, *To the Governors and Subscribers of the Queen's Hospital, Birmingham. November*, 1857. (JFF West Archive).

total ruin of the Hospital. This group – formed to urge subscribers to withhold their subscriptions to the hospital – soon became a vehicle of protest, not only for the injustice perpetrated against West, but for more general issues, namely; the unprofessional behaviour of the professors.

These powerful men, backed by large numbers of subscribers and members of the public, were prepared to express their outrage with the help of the press. Sands Cox and Davies were dubbed as a 'despotic pair' guilty of 'arrogance, self-will and trickery' by the *Birmingham Daily Post*. The paper frequently referred to them as 'the firm of Cox and Davies.' Terms used to describe the two in *The Journal* were equally harsh. The paper describes the pair as 'the individuals who have occasioned all the mischief'[38] and calls them amongst other things 'obdurate,' 'offensive' and 'dominant'.

'Fustian and inconsequential nonsense'

The statements published by both Gamgee and the professors alienated the press.[39] The professors' report was described by the *Birmingham Daily Post* as 'long, wearisome, and incorrect, treating in a style of solemn verbosity matters that' had 'no relation to the question of Mr West's election...'[40] The main thrust of the argument in both, was election by merit as opposed to election through the use of influence. Talk of 'saving' the Institution was another theme common to the two statements. West, both claimed, was not only unfit for the job when compared to Gamgee, but had also been guilty of canvassing. West responded with a statement of his own dated 17 November. He stated that the professors, having failed in their efforts to declare his election null and void, had tried to pressurise him into accepting a less prestigious position, while Gamgee, he said, had done his best to discredit his good name and the good names of those who had voted for him.[41]

'Mr Gamgee' says West 'wrote a very lengthy pamphlet, in which he certainly did his best to damage my position and character as a professional man, without going so far as to render himself liable to an action of libel; while at the same time he ventured, with the most flagrant and uncalled-for impertinence, to assail two gentlemen (the Rev Dr Miller and the Mayor) whose position and influence as men of honour

---

[38] *The Birmingham Journal*, 19, December, 1957. (BCL)
[39] Gamgee's statement, entitled, *'Address to Lord Brougham,'* is also to be found in, *D/1 Part Two*. (BCL).
[40] *Birmingham Daily Post*, 9 December, 1857. (BCL).
[41] In particular the Reverend Miller.

and strict integrity no one who knows anything of them will for a moment dare to question.'[42]

Gamgee's pamphlet not only derides the abilities of West, but is peppered with moral blackmail. He curried favour with the professors by referring to the institution as the 'University of Central England.' He asked if, and in capital letters 'PRIVATE INTEREST OR PUBLIC DUTY?' is to prevail, reminding the reader that his opponent was elected by a 'majority of *one*' (italicised on each occasion, and included a total of seven times). He even ascribed dramatic 'stage' roles to the real characters involved, as well as adding a few fictional ones for good measure. At one point he allocates two and a half sides of print to acquainting the reader with the sort of response he believes a number of fictional representatives of society would make of the situation. By today's standards it is manipulative and patronising.

Gamgee first calls upon the 'artisan' to speak; a man, whom he says is 'the sinew of Birmingham's glory.' Our 'artisan' has, according to Gamgee 'laid down the sledge hammer, wiped from his begrimed manly face the down-trickling sweat, and crossed his arms to listen to the facts.'[43] The 'artisan' says that he's not sure that justice has been done. If it has, our 'artisan' states, he trembles for his own son. Gamgee goes on ' "He's a good and clever lad, and he goes to Mr Miller's Ragged School in Well Lane. I'd lay a wager there's not a boy that's cleaner and does more credit to his mother....I'm in hope as he gets on I'll be able to send him to the College, in Bath Row, where he may get the wisdom which Solomon tells us is better than gold; and who knows but that one day he may be trying to be a Surgeon to the Queen's." '[44]

Gamgee even ascribes a text to his opponent, James West, starting with the quote ' "My heart shall not reprove me so long as I live," ' in Gamgee's address, West conveniently sees reason. He admits he's young and somewhat lazy, saying ' "I am young. I have certainly suffered no hardships for my profession, as have done Laken and Moore, in India, Persia, and the Crimea – I have not ransacked libraries, grown pale in dead-houses, traversed, without resting, the countries of Europe... I have not gained more than good repute for diligence as a student, and moral character as a man. I will not be the instrument, even though the passive one, of an injustice. I will work, in the hope of acquiring esteem as a labourer in the vineyard of science; I am happy in the success of right – let right be done." '[45]

---

[42] (JFF West Archive).
[43] Gamgee, *Address to Lord Brougham*; p.13. (BCL).
[44] Ibid., p.14.
[45] Ibid., p.19.

Gamgee certainly alienated *The Birmingham Journal,* as a result of this and other tirades. He was accused of insulting the Reverend Dr Miller, the governors and Mr West, and of brow beating the Council. One letter which Gamgee wrote to the paper on 14 November, and which claims a status for Birmingham more elevated than most of the capital cities of Europe, was printed by the *Journal* purely for the pleasure it afforded in making fun of West's rival. They accuse Gamgee of 'flunkeyism' and invite their readers to judge for themselves with the words 'As a specimen of fustian and inconsequential nonsense, read this.'[46]

The professors were more subtle, or perhaps it should be said, cunning, in stating their case. They point out that they have already been misunderstood by the public, saying that they have suffered the 'malicious and utterly unfounded interpretation which has been affixed to every part of their conduct...'[47] The professors know they tread a delicate path. They are careful to portray themselves as reasonable men. They speak as though they are above the sort of row which has broken out over the election, actively avoiding, as far as possible, the denigration of West. They stress, that they only have the best interests of the institution at heart. They claim they merely want to act according to the laws of the college and uphold the principles behind meritocratic election, as any reasonable person would expect. They insist they only have the rights and interests of the sick and injured of Birmingham at heart. The full extent of their anger is revealed on occasions, though, through phrases like 'The deed (election of West) was scarcely done' and by referring to the election of West as 'one of those disasters which annihilate hope.'[48]

Resolution in compromise

The incident was finally resolved thanks to a compromise, and it was recorded that both Gamgee and West were appointed on equal terms. In reality, West's name always appeared first on printed hospital documents, and in at least one of the obituaries written on the death of Gamgee in 1886, it says this in relation to their appointment on equal terms 'As a matter of fact Mr West was conceded the seniority and retained it till his death.'[49] Dr Heslop had distanced himself from Cox and Davies during the course of the dispute and became one of West's closest friends. And there

---

[46] *The Birmingham Journal,* Saturday 14 November, 1857. (BCL).
[47] *Statement of the Professors,* etc, p.22 (BCL).
[48] Ibid., p.15.
[49] *Aris's Gazette,* 20 September, 1886. (BCL).

is evidence to suggest that the two rivals themselves soon learnt to respect, and even like each other.

A surviving envelope dating from 1872 is addressed to JF West at 22, Broad Street, the home of Joseph Sampson Gamgee. It coincides with the period in West's life when he was in the process of moving from Acock's Green, near Solihull to Edgbaston in Birmingham. The printed membership list for the Midland Medical Society for the same year also gives West's address as Broad Street. While this does not prove that West was staying with Gamgee at the time, it is the only plausible explanation.

We know, too, from the minutes of a meeting of the Midland Medical Society on 19 March, 1873, that West made a proposal that day to fellow members that a public acknowledgement of Gamgee's contribution to the medical charities of Birmingham should be recorded. West's resolution went as follows:

that *'The members of the Midland Medical Society hereby express their high sense of the important services rendered to Birmingham and its medical charities by Mr Sampson Gamgee in the recent Hospital Saturday movement and beg to tender their thanks to him for the assiduity and zeal in carrying to a successful issue this praiseworthy effort to extend the usefulness and promote the prosperity of all the medical institutions of the town.'*[50]

West's proposal was seconded by Mr Harmar (d.1890), supported from the chair by Mr Bassett (d.1892), Professor at Queen's College, and was carried unanimously. Later, in a paper dating from 1875,[51] West refers to Gamgee as an 'esteemed colleague.' And, as a reference made by Gamgee proves, the two men were clearly able to work together. In his book *On the Treatment of Wounds and Fractures*, published in 1883, the year of West's death, Gamgee named West as one of three colleagues who assisted him in an operation. When West died in May of that year, Gamgee was among the mourners at his funeral.[52]

Gamgee was indeed an asset to Queen's Hospital and medicine in general. Historians who have studied Birmingham's hospitals will know that before he died in 1886, Gamgee worked tirelessly for the town's hospitals, being the chief driving force behind both the new extension at Queen's in the early 1870s, and the Hospital Saturday Fund which both helped to fund that project and raise funds for further use by the medical

[50]　Midland Medical Society Minute Book 1864–1873. 1/1/1. (B Med I).

[51]　JFF West, Notes of a case of Fibro-cystic Tumour, or Hydrocele of the Neck; *BMR;* 1875; p.107.

[52]　*Birmingham Daily Post*, 30 May, 1883. (BCL).

charities of the town. The name Birmingham Hospital Saturday Fund has survived to this day and consists of a health scheme which provides insurance for a wide range of treatments and compensation for injuries. Known as BHSF, it is located in the aptly named, Gamgee House.[53] Another memorial to Gamgee – a blue plaque – is to be seen on the wall of the Repertory Theatre in Broad Street, Birmingham, the site of Gamgee's home. He was also the only Birmingham practitioner to be included in Bailey and Bishop's *'Notable Names in Medicine and Surgery'* and this, on account of the dressings he designed and which became popularly known as 'Gamgee's dressings.'

We do not know what West's views were on the rights and wrongs of electing surgeons on merit in 1857, but he does say in 1873 [54] that the French method of electing surgeons, using merit alone, is superior to the methods used in England where, he says, influence is still common. In any case, West's opponents never did manage to substantiate their claim that he had been guilty of canvassing. Gamgee, on the other hand, turned out to be less of an advocate of meritocracy than he led his supporters to believe in 1857. If comments made by one of Queen's later recruits, Joseph Priestley Smith (1845–1933), are anything to go by, Gamgee seems to have been quite prepared to abandon the principle when it suited him. In a paper entitled 'Notes from the Tent Hospitals of the Franco-German War' Priestley Smith writes 'In consequence of the exertions and influence of my kind friend Mr Gamgee, I obtained an appointment as assistant to a large tent-hospital...'[55]

When Gamgee consigned West to a place among the ranks of the work-shy, he was being unfair and he almost certainly knew it. West made regular contributions to the leading medical journals,[56] visited hospitals and medical schools on the continent, and was a regular attender at medical society and association meetings both locally and nationally. And as was

---

[53] A history of the movement can be found in Peter J Maskell, *Best of Health. 130 Years of BHSF 1873–2003* (England: BHSF Group Ltd, 2003). Peter J Maskell is the current Chairman of BHSF. The present building was opened in 1976 by Gamgee's descendant, Joseph Leonard Gamgee, Barrister at Law, who unveiled a panel commemorating his illustrious relative with the words 'in honour of Joseph Sampson Gamgee FRCS founder of the Birmingham Hospital Saturday Fund – 1873 – and distinguished surgeon to the Queen's Hospital Bath Row, Birmingham.'

[54] JFF West, On some points of Contrast between French and English Surgery; *BMR*; 1873; p 35.

[55] Joseph Priestley Smith, Notes from the Tent Hospitals of the Franco-German War; *BMR*; 1873; pp.44–45.

[56] The first is dated 1857. Case of Asphyxia Complicated with Concussion, and Followed by Stupor, successfully Treated by the Marshall Hall Method of Artificial Respiration; *The Lancet*; 1857; i: pp.530–531.

seen at the beginning, by the time he died in 1883, West had been Vice President of the Birmingham Medical Institute, Senior Surgeon to Queen's Hospital, Consulting Surgeon to the Dental Hospital, Professor of Anatomy and of Clinical Surgery in Queen's College, President of the Clinical Board and of the Midland Medical Society, Director of the Clinical Section of the local branch of the British Medical Association, a Director of the Birmingham Medical Benevolent Society and President to the Shakespeare Dramatic Club. West was an avid reader, and owned a substantial library. None of this would suggest that he deserved a place among the ranks of the work-shy.

The behaviour and attitudes of William Sands Cox, remained a source of dismay to many of those with whom he was involved professionally. Only two years after the election row, Cox's conduct and mismanagement of the college provoked some fourteen members of the institution to band together and demand his removal from office. Rows, resignations and financial ruin threatened the institution to such an extent in the late 1850s, that Professors West, Gamgee and twelve others (not all of them medical) felt compelled to write to Sands Cox with a demand for his resignation. The fourteen pointed out that differences between Cox and others interested in the college had threatened the very existence of the institution. They went on to say 'We cannot conceal from ourselves the fact that in these differences you are on one side and the professors and other officers of the college on the other.' They pressed him to withdraw for a period of two or three years, after which time they said they hoped the college will have attained a degree of popularity and financial success, to which, they say 'it has long been a stranger.'[57] The fourteen were not the only colleagues of West who were prepared to express their dissatisfaction either. Criticisms made by two other Queen's men, Thomas Heslop and Furneaux Jordan, can be found in the Charity Commission's Report of 1863.[58] Heslop had resigned from Queen's in 1858 'owing to intolerable disgust with the administration of the College by Mr Sands Cox and some who acted with him'[59] and was willing to denounce Cox's management and behaviour openly when consulted by the Commissioners. Thomas Heslop is reported as saying that 'Mr Cox grossly insulted him' in saying that he (Heslop) was capable of doing anything, while Dr Jordan complained of Mr Cox's rudeness to him.

[57] *Report to the Charity Commissioners*, 1863, pp.47–48. (BCL).
[58] Ibid., pages 62 and 74 respectively.
[59] *Birmingham Post*, Obituary on the death of Thomas Heslop, 19 June, 1885.

'Birmingham Duelling Pistols; Out twelve times but, as yet, unfired'

The medical men of Queen's were not the only Birmingham doctors to become involved in damaging disputes. Thomas Gutteridge (1805–80) was another undisciplined medic from the Victorian era, and was probably the most vile. He stirred up a tremendous amount of trouble for others between the years 1843 and 1872. Birmingham Central Library has a 4cm thick printed volume of his vindictive letters and pamphlets. No doubt there were more. The surgeons, Dickenson Crompton (1805–94) and Alfred Baker (1815–93), who were both given appointments at The General Hospital in preference to Gutteridge, were the targets of his poisonous pen in 1843 and 1851 respectively. Attempts to ruin others almost invariably failed, as it did in the two above mentioned cases. In one case, Gutteridge even suffered the humiliation of being ordered by the courts to make a public apology. Gutteridge had attacked the Reverend James Prince Lee (1804–69) when he was acting as hospital governor to The General Hospital at the time of Baker's appointment, but when he accused Lee of intoxication at the time of his consecration to the Bishopric of Manchester, Lee took him to court. Mr Grantham Yorke (1809–79), Rector of Birmingham's cathedral, St Philip's, and the Catholic Convent in Hunter's Lane also came under virulent attack, but in these cases, as in so many others, Gutteridge failed to inflict any serious damage.

Thomas Gutteridge was not alone either. The surgeon, and father of William Sands Cox, Edward Townsend Cox, also seems to have had difficulty in getting on with other people. One quarrel between ET Cox and Dr Gabriel Jean Marie de Lys [60] in the early years of the century culminated in the two meeting in the countryside nearby in order to fight a duel. The dispute arose when Cox refused to surrender the library books he had on loan from a local medical society which was to be disbanded. The task of demanding the return of the books fell to the unfortunate Dr de Lys. According to, *The History of the Birmingham Medical School 1825–1925*,[61] Dr de Lys 'was so rudely received when he called that he informed Mr Cox that there was only one way out of the difficulty which, he said, had become an "affair of honour." ' A date was set for a duel which, it was supposed, would settle the matter. In the event, no harm was done. Dr GE Male, the

---

[60] Dr Gabriel Jean Marie de Lys was the son of a French aristocrat who fled the revolution and worked as a physician at the town's General Hospital between 1815 and 1831. De Lys founded the The Royal Institution for the Instruction of Deaf and Dumb Children in Church Road, Edgbaston in 1812 (now renamed, The Princess Royal Centre of the National Deaf-Blind and Rubella Association). He was born in St Malo, Brittany in 1784 and died in 1831.

[61] *The History of the Birmingham Medical School 1825–1925*, pp.23–24.

man Cox proposed to act as his second, not only refused, but exposed the pair to the authorities, and when the two combatants met up, they were greeted by officers of the law. All that remained to remind the townsfolk of the incident, was a display of the pistols Cox had hired in a New Street gun shop, with a label ' "Birmingham Duelling Pistols. Out twelve times, but, as yet unfired." '[62]

The most notorious of Birmingham's medics had had their day by the time Victoria's reign was two thirds the way through. Cox senior died in 1863 at the age of ninety-four and his son was dead by 1875. John Birt Davies died in 1878 and Thomas Gutteridge followed him to the grave just two years later. The type of unprofessional behaviour so beloved of these men was seen as unacceptable by the later generation of medical practitioners. The new generation were the first to be able to develop their expertise without the distraction of the undisciplined behaviour of their colleagues. In any case, the hospital staff of Queen's was left in no doubt about the need to discipline themselves after a resolution to that effect was made in 1872. A report of the House Committee from that year resolved that 'any Resident Member of the Hospital Staff either spreading, being privy to or countenancing reports prejudicial to the reputation either of any other member of the staff or likely to damage the Institution, and not reporting the circumstances at once to the House Committee shall be considered guilty of a grave misdemeanour and shall lay himself or herself open to dismissal at the discretion of the House Committee or General Board as the case may be.'[63]

Recovery of Queen's College
Towards the end of the election dispute there were those who said that if the Committee of Subscribers continued to urge subscribers to withhold their subscriptions, the hospital would suffer complete ruin. They pointed out that the hospital in which they hoped James West would work as surgeon would not even survive long enough for him to take up his post. As we have seen, the election dispute was only one of the troubles which plagued the institution. The letter which West, Gamgee and his colleagues sent Cox asking him to resign from the college in 1859 failed in its immediate objective, although it was used as evidence in a later report on the troubles at Queen's. This document contained a copy of the letter, and was entitled, *First Cause. The Mismanagement of the College Affairs.*[64]

---

[62] *The History of the Birmingham Medical School 1825–1925*, pp.23–24.
[63] *House Committee Report Book, June, 1871 – May, 1873*. Entry under 22 November, 1872. (BCA)
[64] *Birmingham Miscellaneous* 1866 G/I (BCL).

So great were the institution's troubles in the final months of 1859 that the then Dean, Dr Francis Thomas Bond, took the unprecedented step of calling on the Bishop of Worcester for an official visitation. This never materialised, but a suggestion made by the Vice-Principle, Reverend the Honourable Mr Grantham M Yorke, to apply to the Charity Commissioners for an official enquiry was adopted and bore fruit. The enquiry was conducted by Her Majesty's Inspector of Charities, Mr FO Martin. His examination of witnesses began on 6 December, 1859. The report itself did not appear for some months, but when it did, it was a damning indictment of Sands Cox and his management of Queen's.

In the *Second Cause. The College Quarrels*,[65] it is stated that most of Martin's report is devoted to the college quarrels and the resulting loss of public confidence in the institution. Student numbers bear this out. Around the ninety mark in the years 1851–53, numbers plunged to sixty-four in 1857. Things were to get worse. Student numbers were down to thirty-five by 1859. A reduction in student numbers was not the only problem. By January, 1866 the college was in debt to the tune of more than £10,000. Some clearly suspected Cox of something more serious than mere mismanagement. Dr George Vernon Blunt (1823–98), Dean of the Faculty at the time of Martin's Report, was one. He detailed charges amounting to over ninety pages in the report compiled by Mr Martin. The plausibility of Blunt's allegations were no doubt strengthened by the fact that Cox himself guaranteed the payment of the College's debts in 1861 in return for being allowed to take possession of all the personal effects of the College.

There were men who had worked alongside Cox from the beginning who came to regret their connection with him and his institution. Mr James Thomas Law (1790–1876), Chancellor of the Diocese of Lichfield and the first Vice-Principle of the institution, was one. It is said in the *Third Cause. The College Disagreeables* [66] that Law considered 'his thirty years connection with the Queen's College, to be one of the greatest misfortunes of his life.'[67] Cox did have supporters of course, and there were others who colluded with him in keeping things under the carpet rather than expose the institution and its founder to more ridicule. Fortunately adjustments made to lessen his involvement after 1859 went uncontested by Cox, and although he retained some links with Queen's up until 1867, most of it was in name only.

---

65 Ibid..
66 Ibid..
67 Ibid..

A rival medical school, Sydenham College, which was affiliated to the town's other general hospital, The General Hospital, opened in 1851, just in time to profit from the defection of would-be students of Queen's. It flourished for a while, largely at the expense of Queen's, but it declined just as quickly, and in 1868 suffered the indignity of being amalgamated with its rival. When the merger took place, the number of students was only sixty. Queen's College had struggled on during the years from 1859 to 1868 thanks to a series of temporary measures, but what was in effect a new institution finally emerged in 1868 as a result of an Act of Parliament.

The college opened under new management, and it was Lord Lyttelton – a man who had already devoted sixteen years of his life to Queen's, for the most part as its Principle – who gave the introductory address to the inaugural lecture at the beginning of the academic year. Lord Lyttelton was one of many who had retired from Queen's in the troubled years of the 1850s and 60s. He alluded to the controversies of former days in his address, but stated that he had no desire to dwell on the circumstances which led to his retirement in 1856. The Inaugural Address given to the new students on this occasion was given by James West. It was a clear signal that he was ready to back the new organisation, and its tone is upbeat. He informed students that the profession they were entering was 'a profession which, if followed honestly and conscientiously, is one of the most honourable, useful, and God-like of all professions;...'[68]

Queen's College enjoyed a period of success in the years between Cox's departure in 1869 and 1892. After that, medical courses were taught in the town's new college of science, Mason College. This institution was founded in 1875 thanks to the outstanding generosity of its enlightened benefactor, the industrialist, Josiah Mason (1795–1881). This costly enterprise amounted to £200,000 and was supervised by Mason personally through daily visits to the building site over a five year duration even though he was eighty years of age when the project was started. The Medical Faculty of Queen's College had transferred some of its scientific teaching over to Mason College in 1882 and the final transfer of 1892 resulted in better facilities and better prospects for staff and students alike. Mason College was granted university status in 1900 mostly thanks to Birmingham's well known mayor and statesman, Joseph Chamberlain (1836–1914), but there were men who had worked alongside West whose efforts also contributed

---

[68] Inaugural Address by JFF West, *BMJ*, 10 October, 1868. The abstracts of Lord Lyttelton's Introductory Address is printed immediately above.

towards that goal. The surgeons, Robert Lawson Tait (1845–99) and Oliver Pemberton and Drs Alfred Carter (1849–1918) and Thomas Heslop all played an important part.

Queen's Hospital

Queen's Hospital had seventy beds when it opened in 1841, and by 1845 work had begun on a detached fever ward which was designed to cater for up to twenty-eight patients. A chapel and two additional wards were added in 1850, and by 1856 – the year before the election dispute – there were 150 beds. The number of beds fluctuated over time, falling to 120 in 1892 before climbing back to 132 by 1900. A new extension was opened in 1873. This, as we have seen, was made possible through the efforts of Joseph Sampson Gamgee, who raised much of the necessary funds for it by rallying the support of the working classes. His main aim had been to provide a new Out Patients block, but the space released by moving Out Patients to the new

Staff of Queen's Hospital, Birmingham, 1861. Back row from left to right: Joseph Sampson Gamgee, David Malins, James Fitzjames Fraser West, Balthazar Walter Foster, Thomas Furneaux Jordan, John St Swithin Wilders and front Willoughby Francis Wade, William Sands Cox, John Manle Sutton, Rev WH Poulten. Source: By kind permission Birmingham Central Library.

Queen's Hospital, Bath Row, Birmingham in 1873 after the new detached fever wing was opened. Source: The History of the Birmingham School of Medicine.

building, meant that the Dead House, the Post-mortem Room and the Laundry could all be transferred to better locations and the kitchens remodelled. James West donated £20 [69] towards the building of the new extension, and when the foundation stone was laid in 1871, it was West who proposed a toast to Lord Leigh at the VIPs luncheon which was held to mark the occasion. He was also listed [70] as among those present when the new wing was officially opened on 7 November, 1873. James West worked in the enlarged hospital for ten years before he died in 1883, but he did not live long enough to benefit from the modernisation of the operating theatre in 1893 or see the effects of the installation of electric lighting in 1898.

Gamgee was not the first person to persuade the working classes to contribute to the funding of the hospital. Some £905/1/3d was raised by the Artisans of Birmingham by a penny subscription in the year 1847. Apart from investments and income from lands and property owned by the institution, fund raising events, church collections, donations, legacies and subscriptions were the chief sources of hospital funding. Privileges granted

---

[69] *Twenty-sixth Month's Statement of Accounts, March 30th, 1871.* From a sheet entitled, *Working Men's Fund for the Extension of the Queen's Hospital.* (BCL).

[70] *Aris's Weekly Gazette.* 8 November, 1873. (BCL).

to those who subscribed varied according to the size of the subscription. Regulations were adjusted from time to time, but in 1873 a donation of £20 was enough to secure a position as a Life Governor as was a promise of a legacy of £20 or more. A donation of £2/2/– entitled the subscriber to a position as Governor, and an individual chosen to represent the collective efforts of clubs or institutions had the same privileges as other benefactors and subscribers.

In addition to that, physicians and surgeons, including those with consultancies held positions as Governors *ex officio*, and those who donated a lump sum of £20 were permitted the same privileges as a subscriber of two guineas. The document of 1873 states that Benefactors, Governors and Subscribers had the privilege of recommending patients annually in accordance with the scale below and the same in proportion for all sums subscribed.

Benefactors, Subscribers and Governors Privileges

Amount subscribed	In-patient tickets	Out-patient tickets
£0. 10. 6		3
£1. 1. 0		10
£– 2. 0*	1	1
£– 10. 0*	1	5
£3. 3. 0	1	11
£4. 4. 0	2	2
£5. 5. 0	2	12
£6. 6. 0	3	3
£7. 7. 0	3	13
£8. 0	4	4
£10. 10. 0	5	5

A set of regulations was also laid out for the clergy. Every clergyman who organised church collections for the benefit of the hospital was entitled to the privileges set out below.

---

* The original table shows a blank on the two marked with an asterisk rather than a zero as shown in the first row. Given that the privileges stated in rows three and four defy a logical progression, error cannot be excluded.

Privileges Granted to Clergymen and Ministers who Permit Collections

Amount subscribed	In-patients	Out-patients
£5	1	10
£10	2	20
£15	3	30
£20	4	40
£25	5	50
£30	6	60
£35	7	70
£40	8	80
£45	9	90
£50	10	100

In addition to this, every Governor and Subscriber could have twenty out-patient tickets in exchange for one in-patient ticket and could buy additional in-patient tickets upon application. Other donations were given for specific purposes. One of these was a benevolent fund which was created for the relief of accidents and acute cases.

Apart from cash, gifts of all sorts helped to keep the hospital afloat. One Hospital Report [71] shows that donations of coal from the Staffordshire Coal and Ironmasters literally floated in on a regular basis. The first boat load was donated in 1841, the first year of the hospital's existence, and this was followed in the next ten years by a further twenty-eight. It may have been a coincidence, or it may have been because of the damage caused by the election dispute of 1857, but by 1858 donations of coals from the Staffordshire Coal and Iron Masters had ceased. In that year the hospital paid £100/2/3d for coal and the hire of the boats to bring it to the hospital premises. Detailed lists of gifts appeared in hospital reports from the 1880s and 90s. A glance through them shows how varied the gifts were. One list, dated 1882, includes firewood, illustrated papers, a large dolls' house for the Children's Ward, crutches, turpentine, food, clothes and bed linen, amongst other things. Gifts of religious reading matter frequently appear in the lists. These, no doubt, provided moral edification, while other gifts, like flowers, were intended to bring cheer. Gifts of discarded bed linen are

---

[71]   Queen's Hospital Report, 1854; p.22. (BCL).

ever present in the lists and were actively encouraged by the hospital authorities. A reminder to the Friends of the Charity to the effect that discarded bed linen 'continues to be especially welcome' was almost always to be found at the end of lists of gifts.

Hospital conditions

The recipients of the care and treatment provided at Queen's Hospital were, as we have seen, the sick and injured poor. This does not mean that all of those who came into that category were welcome. Anyone seen as the responsibility of the Parish or Poor Law Union could be rejected. Unions were warned that it was their duty to remove such patients when required to do so, and defray the expense of burying their dead should they be unfortunate enough to die in the hospital. Subscribers who sought to recommend persons who were not considered proper objects of charity could expect rejection and those afflicted by chronic disease and incurable illnesses were also unwelcome.

As we have seen already, doctors who were kind and sympathetic were held in high esteem in Victorian England, and the testimonials written for James West suggest that he did have a good bedside manner. Conditions and patient satisfaction were monitored at Queen's and other hospitals by a team of men known as 'visitors.' These men undertook the task of inspecting the hospital on a rotational basis and were chosen from amongst the subscribers. Few of their reports have survived, but of those that have, there are some dating from the time of the election dispute in 1857/8. Inspections took place once a week and visitors were obliged to answer a prescribed set of questions. The information collected was presented in the hospital reports in tables like the one seen below.[72] How reliable this material was as an indicator of the true state of the hospital is not certain. The degree of satisfaction and contentment conveyed in the report is certainly high, but perhaps Visitors and patients alike were under pressure to register satisfaction where little was felt. The difference in status between those who asked the questions and those who answered them may also have compromised responses. The Visitors were, after all, representatives of the hospital. They were men with status inspecting the conditions of those without it. Nevertheless, by specifying that patients were to answer for themselves and without restraint, those who designed the inspection sheets had clearly tried to eliminate the possibility of patients being coerced or intimidated into giving favourable replies.

---

[72] *Queen's Hospital Birmingham Annual Report 17.* 1858 (BCL).

Visitors' Inspection Chart, Queen's Hospital from 4 September, 1857 to 5 March, 1858

Date of visit	Was every part of the house and premises in good order?	Did every person appear to be in his or her proper place, and in the regular discharge of their proper duties?	Were the beds all whole and in proper condition, and the Table of Regulations hung up in the ward?	Did you inquire from patients themselves, when they were under no restraint; whether they were perfectly satisfied with the attendance of the Medical Officers and other persons belonging to the Hospital, or whether they had any reason to complain of inattention or neglect?	Have you any other observations to make?	Visitors in Attendance
Sept 4	Yes	Yes	All beds that need, are in process of purification.	None complained of their treatment: all expressed themselves satisfied.	The wall fence against the canal should be renewed, to prevent depredations	John Boucher
Sept 11	Yes	Yes	Yes	I inquired in every ward; received no complaint whatever but, on the contrary, all expressed themselves fully satisfied. Decidedly so.	None	Isaac Trow
Oct 8	Perfectly so	Yes	Yes	Quite satisfied: no complaint, except in the two front wards the patients complain of the draught of air from the door on the beds. Query – Would a screen be desirable?	None	Joseph James
Oct 22	Yes	Yes	Yes	No ground of complaint from the patients, but perfectly satisfied.	I found in many of the wards that the Bibles had been taken away on the Fridays and not returned. Might not the ventilation of Ward V. 5 and 2, be improved by openings covered with gauze wire, and the other ventilators kept open during the winter, if the same protection was given?	Joseph James
Oct 29	Yes	Yes	Yes	Perfectly satisfied	Eliza. Foxley, A. 5 Ward: Why continued? We understand she is considered incurable. We wish to call attention to the Secretary's office, which is imperfectly warmed.	James Busby, Joseph James
Nov 6	Yes	Yes	Yes	No complaint, except in the Accident Ward, "Not bread enough"	None	R.G. Reeves
Nov 13	Yes	Yes	Yes	No complaints		R.G. Reeves
Nov 27	Yes	Yes	Yes	Perfectly satisfied		R.G. Reeves
Dec 4	Yes	Yes	Yes	Yes: and all were well satisfied	Regret was expressed in Ward V. 5, and concurred in by several of the other wards, that the bedside visits of the Chaplain have latterly been omitted.	Josh Barrows

Date of visit	Was every part of the house and premises in good order?	Did every person appear to be in his or her proper place, and in the regular discharge of their proper duties?	Were the beds all whole and in proper condition, and the Table of Regulations hung up in the ward?	Did you inquire from patients themselves, when they were under no restraint; whether they were perfectly satisfied with the attendance of the Medical Officers and other persons belonging to the Hospital, or whether they had any reason to complain of inattention or neglect?	Have you any other observations to make?	Visitors in Attendance
Dec 11	Yes	Yes	Yes	Yes.; and they expressed themselves satisfied, and appeared to be grateful.	See last week	Josh Barrows
Dec 18	Yes	Yes	They were.	I did: and all appeared to be satisfied and thankful		Josh Barrows
Dec 24	They were	Yes	Yes	I did: and all were perfectly satisfied.	Not any, except that I have not visited the Detached Wards.	Josh Barrows
Jan 1	Remarkably clean, and in order.	Yes: every one.	Yes	All expressed satisfaction and gratitude.	None	John Boucher
Jan 8	Yes	Yes	Yes	Some complaint respecting supply of bread, in V. 1 Ward, was inquired into.	The water pipes appear to be out of repair. Recommended they be attended to.	John Boucher, Wm. Southall
Jan 15	Yes	Yes	They were.	Yes: all appeared quite satisfied.	The nurses of the Detached Wards complain of the darkness of the stairs, landing &c; one or more gaslights might be furnished at a small expense.	Wm. Southall
Jan 22	Remarkably clean	Remarkably Yes	Yes; they were.	Every person appeared to be properly treated, and several expressed their gratitude for kindness received.	No	John Boucher, Wm. Southall
Jan 29	Yes	Yes	Yes	No complaint of any neglect.		John Boucher, Wm. Southall
Feb 5	Yes	Yes	Yes	A complaint of the quality of the sugar in all the male wards, and that the tea was very poor.	A very offensive effluvium in Front Women's Ward V. W. 7.	Thomas Phillips, Thos. Crowley
Feb 12	Yes	Yes	Yes	No complaints; all appeared satisfied.	No	Thomas Phillips, Thos. Crowley
Feb 19	Yes	Yes	No. 5 Men's Ward, some beds require repairing. The nurse promised me she would get them repaired. Referred to House Committee.	No complaints of neglect.	None	Thos. Crowley
Feb 26	Yes	Yes	Yes	No complaints.	None	Thomas Phillips, John Boucher, Joseph Watson
Mar 5	Yes	Yes	Yes	No complaint, except that the House Porter has neglected a proper supply of coals.	No	
					Smoking is practised in the Men's Detached Ward, contrary to the rules of the Hospital.	

Doctors and surgeons who worked only in private practice had, through necessity, to oblige and pander to the whims of their patients. They lost the goodwill and support of their patients at their peril. The charity hospitals, on the other hand, presented doctors with a more subdued clientele. There, doctors could, and sometimes did, exploit their positions of power over their patients. The historian, Ivan Waddington,[73] says that in the charity hospitals of the nineteenth century, doctors could, for the first time, treat patients according to criteria defined by the profession rather than by the patient. He says, that faced with a vulnerable and powerless clientele, doctors came to enjoy great power and status in the charitable hospitals of Victorian England.

The Visitors' report from which the extract above was quoted covered the period between July, 1857 and June, 1858, but apart from that, records which relate to issues of this sort are scarce. Two Visitors elected by the House Committee are recorded as having made a specific complaint in January, 1875.[74] It was recorded that the Rev TD Halstead and AN Hopkins gave a report which was 'most unfavourable with regard to the cleanliness of the Hospital.' It states 'they found the wards, corridors, in short all parts of the Hospital extremely dirty, the floors insufficiently scrubbed and the windows filthy.' The Lady Superintendent was absolved of responsibility for the lamentable state of affairs by the Committee on account of the fact that she had been given insufficient authority over the scrubbers. A swift and marked improvement was reported by the Committee after they had sanctioned a decision to give the Lady Superintendent greater powers over her juniors. A year later, another criticism was recorded in the General Committee Book.[75] The Visitors are quoted as saying 'We think there might be considerable improvement in many of the wards in the way the sinks and closets are kept, old carpets, dressings ——[?], dirty bed pans go and stored away here... The wards themselves appear properly clean.'

The provision of beds was, on occasions, inadequate, and overcrowding occurred from time to time. In April, 1866,[76] for instance, the House Committee resolved that it was no longer acceptable to have more than one adult in a bed. Further complaints about overcrowding appeared in later House Committee Report Books suggesting that the problem had not been resolved by 1873, or even 1884. The reference to the problem in January,

---

73 Ivan Waddington, *The Medical Profession in the Industrial Revolution*, (Dublin: Gill and Macmillian, 1984) p.198.
74 General Committee Book, January, 1873 – July, 1876 p.363 (BCA).
75 Ibid., p.1
76 *House Committee Report Book, June, 1863 – September, 1866*. Entry under 6, April, 1866. (BCA).

1884 is a general one, but in April, 1873 the Committee agreed that it was unacceptable to make up beds on the floor.[77]

Complaints made by disgruntled patients or their representatives also appear in the Committee Books from time to time. A browse through the records suggests that the Committee was remarkably adept at sidelining them in the troubled 1860s. Mr JM Williams wrote to the hospital on 22 December, 1865 [78] stating that he gave an In-patient ticket to a man named Mitchell. He reminds them that Mitchell died in the hospital, and goes on to say that the man's son and a friend called on him to say that 'before his death (he) complained bitterly of his treatment, and neglect.' Unfortunately Williams gave the Committee licence to turn a blind eye to the accusations at the end of his letter when he wrote 'will you kindly investigate the matter in order that I may allay their anxiety on the subject.' It comes as no surprise to find that after 'carefully and minutely' investigating the case using the evidence of Dr Jolly (1841–94) and two fellow patients, it was resolved that 'proper attention was paid to patient Henry Mitchell by the Medical Officers and Nurses.' It might have been possible to take this reassurance at face value but for the fact that the Committees of the day had a marked propensity to find all such complaints unjustified.

Attitudes towards patients

Records show that attitudes towards patients did begin to change in the latter part of the century. An entry in the House Committee Book for March, 1881[79] refers to the resentment which has been expressed by patients who feel they are being treated as second class citizens by the hospital's porters. The complaint was taken seriously, and the General Superintendent soon reported back that he had impressed upon the porters the importance of showing kindness and forbearance towards patients. Further complaints, communicated to the Committee by Councillor Cook a month later, reinforce the theory that patient satisfaction was not what it might have been in the early 1880s, and the fact that, in this particular situation it was having a direct effect on fund-raising, would not have been lost on the Committee members. He states that, 'various ill defined complaints of incivility have been made to him during his canvass for Hospital Saturday by persons who have been patients of the hospital.'[80] The response was immediate. It was resolved that

---

[77] *House Committee Report Book, June, 1871 – May, 1873.* Entry under 23 April, 1873. (BCA).
[78] *House Committee Report Book, June, 1863 – September, 1866.* Entry under 29 December, 1865. (BCA).
[79] *House Committee Report Book, April, 29th, 1879 – February 6th, 1883.* Entry under 15 March, 1881. p.184. (BCA).
[80] *General Committee Book, May, 1880 – February, 1886.* Entry under 1 April. (BCA).

the secretary be instructed to inform each member of the Honorary staff to help by noticing and preventing any cause for complaint.

Bedside manner

We do not know much about the 'bedside manner' of individual doctors who worked at Queen's, but West left a number of clues and there were others – those whose style was legendary – for whom there is circumstantial evidence. James West is described as a man with marked 'bonhomie,' 'genuine humour' and a 'cheery, hearty laugh,' in the obituary which appeared in the magazine, *Edgbastonia*,[81] and yet later on in the same article it states, 'Spite of a certain abruptness of manner, he was much beloved....' So were the testimonials of the 1850s right to suggest that James West was a compassionate man with a good bedside manner? A paper [82] written by West, dating from 1873, speaks volumes about his own attitude to patients, but there are also unspoken assumptions to the effect that he believes his views are widely shared by others. West described the inhumane treatment of patients in France that he had witnessed during recent visits to that country in the paper.

In the Hospital St Louis, he says,

'women with skin diseases, whether syphilitic or not, are placed on a stool in a strong light, and then before the whole class requested by the physician to take off every article of clothing. There they stand perfectly naked, while the professor diagnoses their disease and points out its peculiarities and proper mode of treatment to the assembled students. Such a disregard of the feelings even of prostitutes would not be sanctioned in this country. Indifference to the sufferings of the patients is again seen in the fact that at many of the hospitals the surgeon is attended through the wards by an infermier, in his short sleeves, carrying a brazier full of hot coals and the accompanying cauteries. These formidable instruments are not only displayed before the eyes of the patients who are about to be operated on, but they have to submit to them without having their eyes bandaged and without chloroform being administered..... Anæsthetics are certainly much less used than with us. I saw the actual cautery [83] frequently applied, and also an amputation of the cervix uteri performed without chloroform. But worse than all, on

---

[81] *Edgbastonia*; 1883; iii: pp.97–99. (BCL).

[82] West, *On some points of Contrast between French and English Surgery*; BMR; 1873; p.33.

[83] The authority, John Kirkup MD MA FRCS Dip Hist Med, has informed the author that many Victorian doctors used the term 'actual cautery' to distinguish it from the 'potential cautery' which was the application of chemicals to the skin. The 'actual cautery' was a heat or thermo-cautery. It caused less damage than caustics which, although painless on application, were difficult to control and could lead to long-lasting ulceration or even permanent damage. Kirkup also says the 'actual cautery' was often used as a counter-irritant whereas the hot iron cautery was favoured as a means of arresting hæmorrhage.

one occasion some years ago, I saw M. Nelaton [84] try for half-an-hour to extract a hair pin from the bladder of a woman, by means of forceps, without success, while the patient lay shrieking most piteously every time the sharp points of the pin lacerated the mucous membrane of the bladder and urethra, in the futile attempts made by him....'

West's indignant response to what he saw indicates that treating patients in a manner like that outlined above, would have been considered barbaric in England. Subjecting patients to humiliation and embarrassment, or expecting them to suffer severe pain when there were ways and means of preventing it, would have been unacceptable to English practitioners. But the English were not opposed to the idea of exhibiting their patients per se. James West and his contemporaries regularly took live exhibits along to the meetings organised by the various medical societies. Exactly how they were treated has not been recorded, but let us hope that it was rather better than that meted out to the French.

Jordan Lloyd – the man who filled the vacancy created by the death of West in 1883 was less compassionate. He is described as 'genial,' in an article printed in the magazine, *Aesculapius,* and it is stated that he adopted the vernacular when talking to patients. But in reading further it becomes clear that his use of the vernacular was patronising rather than chummy. The article's author, Dr Arnold Gourevitch, overlapped with contemporaries of Lloyd, and their knowledge of him made it possible for Gourevitch to include a passage which illustrates how Jordan Lloyd communicated with the out-patients who consulted him at Queen's. These extracts, based on the memories of the surgeon Frank Barnes conjure up an image far from genial.

'Next! What's the matter with you?'

'Got appendicitis.'

'Oh, you 'ave, 'ave yer, and who told you? Damn the man! I don't want to know what your doctor says, if you can't tell me what you're complaining of, be off and I'll have na-more ta-do with you....Next!... Come on, if you want to see me, and don't sit staring there.'

A second patient does no better,

'Hurry up now, missiz. Something in the breast? How long?'

'Well, my doctor, 'e says –'

'Don't want to know what your doctor says, I want to know how long you've had it?'

'It's my 'usband wot told me –'

'How long???!!! Can't yer answer a plain straightforward question? Or don't you understand English, which? You 'er friend? Well then, stand

---

[84] Monsieur Nelaton was probably the urologist Auguste Nélaton (1807–73).

Robert Lawson Tait (1845–99) MRCS; FRCS; LRCP; LRCS Edin.
Source: By kind permission Special Collections, University of Birmingham.

behind the chair and don't keep fidgeting. Can YOU tell me how long it's been there?'[85]

Doubtless Lloyd was not the only doctor who adopted the tone found in the extracts above. There is evidence, by admission, that there was one who was even prepared to spank patients considered, by him, to be hysterical. The Birmingham gynæcologist, Robert Lawson Tait, says he once resorted to corporeal punishment on a woman who had undergone an ovariotomy three days earlier. He says his patient's predilection for drama had been demonstrated from the start, and when he had to contend with her refusal to have her wound dressed for the third day running, he lost patience. According to his own account of the incident he 'seized her by the shoulder and a hip, turned her over on her face and gave her a practical reprimand on her nates.'[86] He says he has never had to do anything like it before, but he adds that it had the desired effect in that she was not only subdued at once but never gave any further trouble.

Some stories, like those outlined above, undoubtedly reflect the stance males took towards women, but anyone belonging to the lower strata of

[85] Arnold Gourevitch TD MC FRCS (1914–2004) article entitled, *Jordan Lloyd* printed by *Queen's Medical Magazine* in *Aesculapius*, June, 1981. p.28. (Barnes Medical Library, University of Birmingham).

[86] Robert Lawson Tait, Fifty Cases of Ovariotomy; *BMR*; 1878; vii: p.301.

society – male or female – would have been in awe of their 'betters.' The attitude of the successful towards their less fortunate fellows in Victorian England was probably at best, paternalistic. The use of the term 'lower orders' to describe the poor, strikes us as offensive today, and yet it was used openly and without shame in government documents [87] in nineteenth century England. Even so, the fact that Lloyd's own particular style of dealing with patients has been remembered and recorded for posterity probably suggests that it was atypical rather than the reverse.

'Persons of dissolute character'

Some patients or their representatives used the hospital's facilities when they were not entitled to do so and this led to hospital investigations from time to time. Of the eighty-eight in-patients investigated on 19 May, 1873, sixty-seven were described as legitimate objects of charity. Of those who were not, five gave false addresses, six were ticket cases which were deemed unsuitable, eight were accident and emergency cases who could have contributed towards their treatment, and two were unsuitable emergencies. The number of out-patients investigated amounted to some 366 altogether. Two hundred and sixty of these were considered legitimate. Of those who remained, two refused to provide information, thirty-four gave false addresses, six were parish cases and sixty-four are simply listed as 'unsuitable.' In the report it states that in cases of severe disease, and this includes hypochondria, of all things, patients are classed as legitimate cases, irrespective of their pecuniary circumstances. Also legitimate, were cases of chronic or prolonged illness, where the patient had paid for medical advice according to the means at his disposal. The circumstances of some of the 'unsuitable cases' who were treated appear in detail in the report. Of those catalogued, there is a woman whose husband's earnings were stopped because of his poisoned hand; a single man who earned 18/– per week, but who was consumptive; and a young man with an income of 22/– per week who was passed because he and his brother had to support their aged parents.

A decidedly moral tone is applied to the patients under the heading of 'Unsuitable Cases – Class 11.' The report states that 'This class includes single men who, being able to earn sufficient wages, are idle or drunken; "kept" women; and persons of dissolute character.' The report's author goes on to say that 'By helping such cases a direct encouragement is given to improvidence and vice.' The author also writes that furthermore 'the

---

[87] One is the, *'Third Report from the Select Committee on the Education of the Lower Orders.'* 1818.

present system....tends to discourage provident habits amongst the working classes, by affording *gratis* the medical treatment which many ought to procure for themselves in a Sick Club, or by other means.' The hospital, like many of its modern counterparts, was also inundated with patients suffering from trivial complaints. It is stated in the report that the ease with which tickets are obtained encourages those with minor ailments to seek medical treatment in out-patients. These people, it is said 'unnecessarily occupy the time of the Medical Staff, to the detriment of the more serious cases.'

A number of cases singled out for special mention are attached to the end of the report.[88] Moral judgements abound, but the hospital's concerns are not unreasonable. There were those who were prepared to abuse the system. Number 355 is a young woman of twenty-three whose father, a certificated engineer, and two brothers are both in work. They are reputed to be living in a '£20 house.' Another – number 214 – is an elderly lady, whose son has a manufactory in the town. The words which the author of the report placed inside inverted commas are enough to condemn number eighty-six without any further elaboration. This woman, aged twenty-six, could hardly qualify on account of the fact that she was being ' "kept" by a gentleman, and has her "fancy man." ' Number fifty-eight was a woman with a husband and four children. Apart from having two children in work, her husband was found to be an employer of three men. She thought she had concealed her true identity by giving a false address, but was reported by neighbours after boasting to them about what she had done.

The report ends with a proposal to change admission procedure. Changes could not be implemented immediately, but in November, 1875 a sub-committee consisting of some eleven men, and which included James West, proposed the adoption of a 'Free System' on an experimental basis. Admission tickets were to be dropped in favour of a scheme which would ensure that those who needed immediate treatment received it irrespective of their pecuniary circumstances, and that those who elected to visit Out-patients were deterred from doing so for trivial reasons by a registration fee of one shilling.

The hospital governors were ever mindful of the pecuniary embarrassment that some patients suffered. A hospital report dating from 1876 describes a Relief Fund which was instituted twelve months earlier for the relief of those patients who leave hospital in a state of destitution. It cites cases where wives have had to pawn their furniture and many of their

---

[88] *Report of Sub-committee*, July, 1873. pp.3–10. 660395. (BCL).

James Fitzjames Fraser West ca.1864, the year of his marriage.
Source: JFF West Archive.

belongings as a result of a husband's ill heath or accident. The fund had also been used to provide artificial limbs, crutches and other appliances and had even enabled the Midwifery Department to send some patients to the seaside. Subscriptions to the fund were set at five shillings so that the sum would fall within the means of most townsfolk. West had married in 1864 and his wife and their first-born son, Walter (then a boy of nine), were among the subscribers listed in the report.

Staff who failed to treat patients with respect probably got away with it, but patients who disobeyed the hospital rules or made nuisances of themselves could be disciplined or even expelled. At both Queen's and The General Hospital, patients guilty of insubordination could expect dismissal. Reports of insubordination and waste of provisions by patients reached the House Committee of Queen's in March, 1866. The Committee resolved, 'that a notice to the effect that any patient found guilty of any act of insubordination or waste should be forthwith discharged by the Resident Medical Officer.'[89] If surviving evidence is anything to go by, records of misconduct were reported more assiduously at The General Hospital, although there is always the possibility that discipline was more draconian

---

[89] *House Committee Report Book, June, 1863 – September, 1866.* Entry under 15 March, 1866. (BCA).

at The General. Examples dating from the years 1876–86, give the names and other details of those found guilty of misdemeanour and include Roland Balnavis aged twenty-eight and William Bagnall, twenty-two, who were both discharged for misconduct; and John Euston, a boy of sixteen, who was expelled for insubordination.

Broth and beef tea
Strict attention to discipline notwithstanding, there were compensations for those who occupied beds as in-patients at Queen's and other charitable hospitals. Many patients enjoyed standards of physical comfort well in excess of what they could aspire to in life outside the hospital. Doctors at Queen's often prescribed special light diets during the recovery period, but once patients were considered fit enough, they would have been fortified by a diet rich in foodstuffs beyond the means of most of the town's poor. Provisions listed in the annual reports are, for the most part, high calorie foodstuffs. Protein rich foods are plentiful, but the provision of vegetables seems woefully inadequate to us today. There is no mention of fruit whatsoever. In the year ending 1875, the patients and residential staff of Queen's consumed 3,086lbs of sugar, 1,179lbs of rice and sago, 40,1671½lbs of meat, 1,051¼lbs of bacon and ham, and 1,236¼lbs of cheese. Fish, poultry, bread and flour were listed according to expenditure. Over fifty-three pounds was spent on fish. This may not sound much compared to the figure for meat, which was £1,493/13/4d, but it must be remembered that fish was both cheap and plentiful in Victorian England. Expenditure on bread and flour was £265/14/5d. Apart from that, staff and patients ate their way through some 353½cwts of potatoes and 19,300 eggs. Butter consumption amounted to some 1,133lbs, while cheese came to 1,236¼lbs. Milk was an important and costly item. In 1875, the hospital spent £537/10/6d on the 11,410 gallons consumed that year. Beverages included wines, spirits, porter – a dark brown malt liquor – and ale, but tea was clearly very popular. Some 457lbs of tea were bought by the hospital in the year 1875 at a cost of £48/12/9d.

A glance through the medical journals of the nineteenth century is all that is needed to see that doctors attached great importance to diet. Fortunately a surviving diet table from 1876 was printed for inclusion in one of the annual reports. The diets include a 'meat diet,' a 'varied diet,' an 'extra' or 'full diet' and a 'milk diet.' An 'extra' or 'full' diet was the same as the 'meat' diet except that the portions of meat were bigger and patients were given ½ pint of beer and 1½oz of cheese for supper. Extras were available to those who were not already taking the 'full' or 'strong diet,' and these included mutton chops; fish; strong beef tea; extra milk; rice; sago; light pudding, consisting of one egg, ½oz of sugar and ½pint of milk; batter; eggs; bread; green vegetables; wine; spirits; porter and ale. Children under ten years were put on a 'simple' diet or a 'strong' diet. In both, there is an abundance of milk – two pints – but broth and beef tea take the place of meat in the 'simple' diet. There was very little difference between the 'meat diet' and the 'varied diet' offered to the adults. For this reason, only one – the 'varied diet' is reproduced below. In 1876 it was hospital policy to put all new adult admissions on to a milk diet to begin with. Broth and beef tea were much in favour, and fortunately for those of us today who may be unfamiliar with them, recipes were recorded in the report. Ordinary beef tea consisted of ½lb clod and sticking of beef, without bone, to a pint, while strong beef tea had 1½lbs of meat to the pint. Broth was made from ¼lb of neck of mutton, with bone, to every pint. Fresh vegetables, it is stated, could be added to broth where practicable.

Day	*Per Day*	*Break-fast*	*Dinner*	*Supper*
Sun	Bread, 12oz. Potatoes, 8oz.	1 pint Milk & 1 Egg	Chicken, 6oz; or Boiled Mutton, 4oz; and Light Pudding	½pt Broth, Milk, Cocoa or Gruel.
Mon	ditto	ditto	Roast Mutton, 4oz; and Batter Pudding	ditto
Tues	ditto	ditto	Fish, 6oz; and Rice Pudding	ditto
Wed	ditto	ditto	Chicken, 6oz; and Rice Pudding	ditto
Thur	ditto	ditto	Rabbit, 6oz; or Boiled Mutton 4oz; and Rice Pudding	ditto
Fri	ditto	ditto	Fish, 6oz; and Light Pudding	ditto
Sat	ditto	ditto	Roast Mutton, 4oz; and Rice Pudding	ditto

Apart from the meat and fish, we do not know how big the portions were or what time of day meals were served. Some patients do seem to have found the amount of food served inadequate, and most people today would want something more substantial than a milk diet on admission to hospital. The only clue about meal times is to be found in a surviving document from the General Hospital.[90] At their House Committee meeting on 14 October, 1864, those present decided to abandon the hospital practice of getting patients up at 4am for breakfast on the grounds that it was unreasonably early. An interim decision made that day to leave patients to sleep until 7am must have come as a great relief to both patients and staff alike.

When he submitted papers for publication in the medical journals, West often gave precise details of the diets he prescribed for patients. In others he bewails the fact that an inadequate diet can hamper recovery. In a paper published in 1870,[91] West describes the way in which he treated Mary Horton, a woman who was suffering from complications following an injury to the wrist. West decided to perform an excision of the injured parts in order to spare the woman from the only other option, amputation. The incentive for doing so was particularly strong in her case. She was a married woman with four children. Her husband was out of work and she was endeavouring to support the family by working as a washerwoman. Mrs Horton took longer than expected to recover and West was in no doubt as to why. He says that since the operation, Mrs Horton's husband has only succeeded in getting partial employment yielding an income of under a pound a week. In writing up her case, West says that after her discharge 'she has not been able to have such a diet as was really necessary for a woman in her condition.' Later in the same paper he compares Mrs Horton's situation with that of the more fortunate Mr Hancox, who ate well and completed his convalescence in a sanatorium some miles from Birmingham.

Apart from advocating a nutritious diet, West prescribed wines, porter and port wine. Some of the doses were large. One patient – a man who was suffering from Syphilitic Fungus of the Testicle – was given wine 'in large quantities' after he was relieved of the diseased testicle in an operation performed by West on 27 October, 1858.[92] Another syphilitic patient was ordered to have one pint of porter and three ounces of port wine daily.

90 *House Committee Minutes, 1854–66.* (BCA).
91 JFF West, On Excision of the Wrist-Joint; *The Dublin Quarterly Journal of Medical Science*; February and May, 1870; XLIX: pp.85–97.
92 JFF West, On Syphilitic Fungus of the Testicle, *The Dublin Quarterly Journal of Medical Science*; 1859; XXVIII: pp.323–332.

Patients who had suffered head injuries were often prescribed what West called 'a low diet.' One, we are told, was nourished with beef tea and milk, while another was given four ounces of port wine in addition to a pint of milk and a pint of beef tea daily.[93] The low diet did not suit everyone. George S—, aged nine, was brought to Queen's on 11 January after he had been struck with a pickaxe on the back of the head by his brother. The boy remained in hospital for thirty-four days altogether. West had first to deal with the danger to the brain caused by blow, and then with a complication – an infected wound. He ordered a low diet which we can only assume was well tolerated to start with, but by 21 January, George was hungry. He requested more food and was heard. West prescribed a chop.[94]

Once admitted, patients remained in hospital for long periods of time in Victorian England. In a sample of one hundred surgical patients at The General Hospital in 1865,[95] only twenty-one patients had a stay of under ten days. Eighteen stayed between ten and twenty days, and there were a further eighteen who remained in hospital for between twenty and thirty days. Nine people stayed between thirty and forty days, with an equal number staying between forty and fifty days. Those who stayed for over fifty days amounted to twenty-five, and there were six among them who remained in hospital for over 150 days. The longest stay of all was a patient who remained in hospital for some 214 days. By the 1870s, tables showing the average number of days in-patients spent in hospital were recorded in the annual reports of Queen's. The figures for the years 1872 to the time of West's death in 1883 can be seen in the table below.

'Gun shot case doing fairly well'

A composite table taken from a number of Annual Reports showing the average residence of In-Patients at Queen's Hospital.[96]

1872 – 28.2 days	1873 – 25.0 days	1874 – 25.7 days
1875 – 24.6 days	1876 – 22.8 days	1877 – 22.6 days
1878 – 23.0 days	1879 – 21.4 days	1880 – 22.2 days
1881 – 24.3 days	1882 – 24.6 days	1883 – 24.1 days

---

[93] JFF West, Observations on Injuries of the Head; *The Lancet;* 1862; i: pp.483–486.
[94] Ibid., pp.168–169.
[95] Surgical Inpatients 1862–1879. (BCA).
[96] Annual Reports for 1877, 1882–3 and 1884. (BCL).

Another table routinely shown in the reports was one which records the number of days after admission that death occurred in those patients who had the misfortune to die at Queen's. In the report for 1883–4, fourteen of the 134 patients who died at the hospital that year, died on the day of admission. The first few days seem to have been crucial. A further twenty-three died on the second day and another thirteen on the third day. After that the numbers are in single figures. For some, the battle to stave off death was, not only lost but prolonged, and there were three individuals who died after a stay of 105, 123 and 252 days respectively. None of the Queen's statistics quoted above differentiate between surgical and medical patients, but separate tables are included in the reports which list the types of complaint or accident suffered and detail the numbers who were cured, relieved or died.

Some who spent time in the hospital as in-patients came in as a result of accidents. A total of 5,004 accident victims applied to the out-patient department of Queen's in 1877, although only 529 of these were admitted to the wards as a result of their injuries. Of the 529 treated as in-patients, thirty-nine died and thirty-four remained in hospital at the end of the year. The rest were said to have been either cured or relieved.[97] It is necessary to be somewhat cautious about the numbers reputed to have been cured. Cancer patients, for instance, were clearly described as having been cured too readily by today's standards.

Some accidents would have called for the expertise of physicians rather than surgeons. Poisonings, drownings and inhalation of toxic fumes may well have been dealt with by physicians for example. The 1868 hospital report lists twenty-four cases of poisoning. Some of these are clear cases of suicide or attempted suicide (strychnia and prussic acid) but others such as opium, lead and mussels were likely to have been genuine accidents.

Many injuries were sustained in the workplace or on the roads, but accidents included everything from injuries caused by fighting to gunshot wounds caused handling loaded firearms. On Friday 23 February, 1883, James West wrote the following in his diary 'and lastly to Hospital to a case of pistol shot wound of girl at 18 just over... the result of accident at Mr Parton's Kingswood: tried to find bullet but without success. To bed at 2am.' He must have called into the hospital or inquired of a colleague the next day, because on Saturday he wrote 'Gun shot case doing fairly well. No wound of bladder.'[98]

---

97 Queen's Hospital Birmingham Annual Reports 29–39, 1877. (BCL).
98 JFF West, Diary; 1883. (JFF West Archive).

The girl, a domestic servant called Rose Lowe, did not do well. A contemporary newspaper cutting containing a report on the inquest which followed her death is glued into West's diary a few pages further on. West became unwell himself on 26 February and asked Jordan Lloyd, to look after the girl. Lloyd ultimately came to the conclusion that had he, and his medical colleagues, acted differently, Rose Lowe may well have been saved. He states that the unfortunate girl died from shock following an exploratory operation three days after the accident. Infection set in quickly after the accident, and finding her condition had worsened considerably by the 26 February, Lloyd operated in the hope of finding its cause. He did so with the help of Lawson Tait, a man considered by many, to be the greatest surgeon of abdominal cases in Birmingham. They discovered, to their dismay, that the abdominal cavity was filled with infected fæcal matter. To put it in Lloyd's own words 'there was at once a free gush of stinking thick brownish-red fluid.'[99] Lloyd concluded his article by saying that, in future, he would open up the abdomen straight away rather than delay and risk infection.

Listerism – 'Only fools would ignore it'

With the exception of gynaecological procedures, there is no evidence to suggest that surgeons specialised at Queen's Hospital. James West and his surgical colleagues performed operations of every type. Limbs were amputated; eyeballs excised; kidney stones, tumours and nævuses removed; tracheotomies performed; and hernias and hair-lips repaired. The suffering endured by patients who needed surgery before the introduction of anæsthetics in 1846 is legendary, and it is no surprise that the adoption of anæsthetics was rapid. James West and his patients were spared the horrors that procedures involving the lancet or the saw had inflicted on the previous generation, but the eradication of one of the other horrors of the nineteenth century hospital – wound infection – took longer to implement.

So great was the danger of hospital infection in the mid-nineteenth century that it was common knowledge both in Birmingham and elsewhere that lives were risked as well as saved in hospitals. The slightest malady or injury was, or could become, life-threatening. The greatest hazard was for those with open wounds, and infection by one of the notorious hospital diseases – erysipelas, pyæmia, black gangrene or septicæmia – could mean fever resulting in a prolonged spell in hospital, further surgery bringing with it the risk of a second bout of infection, or death. The incidence of

---

[99] Jordan Lloyd, *Contributions to Operative and Clinical Surgery*, (Birmingham: Cornish Brothers, 1883) pp.11–13. (BCL).

infection in the tent hospitals servicing the military was even worse than in non-military hospitals. Mortality rates following amputation in the Crimean war were so high that the death rates found in British hospitals seem good by comparison. French soldiers were the most unfortunate with a mortality rate of 91.90%, but the 65.20% recorded for the English would hardly have been cause for congratulation.

In hospital, survival depended on a number of factors – the patient's capacity to withstand the operation, the skill of the surgeon, the conditions in which the operation was carried out and post-operative care. A paper written by William Mac Cormac (1836–1901), an Irish surgeon then at Belfast General Hospital, revealed that mortality rates following amputation of the thigh could be anything between 50 and 70% in some hospitals, or as low as 41.6% in others.[100] Death rates following excision of the knee joint – an operation devised to save a diseased limb – Mac Cormac pointed out were even higher. He wrote the paper before Joseph Lister's discovery of the importance of the antiseptic treatment of wounds was widely known, but he was to become one of the earliest converts to Lister's methods, and would later become an ally of James West in his efforts to convince London surgeons of the efficacy of Listerism.

Even though the plague of hospital infection filled doctors with consternation, the adoption of practices shown to eradicate the threat were not universally accepted to begin with. Joseph Lister's method of treating wounds, sometimes referred to as 'Listerism,' proved to be one of the most significant advances in surgery in the second half of the nineteenth century, and yet it was a subject of heated debate and inflamed tempers in medical circles during the mid-Victorian period, and beyond. On his death in 1883, the obituaries which appeared in the two leading medical journals accused James West of being behind the times generally, and of being somewhat slow to embrace Listerian methods. The evidence suggests this was unfair.

Joseph Lister first described his methods in a paper in 1867. His discoveries, and the research which he conducted in order to substantiate his claims, were the product of the brilliant mind of one man, but other medical professionals had sought remedies to combat hospital infection before Lister came along. In the late 1840s the Hungarian, Ignaz Semmelweis, discovered that puerperal fever – commonly known as childbed fever – was caused and spread by students and staff at the Vienna

---

[100] William Mac Cormac, Observations on Amputation of the Thigh and on the Merits of that Operation as Compared with Excision of the Knee; *The Dublin Quarterly Journal of Medical Science*; 1 August, 1868; pp.1–18.

General Hospital. He instituted a rigorous hand-washing regime in which those responsible for the examination of patients were compelled to wash their hands in chlorine water (later chlorinated lime), between examinations. Semmelweis never got the credit for the discoveries he made in his own lifetime. By the time he died, he had not only failed to communicate his findings adequately, but had alienated other medical professionals. If that was not enough, he even suffered the indignity of dying as a result of an infected wound on the finger of his right hand.

Given the high incidence of hospital infection before the advent of high standards in hygiene and antisepsis, the lack of support for Lister's ideas is puzzling. Yet opposition and even hostility towards Lister and his ideas persisted into the eighteen nineties. Lawson Tait (1854–99) – one of the greatest Birmingham surgeons of his day was just about young enough to be West's son – and yet he was openly hostile to Lister's ideas. He was not alone. West's young colleague, Jordan Lloyd, was another. He took up his first appointment in 1881, some fourteen years after Lister's first paper appeared. Some of the most entrenched views of all, though, were to be found among the London elites. Lindsay Patricia Granshaw [101] highlights the reluctance of some members of the medical staff at St Thomas' Hospital, London to embrace Listerism. She states that by 1877, the year Lister took up a post at King's College Hospital, London, opposition to his methods had hardened in some quarters.

Queen's Hospital, Birmingham, must have been one of the first hospitals in the country to test the efficacy of Lister's antiseptic methods. An inaugural address West gave to the students of Queen's College in 1868 proves that Lister's antiseptic methods had already been on trial at Queen's Hospital by October, 1868. West speaks as though the staff of the hospital, himself included, remained unconvinced when he says 'Carbolic acid, as recommended by Professor Lister, has been used in compound fractures, and also after amputations and for abscesses. Although it has appeared to act beneficially as an astringent and disinfectant, it has not given us all the advantages which have been attributed to it by its talented originator. Many of the alleged benefits of carbolic acid have been obtained by dressing wounds with dry lint, instead of with water dressing as hitherto, by avoidance of frequent disturbance of the parts, by the exclusion of air, as far as possible, and by the use of silver [102] sutures. These seem to be the essential points to

---

[101] Lindsay Patricia Granshaw, *St Thomas' Hospital, London, 1850–1900*. Unpublished PhD thesis, (Bryn Mawr College, University Microfilms International,1981). (Wellcome Library).
[102] Silver is significant in that it has bacteriostatic properties.

be observed in the treatment of all wounds; still, carbolic acid is doubtless a useful remedy, and must have a further trial before it is condemned as inoperative.'[103] There is no record to say who initiated the trial, but West was, with Gamgee, senior surgeon to the institution at the time and it is not unreasonable to suppose that he himself gave it the go ahead.

It is not possible to say exactly when West finally became convinced of the value of Listerism, but papers written by him some ten years later reveal that he was by then, a staunch advocate of Lister's methods. Three papers written around this time refer quite specifically to his own use of Lister's methods.[104] Descriptions of remedies West used in the dressing of wounds, suggest he was experimenting with a number of antiseptic methods before 1877. Carbolised paste, carbolic acid lotion, Condy's fluid,[105] stypium, setons,[106] Red Lotion [107] and salicylic acid [108] are all mentioned in papers dating from between 1868 and 1877, as is carbolised catgut, which he used in the stitching of wounds.

West's interest in Lister's methods of treating wounds in the early 1870s is also evident in a paper he read before the Midland Medical Society in 1873. *Some Points of Contrast between French and English Surgery*,[109] was a paper based on West's own observations of French practice during a visit to France in 1872. In it, he describes a lamentable lack of attention to simple hygiene and an ignorance of Lister's method of treating wounds. He compares French practice unfavourably with the many Swiss and German hospitals where, he tells us, Lister's treatment was in common use.

West wrote two more papers on Continental surgery during the 1870s.[110] Both contain numerous references to Listerism, and comment on

---

[103] JFF West, Inaugural Address to the students of Queen's College, *Medical Times and Gazette*; 1868; ii: p.426.

[104] JFF West, (1) Value of the Antiseptic Treatment in Herniotomy; *The Lancet*; 1877; ii: pp.230–232. (2) On the Surgical Cases in which Lister's Plan of Treating Wounds is Preferable to Any Other Method of Dressing, *St Thomas' Hospital Reports;* 1879; X: pp.73–83. (Barnes Medical Library, University of Birmingham). (3) Compound Comminuted Fracture of the Humerus; Listerism; Recovery; *The Lancet*; 1880; ii: pp 768.

[105] Condy's Fluid contained sodium permanganate which has antiseptic properties. It was tried for the first time on putrid meat in 1857.

[106] Thread which acts as a wick to draw off fluid, especially pus.

[107] Red Lotion contained 2 grains of Zinc Sulphate, 2 minims Compound Tincture of Lavender and water to 1 fluid ounce. Zinc Sulphate does not have antiseptic properties although Lavender does.

[108] Salicylic acid had only mild antiseptic properties. It was used chiefly to break down tough skin in order to facilitate the absorption of other substances.

[109] *BMR*; 1873; pp.31–44.

[110] Impressions of German Surgery; *BMR*; 1875; pp.41–58, and Jottings from a Surgeon's Holiday Note Book; *BMR*; 1879; pp.161–175.

how effective his Continental colleagues had been in eliminating wound infection. One paper West wrote on his return from Europe states that the majority of German and Austrian surgeons were in favour of Lister's methods, but he does single out Baron von Langenbeck as one who remained unconvinced. West translated Langenbeck's paper, 'Surgical Observations on Gun-shot Wounds of the Hip-joint' [111] in 1876 – a project which probably resulted from contact West made with the Baron on his trip to the Continent in 1874. Langenbeck's paper is based on his own experience as a Military Surgeon, and catalogues a tale of avoidable death from wound infection. It makes the Baron's reluctance to embrace Listerism surprising.

West's own paper on German surgery contains a table which is designed to show at a glance how successful a number of hospitals had been in the treatment and prevention of infected wounds. West mentioned a number of surgeons as devotees of Lister's treatment – Bardeleben of Berlin and Busch of Bonn were two. Bardeleben, he said, operated under the carbolic spray [112] and carried out Lister's antiseptic treatment of wounds, 'with perfect thoroughness and fidelity to his principles,'[113] while Busch applied 'Lister's antiseptic dressing in its entirety.'[114] West was no less attentive to the subject of Listerism in his paper, 'Jottings from a Surgeon's Holiday Note Book.'[115] He wrote that the antiseptic treatment of wounds was largely carried out in Amsterdam, and that in the Julius Hospital in Würzburg where operations are performed under the carbolic spray, erysipelas had been eradicated as a result of Lister's treatment of wounds.

James Fitzjames Fraser West went to the Continent with an open mind. In his introduction to 'Impressions of German Surgery' he said 'I went to the continent as a student, and with as much eagerness for knowledge as any alumnus on first entering the portals of his alma mater.'[116] We know from West's own published output, and his attendance at various medical society meetings and congresses, that he continued to look upon himself as a student right up until the time of his death in 1883. The papers on Continental surgery and practice alone prove that West was not a new convert to Lister's methods when he published his first paper on his own use

[111] *BMR*; 1876; pp.29–45; 88–108 and 166–188.
[112] A device designed by Lister which could administer a fine antiseptic spray over the patient during surgery.
[113] Impressions of German Surgery; *BMR*; 1875, p.52.
[114] Impressions of German Surgery; *BMR*; 1875, p.47.
[115] *BMR*, 1879, pp.161–175.
[116] Impressions of German Surgery; *BMR*; 1875; p.42.

of Lister's methods in 1877. In any case, he would not have enthused in the early 1870s about the favourable results which were being achieved on the Continent as a result of Listerism, while rejecting the principles himself.

The five successful cases recorded in his first paper on the subject were all herniotomy cases. West said he could have cited more. He said one patient had been transferred to him by Mr Sampson Gamgee, on account of his interest in the antiseptic treatment of herniotomy. West gave a detailed account of the methods he used. In each case, he operated under the carbolic spray, used a drainage tube and applied dressings according to the rigorous regime advocated by Lister.[117] West stated that, while he would be interested to hear about any failures which surgeons had encountered in the use of Lister's methods, he hoped that his own successes would help to convince others.

One paper written by West in the 1870s is an impassioned missive in support of Listerism. It had already been published in *The St Thomas' Hospital Reports* by the time he read it to the Birmingham Medical Society on 3 December, 1879. In it, he said that his own mind was fully made up, and he challenged those die-hards who were still resistant, directly and by name. Lindsay Granshaw says that the paper by West was the only paper *to date* on the subject to appear in *The St Thomas' Hospital Reports*. Granshaw believes that West may have published this paper at the instigation of William McCormac,[118] who by that time had a post at St Thomas', and who had been committed to Listerism since 1869. She says that it was ambitious provincial colleagues who brought Lister's methods to the notice of the London elites, and that they did so by publishing their results in such a way as, 'only fools would ignore it.'[119]

West certainly did make his case vehemently. After openly attacking the die-hard Mr, later, Sir William Scovell Savory (1826–95), with challenges like, 'If Mr Savory [120] had given himself the trouble to examine

---

[117] A strip of protective was placed over the entire length of the wound, and then two or three small pads of carbolic gauze which had been saturated with carbolic water, and on top of that, the eight layers of gauze, with a sheet of protective between the seventh and eighth folds. West goes on to say that the wounds were dressed again if any discolouration at the edges of the dressing was present within twenty-four hours. If no discolouration occurred, the dressings were changed daily for the first few days and after that, every other day.

[118] Evidence found elsewhere suggests that West and McCormac knew each other personally.

[119] *St Thomas' Hospital, London, 1850–1900*, p.251.

[120] Sir William Savory (1826–95) opposed the teaching of Lister in his celebrated address at the Cork meeting of the BMA in 1879. West was probably quite justified in his assessment of Savory as an entrenched traditionalist. *The Lancet* said Savory 'was slow to adopt innovations' in his obituary of 1895. *The Lancet*; 1895; i: p.648.

the recent writings of surgeons,' etc, West supported his case with evidence gathered by both himself and others. Dr Johann Nepomuk Ritter von Nussbaum [121] of Munich, West informed the sceptics, had a very high incidence of pyaemia, erysipelas and hospital gangrene in his hospital prior to his introduction of Lister's treatment. Physicians, he said, used to question if it was right to perform operations in the stricken hospital. West spelt out the facts – pyaemia striking down all compound fractures and nearly all amputations, gangrene attacking 80% of cases by 1874 and erysipelas in nearly every bed. The rare cases of amputation which were not fatal, West wrote, succumbed to two or three attacks of erysipelas. From the time that hospital introduced Lister's antiseptic methods, West quoted, there had 'not been "one case of hospital gangrene, of pyaemia, or of erysipelas; in a word, the hospital has been transformed" ' and all this, he wrote, was achieved without any change to the wards, nursing, diet or the surroundings.

The effort made by West to be diplomatic in his account of the measures taken by Nussbaum to combat hospital infection is laudable as it is in his earlier paper, *Impressions of German Surgery*.[122] It would be fascinating to know what West wrote of Nussbaum in his diary after he visited the professor's hospital in Munich in 1875. Did it, one wonders, resemble the account given by the Swedish surgeon, John Berg in his travel diary of 1879–80, who said 'Nussbaum's whole personality is eccentric. He is so deaf that only a screaming voice can stir him. He is so lame that he needs both a cane and an assistant to make his rounds. And he is quite addicted to morphine. His movements are very lively, his speech reveals an inner fire, but the face is a frozen mask and the eyes, shiny with tiny pupils, bear witness to the drug. He makes no secret of it…He is a bigoted Catholic, great nationalist, kind to the poor, and folksy in manner….at the same time as he suffers all those oddities, shows a wondrous combination of energy and weakness….'[123] Failings aside, Berg, like West, does give credit to Nussbaum for his 'warm' admiration of Lister.

Debates on Lister's treatment continued both in Birmingham and elsewhere. Those who sought to reject the argument for Lister's methods had to convince others that their alternatives were equally effective. The resulting attention to hygiene and cleanliness meant hospitals really did

---

[121] Professor Johann Nepomuk Ritter Nussbaum (1829–90).
[122] JFF West, Impressions of German Surgery; *BMR;* 1875; p.45.
[123] Diary of John Berg 1879–80. Cited in Hæger Knut, *The Illustrated History of Surgery.* (England: Harold Sparke Publishers, 2000). p. 214.

become safer places for the sick and injured. In November, 1881, West's colleague, Lawson Tait, opened a debate on the subject in Birmingham.[124] James West seldom missed these meetings, and was present at this one. West again argued for Listerism, saying he had tried alternatives to Lister's treatment and had found them flawed. He cited the successes of Dr Thomas Keith (1827–95) in his performance of ovariotomies which, he said, were the result of that surgeon's use of Lister's methods.[125] Tait was unconvinced, and argued that the improvements were just as likely to have been the result of Keith's own growing expertise. Some surgeons preferred to substitute their own antiseptic methods to those of Lister, and West's colleagues were no exception. Alternative methods devised by Joseph Sampson Gamgee and Mr Furneaux Jordan were also subject to discussion at the meeting. West acknowledged the efficacy of Gamgee's dressings for minor wounds and injuries, but claimed that they were inadequate in cases of amputation. Of the thirteen who contributed to the debate that day, West and seven others were fully in support of Listerism. Of those who remained, only Tait was opposed to it in its entirety. Tait's argument amounts to some five sides of print in the journal, but the one who made the next biggest contribution was West, with two sides.

Fortunately when West died in May, 1883, *The Lancet* and *The British Medical Journal* were not the only medical journals to give him an obituary. The one printed by his own local medical society states that West was a hard-working member of his profession, but it also says 'Mr West was a very strong supporter of Mr Lister's method of treating wounds, and took an active part in the controversies which have arisen respecting it.'[126] This, it could be argued, is a more fitting tribute.

---

[124] Debate on the Clinical Results Obtained by the Listerian Method of Performing Operations and Dressing Wounds; *BMR*; 1881; X: pp.79–92.

[125] Keith achieved an 81% recovery rate on 136 ovariotomies as well as having performed 33 hysterectomies with only 3 deaths between 1870 and 1880 according to the author of an article entitled Correspondence Relating to Professional Disputes Involving James Young Simpson and Thomas Keith, Doctor of the Month, March, 2004, Royal College of Surgeons.

[126] *BMR*; 1883; IVX: p.47.

CHAPTER FOUR

The fragility of life

James West lived and died at a time of high mortality rates, but he died prematurely nonetheless. In the week ending 24 April, 1858, some twenty-five years before West's own demise, six of the individuals who died in London that week were ninety or more.[1] Of these, one was ninety-eight and another was one hundred and one. In 1883, the year in which West died at the age of forty-nine, the *BMJ*,[2] analysed and published statistics on the ages at which members of the medical profession had died during the previous year. It adds weight to the argument that West's death was untimely. Seventy percent of the profession lived beyond fifty in 1882. More than half (54%) of the sample (some 277 individuals) survived long enough to celebrate their sixtieth birthdays, while twenty-eight percent lived beyond the age of seventy. Nine percent of the practitioners lived long enough to enjoy their eightieth birthdays. Three percent passed the age of eighty-five and there was one individual who survived until the grand old age of ninety-three. The report shows that the average age at death was 58.6.

These figures are in line with the age at which the thirty-three Birmingham doctors, who were included in the author's earlier study, died. Three quarters (25 members) of that group lived to see their sixtieth birthdays, and of those, fifteen reached an age in excess of seventy. Six members lived to see their eightieth birthdays, and four lived beyond the age of eighty-five. West was one of three who died in their forties, but apart from that, the only person who died tragically young was the unfortunate Frederick Gerald Messiter who died in 1896 at the age of twenty-three as a result of Typhoid Fever. The average age of death for the group of thirty-three was 54.9. West's contemporary, Dickenson Crompton of The General, had the longest life, dying at the age of eighty-nine in 1894, after having lived through virtually the whole of the nineteenth century. Casting the net a little wider to include others whose lives overlapped with West, reveals that longevity in Birmingham's medical practitioners was not unusual. We have seen that Edward Townsend Cox died at 94, but so did Edward Johnstone 1851–1945) and Thomas Taylor (1797–1890). Thomas

---

[1] *Health of London – Week Ending April 24th, 1858*; *BMJ*; 1858; May: p.362.
[2] *BMJ*; 1883; i: p.572.

Bell Elock Fletcher (1806–97) reached the grand old age of ninety-one while Bowyer Vaux (1782–1872) died at ninety. Richard Middlemore (1804–91) and Joseph Priestley Smith (1845–1933) were close behind, dying at eighty-six and eighty-eight respectively.

Even so, high infant and child mortality meant that average life expectancy remained stubbornly low throughout the nineteenth century. Medical men and other professionals may have enjoyed comparatively long lives, but the figures for the population as a whole were less good. According to the local historian, Victor Skipp,[3] the death rate in Birmingham between 1851 and 1860 was 28 per 1,000 for males and 25 per 1,000 for females. The incidence of cholera was low in Birmingham on account of its position on high, well drained land, but diseases like typhus, scarlet fever, measles and tuberculosis were a constant danger to the town's inhabitants. The incidence of diphtheria – another killer – was high when West first qualified and it was to get worse before it got better. The town also suffered outbreaks of smallpox from time to time – the most serious being in 1864/5. The situation was not much better in the 1870s. By that time, the average death rate had gone down to 25.2 per 1,000, but that was 50% higher than the nearby rural villages, and for some of the central wards the discrepancy was over 100%. The differences within the town were huge too. The central ward of St Mary's is recorded as having mortality rates of 26.8 per 1,000 in 1875, while those of the town's most affluent suburb, Edgbaston, were a mere 13.1. It paid to live in the right place even if one could not manage to live at the right time.

Emily Brontë – 'no poisoning doctor'
While doctors were able to reduce mortality rates in hospitals during the second half of the nineteenth century through the use of antiseptic methods and careful attention to hygiene, the challenge to relieve and cure the sick still remained formidable right up until the dawn of the twentieth century. There was little doctors could do to reduce death rates from certain diseases before sanitation and living conditions had been improved or before some of the vaccines that we take for granted today had been found and antibiotics discovered. At the beginning of West's career in the mid-1850s, those who sought relief from medical conditions were just as likely to approach non-medically qualified quacks or 'wise women' as a medical man. In the circumstances, it was not unreasonable. Expertise was in its infancy and so was the means (principally the medical journals) of sharing that newly acquired expertise.

<hr>

[3] Victor Skipp, *The Making of Victorian Birmingham*, (Birmingham: Published by the author, 1983).

In any case, remedies could also be sought on the shelves of the apothecary's shop, the druggist's or from any of the unregulated and sometimes dubious traders for a fraction of the cost of a doctor's fee. Purgatives, tonics, purifying pills and 'cures' were all abundant in Victorian England. Much to the chagrin of apothecaries, some doctors dispensed their own drugs. For those who did, it was often a question of you are damned if you do, and damned if you do not. While some who dispensed drugs were accused by their patients of doing so in order to supplement their incomes, others caused disappointment by their failure to produce a tangible solution. George Elliot [4] knew only too well the risk a doctor took when he left the dispensing of drugs to the apothecary. Mr Lydgate, surgeon, caused quite a stir in Middlemarch when it was rumoured that he did not dispense drugs. Mrs Mawmsey asked ' "Does this Mr Lydgate mean to say there is no use in taking medicine?... I should like him to tell me how I could bear up at Fair time, if I didn't take strengthening medicine for a month beforehand." ' Another, Mr Gambit, asked ' "How will he cure his patients then?" ' Mrs Mawmsey answered with another question 'Does *he* suppose that people will pay him only to come and sit with them and go away again?" ' Mr Toller, one of Lydgate's rivals, was lazy when compared to Lydgate and 'was a little slow in coming but' Elliot tells us 'when he came he *did* something.'[5]

We do not know what George Elliot wanted of a doctor herself although we can make speculations based on her portrayal of Mr Lydgate but another well-known nineteenth century author, Emily Brontë, had no time for doctors. As she lay dying of consumption in December, 1848, her sister Charlotte wrote to her friend Ellen Nussey explaining that she had, in opposition to her sister's wishes, summoned the help of an eminent London physician. 'Her repugnance to seeing a medical man continues immutably as she declares "no poisoning doctor" shall come near her...'[6] writes Charlotte.

Some three years later, Charlotte was herself being poisoned quite literally by the surgeon, Mr Ruddock. Ruddock had told Charlotte that she suffered no organic disease but diagnosed 'a highly sensitive and irritable condition of the liver.' For this, he ordered a mixture containing mercury, and when that did not seem to have the desired effect, he produced an alternative – another type of pill incorporating mercury. Charlotte wrote to

---

[4] George Elliot (Marian Evans), author of *Middlemarch*. The book was set in the late 1820s and 1830s. Elliot gave the book the subtitle 'a study of provincial life' and looked upon herself as an imaginative historian or scientific investigator even. George Elliot, *Middlemarch*. (England: Blackwood and Sons, 1871), p.446.

[5] Ibid., p.447.

[6] Juliet Baker, *The Brontës A Life in Letters*. (England: Penguin, 1997), p.215.

her friend, Margaret Wooler, on 20 January, 1852 'every day I grew worse before the week was over I was very ill – unable to swallow any nourishment except a few teaspoonfuls of liquid per diem, my mouth became sore, my teeth loose, my tongue swelled, raw and ulcerated while water welled continually into my mouth.'[7] A layman's glance at any modern medical dictionary is all that is needed to confirm the fact that one of England's greatest authors was being poisoned by the very man who was charged with making her better.

The doctor who treated Charlotte in her one and only pregnancy three years later did no better, and she died from an excess of vomiting – hyperemesis gravidarum – in early pregnancy. The Brontës' lives were plagued by illness and premature death. Charlotte's mother died as a result of ovarian cancer when Charlotte was only five, while all five of her siblings had died from tuberculosis by the time Charlotte was thirty-three years of age. Not everyone suffered losses on this scale in nineteenth century England, but the fact that some families did, can hardly have inspired confidence in the ability of the medical profession to cure the sick.

Preventing disease

Medical expertise was not the only thing in its infancy in the mid-nineteenth century. Preventative medicine was acknowledged as a sound principle and its advocates were publishing papers on it throughout West's life, but it could be, and sometimes was, based on an ignorance of scientific fact or on flawed judgement.

The link between poor sanitation and disease, for instance, was not properly understood when James West first qualified in 1854. The London physician, John Snow (1813–58), was one of the first to suspect that cholera and typhoid fever were caused by drinking water contaminated with sewage, but his efforts to convince others were ignored initially. Through mapping out the incidence of the disease, Snow established that the stricken were all drinking water from the same source. During the epidemic of 1849, he is said to have resorted to smashing the handle off one of the city's water pumps in the hope that the resulting freedom from the disease would convince others that his theory was sound. London suffered several major cholera epidemics in the mid-nineteenth century. The death toll for the 1849 epidemic was 14,000, but it took two further outbreaks – one in 1854 and another in 1865 – before serious action was taken to prevent further attacks.

---

7 Juliet Baker, *The Brontës A Life in Letters*. (England: Penguin, 1997), p.341.

Some thought that the inhalation of gases which emanated from drains and sewers was entirely to blame for the diseases we now associate with poor sanitary conditions. Those who subscribed to this view were reluctant to relinquish it. One paper,[8] published in 1858, describes how a number of dogs, jackdaws, a mouse and a single hedgehog were subjected to the noxious fumes given off by sewers in an attempt to assess the dangers of sewer gases to health. A chemical analysis of the gaseous emanations from a cesspool was carried out for the purposes of the research, although this was not the first of its type. The animals were first exposed to the mixture of gases just as they were given off by the cesspool, and afterwards to various of the gases separately. The scientific methods used were hardly rigorous by today's standards, but the symptoms suffered by the experimental animals were recorded and post-mortems performed on the animals that died. Of the eighteen creatures exposed to the miasma, twelve survived. All the survivors suffered symptoms to a greater or lesser extent and these included vomiting, diarrhoea, increased heart rate and breathing difficulties. The experimenters may have been mistaken in thinking that the odours associated with sewage caused cholera, but the research they undertook in 1858 suggests that the gases were not entirely harmless.

London lagged behind Birmingham initially in its provision of sewers. It took the infamous 'great stink' of 1858 before London's large scale sewer building project was authorised. In contrast, some forty-three and a half miles of sewers had been laid under Birmingham's 124 miles of roads by the town's enlightened Street Commissioners by 1848.[9] It was a laudable achievement, but the Town Councillors who superseded the Commissioners in 1851 failed to continue the good work, and the town had to wait until Joseph Chamberlain took matters in hand when acting as its mayor in the 1870s for further improvements.

'Such is the history of this poor girl'

Even if doctors could do little to help the sick and injured when West first qualified, it was not for lack of trying or concern for their patients. Medical papers of the period show that medical practitioners were concerned with the whole person and not just the malady. James West routinely recorded the general health and well-being of his patients in the papers and reports he wrote. He even commented on their pecuniary circumstances and

---

[8] Under, *Periscope. Epidemiology, Hygyienics, and Statistics. The Influence of Sewer Emanations. BMJ*; 1858; April: pp.311–313.

[9] Skipp, *The Making of Victorian Birmingham*, p.94.

family history if he believed that it was significant. The circumstances of H.P., one of the subjects of West's paper on Syphilitic Stricture of the oesophagus in 1860, were, for instance, described by West in some detail. He tells us that H.P. – a young woman who died as a result of her condition – was 'an "unfortunate" twenty-five years of age, tall, and formerly of comely aspect, dark complexioned, and of nervous temperament, the child of healthy parents, was seduced at the age of fifteen. She left home soon after, and before twelve months had elapsed she became the subject of primary syphilis.' West does not condemn the behaviour which brought his patient to this sorry state, but rounds off his report with the words 'Such is the history of this poor girl.'[10] The importance attached to diet has been mentioned, but papers also contain details about the state of the tongue, the skin, the eyes, as well as commenting on how well the patient has slept and whether or not the bowels had been opened.

The capacity of surgeons like West to cure the sick and injured improved during the second half of the nineteenth century. West practised at an exciting time and he felt that excitement. The sheer quantity of papers written by him and his contemporaries is testimony to the enthusiasm of his generation, and a glance through those written by West himself, display a boyish devotion to his calling. His sole surviving diary is no different.

Bleeding

As medical men embraced new ideas, some old practices began to fall into disuse. Bleeding was one. In 1858, it was stated in the *BMJ* that bleeding was 'now less common' but the practice, in fact, was to continue for decades to come. We know that West was expected to perform one type of bleeding procedure – cupping – when he was a resident medical officer at Queen's in the mid-1850s, but there is no way of knowing whether he actually did so. And neither is there any evidence to that effect in the papers written by him after his election to the position of surgeon.

Bleeding – whether achieved by the lancet, leeches or cupping – was more popular with physicians than surgeons. The lancing of a vein and the application of leeches are procedures which to some extent are self-explanatory and will be familiar to most readers. Cupping, which remained in use until the early years of the twentieth century, is less well known and may require definition. The operation could be divided into two distinct

---

10   JFF West, one of a series entitled, Contributions to the Surgical History of Syphilis. 11. On Syhpilitic Stricture of the Œsophagus. *The Dublin Quarterly Journal of Medical Science*; 1860; XX1X pp.86–98.

procedures. In the first, anything between four and sixteen spring loaded blades were released into the skin before the application of the cupping glass. The glass was a vessel with thick walls which could be anything between an egg cup and a teacup in size and had a rolled rim to procure an airtight fit against the skin. Before application, the glass was warmed with a candle or spirit lamp. Once in place, the cooling glass would create a vacuum within the cup and this would result in blood being drawn into the vessel. The other procedure was known as dry cupping. In it, a heated cup was applied to uncut skin. The process, which simply caused bruising under the cup's thick rolled rim, meant that the bleeding was contained within the skin itself.

West never mentioned using the cup or lancing veins in his early papers, but he did mention the use of leeches. He may have preferred leeches on account of the fact that they could be applied to small and awkward surfaces and be left to get on with it. In 1862, *The Lancet* published a series of three papers by West on head injuries – two contain references to the use of leeches. Thomas B–, a fifty year old coal dealer, was admitted to Queen's on 12 June, 1855 following an accident. His injuries were extensive and included an injury to the head. On admission Thomas B's head was strapped with a cold-water dressing and some dozen leeches were applied to his bruised shoulder. It was all to no avail. On the night of the 23 June, while still in hospital, the patient took another fall. The new and accumulated injuries sustained on this occasion proved fatal within days. Selina T– was more fortunate. She was admitted to Queen's following a fall on the head from a height of ten feet. On the day of admission, she was ordered to have her head shaved so that twelve leeches could be applied to the left temple. It was not the only treatment administered to the suffering Selina T–. She was also given an enema of turpentine and castor oil and a pint of gruel. That West considered bleeding an important part of the treatment is clear when, in summing up the case, he declared 'Perfect rest, bleeding, antiphlogistic regimen [11] and calomel [12] pushed to salivation appeared to give excellent results in this girl, and I would employ them unhesitatingly in any similar case.'[13]

James West and other members of the medical staff at Queen's may not have reduced their use of leeches from choice. They were probably under

---

[11] Cooling, anti-inflammatory treatment.
[12] A purgative.
[13] JFF West, Observations on Injuries to the Head. *The Lancet*; 1862; i: pp.195–198
      and 247–250 respectively.

pressure to cut down the number used by the late eighteen fifties and early sixties. The institution, as we know, was in financial difficulties and expenditure had to be reined in. In 1859, spending on leeches fell below £10 for the first time. Annual reports show the numbers of leeches bought by the hospital had been 948 in 1856. After that there was a steady decline. There were no leeches in the lists of items by 1864 but even two years before that, expenditure had already dropped to a mere eighteen shillings.

Evidence garnered from the minutes of the Midland Medical Society in 1876/7 [14] suggests that West did not much mourn the demise of bleeding, but it also reveals that many of his colleagues still favoured it. The topic was brought up by Mr Arthur Oakes (1830–1925) at a meeting on 13 December, 1876. It excited so much interest that the debate continued for three subsequent meetings.

Oakes first asked whether any member present had bled a patient in the past twelve months. He recorded that while only three had done so in practice, several were in support of its use in certain circumstances. Oakes, himself, believed that practitioners should not abandon the remedies tried and tested by their forefathers too hastily. He said doctors should look at individual cases, claiming that while some patients are harmed by bleeding, others die through the lack of it. Oakes described how two of his patients were relieved as a result of bleeding. One, a case of pleuro-pneumonia, he bled at the patient's own 'urgent request' and the other was a 'young florid subject.'

Another colleague, Mr Larkin, thought it was important to keep an open mind. He said that since humans have a surplus of power in both heart and lung as well as a surplus of blood itself, bleeding was unlikely to be detrimental. He probably caused a smile if not a laugh when he recounted how the celebrated Hickenbotham of Gornal bled everyone who consulted him and claimed that no-one ever died from it. Larkin himself, favoured its use in cases of stasis, pleurisy, eclampsia and tracheitis.

James Sawyer [15] (later Sir James) said he grew up professionally in the days of bleeding and thought there should be a reassessment of its benefits. He believed it was not suitable in cases of inflammation as in pneumonia, typhoid or pericarditis of chronic Bright's disease, but could provide relief for those suffering engorged capillaries, high blood pressure and in extreme cases of engorgement of the heart in patients who are dying.

---

[14] MMS 1/1/2 Minutes 1874–1883. (B Med I).

[15] James Sawyer, physician at Queen's Hospital and colleague of James West treated West during his last illness some seven years later. The nature of that illness could well have prompted Sawyer into bleeding his patient.

Sawyer stated that he had used it many times for patients in the latter group. He not only considered bleeding helpful in cases of uræmia, especially that complicating tubular nephritis, a sequel of scarlatina, and in puerperal eclampsia but also in what he calls 'head cases.' Sawyer believed that it was unsafe to bleed children, the elderly or drunks, and thought that bleeding early should be the rule. He was not alone in thinking that it was important to bleed sooner rather than later.

Mr Williams was of the same opinion. He used it in cases of pneumonia and pleurisy according to the record. Williams was also reported as having said that he thought it unwise in postpartum hæmorrhage. Whether this means, by implication, that there were practitioners who would have advocated the use of bleeding in cases of postpartum hæmorrhage, is an interesting question. Dr Norris explained the effects of bloodletting on stasis to his colleagues, and said that he favoured its use in cases of 'overdistention of the right heart' where it was unable to contract and where there was an excess of corpuscles.

Of all those who contributed to the debate that day, James West had the least enthusiasm for the procedure. Like the others, West thought its adoption should depend upon the case. He said that he had not used it in his surgical practice at Queen's Hospital, although he thought it could be usefully employed in cases of poisoning by carbonic acid, suffocation (especially through crushing), uræmic convulsions and where the right heart was surcharged.[16] West argued that good results had been achieved in cases of wounds of the lung without bleeding. He went on to point out that John Hunter (1728–93) and John Abernethy (1764–1831) had been among the first to abandon bleeding and that its use had declined steadily ever since. West drew attention to the fact that bleeding was not practised in France, Germany or America where, he declared, physiology and pathology were so advanced.

The following year, Sawyer's views on the subject were again given expression. In a paper entitled 'The Value of Venesection in the Treatment of Disease'[17] he said he believed modern practitioners had committed a 'grievous error' in their rejection of the remedy. W H Broadbent [18] and other contemporaries supported his thesis. Today's practitioners have also reassessed the use of leeches and are occasionally putting them to use again

---

[16] Leon D Abrams MD ChB FRCS, retired heart surgeon at the Queen Elizabeth Hospital, Birmingham , has informed the author that bleeding is particularly effective in the latter case.
[17] James Sawyer, The Value of Venesection in the Treatment of Disease, *BMR*; 1877: pp.168–182
[18] WH Broadbent, On Venesection, *The Lancet;* 1883; i: pp.4–5 and 54–56.

in certain situations. The same cannot be said for some of the other remedies used by West and his contemporaries.

Medicinal use of coffee and tobacco

The predilection for purging has been alluded to, but Victorian medical practitioners also made use of some substances in ways which we would consider bizarre today. Coffee and tobacco are two. Joseph B Sammut, MD, expressed his confidence in the efficacy of coffee in the treatment of strangulated hernia in a paper which was published in the *BMJ* in 1857.[19] His only surprise was that it acted so quickly. He states that normally, six cups, allowing fifteen minutes between each, were necessary to produce the desired effect, and yet his patient, who was given a single cup of coffee made up of one ounce of coffee per cup, was relieved of pain almost immediately.

James West does not seem to have used coffee or tobacco in the treatment of his patients, although the diary reveals that he did smoke the occasional cigar. He even implies, on one occasion, that he considered the practice beneficial. West and his wife, Sarah, were forced to sit next to 'a regular caution' of a woman from Liverpool on a journey between Paris and Avignon in March, 1883. She would, he says 'have the window open and would not let me smoke so we both got bad colds.'[20] Contrary to what we may think today, debates on the dangers of tobacco did not start in the middle years of the twentieth century. *The Lancet* ran a series of letters and articles on smoking in 1857, the year of the election dispute, and one correspondent reminded readers that they themselves were merely re-enacting a controversy which had raged some 150 years earlier. Among the numerous articles which were written on the subject during that year, one amounted to three pages. One contributor to the debate even expressed himself in verse, while another – a student – wrote a letter entitled, 'Student's Bird's Eye View.' James West did not publish his views on the matter, but Joseph Sampson Gamgee, West's rival in the election dispute, declared himself a non-smoker and was among those in opposition to the practice.

Dictionaries of herbal remedies invariably contain sections on the merits of tobacco and nineteenth century practitioners put tobacco to use in a variety of ways. In his article on anæsthesia at St Thomas',[21] for instance, Dr Charles Pither states that tobacco smoke was sometimes administered in the

[19] Joseph B Sammut, Use of Coffee in the Treatment of Strangulated Hernia; *BMJ*; 1857; November, p.926.
[20] JFF West, Diary; 12 March, 1833. (JFF West Archive).
[21] Charles Pither, Consultant Dept of Anæsthetics, St Thomas' Hospital; Anæsthesia at St Thomas'. The Early Days. 1847–1878; *St Thomas' Hospital Gazette;* 1987; summer: p.35.

resuscitation of patients by means of a rectal tube. Tobacco, it seems, was used successfully as an enema for intestinal obstruction (*BMJ* 1863; i: 43); as a internal remedy for the effects of a rattlesnake bite (*The Lancet* 1860; i: 321); and as a cure for traumatic tetanus (*The Lancet* 1865; ii: 497). More surprising still, are articles which suggest that it is effective as a prophylactic for phthisis and as both prophylactic and cure for asthma (*The Lancet* 1869; i: 482 and *BMJ* 1859; 794 respectively). But even if nineteenth century doctors did fail to realise that smoking was injurious to the lungs,[22] some not only blamed smoking for cancers of the mouth and lip, but were prepared to say so as early as 1859.[23]

Blisters

Another treatment which remained popular with nineteenth century doctors, even if it was not popular with patients, was the blister. Basically, the area deemed suitable for this type of treatment was subjected to the application of chemicals or other substances with caustic properties. Medical historian, John Kirup MD MA FRCS, says blisters were favoured chiefly as counter-irritants and generally consisted of mustard, stinging nettles, boiling water or cantharides (the Spanish fly). The latter was very much in vogue in the nineteenth century, according to Kirkup. Publications of papers by West show that he used blisters from time to time in the early years. The first time he refers to his own use of blisters is in the journal of a local medical society [24] and concerns his successful treatment of a twelve year old girl with a facial nævus. In this case he used a blister to remove successive layers of the affected skin's surface. Two other patients treated with blisters were less fortunate. When the aforementioned fifty year old coal-dealer Thomas B deteriorated after the second fall, he was ordered ammonia, wine, and beef-tea, but in addition to that, he had to endure a blister which was applied to the nape of the neck. Another victim of head injuries treated by West with a blister was a small boy of 3½. The unfortunate child died on the fifth day, after suffering a series of convulsions and coma. In his attempts to save the boy, West had

---

[22] It was left to William Richard Shaboe Doll and Austin Bradford Hill, epidemiologists, to make the first credible connection between smoking and lung cancer in 1950.

[23] Report from the Foreign Department entitled Smoking, the Exciting Cause of Cancer. M. Boussin is reported as having published an article in the Montpellier Médical in which he states that smoking actively causes cancer of the tongue, lips, sides of the cheeks and soft palate. *The Lancet;* 1859; ii: p.240.

[24] JFF West, On the Treatment of Nævus by Chloride of Zinc; *Midland Quarterly Journal of Medical Sciences*; 1857; i: pp.240–244.

administered that treatment so beloved of the Victorians – a purge
(consisting of calomel and rhubarb) – and applied a blister four inches by
four inches to the nape of the neck.

Acupressure
It may surprise the reader to know that a procedure known as acupressure
was in use in nineteenth century England. The term, familiar to most
surgeons by the late 1860s, defined a procedure which bore little
resemblance to that in use today. West refers to his own use of the
technique in a paper of 1869.[25] He gathered data on its use as a means of
arresting hæmorrhage over the course of twelve months and published the
results in table form. He did not explain the technique as such but was
content to say simply that he had used the first and fourth methods without
ligature as laid down by James (later Sir James) Y Simpson (1811–70).

Simpson devised the procedure in 1859 as a means of avoiding the
pitfalls of using ligatures to tie severed vessels. In his view, ligatures, by
their very nature, were strangulation points which invariably lead to the
mortification and sloughing of tissue. He insisted that complications caused
by the ligature frequently led to infections which could hinder healing or
result in death. Simpson described the technique in detail with the aid of
diagrams in his book *Acupressure, a New Method of Arresting Surgical
Hæmorrhage, and of Accelerating the Healing Process* which was reviewed in *The
Lancet* in January, 1865. A lexicon of 1881 [26] is more concise and describes
acupressure as a method of arresting hæmorrhage by means of the
pressure of a needle. The needle, it states, should be long, with a sharp
point at one end and a head at the other, and should be rendered
unoxidisable. The needle, which is positioned so that it presses down at
right angles upon the vessel, should first be passed through the tissue at
one side of the vessel and then secured by passing it through the tissues on
the other side. By applying compression to the vessel in this way,
hæmorrhage is stopped and coagulation takes place rapidly.

By 1869 West said that he was using acupressure in almost every case of
amputation. In the table he sets out to show how some nineteen patients
responded to acupressure as a means of arresting post operative
hæmorrhage. Two of West's patients died post-operatively as a result of
shock, but he is at pains to point out that blood loss had not been

[25] JFF West, On Acupressure; *BMJ*; 1869; i: pp.563–564.
[26] Edited by Henry Power and Leonard Sedwick, *The New Sydenham Society's Lexicon of Medicine and the Allied Sciences*. Volume 1 (London, The New Sydenham Society, 1881).

responsible for either of the two deaths. West used anything between one and three needles, and left them in place for an average of about fifty hours. Two individuals did suffer blood loss in spite of the treatment, but West or his assistants managed to arrest it. He did so by applying manual pressure [27] in one case and by the use of a tourniquet in the other.

A narration by West at one of the local branch meetings of the BMA [28] gives us a better idea about exactly how the needles were used. He not only described what he did to stop bleeding following a particular amputation, but because the case had ended fatally, was able to show the very arteries to which acupressure had been applied. West showed his colleagues the femoral, profunda and two other arteries just as they had been dissected in post-mortem, with the needles still in place. He was able to demonstrate how occlusion had been perfect in both the femoral and the profunda. The specimens prompted the assembled company to discuss whether the pressure of the needles on the outer wall of the arteries had caused some ulceration, and in response, West is reported as having said that he thought that the pressure need not have been continued for so long.

Acupressure was not merely a fad of the 1860s. Papers written by West's colleague, Joseph Sampson Gamgee, show that he, Gamgee, was still using it in the 1880s. Like West, Gamgee also believed that the practice of acupressure was common knowledge among the surgical fraternity by the mid-1860s. He occupied a position as Foreign Corresponding Member of the Society of Surgery in Paris for a time, and in 1867 he expressed surprise at French ignorance of the technique in a series of papers he wrote on the state of Parisian surgery.[29]

Homœopathy

Medical men of the second half of the nineteenth century were not prepared to embrace any ideas which they considered flawed any more than their modern counterparts would. Indeed, they felt so threatened by quacks and quack remedies, that letters and articles denouncing them were a regular feature of the medical journals. By the time West qualified, medics were becoming welded to the new scientific approach and their rejection of anything which smacked of quackery was gathering force. Birmingham sported a homœopathic hospital in the late 1860s and when

[27] In one case, on the femoral artery for five hours.
[28] Association Intelligence. Birmingham and Midland Counties Branch: General Meeting. *BMJ*; 1868; i: p 105.
[29] *The Lancet*; 1867; ii: p.670.

Mr RL Chance, one of Birmingham's greatest industrialists and representative of the institution, approached Queens in 1869 in order to try and persuade them to allocate two of their wards to the homœopathic treatment of patients, his request was firmly rejected.

The Committee of Management of the Homœopathic Hospital were prepared to offer a substantial sum of money towards the proposed extension of Queen's in return for the two wards. They had already tried and failed to persuade The General Hospital to undertake a similar scheme. James West, Joseph Sampson Gamgee and a number of Governors of Queen's attended a meeting to discuss the proposals on 25 March, 1869. The minutes of the meeting show that although tolerance and respect towards those involved in the homœpathic movement was shown by all those representing the Governors of Queen's, they made a unanimous decision to inform Mr Chance that his proposal could not be entertained. Gamgee was less courteous in the letter he sent to Mr Chance. In it he states:

'I hold the so-called doctrine of homœopathy to be opposed to the fundamental principles of physical and natural science; and I see no more reason for encouraging their practice in the hospital to which I am surgeon, than were I a minister of the Gospel, I should feel justified in allowing doctrines opposed to the essential truths of Christianity to be preached in a church under my charge; or were I the head of an engineering establishment, I should feel justified in allowing time and capital to be wasted by an experimenter, who entertained opinions fundamentally opposed to the laws of gravitation, the power of the lever, and the expansion of steam..... I believe... that free scope be allowed for the development of differences; but while I would do nothing to curtail the liberties of others, I decline to do anything which can imply my approval of opinions which I hold to be fundamentally erroneous.'[30]

Gamgee again sought the support of the local newspapers. This time it was to publicise his denunciation of homœopathic medicine. Mr Chance was not a man to be trifled with though and in his reply to Gamgee, he first points out that although he has no objection to Gamgee having sent a copy of his letter to Queen's to the press, he says he will not enter into a controversial correspondence in the newspapers with him on the subject of homœopathy. Overall, as we might expect, Queen's rejection of the proposal made by the Homœopathic Hospital was not well received, and led to some bitterness on the part of the rejected body. By the time West qualified in 1854, medical men were beginning to embrace scientific

---

30 *Birmingham Miscellaneous*. D 13. p.8. (BCL).

methods and ways of thinking as never before. In the second half of the century they would go on to develop a level of expertise which would set them well and truly apart from the lay public, and it was achieved partly at the expense of what we would today call alternative medicine.

Developing expertise

There is only one surviving diary of James Fitzjames Fraser West – his last – and since West died in May, it provides but a brief insight into his life. Nevertheless, it is rich in detail and reveals that the diarist had a tremendous love of his profession. It shows that West led a very active life – attending medical society meetings, writing papers, performing operations, visiting patients etc – but most of all, it is full of boyish enthusiasm. An earlier study [31] written up by the author, and which included James West's contemporaries at both The General Hospital and Queen's Hospital, as well as the infamous Thomas Gutteridge, shows West's colleagues shared his enthusiasms. Index Medicus – a directory of medical literature – was published for the first time in 1879 and reveals at a glance that West and his colleagues published numerous articles. For the first time it became easy to find out what a given surgeon or physician's published output was for any given year.

The lists include everything from published correspondence of a medical nature to books. Books can be identified on account of the fact that, for them, the number of pages is given. Even so, there is nothing to distinguish between important works of quality and second rate work and, as we all know, quantity and quality are not necessarily bed-fellows. As a source, Index Medicus has its limitations, but it does provide us with a record of the sheer quantity of publications produced and enables us to compare the output of individuals.

It is impossible to choose a year, or block of years, in which all thirty-three contributors were represented in the index, but in order to include West, the years between its inception in 1879 and 1883 have been selected to serve as an example. In 1879 some of the thirty-three were either too old or too young to publish and some were dead. As we know, James West himself died in May, 1883, after a month-long illness, and there were others who were unable to publish owing to poor health. Nevertheless, of the twenty-one who were between the ages of twenty-eight and sixty-five in 1883, two thirds published in the five year period. The man who published most was the physician, Robert Saundby (1849–1918), of The General

---

[31] GM Goodman, *Birmingham Hospital Doctors 1850–1900: The Rise of Professionalism;* Unpublished MA dissertation; 1996. (BCL).

Hospital, with a total of forty-three publications. James Russell, another physician from The General, came second with thirty-five, and West, who, as we have seen, was out of action from around the middle of April, 1883, was in third place with twenty-six publications. West's rival in the election dispute, Joseph Sampson Gamgee, published twenty articles as well as a book, putting him in fourth place, and Furneaux Jordan, another Queen's surgeon, came next with thirteen publications – one of which was a book. Gamgee would undoubtedly have produced a greater number of papers but for the fact that he suffered a serious illness which incapacitated him for a prolonged period during 1881. Members of the group who published little no doubt had good reasons for not doing so, and, for all we know, others may have been afflicted, as Gamgee was, by illness.

Some books produced by individual Birmingham doctors are on diverse topics. Tait wrote primarily on the abdominal diseases which afflicted women, as we might expect, but he also wrote about hospital mortality and other subjects. Gamgee wrote on the subject of wounds and fractures, but there are also volumes on hospital reform and researches in pathological anatomy. Robert Saundby wrote on Bright's Disease, Diabetes, renal and urinary diseases and diseases of the digestive system, but he also published books on subjects such as medical ethics and old age – its care and treatment. One Birmingham doctor and close neighbour of the Wests, Pye H Chavasse, made it his mission to enlighten and educate women on how to manage everything from menstruation, pregnancy, labour and suckling to how to bring up their children. The latter, which has survived in manuscript,[32] is surprisingly modern. His observations are wise. The book contains chapters on topics such as play, clothing, education and hair, and includes comments like 'Many silly people delight to teaze (sic) a little child: it is a senseless and cowardly thing to do' and 'Children soon find out those who are fond of them.'

The proliferation of medical societies and associations in the second half of the nineteenth century, together with their journals, provided medical men with unprecedented opportunities for debate and a medium for the dissemination of knowledge denied to earlier generations. James West began publishing early. He may even have been encouraged to put pen to paper for the first time by William Sands Cox. The case was that of a patient who, after suffering a wound to the palmer arch, succumbed to

---

[32] Pye H Chavasse, *Things New and Old Touching Principally on the Welfare of Children.* He intended to dedicate the book to his 'dear wife.' It was written on a collection of sheets of various sizes and even envelopes. MS 556/5–281. (BCA).

traumatic aneurysm. He had been admitted, as its author makes clear, under the care of Mr W Sands Cox. When it was printed in *The Lancet* in April, 1857,[33] the appearance, in parenthesis, of West's name suggests he simply wrote up the case. James West seems to have been a confident and eager recruit to the profession in the first nine months of 1857. In May, he published another paper in one of the local society journals [34] as well as a second one in *The Lancet*.[35] This last was a report on a patient who was under the care of Thomas Heslop, so it too, may have appeared as a result of someone else's encouragement. When these early papers were printed, Cox, Heslop and West were unaware of what lay ahead in the autumn of 1857, but the absence of papers in the *British Medical Journal* and *The Lancet* between 1857 and 1862 may reflect a reluctance by their editors to publish works by West following the election dispute. Even if this was true, it had little effect on West's eventual output. A series of papers he submitted to *The Dublin Quarterly Journal of Medical Science* were accepted by them for publication in the years 1859 and 1860 respectively.

Contributions to the Surgical History of Syphilis

The first paper by West accepted for publication in *The Dublin Quarterly* was one of three entitled, Contributions to the Surgical History of Syphilis.[36] West wrote his first article on syphilitic fungus of the testicle, but the two subsequent articles were on an issue which he knew to be controversial – namely, constriction of the œsophagus.[37] When West wrote on this subject, he was airing the belief that stricture of the œsophagus could occur in cases of aggravated syphilis. If the election dispute had undermined his confidence, there is no evidence of it in these papers. At the age of just twenty-six years, he was prepared to challenge his colleagues and defend his argument. He starts off with an acknowledgement of the fact that some remain unconvinced, but says that he hopes his paper will provide the evidence necessary to support his belief. James West was a staunch advocate of the post-mortem, and he states in the paper that the 'quæstio

---

[33] JFF West, Report of a Case of Wound to the Palmer Arch followed by Traumatic Aneurysm, in which Compression of the Brachial Artery was Successfully Employed. *The Lancet*; 1857; i: p.406.

[34] JF West, On the use of the Chloride of Zinc as a Caustic in Cases of Aneurysm by Anastomosis; *The Midland Quarterly Journal*; May, 1857; pp.240–244.

[35] JFF West, Case of Asphyxia Complicated with Concussion, and Followed by Stupor, Successfully Treated by the Marshall Hall Method of Artificial Respiration. *The Lancet*; 1857; ii: pp.530–531.

[36] JFF West, On Syphilitic Fungus of the Testicle; *The Dublin Quarterly Journal of Medical Science*; August and November, 1859. pp.323–332.

[37] JFF West, On Syphilitic Stricture of the Œsophagus; Ibid., February and May, 1860: pp.86–98. Also, on the same topic – ibid.; August and November, 1860. pp.29–33.

vexata' would have been settled earlier on, if earlier writers on the subject had thoroughly investigated the outcome of the disease in the post-mortem room. He cites a number of cases in which he believes medical practitioners have failed to make the connection between stricture of the œsophagus and advanced syphilis. He even names individuals whom he believes were responsible for oversights of this sort. West's paper describes the symptoms and treatment of each case, as we might expect, but it is in detailing the results of post-mortem examination that he hopes he has provided sufficient evidence to convince those who remain sceptical.

It would appear from a paper West wrote in 1872 [38] that he believed many of his colleagues still remained unconvinced about the connection between œsophageal stricture and syphilis. In that paper, West stated that he had found little support for his belief in the phenomenon among his British colleagues, but says that there had been considerable interest from the French and the Americans. He states that one of his own earlier papers on the subject had even been republished in the French journal, *Archives Générales de Médecine*, in June, 1860. West states that its surgical editor, M. Follin, not only cited cases of his own in which œsophageal stricture had occurred as a result of syphilis in his book, *Traité Elémentaire de Pathologie Externe*, but finished off by stating that James West had effectively proved it. 'Enfin,' writes Follin, 'West a publié sur cette question deux observations qui lui sont personelles; la premiére, dans laquelle l'autopsie du malade a été faite, est seule probante, et *elle suffit pour faire admettre l'existence du rétrécissement syphilitique de l'œsophage*.'[39] Another French surgeon, Lancereaux, West points out, quoted details from the first case West described in the *Dublin Quarterly* 'in extenso' and Dr Bumstead, of New York, gave an abstract of West's papers on the subject. Bumstead, says West, even went as far as saying, 'In reviewing this subject, it appears extremely probable that Mr West is right in his conjecture as to the cause of the stricture in the cases which have come under his observation, since we may readily admit that syphilitic ulceration of the fauces may extend to the œsophagus or attack the latter as a primary affection.'[40]

There is further evidence to suggest that West was not entirely justified in complaining that he was alone in thinking that syphilis could cause œsophageal constriction. Numerous papers written by others on

---

[38] JFF West, On Syphilitic Constriction of the Œsophagus and Pharynx; *The Lancet;* 1872; ii: pp.291–293.

[39] Ibid., The extract West cites from M. Follin's book translates as: 'Finally West has published two personal observations. The first, made after the autopsy had been carried out is the only one which is relevant, and allows us to admit to the existence of a constriction of the œsophagus due to syphilis.'

[40] Ibid., p.292.

œsophageal constriction appeared in British medical journals between 1859 and 1883, the year of West's death. It is true that seven of the papers which appeared in the *BMJ*, were written by men who showed little or no interest in the causes. Others describe strictures which had other causes – cancer, for instance – but there are some among them who state quite categorically that stricture was due to syphilis. A few acknowledged that syphilis could result in constriction of the œsophagus by implication when they made a point of saying that there was no evidence of syphilis in the cases they were then describing. West's name is not mentioned in any of the above mentioned papers, but it is not true to say that he that he received no British support whatsoever.

Langston Parker, of Queen's Hospital, Birmingham, referred specifically to West's first case in his own work on syphilis, while John K Barton MD FRCSI from Ireland, mentioned West's work on œsophageal constriction in his publication on syphilis in 1868. The latter even contained a one hundred and eleven words extract from West's paper of 1860. Barton's own conviction that œsophageal stricture can result from syphilis is clear from the following passage. 'The mucus membrane of the œsophagus' states Barton 'may suffer subsequently to or at the same time with that of the pharynx, and from the consequent contraction which follows, a syphilitic stricture of the œsophagus may be produced.' Barton refers to a drawing by Wilks of an œsophagus so afflicted, which he says is based on a specimen of the same in the museum at Guy's Hospital.

John Barton even places West's name in the same sentence as the great German surgeon, Rudolf Virchow (1821–1902) when he states 'Virchow relates a similar case; and West, of Birmingham, gives the following description of the post-mortem appearance in the case of a patient who had syphilis for some years, and whose throat was extensively ulcerated.' Barton rounds off the section he wrote on œsophageal stricture with the following words 'As to the other organs in this case showed undoubted signs of syphilis, there can be no doubt that the stricture of the œsophagus was due to syphilis also, and the possibility of such an occurrence may be considered proved.'[41] An acceptance that syphilis could lead to constriction of the œsophagus was universally acknowledged in time. By the time that West died in 1883, it was a sufficiently well established fact for it to warrant inclusion in Quain's [42] Medical Dictionary of that year. The editors, in fact,

---

[41] John K Barton, *The Pathology and Treatment of Syphilis,*
(Dublin: Fannin and Co. 41, Grafton St, 1868). p.138.
[42] Richard Quain, 1816–98.

Diagrams to illustrate West's first paper in the Birmingham Medical Review,
1872. Source: By kind permission of the General Committee of the
Birmingham Medical Institute.

devoted a whole page to stricture of the œsophagus and the section begins
with the words 'This affection may be the result of either of the two first-
named disorders; or of a changed condition of the wall of the œsophagus,
brought about by the existence of some new growth, such as that resulting
from cancer or syphilis.'[43]

   We have seen already that West's published output appeared in a
number of different journals. Apart from the numerous examples to be
found in *The Lancet* and the *BMJ*, there are the papers from *The Dublin
Quarterly* (4), the *St Thomas' Hospital Reports* (2), the *Medical Times and Gazette*
(3) and in the *Medico-Chirurgical Transactions* (2). Once the *Birmingham
Medical Review* was launched in 1872, West became a regular contributor to
that journal too.

   He wrote on a wide range of subjects. Papers on head injuries, his own
use of Lister's antiseptic methods, syphilis and acupressure have been
mentioned already, but he wrote on numerous other topics including
excision of joints, trephining, wounds of the heart, lithotrity, ovariotomy,
the treatment of fractures and cancer. He also translated Baron Von
Langenbeck's paper on gun-shot wounds of the hip from the German and,
as we have seen, he wrote on foreign hospitals.

---

[43] Richard Quain MD FRS (Editor), *Quain's Medical Dictionary,* 1883. p.1056.

'Copious notes'

Many of the Birmingham hospital doctors who were the subject of the author's earlier study, continued their studies on the continent or travelled abroad for further study mid-career. In her study of the medical profession in mid-Victorian London, [44] the historian, Peterson, found that whilst Paris was the favourite venue for further study in the 1850s, Vienna and a number of German cities were the most popular destinations of those who embarked on study abroad after the 1880s. No such shift in popularity is evident among the thirty-three Birmingham hospital doctors. For them, a preference for Paris prevailed, but other centres such as Vienna and Berlin were also popular. Five members of the Birmingham group confined themselves to a single centre, but one studied in two separate centres (Berlin and Vienna) and another four studied in three centres.

West's rival in the election of 1857, Joseph Sampson Gamgee, was well acquainted with continental surgical practice. He trained for the profession at University College, London, but during his days as student he also studied in Florence (his birthplace), Parvia and Paris. He was not only the English correspondent of the Society of Surgery in Paris for a time, but according to one obituary,[45] he also occupied similar posts for several other foreign learned societies. James West did not study abroad during his days as a student, but he became an inveterate traveller later on. He is described in obituaries as a surgeon who made frequent trips to the continent in order to visit the medical schools and hospitals of the great capitals. In one, he was said to have brought back from these excursions, 'copious notes, which he freely communicated to his clinical class and to the medical societies.'[46]

Some of these trips doubled as holidays, and one paper, as we have seen, was even called, Jottings from a Surgeon's Holiday Notebook. In this paper, West introduces the subject by stating that he can think of no better way to spend his time than in visiting continental hospitals and medical schools. The content of 'Jottings' is not trivial though. West describes three separate places in the paper – St Peter's Hospital in Amsterdam, the University of Würzburg and the Alpine health resort of St Moritz. In writing about St Peter's Hospital he reports on ward lay-out and attention to hygiene, the methods employed by their practitioners to treat the sick and injured and their use of new or controversial techniques such as Lister's antiseptic treatment and plaster of Paris. West says the reputation of the University of

---

[44] MJ Peterson, The Medical Profession in Mid-Victorian London. (Berkeley: California, 1978), p.86.

[45] *The Lancet*; 1886; ii: pp.607–608.

[46] Ibid., 1883; i: p.1024.

Würzburg is so great that it attracts students from all over the world. He says its popularity is undoubtedly due to the eminence of its professorial staff and yet he is surprised and puzzled to find that his colleagues in Würzburg are still reluctant to use the microscope. With respect to the health resorts, he says he hopes that what he has to say about them will be of help to medical colleagues who may be at a loss to know what the various health resorts have to offer and which, if any, to recommend.

The arrangements made for childbirth at the Julius Hospital in Würzburg under the renowned, Scanzoni, is another topic described by West in 'Jottings.' Its purpose, he tells us, is threefold. It receives and cares for the poor in their confinements, it provides medical students and midwives with practical opportunities to study obstetrics and it serves as a place where 'pregnant women who wish their confinements kept secret'[47] can shelter. The women who are intent on keeping their condition incognito are described by West as 'young ladies who have loved not wisely, but too well.'[48] It is a comment which suggests that West not only has a degree of compassion but also a sense of humour.

Papers published in the medical journals provided a platform for the dissemination of knowledge, as we have seen, but doctors could also express their discontent on issues like quackery and fees, and enter debate on controversial topics. The smoking controversy has been mentioned already, as have the heated debates on Lister's antiseptic treatment of wounds, but topics such as vivisection, the advisability of awarding prizes to medical students, breast feeding versus bottle feeding and whether or not women should be admitted to the profession were all debated by West's medical brethren in the medical journals throughout his professional life.

Female practitioners

Opportunities for women to practise medicine were virtually non-existent in the second half of the nineteenth century. We have seen that Birmingham had just three practitioners in the final years of the nineteenth century – Annie Elizabeth Clarke (1845–1924), Mary Darby Sturge (1862–1925) and Annie Reay Barker (1853–1909). Clarke worked in the Birmingham and Midland Hospital for Women and The Children's Hospital after having gained an MD at Berne in 1877. Mary Sturge, who was awarded an MD by the University of London in 1891 worked initially in London but returned to Edgbaston, the place of her birth, where she set herself up in private

---

practice and worked as anæsthetist to the Birmingham and Midland Hospital for Women.[49] The life of Annie Barker is more obscure. The Medical Register shows she gained a Licentiate at King's and Queen's College of Physicians in Ireland, in 1878, although the Census of 1881 states that she had an MD from Paris. She also worked at the Women's Hospital in Birmingham to start with but her days as a hospital doctor were short-lived. She moved to Aldershot in 1884 after having spent three years as a lodger in the home of John Cleveland and his daughter, Rosa, at 7, Calthorpe Road, Edgbaston. Barker may have worked as a private practitioner between 1881 and her death in 1909 but there is no concrete evidence to support it.

Edinburgh was the first university in the British Isles to allow women to embark on medical courses, but the experiment was short-lived and the decision to admit them had been overturned by 1872. The Birmingham practitioner, Annie Clarke, was one of the casualties of this policy. She began her medical training in Edinburgh, but was compelled to leave in 1872 and continue her studies abroad. Before that, just two women succeeded in gaining registration in England – one who had qualified in America in 1849, and Elizabeth Garrett Anderson (1836–1917) who gained the LSA in 1865. Both succeeded in being registered in England under the Medical Act of 1858, but this was only because, at the time, no-one had thought to exclude women. The decision to impose a ban on females at Edinburgh prompted some women to press harder for their right to train in England. They did so with the help of a small number of sympathetic and influential men folk. Their reward came in 1874, when the London School of Medicine for Women was opened. Medically qualified women continued to suffer prejudice even after official opposition had been dropped, but progress was unstoppable by then and in 1882, The Royal Commission on the Medical Acts decreed that women were to be admitted to the examinations on exactly the same terms as men.

The historian, WR Reader says that Birmingham's mayor, Joseph Chamberlain, successfully persuaded Queen's College to admit women on to its medical courses in 1876.[50] The scheme, such as it was, came to nothing. The General Committee of Queen's agreed in principle to the possibility of providing clinical instruction to female students at a meeting on 7 January, 1876,[51] but then failed to put any means in place for the

---

[49] *Edgbastonia*; 1900; XX: pp.201–207. (BCL).

[50] WR Reader, *Professional Men – The Rise of the Professional Classes in Nineteenth Century England*, (London, Weidenfeld and Nicolson, 1996). p.179.

[51] *General Committee Book, January, 1873 – July, 1876.* Meeting held on 7, January, 1876. p.500. (BCA).

certification of those women who did attend medical courses. On 2 May, 1876,[52] Chamberlain wrote to the Reverend Clarke, of the Board, expressing his exasperation at the delay in instituting the changes that had been agreed earlier. He reminded Clarke of the resolutions which had been made on 7 January, and urged him to apply to the Royal College of Surgeons for the endorsement of certificates awarded by the staff at Queen's. The Board may have told Chamberlain that they anticipated, or had already encountered difficulties in getting approval from the Royal College of Surgeons for their certificates, but in view of the conservatism of Victorian society it is possible that both committee and the RCS alike were doing their utmost to obstruct the plan. Whatever the reason, Chamberlain's efforts were to no avail, and it took another twenty-five years before women were admitted onto medical courses in Birmingham.

Vivisection and experimentation

Vivisection was another subject which was debated in the medical journals. In the four years 1860–64, for example, the *BMJ* and *The Lancet* carried nineteen and twelve articles respectively on vivisection. Experimentation on animals was hardly systematic in mid-nineteenth century England. Animals were not bred for experimentation any more than there were laboratories to house animals for vivisection. The motley collection of animals which were rounded up and used to test the toxicity of the London sewers hardly represent organised vivisection, yet medical men had for many years experimented on animals before attempting new and dangerous procedures on humans. Astley Cooper, maestro of John Flint South's teacher, Henry Cline, perfected ligation of arteries on dogs and corpses in the early years of the nineteenth century. John Hunter, born 1728, and teacher of both Cooper and Cline, was another who was known to use animals in perfecting surgical technique. Cooper was convinced that collateral circulation could develop after ligation of major vessels, but felt it prudent to try the procedure on animals first. That Astley Cooper could make a real difference to the long term survival of patients with aneurysms was probably due to his insistence on perfecting the techniques on animals first. One patient upon whom Cooper successfully tied the external iliac artery for aneurysm in 1808, survived a further eighteen years after the operation. Cooper operated on a second patient later the same day, this time tying a aneurysmal common carotid artery. It was another success story – the patient lived for a further thirteen years.

---

[52] *General Committee Book, January, 1873 – July, 1876.* Meeting, 5 May, 1876. p.556. Chamberlain's letter, p.559. (BCA).

James West did not leave any record of having experimented on animals or of holding strong views on the subject, but Joseph Sampson Gamgee and other colleagues did. Gamgee almost certainly had sympathy for, if not love of, animals. His father was an eminent veterinary surgeon, and Gamgee began his own career in veterinary science. But that did not stop him from being a strong advocate of vivisection in the interests of medical science. One pamphlet he wrote in defence of experimentation on animals, amounts to some thirty-seven sides.[53] It was the text of a talk he delivered at the Birmingham Medical Institute (BMed.I), and like the address to Lord Brougham in 1857, it is an emotionally charged document. George Jesse of the Society for the Abolition of Vivisection, was given the opportunity to contest Gamgee's argument at a meeting at the Birmingham Medical Institute a month later on 9 March, 1882.

Jesse, it turned out, was a tough adversary. Apart from denouncing the use of vivisection, he complained that the conditions under which he was expected to deliver his address, did not match those of his opponent. He said that he had been stopped from reading his manuscript initially, and was told that he must speak. He reminded the President that Gamgee had read *his* paper, and said that although he was eventually given permission to read his text, he was ordered not to exceed fifteen minutes. Gamgee, on the other hand, he said, had taken over an hour to deliver his address in February.

That some scientists were hesitant to conduct experiments on animals was freely acknowledged by Gamgee in his address, but he was convinced that individuals of that persuasion could be won over, if not by the arguments, then as a result of spiritual guidance. The sceptics could seek it, he informed them, from the works of composers like Mozart, Auber or Rossini or from God himself. He even went so far as to suggest that John Henry Newman's hymn, *Lead, kindly Light...* was suitably inspirational material for those in doubt. It was a paper which provided Jesse with plenty of ammunition, and he did not hesitate to use it. *The Medical Press and Circular* expressed a certain amount of admiration for the way in which Jesse argued his case in their account of the debate but, even so, its correspondent could not resist concluding in a more patronising tone. 'Taking them all in all' it states 'these anti's are a curious class of cranks, worthy of careful study on the part of some of our experts in mental diseases...'[54]

[53] Joseph Sampson Gamgee, The Influence of Vivisection on Human Surgery; *Birmingham Institutions*, D/12, (BCL).
[54] *The Medical Press and Circular*; 19 April, 1882.

Gamgee was not the only one of West's colleagues to speak out in favour of vivisection. Dr Alfred Carter, of Queen's, was another advocate, but there were also regular petitions from the staff of Queen's, as a body, for a licence to practise vivisection in the institution. Since the only real alternative to testing the efficacy of certain drugs and surgical procedures on animals was to experiment on humans, it is hardly surprising that vivisection was considered the better option. The more that skills could be perfected and the more that hazardous procedures could be attempted without putting human lives at risk, the better.

Regulations against vivisection were more rigorous in Britain than in other parts of Europe. In the second half of the nineteenth century, difficulties in obtaining a licence for experimentation on animals caused considerable frustration for individuals and institutions alike. By contrast, Continental medical scientists were able to practise vivisection virtually unimpeded. Louis Pasteur, Paul Ehrlich and Emil Behring, whose work on rabies, TB, syphilis, diphtheria, tetanus and anthrax amongst other things, marked them out as exceptional, all used animals in their efforts to conquer disease. Behring's laboratories were reputed to be more akin to the farmyard than the laboratory according to Robert Koch, a fellow scientist and vivisectionist.

Even today, with sophisticated diagnostic tools at our disposal, medical practitioners are sometimes surprised by what they find when a patient is opened up during surgery, or in the case of those unfortunate enough to die from their maladies, from what they discover in a post-mortem. In the case of the living, doctors are, in effect, left with no option but to act on the spur of the moment. If present day medical practitioners are occasionally faced with situations in which it is necessary to undertake a procedure without the benefit of experience, we can easily imagine how common an occurrence that was in the past. The very boundaries of what was possible were extended thanks to physicians and surgeons who were prepared to try out new and unproven techniques and drugs on patients themselves. Where particularly dangerous procedures were concerned, some scientists and medical practitioners even conducted experiments on themselves or their relatives. Langston Parker, of Queen's, was one. In 1847, less than a year after William Morton pioneered the use of ether in anæsthesia, he subjected his son to an anæsthetic before using it on patients. To be fair to Parker, the dangers of anæsthesia were not apparent initially. It was an experiment he may have shied away from, had he had the benefit of hindsight to guide him. The French vet, M. Delcroix, conducted an experiment on himself which must have been regarded as reckless by many. He swallowed a piece of raw meat which had been soaked in saliva from a rabid dog in his quest to better understand the rabies virus.[55]

Lady Mary Wortley Montagu, herself a survivor of smallpox, was not medically qualified, but in 1721 she persuaded the English surgeon, Mr Maitland,[56] to inoculate her daughter against the disease during a smallpox epidemic. The process involved smearing smallpox-infected pus into cuts on the girl's arm. Lady Mary had not only observed the practice while living as the British Ambassador's wife in Constantinople (now Istanbul), but had had her son inoculated against the disease during her stay there.

Inoculation against smallpox was not unknown in Britain. The medical historians AFM and WD Stone say that accounts of the Turkish practice had already been published in London by two separate physicians by 1715.[57] Few were convinced by it. Lady Mary needed no persuading though. Her own experience of successful inoculation against smallpox in Constantinople was enough to convince her of its efficacy, and on her return to England she determined to persuade English doctors to adopt the practice. Mr Maitland had been surgeon to the British Embassy in Constantinople at the time of Lady Mary's residency there and had seen successful inoculation for himself. He was, nevertheless, somewhat reluctant to inoculate Lady Mary's child. The occasion caused a flurry of interest and at least one of the physicians who witnessed the historic moment was sufficiently impressed by it to treat his own children.

Anxious to protect her own children from smallpox by having them inoculated, Princess Caroline persuaded her father, George I, to sanction an experiment on a number of condemned prisoners. The prisoners were given a choice between acting as human guinea pigs for a trial of smallpox inoculations or going to the gallows. Seven opted for inoculation. They soon had reason to celebrate – they survived both the gallows and smallpox. It was not long before the hazards of these early inoculations began to manifest themselves,[58] and the practice did not gain

[55] *BMJ*; 1864; i: p.236. M. Delcroix survived, although it may not surprise us to know that he did experience some constriction of the throat and some difficulty in swallowing when he read the results of his experiment to the Academy of Sciences.

[56] Maitland had a post as embassy surgeon in Constantinople.

[57] AFM and WD Stone, Lady Mary Wortley Montagu: medical and religious controversy following her introduction of smallpox inoculation; *Journal of Medical Biography*; 2002; 10: pp.232–236.

[58] Some died or suffered serious illness as a result of their inoculations and some infected those around them with the disease. The Stones say in their paper that by 1730, some 845 had been treated and that out of those, seventeen had died.

full acceptance until the last decade of the eighteenth century when Edward Jenner (1749–1823) discovered a safe alternative. Jenner began in much the same way, namely, smearing infected pus into incisions on the arms of volunteers, but his programme involved the use of cowpox rather than the more dangerous smallpox.[59] A national programme of vaccination was introduced as a result of Jenner's work and by the time West was practising, parents who failed to have their children protected against smallpox were liable to prosecution. It was not an empty threat. A glance through Victorian newspapers confirms the fact that individuals were indeed fined.

DISSEMINATING KNOWLEDGE
Medical professionals from Birmingham and its environs shared knowledge and discussed cases with colleagues at the medical society meetings they frequented. Knowledge was disseminated through papers and specimens brought along by members and those societies fortunate enough to have their own premises housed substantial libraries and subscribed to prestigious professional journals from across the world. West was a member of a number of medical societies and contributed to them on a regular basis. He occupied a place on the councils of various of them and took his turn as President of some.

Midland Medical Society
West was a particularly active member of the Midland Medical Society. Originally founded in 1848, it flourished throughout his professional life. He became a member in October, 1868, was on its Council in the years 1869/70, 1873/4, 1875/6, 1881/3 and its president during the year 1871/2. During West's presidency, Thomas Furneaux Jordan read a paper entitled *A Couple of Operating Days*.[60] Jordan had been elected to the post of honorary surgeon at Queen's six years after his unsuccessful application for the position at the time of the election dispute in 1857. It makes him one of West's closest professional colleagues along with Joseph Sampson Gamgee.

The paper gives us a valuable insight into the work of a surgeon at Queen's in West's day and the cases almost certainly bear a resemblance to those that West himself tackled. One, an excision of the hip, would have

---

[59] Jenner based his decision to use cowpox on his observation of the fact that individuals who had been infected with the bovine disease enjoyed immunity to smallpox.

[60] Thomas Furneax Jordan, A Couple of Operating Days. Paper read at a meeting of the *Midland Medical Society* on 15 February, 1872. MMS 1/1/1. (B Med I).

been of particular interest to West, but there were other procedures, which we know from West's papers, that he too carried out at the hospital. Another operation performed by Jordan in those two days was that of excision of the tongue. As we will see later, West was to give a clinical lecture on epithelioma of the tongue and its operative treatments in 1875 and he described the method Jordan had used on this occasion as one of several options. The account of Jordan's two operating days to be found in the minute book of the Midland Medical Society is in West's hand, and it is significant that the operation to remove a patient's tongue is the only procedure which he describes in detail. Jordan also says he operated on an anal fistula, treated haemorrhoids with a ligature, used the actual cautery in hip disease, removed a scirrhus tumour of the breast, reduced an old sub coracoid dislocation, removed a sequestrum from the radius and used the aspirator in a large abscess of the abdomen.

Jordan's paper excited plenty of interest in the members present that day. As West says at the conclusion of his account 'owing to the lateness of the hour the discussion on Mr Jordan's admirable paper was deferred until the next meeting.'[61] Doubtless some continued the discussion informally after the meeting was over. The Midland Medical Society had introduced the practice of allowing time for members to gather socially after the meetings by the 1870s and if the society's members were anything like their modern counterparts, it is likely that groups collected afterwards to network and talk shop.

The first paper West read to its members, on 100 cases of aneurism, was on 17 February, 1869. He read a further fifteen papers before the society during the next fourteen years, as well as contributing to discussions and exhibiting numerous specimens. West showed exhibits throughout his membership, but in terms of the sheer number brought in, his contribution in the year he spent as president exceeded that of all the other years. Two were living exhibits. One was brought in to demonstrate the success he had had in a case of excision of the knee, and the other was a case of syphilitic constriction of the fauces in a woman of twenty-six. He also showed a gun-shot fracture of the skull and perforation of the dura mater from a case of suicide and an eyeball he had extirpated after it had suffered irreparable damage through injury. The other exhibits consisted of a nasal calculus, a scapula, fractured at its neck, a case of caries of the Astragalus and Os Calcis, stricture of the Urethra and its sequelæ, necrosis of the Lower Jaw and necrosis of the Tibia.

---

[61] Ibid..

West also sent specimens to society meetings in the care of colleagues from time to time. At a meeting of the Midland Medical Society on 7 March, 1883, Mr Jordan Lloyd, the man who would become West's successor at Queen's Hospital, exhibited a kidney West had removed from a boy some four days earlier along with a number of specimens he had brought in himself. West recorded the fact that he had performed a nephrectomy in his diary on Saturday 3 March, 1883. Few details are given in the diary, but the *BMJ* report of the meeting indicates that West did not undertake the operation lightly.[62]

The patient had been admitted to the hospital on 5 November, 1882, following an injury to the kidney. His symptoms included hæmaturia, the development of a lumbar tumour, pus in the urine and a fever. Purulent fluid soon built up in the damaged kidney. In December, fifty-five ounces of fluid were drawn off by means of an aspirator, but the relief was short-lived and the procedure had to be repeated a week later. This too failed to effect a permanent solution. A drainage tube was then inserted, but the passage of eighty ounces of ammoniacal fluid daily together with the rapid onset of emaciation made a nephrectomy the only serious option. West said in his diary that it had been a difficult operation, but by Wednesday 7 March he was able to report that his patient was 'going on well.'[63] A further entry, dated Thursday 8 March, suggests the operation won West the admiration of his colleagues. In it he writes 'My case of nephrectomy wh. is still talked about as the last new thing exciting some attention.'[64]

Jordan Lloyd had also shown a specimen for West during the latter's absence on an earlier occasion. He exhibited for West a living specimen showing a case of disease of the tarsal bones successfully treated by resection at a meeting of the Midland Medical Society on 16 April, 1879. Mr J Bassett (1826–92), West's successor as President, also showed a specimen for West. On 8 January, 1873, he showed a uterine tumour removed by West a few days earlier. There is no concrete evidence of West having exhibited anything for either Lloyd or Bassett, although he did show an example of osterid cancer of the tibia and read notes on the case for a Mr Partridge of Stroud, Gloucestershire.

New ideas, inventions and procedures were often demonstrated or discussed at Midland Medical Society meetings. Some of these were the

[62] *Midland Medical Society* meeting held on Wednesday 7 March, 1883 reported in the *BMJ*; 1883; i: p 669.
[63] JFF West, Diary; Wednesday 7 March, 1883. (JFF West Archive).
[64] Ibid., Thursday 8 March, 1883.

product of the society's own members. Joseph Sampson Gamgee, a man whose name became synonymous with a type of dressing, kept members informed about the refinements he was making to his invention. On 25 February, 1880, for instance, Gamgee explained how he had produced 'a remarkably clean, light and absorbent antiseptic dressing'[65] by impregnating the pads with carbolic and benzoic acid. Another member, Mr C Sims of the Dental Hospital, brought along a living specimen who had been fitted with an artificial palate after having suffered extensive syphilitic destruction of the roof of the mouth on 19 February, 1873. A few weeks later, Dr Charles Warden (1828–1912), gave a paper on polypus of the ear and the treatment of perforation of the eardrum using a new artificial tympanium.[66]

Like West, Joseph Sampson Gamgee was an active member of the Midland Medical Society. One specimen brought in by him was a leg he had amputated in October, 1873.[67] It was followed a month later by the amputee himself. This may conjure up a somewhat comic image today, but a few exhibits, even by nineteenth century standards, may have sparked controversy or caused raised eyebrows. After gaining permission from the Society's president (then, Mr John St Swithin Wilders), Dr Edward Malins (1842–1922) demonstrated the operations of cephalotripsy and cranioclasm [68] on a foetus at meeting on 1 April, 1874, while the gynæcologist, Robert Lawson Tait, showed a pair of normal ovaries that he had removed from an inmate at the Borough Lunatic Asylum on 21 April, 1880. Astonishment probably greeted a specimen brought in by Mr R Prosser on 25 March, 1870. Weighing in at four pounds seven ounces, Prosser exhibited hair taken from the stomach of a woman aged thirty-one. The hair, which had formed itself into a perfect cast of the stomach, was twelve inches long, five inches deep and four inches wide.

Midland Medical Society meetings were held in rooms at the Birmingham and Midland Institute in the 1860s and 70s. As a letter of complaint from Edwin Smith, the Secretary of that institution shows, the Society came in for severe criticism in March, 1874. It seems enthusiasm for bringing in exhibits did not always extend to taking them away again at the end of the meeting. The correspondent bewails the fact that members'

---

65 *Midland Medical Society Minute Book* 1874–83 MMS 1/1/2. (B Med I).
66 Ibid., 2 April, 1873.
67 *Midland Medical Society Minute Book*, 29 October and 26 November, 1873 respectively. MMS 1/1/1. (B Med I).
68 Both involve crushing the foetal head to facilitate delivery. The former would have been carried out by an instrument known as a cranioclasis and the latter by a cranioclast.

'specimens are constantly left after meetings.' Chastened committee members heeded the complaint and it was resolved that the Secretary and Treasurer should make proper arrangements to remove exhibits in future. Smith's dismay is understandable. A glance at the specimens brought in during the six months prior to the letter of complaint shows that those left behind would have included some, or all, of the following:

- Excised tongue & dead baby with severely crushed skull (Wilders).
- Certified tubercle, several specimens of biliary calculi, inflammatory disease of aorta & mitral disease (Sawyer).
- Necrosed jaw (JP Bradley).
- Uterus, cystic tumour of mamma (Savage).
- Premaxilliary bones of an infant (F Jordan).
- Section of fibroma & dermoid cyst (Tait).
- Two biliary calculi passed per rectum, osteophyte of femur & aneurism of the arch of the aorta (Thomas).
- Nævoid tumour, upper end of tibia, lower end of femur & patella (West).

The Midland Medical Society organised an annual conversazione or inaugural lecture followed by dinner from just before the time West took office as President. These gatherings proved very popular, and West seems to have made a point of attending these functions whenever he could. Illustrious speakers were invited each year and these included Professor Joseph Lister, Sir Henry Thompson (1820–1904) and Sir William Jenner (1815–98). While it is not possible to say for certain that West was present in every case, we do know that he heard Dr BW Richardson speak on bleeding and transfusion on 21 October, 1869, Professor Lionel Beale (1828–1906) on the nature and origins of contagious disease germs on 8 November, 1871, Dr Richardson on the treatment of the dying on 10 November, 1875, Professor Joseph Lister on healing wounds without antiseptic treatment on 30 November, 1878 and J Matthews Duncan (1826–90) on the treatment of puerperal fever on 6 November, 1880.

Some, if not all, of these distinguished visitors must have both stimulated and enlightened West and his colleagues, but the medical professionals of Birmingham and the surrounding area also learnt much from each other. Minds were broadened through the dissemination of ideas. West, for instance, enjoyed visiting medical schools and hospitals both in Britain and abroad. He jotted down his observations at the time, and invariably wrote papers about what he had seen on his return. Others, unable to travel through age, lack of time or income, could and almost certainly did benefit from this. West wrote seven such accounts and six of those were given to colleagues at meetings of the Midland Medical Society. He may have got carried away on occasions though. On 15 February, 1882, he was said to have accompanied his talk on Aix les Bains and the Sulphur Springs of Savoy with 'many photographs.' If he did outstay his place in the limelight that evening, it would not have been for the first time. On 18 April, 1877, West was recorded as having run out of time when he gave his paper on recent joint resections at a meeting.

If West did enlighten colleagues about European practice he, too, benefited from listening to the papers of others. He may well, for instance, have been inspired to make greater use of the clinical thermometer as a result of a paper given by Dr James Sawyer on 5 January, 1871. Sawyer's paper was based on three years' work at West's own hospital, Queen's, and shows that he was positively in favour of its use. Interestingly, he favoured centigrade over fahrenheit. We know West was making good use of the thermometer by the time his paper *On Resection of the Knee-joint* was published in 1872 because he included temperature charts to show the progress made by two of his patients after the operation.[69] His confidence in the role of the thermometer three years further on is evident in the closing remarks he made in a paper written on two ovariotomy cases. 'The thermometer should be frequently in use, as its rise and fall are the best and the only sure guides as to the patient's absolute condition.'[70]

In this paper, West said that ovariotomy was once the 'bête noir' of operative surgery. It was an opinion he would come to endorse again at a later date. Robert Lawson Tait, also a member of the Midland Medical Society, was developing his expertise in ovariotomies in the 1870s and 80s and we know that West and other practitioners heard him speak on the subject at Society meetings. By publicising his own successes [71] West and others were probably emboldened to undertake this procedure more readily than they might otherwise have done at that time. And they, in turn, would have helped to sharpen up Tait's skills through challenging his statements and demanding greater clarification of his techniques.

---

[69] JFF West, On Resection of the Knee-joint; *BMR*; 1872; pp.16–31.
[70] JFF West, Notes on Two Successful Cases of Ovariotomy, with Remarks; *BMR*; 1875; pp.248–259.
[71] RL Tait, Fifty Cases of Ovariotomy; *BMR*; 1878.

West belonged to The *Pathological Society of London* but this was not the only outlet for his interest in pathology. The specimens brought along to the Midland Medical Society often excited so much interest that selected members were elected to investigate further and report back at the next meeting. During his year as president, for instance, West himself proposed that a diseased liver brought in by Dr Underhill should be examined microscopically by a sub-committee consisting of Dr Underhill, Dr Johnston and Mr Jolly.[72] Another exhibit given to a committee to investigate was a section of small intestine which had an obstruction. On this occasion Dr JW Keyworth, West's predecessor as president, asked Messrs Furneaux Jordan, Robert Lawson Tait and William Slingsby Mann to undertake a more thorough examination and report back at the next meeting.[73]

West must have found it more difficult to attend national society meetings and papers by him were communicated by a representative on occasions. Examples appear in the reports of both The Pathological Society of London [74] and The Royal Medical and Chirurgical Society.[75] The majority of exhibits brought along to the meetings of these two societies were pathological specimens removed because of disease. One of the meetings West attended in person was a meeting of the Pathological Society of London on 21 February, 1871 when he exhibited a section of upper jaw which he said he had removed from a man of twenty-four because of a rapidly growing cancer.[76] It was not unusual for members to bring in more than one specimen, and some individuals exhibited animal parts. On this particular occasion, seven individuals brought eleven exhibits between them. With one exception, the diseased vocal chords of a dog, all were human.

James West was one practitioner who brought live patients along whenever he thought it was called for. West was Chairman of the Birmingham and Midland Counties Branch of the BMA Pathological Section in 1882 when Dr Gilbert Barling, (1855–1940) of The General Hospital, exhibited a boy whose arm had been amputated at the shoulder joint by Mr Baker for sarcoma of the humerus some twelve months earlier. Barling, West and Furneaux Jordan all expressed the belief that the boy's prognosis was good and they agreed that Baker should be congratulated

---

72 *Midland Medical Society* meeting, 8 December, 1871. (B Med I).
73 *Midland Medical Society* meeting, 2 November, 1870. (B Med I).
74 JFF West, A Case of Rapidly Growing Cancer; *BMJ;* 1871; p.254.
75 JFF West, On Excision of the Wrist-joint; *Medical Times and Gazette;* 1868; i: p.353 and A Second Case of Trephining for Epilepsy, *Medical Times and Gazette;* 1881; i: p.334.
76 11 March, 1871. Report from, The Pathological Society of London on 21 February, *BMJ;* 1871; i: p.245.

on his work. A total of five pathological specimens were exhibited at the meeting on that day. Three – a skull, fractured at the base; a hypertrophied heart and some atheromatus arteries – had been brought in by West.

Eleven men contributed to an Ordinary Meeting of the Midland Medical Society which was reported in the *Birmingham Medical Review* and chaired by James West on 31 March, 1882. Three doctors, one of whom was West, exhibited living specimens that day. Whether West or his colleagues ever had to offer some kind of inducement to live exhibits is not known, but some must have suffered considerable embarrassment as a result of their agreement to appear as living visual aids. Did West remember his observations on the female who had been made to stand 'perfectly naked' in a Paris hospital when he asked the subject of this venture to accompany him, one wonders? The individual, a man, had been operated on by West after he suffered injury to the foreskin as a result of serious abdominal burns. Dr Barling's exhibit consisted of a pathological specimen of breast tissue which, he said, had been removed by Mr Thomas Hiron Bartleet (1837–91),[77] of The General, on account of malignant infiltration. The assembled company did not agree on the question of the malignancy. West said that he had some doubts as to whether or not the tissue was malignant and was not sure if Bartleet had been right to operate. Jordan Lloyd, the man who would become West's successor the following year, held stronger views altogether and stated that he very much doubted that there was malignancy. Robert Saundby and Gilbert Barling, both of The General, and Bennett May (1846–1937), a colleague of West at Queen's all leant towards the belief that the breast had been cancerous and supported Bartleet's decision to remove it.

An examination of the issues which occupied the minds of the medical establishment between the year when James West qualified and his death in 1883, shows that he lived through a time of great innovation and progress. In the lead up to the 1858 Medical Act, and beyond it, the medical journals contained numerous articles relating to medical politics – reform of examinations and qualifications, the registration of practitioners, doctors' fees, and unprofessional conduct, etc. – but they also reveal the extent to which the boundaries of medical treatment were being extended. Even before the control of post-operative infection had been made effective, surgeons of West's generation could, thanks to

---

[77] When the unfortunate Bartleet died in 1876 at the age of seventy four, *The Lancet* found little in Bartleet's life's work to celebrate and concluded that his was 'not a very eventful career.' Obituary, *The Lancet*; 1876; ii: p.521.

anæsthesia, readily undertake operations which had previously been thought impossible. The incidence of post operative infection in West's early career meant that mortality rates following surgery were high but this did not deter those courageous pioneers who, in their attempts to save lives, were prepared to perform complicated, high-risk operations. In doing so they perfected their techniques and transformed procedures which had once been considered unsafe into the realms of the routine. Colleagues often questioned the wisdom of what was being done and debated the difficulties involved, but they also learnt what was possible from what was being achieved.

Embracing risk: Ovariotomy – the 'bête noir' of surgical procedures

One abdominal operation that filled surgeons with dread in the mid-1850s and beyond was the ovariotomy. It was considered so hazardous that many surgeons refused to undertake the procedure altogether. The first successful operation to remove a diseased ovary was performed by the American surgeon, Ephraim McDowell (1771–1830), in December, 1809, and yet the surgical risks involved and the difficulties in providing a safe post operative environment were still the subject of debate in the 1880s. At Queen's Hospital, the matter was raised by the House Committee on 20 February, 1883, after statistics revealing that between 1875 and 1883 five out of the eight cases dealt with in the hospital had resulted in death. The hospital's surgeons were asked to report back to the Committee on the advisability of performing ovariotomies on the premises. Comments made by James West indicate that by that time, he was no longer prepared to undertake the operation himself. As the book records, 'Mr West wrote, "My present practice is not to perform ovariotomy in this hospital, but to hand such cases to the Obstetric Surgeon, and such has been my practice for some years." '[78] West's colleagues Messrs John St Swithin Wilders, Thomas Furneaux Jordan and Bennett May say much the same, while West's future successor, Mr George Jordan Lloyd says 'for several years I have designedly avoided ovarian operations.'[79] The most junior among them, Mr Alexander Frederick Hawkins, says that no such cases have come under his care but that if they did he would refer them to the obstetric surgeons. The obstetric surgeon himself, Mr Clay (1821–84),[80] says that he is not afraid of

---

[78] *House Committee Report Book*, 20 February, 1883 – 2 August, 1887. p.9.

[79] Ibid..

[80] Mr John Clay was said to have been one whose enthusiasm got the better of his judgements and a man who persisted in treatments for cancer of the uterus which posterity proved useless. Obituary; *The Lancet*; 1894; i: p.1650.

the risks involved in the operation, but states that the sanitary conditions under which it is performed are of paramount importance. He goes on to say that he believes these conditions cannot be guaranteed in the hospital at the present time.

James West had not always subscribed to the view that was recorded in the Committee's Report Book of 1883. Ovariotomies performed by him in 1873 and 1875 respectively are the subject of a paper he wrote entitled, *Notes of two successful cases of Ovariotomy, with remarks*. He even begins his paper with the words 'Ovariotomy, once the bête noir of operative surgery, is now so well recognised and so frequently performed an operation, that it may seem superfluous to go on narrating in detail any fresh cases of that sort.'[81] He goes on to say, though, that since no two cases are alike and since these presented novel features, describing them was justified. The first case, he says, was complicated by the fact that the patient, Mrs W., was expecting twins. West describes his dilemma – to operate on a pregnant woman or to induce labour and wait until the patient had recovered from her confinement. The patient was referred to West by his partner in private practice, Mr William Slingsby Mann. By the time West became involved with the case, the woman in question was in constant pain and very emaciated. In the end, West decided it was far too dangerous to operate on a pregnant woman and opted instead for surgery after an early delivery had been induced.

He induced labour by administering twenty drops of the liquid extract of ergot in a little peppermint water every four hours over the course of five days. The 'fine twins' which he says were 'of about the sixth month of utero-gestation'[82] and which were sacrificed to save the mother are never referred to again. The patient picked up quickly according to West, and he was able to undertake an ovariotomy with the assistance of a team of four [83] some eight weeks later. It proved a difficult day. The nurses, West says, had disobeyed his instructions to starve the patient, so that she suffered 'violent heaving and sickness, followed by fainting' when his colleague, Dr Sawyer, tried to administer chloroform. The team decided the only solution was to delay the operation until later that afternoon. The operation itself did not prove easy either. West found several smaller cysts in addition to the main tumour, and their removal was hampered by the extent of the adhesions by which they

[81] JFF West, Notes of two successful cases of Ovariotomy, with remarks; *BMR*; 1875; p.248.
[82] Ibid., p.250.
[83] Mann; Dr, later Sir, James Sawyer, a younger colleague; and Messrs G Smith and Whitby who other sources show was West's dresser at the time.

were attached to the omentum. The tumour, he says, was a multiocular ovarian cyst containing some two or three gallons of fluid. The surgical procedure is described in detail by West as is the post-operative treatment.

West must have been gratified by the patient's recovery. The wound healed quickly and without any suppuration or smell. The patient's temperature hardly wavered from normal, and although West had to resort to enemas and opium in order to make his patient comfortable, she was well enough to have her sutures removed a mere nine days after the operation. James West also had the satisfaction of reporting that after her discharge from his care, Mrs W... had not only continued to enjoy good health but had since been delivered of a healthy child.

The second case was Ann N... who was 38, married and the mother of six. The patient, West tells us, had borne eleven children altogether, but had lost the five most recent within days of birth. Again West describes the operation in detail. Ann N...'s recovery did not go as smoothly as West's other patient. During the days immediately following surgery, her temperature was raised and even reached an alarming 104.4 degrees Fahrenheit on the fourth day. Ann N... had been given ether rather than chloroform and suffered sickness during and after the operation. West believed that a diet consisting of milk and ice would relieve her sickness and he allowed nothing else. This patient was also given opium but, once only. West's preference on this occasion was for morphia. Fortunately, Ann N...'s wound healed well and West was able to remove her sutures on the eighth day.

With the possible exception of carbolised catgut, West does not seem to have made use of Lister's ideas about the treatment of wounds in either of these cases. In the first, West says he used carbolised catgut stitches and tenax to dress the wound and in the second, silver sutures and a dressing of stypium. West's efforts to make sense of what he found when he operated on these women was impressive. In the second case, he even went as far as conducting a chemical analysis on the fluid taken from the cysts and examining it under the microscope.

Notes of Two Successful Cases of Ovariotomy, with Remarks lists seventeen points which West says suggest themselves to him. Leaving aside the purely technical, he recommends the following procedures. He advocates, for instance, that the operation should be undertaken before exhaustion and emaciation occur; he says that the bladder should be emptied every six hours by means of a flexible gum elastic catheter and he stresses the importance of taking the patient's temperature regularly, saying that it is the only sure indication of the person's absolute condition. He recommends the use of opium for the first seven or eight days as a means of locking up the bowels and says that solid and even semi-solid food should be strictly avoided for the first three or four days. He expresses a preference for ether over chloroform, saying that it produces less subsequent depression, but he also says that a combination of two parts of chloroform, one part alcohol and three parts ether, as recommended by the Medico-Chirurgical Society, is also worth considering.

We do not know whether West's former rival, Joseph Sampson Gamgee, performed ovariotomies in 1883, but there is evidence to show that, like West, he did in the 1870s. Gamgee scaled down his involvement with Queen's Hospital to that of consulting surgeon in 1881, so that his opinion on ovariotomies is not recorded in the House Committee Report of 1883. He did, however, deliver a lecture [84] consisting of some nineteen pages based on his own experience of the operation in the early 1870s. In it he acknowledges the many difficulties which can present themselves but says that, overall, the operation is justifiable. He says that whilst a medical practitioner who decides not to operate condemns his patient to certain death, one who elects to perform an ovariotomy may not only save the patient but also enable her to enjoy many more years of good health. Early intervention is the ideal in Gamgee's view. He expresses regret that older practitioners, remembering the unacceptably high mortality rate of earlier times, are loath to recommend surgery to their patients at a stage when the operation could be conducted with relative ease.

One such patient, he says, came to him with a bulk 'far greater than that of a woman in the most advanced state of pregnancy with twins.'[85] The operation Gamgee performed on that occasion was terrifyingly complicated and he says that he is surprised the human body can survive a trauma as great as that suffered by the luckless woman. He says, though, that he is glad he went ahead with the operation even though he admits that he would not have embarked on it had he realised how widespread the adhesions were. In order to gain access to the site and deal with the tumour, Gamgee had eventually been compelled to extend the incision to fifteen inches (ca.38cms). His efforts to excise the tumour involved an hour's surgery, with the aspiration of three gallons of fluid and the eventual removal of a tumour of some thirty-seven pounds in weight. The greatest

[84] JS Gamgee, On Ovariotomy, Queen's Hospital, Birmingham, May, 1871. D/1 L46.1. (BCL).
[85] Ibid., p.5.

difficulty Gamgee faced in this operation was on account of the many adhesions. They were extensive and there were some which involved large blood vessels. Gamgee, who was not convinced of Lister's methods, used the disinfectant, Chloralum lotion, to dress the wound and his patient enjoyed an enviable level of post-operative care which even included the watchful eye of Gamgee's student assistant throughout the night on the first night after the operation.

Robert Lawson Tait developed an enviable expertise in the field of abdominal surgery and in ovariotomy in particular. Tait spent three years working as a House Surgeon at Wakefield Hospital, Yorkshire, before moving on to a post at the new specialist hospital for women in Birmingham in 1871. He had already undertaken five ovariotomies by the time he left Wakefield. As we have seen, Tait was openly hostile to Lister's methods and relied instead on scrupulous hygiene. He wrote papers on his first fifty ovariotomies as well as on a later series of one hundred cases and one hundred and thirty-seven cases respectively. He reported an overall mortality rate of 38% [86] in the first fifty cases leading up to 1878 – the sort of figure which could indeed persuade some that the operation could not be justified. Even so, he remained optimistic. He said he had learnt more from his failures than he had from his successes and that he expected greater success in his next fifty cases.

Lawson Tait was certainly right in thinking he was gaining expertise. By 1886 he was able to report that he had performed a series of one hundred and thirty-seven consecutive ovariotomies without the loss of a single life.[87] The success of Tait, and other outstanding abdominal surgeons from elsewhere, must have gone a long way towards convincing those who remained reluctant to undertake or recommend ovariotomies in the second half of the nineteenth century to reconsider. By the time Tait died in 1899, papers like the one written in February, 1857 by J Matthews Duncan MD, of Edinburgh,[88] arguing that ovariotomy could not be justified would have been nothing more than an interesting reminder of how things stood in days gone by.

Successful outcomes notwithstanding, nineteenth century surgeons would have been more accustomed to cases which ended in the loss of life than their modern counterparts. Like Tait, James West recognised the

---

[86] Robert Lawson Tait, Fifty Cases of Ovariotomy; *BMR*; 1878; p.294.

[87] RL Tait, One hundred and thirty-nine Consecutive Ovariotomies without a Death. Paper read before BMA in 1886. Pamphlet published by Birbeck, Birmingham.

[88] J Matthews Duncan, Is Ovariotomy Justifiable? *The Lancet*; 1857; i: p.212.

Dissecting Room, Queen's College ca.1880. Source: By kind permission Special Collections, University of Birmingham.

value of the lessons learnt from failure and he was especially committed to the importance of the post-mortem examination. In his inaugural address to the students of Queen's College in October, 1868, West spelt out the way in which enlightenment can follow an investigation post-mortem.

'You must not, however, be satisfied with watching the sick in the wards of the Hospital; you must follow to the dead-house the bodies of those whose diseases prove fatal. That which was before obscure will now be made plain; why such a remedy did not produce its wanted effect, or why a certain disease, which the Surgeon thought he had thoroughly extirpated, has proved fatal, will now be made manifest. We all learn more from our failures than from our successes; therefore always investigate to the fullest extent those cases which terminate unfavourably; they will serve as landmarks for the future, and will help to guide you in determining the nature of any similar case which may hereafter occur to you, and lead you to the determination of a mode of treatment founded on an exact knowledge of the real nature and true site of the disease. Here, as in the wards, your note-book should ever be in use.'[89]

Other abdominal procedures

Robert Lawson Tait was not alone in persevering with operations which were dangerous. The high mortality rates associated with Cæsarian sections did not deter surgeons from performing them when there was no alternative. Tait estimated that, even in 1890, the mortality rate of mothers whose infants were delivered by Cæsarian section was somewhere between 90 and 95%. Even so, there were surgeons who were prepared to take the risk, and reports of successful Cæsarian births can be found in the journals throughout

---

[89] JFF West, Inaugural Clinical Address, *Medical Times and Gazette*; 1868; ii: p.426.

the second half of the nineteenth century. One surgeon, James Hawkins of Newport in Wales, even succeeded in delivering the infant of a woman who was only four feet one inch high by cæsarian section in May, 1858.[90]

James West was not averse to taking on a dangerous surgical procedure if he thought he might save a life which would otherwise be lost. Operations to relieve intestinal obstruction were, according to West, notoriously difficult with phenomenally high mortality rates. Nevertheless, West says surgeons should be decisive and act promptly. In a clinical lecture delivered to his students at Queen's Hospital on 27 May, 1878 and which, interestingly, was reported by a Miss Beilby,[91] he says 'Do not refuse to operate because thirty-two cases (as statistics inform us) out of thirty-three die; it is your business to give the thirty-third a chance of life'….. 'If the patient is suffering from obstruction he will surely die unless something is done at once to bring relief, and you cannot at any rate increase his risk by an exploratory incision.'[92]

It was a philosophy which saved the life of the patient West was discussing with his students in his lecture that day. The patient, Mrs W., was forty-seven years of age and was originally under the care of West's colleague, the physician, Dr Heslop. Heslop had tried a number of medicinal measures but soon realised that the only hope was surgical intervention. West put his convictions into practice and operated at once. Happily, Mrs W. not only survived, but at the time of West's lecture was in good spirits and had gained flesh. He does not explain the cause of her obstruction, but when he opened up the ascending colon he found he could only bring relief by fitting her up with an artificial anus which he plugged with ivory and held in place with a band of elastic. He told those gathered at Queen's Hospital to hear his clinical lecture that the surgeon, Mr Bryant, had reported one hundred and four cases of operations to relieve intestinal obstruction. In the lecture West explained that it was customary to open up the descending colon, but in opening up the ascending colon of Mrs W., he said had not broken new ground. He declared, in fact, that in doing so he had undertaken a procedure that was already thirty-nine years old.

[90] James Hawkins, Successful Case of Cæsarian Operation: Mother and Child Saved; *BMJ*; 1858; May: p.386–387.

[91] Miss Beilby was probably a nurse, rather than a doctor. Her name does not appear in the Medical Register for that year or in subsequent years. She is not listed in the 1881 census as a resident member of the nursing staff of Queen's Hospital but may have moved out of Birmingham by that date or have married or both.

[92] JFF West, On Intestinal Obstruction and its Relief by Colotomy; *BMR*; 1878; p.382.

Conservative surgeons not only remained reluctant to submit patients to the grave risks involved in abdominal procedures, but often denounced those who opted for them. It was a strategy which probably spared some lives in the short term but did little to extend expertise. The efforts of West, and others like him, who were unafraid of acting upon the belief that such surgery could be justified, on the other hand, helped to advance the range of what was feasible.

Pathological specimens and cases of special pathological interest

West was a member of the Pathological and Clinical Branch of the BMA and was, at one time time, its Chairman. As we have seen, he often took along pathological specimens of his own and was an enthusiastic participant in discussions involving the exhibits brought along by others. Many of these discussions were centred around successful cases, but in cases where individuals had died, West and his colleagues related what they had discovered post-mortem. James West acted on his belief that he and others could learn more from cases which ended fatally than from those which were successful by writing up details of these cases for publication in the journals. On occasions, West wrote up his experiences as an explicit warning to others. In 1874, for instance, he reported that Alfred GT, a boy of nine months, died from embolism after treatment for a nævoid tumour. West used a technique which he said had proved brilliantly successful under MM Broca, Gosselin, Demarquay and Professor Pitha, namely using a hypodermic syringe to inject a solution of perchloride of iron directly into the tumour. In West's case, though, it was clear within seconds that there had been an adverse reaction and, in spite of all his efforts to resuscitate his little patient, the child died a few days later. West said that he was not alone in having an unhappy outcome of this sort and felt he had an obligation to alert others to the dangers. 'It is' he said 'incumbent on those who have had fatal cases to publish them as a warning to others not to use such injections in the future, but to adopt some less hazardous mode of treatment.'[93]

James West's interest in surgical pathology prompted him to write a series of papers entitled *Cases of Special Interest in Surgical Pathology* in 1877.[94] In his introduction, West says 'From such unsuccessful cases many

---

[93] JFF West, Case of Cirsoid Aneurysm Treated by Injection of Perchloride of Iron; Death from Embolism; *The Lancet*; 1874; i: p.402.

[94] JFF West, Cases of Special Interest in Surgical Pathology; *BMR*; 1877; pp.133–137; 162–168 and 249–257 respectively.

important and instructive lessons may be learnt; more, in fact, very often, than from our successes.'[95] The first case cited was that of Benjamin L., who had been admitted with a scirrhus tumour of the posterior cervical triangle. The site and nature of the tumour made the operation difficult. West found the tumour was embedded in the sterno-mastoid and had to strip part of it away. He also divided some of the nerves of the cervical plexus when he cut the posterior adhesions and caused damage to some large branches of the internal jugular vein. As soon as the tumour had been removed and a drainage tube introduced, West used ligatures of catgut on the vessels and closed up the wound. The first three days went well, but it was not to last. Benjamin L. soon became delirious and died eighteen days later.

The autopsy showed that West's diagnosis had been correct. He believed he had been justified in his decision to remove the tumour, but realised that opinions would be divided on the action he took to prevent hæmorrhage. The experience made West question his use of ligatures, and he wondered whether he would have caused less disturbance to the cerebral circulation if he had used an acupressure needle instead.

His notes on the fourth case, a hawker by the name of Joseph Dumbleton, suggest this was the one which interested him most. It occupies eight and a half sides as compared to the next longest article of just four sides, and contains an explanatory diagram and a list of further reading matter. Dumbleton had sustained severe injuries to the left inguinal region four years earlier when he was crushed between a coal wagon and the coal face while working in a coal pit. He suffered a number of symptoms, one of which was retention of urine. His recovery was slow, but he returned to work in due course and continued well until he met with a second accident a few years later. This time Dumbleton felt something give way when lifting a heavy tub and he told West that he had suffered some level of incontinence ever since.

James West says Dumbleton had already passed a small bladder stone by the time the second accident occurred, but on examining him he found another larger one. Far more disturbing, though, was West's discovery that the inner and upper part of the thigh was engorged with urine. West operated on the unfortunate Dumbleton but says he 'never rallied from the shock'[96] and died the next day. As many questions as there were answers emerged as a result of the autopsy and West clearly enjoyed the opportunity to indulge in a little detective work.

---

95 JFF West, Cases of Special Interest in Surgical Pathology; *BMR*; 1877. p.134.
96 Ibid., p.251.

While acknowledging that the evidence was open to interpretation, he says he believes that Dumbleton's bladder was lacerated by fragments of bone as a result of the first accident and that, although healing took place, the bladder was weakened. He thought that the stones started to grow during the period of urine retention and that whilst one was passed early on, the other continued to develop. The remaining stone continued to grow over the course of the years causing inflammation and ulceration of the bladder wall. The wall of the bladder eventually became so thin that it ruptured suddenly when placed under severe stress. Urine began to forge a fistulous track which became extended as the amount of urine escaping increased so that, by the time West was consulted, the track reached nearly half way down the inner thigh and backwards. West says that it is almost unheard of to survive a rupture of the bladder and he expressed astonishment that his patient had survived for so long.

The two other cases dealt with in West's papers on *Cases of Special Surgical Interest* were those of Thomas M, a thirty-two year old well sinker and Patrick M, a stone breaker. Both were admitted to Queen's Hospital under West's care in the mid 1870s with injuries to the knee. Both had sustained their injuries many years earlier and were in a debilitated state on admission to hospital. These were not the only similarities. Urine samples indicated that the two men had diseased kidneys. West wrote up these two cases as numbers two and three respectively. He cited kidney disease as the reason for his decision not to perform a resection in both cases, choosing instead to do what he could by cleaning out the cavities and inserting a drainage tube. Thomas M died the day after the operation – an outcome that would have come as no surprise to West if he had had the benefit of the intelligence provided after the event in post-mortem. The autopsy revealed that in addition to the diseased kidneys and knee, the liver, gut and bladder were also in a diseased state.

Patrick M. injured his knee for the first time some twenty-five years earlier. He had suffered intermittent trouble ever since and had had the knee treated elsewhere on numerous occasions. He survived the operation, but died just over five weeks later. Again, West did not know the extent of the problem suffered by Patrick M. until the body was examined at autopsy. What he found surprised him. The lower end of the femur was, he says 'white and dense like ivory, and the medullary cavity and cancelli of the shaft obliterated.'[97] West said he had never seen a finer specimen of osteosclerosis.

---

[97] Ibid., p.167.

Saving limbs

West may have judged certain cases of joint disease unsuitable subjects for resection but, unlike some of his contemporaries, he was in favour of undertaking the procedure in certain circumstances. Four papers written by him were devoted quite specifically to excision or resection of joints and another on chronic joint disease describes cases in which he has performed resection. In the second half of the nineteenth century operations of this sort were still hazardous. Unforeseen complications, post-operative infection and failure could all lead to useless limbs, secondary amputation or death. The author of an article in the *BMJ* on diseased joints which appeared on 13 August, 1864, said that excision of the wrist, hip and ankle were too dangerous and should be avoided, but expressed great enthusiasm for resection of the knee which he said represented 'perhaps the greatest triumphs of modern surgery.'[98]

There is no mention of an operation to excise a hip joint in any of West's papers, but he did perform excisions on the wrist, knee and ankle. He mentions a number of devotees of the procedure in his papers – Hey of Leeds who, he says, was the first Briton to perform an excision of the ankle in 1766, and from among his own contemporaries, Hancock, Heyfelder, Jægers, Stokes, Lister, Fergusson, Henry Smith, Humphrey and Langenbeck. West said that, while the English and Germans looked favourably on excision, many French surgeons spoke out against it. He cites Messieurs Malgaigne, Chassaignac, Geurin, Follin and Duplay as being in opposition to the idea in his paper of 1872.[99] Another Frenchman, M. Ollier (1830–1900) of Lyons, described by West as an advocate of excision in 1875 [100] was, at one time, one of its severest critics according to the author of a paper published in *The Lancet* in 1883.[101] Ollier, a man who once put mortality rates following excision for suppurative osteo-arthritis at 80%, had been converted to the idea by 1883.[102] By using strict antiseptic measures, its author says, the French surgeon had managed to bring mortality rates down to what must have seemed a trifling 14%.

---

[98] The Excision of Diseased Joints; *BMJ;* 1864; ii: p.180.

[99] JFF West, On Resection of the Knee Joint; *BMR*; 1872. p.16.

[100] JFF West, Excision of the Ankle; *The Lancet*; 1875; ii: p.868.

[101] JFF West, On Resection of the Knee; *The Lancet;* 1883; ii: p.1131.

[102] West made a point of visiting Professor Louis Xavier Edouard Leopold Ollier in the Hôpital de l'Hotel Dieu when he was passing through Lyons on 7 April, 1883. He found the hospital dirty and overcrowded but said that results after operations had improved since Listerism had been introduced. He reports that six patients in for resections of the wrist and many other joint resection cases were all doing well. JFF West Diary, 1883. (JFF West Archive).

West frequently bewails opposition to resection in his papers. He says in one, that as late as 1866, one eminent surgeon from St Bartholomew's referred to the operation as 'barbarous'[103] and in another, that in France 'The prejudice – for I can call it nothing else – against all excisions is great, but against the knee in particular, it is tremendous.'[104] Even in 1875, when the use of antiseptic measures in operations to excise joints had become more widespread and outcomes improved, West says in his paper on excision of the ankle 'Prejudice against the operation has been entertained and freely expressed by some.'[105]

Even though the earliest resections date back to the days before anæsthesia and the antiseptic treatment of wounds, few then attempted them on account of the unacceptably high risks involved. The advent of anæsthesia in the mid-eighteen forties allowed surgeons to cut, probe and cauterise flesh as never before, and also to file, gouge and saw bone without fear of causing pain. Antiseptic methods, on the other hand, lagged well behind and the high incidence of hospital infection in some hospitals was enough to convince some surgeons that excision could not be justified on these grounds alone. We have seen already that there were times during the second half of the nineteenth century when Queen's Hospital succumbed to bouts of infection and wards had to be disinfected and fumigated, but at the time of West's first excisions the hospital was almost totally free of these problems. West's first paper on excision appeared just one year after Joseph Lister published his first report on the success he had achieved in adopting strict antiseptic measures to prevent wound infection. We do not know if West used Lister's methods in his earliest excisions but we do know that Queen's Hospital was receptive to them at the time and was even conducting trials into the use of Lister's antiseptic measures.

The paper in question was read out at a meeting of the Royal Medical and Chirurgical Society in 1868,[106] the same year that he gave an account of the sanitary state of Queen's Hospital in an inaugural address to the students of Queen's College. James West expressed his pride in the hospital when he said, 'Here you will find disease treated under the most advantageous circumstances. The wards are well ventilated, large and airy, each having a bath-room in connexion with it, where hot, cold, or shower-baths can be given at a few minutes notice.... The healthiness of the

---

[103] JFF West, On Resection of the Knee Joint; *BMR*; 1872; p.16.
[104] JFF West, On Some Points of Contrast between French and English Surgery; *BMR*; 1873: p.40.
[105] JFF West, Excision of the Ankle; *The Lancet*; 1875; ii: p.868.
[106] JFF West, On Excision of the Wrist-Joint; *The Medical Times and Gazette*; 1868; i: p.353.

 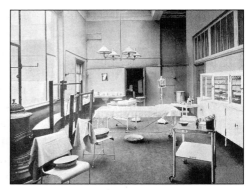

Left: Men's ward, Queen's Hospital in 1899. Right: The Operating Theatre at Queen's Hospital in 1899. Source: By kind permission of the University of Birmingham Library.

Hospital is shown by the fact that erysipelas is hardly ever seen attacking any accident or operation case, and pyæmia almost unknown.' More significantly, he told those assembled that a trial was, at that time, being conducted in the hospital in order to establish whether benefits were to be gained from the adoption of Lister's antiseptic methods. West said that Lister's treatment was being used in cases of compound fracture, amputations and abscesses and that although staff found carbolic acid used in accordance with Lister's recommendations beneficial as an astringent and disinfectant, they believed they had not enjoyed all the advantages attributed to 'its talented originator.'

Some of West's papers on resection were accompanied by drawings or, as in one of his papers on excision of the wrist, with examples of the patient's handwriting following the operation. The descriptions he gives of individual cases, catalogue the difficulty and tedium experienced by most patients and include tales of protracted recovery times. He does not shy away from admitting to his failures. Doubtless there were surgeons who, on seeing West's excised joints, would have defended their own preference to amputate in the first place. Why then did West opt for excision? The papers show that West wanted, above all, to preserve the limb of the afflicted. He believed a repaired joint, even if it was imperfect,[107] was preferable to an

---

[107] The author has been informed by Christopher Gardner-Thorpe MD FRCP FACP, that operations of this sort would have rendered the joint immobile. West, and others who carried out this type of procedure, would have used a technique called ankylosis which fused the joint. After removing diseased bone, he would hold the joint in compression until healing took place.

artificial limb and, as he said on more than one occasion, the limb could always be amputated as a 'dernier resort' should excision fail.

One of West's papers [108] details three separate cases and includes pictures of the three satisfied recipients. Tables showing pulse, respiration and temperature after the operation are given for two out of the three cases and the paper concludes with six and a half sides of reflections and comments. West did not rush into excising joints, but preferred instead to try remedies such as bed rest, splints, the application of warm lead and opium lotion, ice, medication, local abstraction of blood or counter irritation with iodine, blisters or Schott's dressing. In more advanced cases he sometimes used the actual cautery or tried straightening the limb under anæsthetic before resorting to the knife.

Resections performed on adult patients invariably resulted in a shortened limb but there were surgeons who were warning colleagues as early as the 1850s that in children the excised joint could fail to grow properly after resection. One surgeon who voiced concerns of this sort was West's colleague, Oliver Pemberton, of The General Hospital. He wrote a paper in 1859 [109] alerting colleagues to an alarming case of his own in which a child's leg had failed to grow after resection. Pemberton performed the operation in 1854 but by 1859 the child's leg was nine inches shorter than its counterpart. While West heeded these warnings and avoided performing resections on children whenever possible, he did undertake the operation on young subjects if he believed that the alternative was worse.

Ada Brooks, a thirteen year old girl, had been suffering the effects of a diseased knee for five years. West made strenuous efforts to cure her without resorting to surgery, but her condition only worsened. He realised eventually that the only way of saving her limb was to excise the knee. We do not know whether the limb failed to grow after the operation, but West says that at the end of four months Ada Brooks could walk about using a boot with a 1½ inch heel and that she had since walked several miles. The third case written up by West was that of William Hodgkins, a forty year old wagoner. Hodgkins was lucky. His injury was recent and the disease not yet extensive. He gave West the satisfaction of recovering from the operation in under three months and was able to walk four miles after twelve weeks. West's second case was Maria Wells, an emaciated and poverty-stricken woman of twenty-five who had four children and had suffered several

---

[108] JFF West, On Resection of the Knee-Joint; *BMR*; 1872; pp.16–31.

[109] Oliver Pemberton, paper cited in an article entitled 'Progress of Surgery during the Present Century' by WM Fergusson and reported by T Holmes. *BMJ*; 1864; ii: p.158.

*Oliver Pemberton (1825–97) FRCS England & Edin. Source: By kind permission
Special Collections, University of Birmingham.*

miscarriages. She had endured six years of pain by the time she came
under West's care.

West tried to cure the diseased knee without resorting to the knife but
to no avail. Even then he must have been unsure about the best way
forward, for it was only after consulting his colleagues that West went ahead
with a resection on 17 December. He says 'a large quantity of pus escaped'
on opening up the joint and he described its condition as follows: 'The
crucial ligaments were found to be destroyed, the articular surfaces of the
bones almost denuded of cartilage, and the bones themselves surrounded
by a soft gelatiniform material and all more or less carious.'[110] West found
both femur and tibia extensively diseased and cut away a sizeable section
from both using a Butcher's saw. He also found it necessary to remove the
patella in its entirety.

Maria Wells' convalescence was protracted. She suffered great
suppuration of the wound and it was five months before she could even
leave her bed. Things were little better for the luckless woman once she got
home. When she left hospital on 11 June, West ordered her husband to get
her a boot with a one inch heel. Mr Wells never did so. Special footwear
may have been beyond his means, but West's frustration is apparent when
he says 'as he either could or would not do so, the hospital authorities, in
November found her one.'[111]

---

110 JFF West, On Resection of the Knee-Joint; *BMR*; 1872; p.21.
111 JFF West, On Resection of the Knee-Joint; *BMR*; 1872; p.22.

James West always tried to feed up his patients so that they had the best possible chance of recovery, but he said in this paper that while tubercle, Bright's disease, constitutional syphilis and purpura were 'utterly antagonistic' to success, emaciation and debility were not. West also held strong views on after care. He says that immobilisation of the limb in a properly designed splint is crucial to success. West used carbolic paste in dressing joints after resection and covered the wound in an elastic bandage. He said these dressings should not be changed more often than once a week and that the entire apparatus should remain undisturbed for between five and six weeks. Also recommended are a good diet, tonics and removal, if possible, to the country or seaside.

By 1883, one surgeon, HC March, was describing a sophisticated technique he had devised for the removal of the diseased parts of a joint. He advocated opening up the joint to a greater extent than was usual by subjecting the limb to an artificial Pott's fracture. He pointed out that, by doing this, he had easy access to the diseased joint and could avoid causing damage to tendons, ligaments, arteries or nerves. James West may have been attracted to this idea for all we know, but his last paper on diseased joints suggests his attachment to resection had waned. This paper,[112] written shortly before he died, deals for the most part, not with excision, but with other types of remedial action, namely; rest, the application of ice bags, extension and, if pus is present, the aspirator followed by compression using an elastic bandage. He says he had used the actual cautery or thermo-cautery 'with advantage' but added that the prolonged application of iodine, blisters and Schott's dressing 'not infrequently disappoint the surgeon greatly.'[113] Iodine, in particular, he feels should be rejected on account of the fact that it causes a great deal of pain.

West read this paper at a meeting of the Midland Medical Society on 21 February, 1883. We know from the diary that, in his own opinion, it went down 'fairly well.'[114] He says there were few in attendance that evening, but that Edward Malins, Charles Warden, and Messrs Chavasse [115] and Bennett May all contributed to the discussion that followed. James West also

---

[112] JFF West, Chronic Joint Inflammations and their Treatment; *BMR*; 1883; pp.145–153.

[113] Ibid., p.151.

[114] JFF West, Diary; 21 February, 1883. (JFF West Archive).

[115] This was probably Thomas Chavasse FRCS (1800–84) of Wylde Green, near Birmingham. The Chavasse family had numerous medical practitioners among its members and two were members of The Midland Medical Society in 1883. The fact that West's reference is to a Mr rather than a Dr means that it was unlikely to have been Thomas Frederick, later Sir Thomas Frederick Chavasse MD.

brought two live specimens along to the meeting that day. One was a boy aged eleven who had been treated for a pyæmic abscess and the other a boy of seven who had suffered suppuration of a knee wound.

In the first case, West says he evacuated half a pint of pus by free incision and removed the head of the femur, which he said was denuded of periosteum. The seven year old boy was more fortunate. His injury responded to free incision, drainage and antiseptic dressings. The fact that West brought one subject of an excision along to the meeting shows that he continued to excise joints on occasion, but he does emphasise how important it is to try and avoid excision by dealing with injured joints immediately. He says 'It… *should never* be the fault of the surgeon, if the acute stage degenerate into the chronic, for no class of surgical cases is more amenable to treatment, or gives more satisfactory results than do cases of acute inflammation of joints, if they are seen early, and from the beginning treated by competent surgeons.'[116] The concluding paragraph of West's paper on inflamed joints which begins with the words 'Free incision, combined with drainage and antiseptic treatment, have revolutionised the treatment of joint diseases' confirms the extent to which he had revised his convictions.

West was probably one of many to modify his attitude towards resection over time, but diehards remained on both sides. Those unconvinced about the merits of resection frequently criticised devotees of the procedure. Devotees stood accused of a reluctance to publicise their failures. When Mr Samuel Solly read a paper by West on excision of the wrist joint at a meeting of the Royal Medical and Chirurgical Society in March, 1868,[117] Sir William Fergusson, one of the fathers of excision was present. The 'maestro' expressed his pleasure in the fact that the operation was gaining converts, but this did not stop Mr Birkett, another of those present, from saying he wanted to hear more about unsuccessful cases. Fergusson was doubtless used to this. Four years earlier, T Holmes [118] had written a scathing attack on his lectures on excision of the knee. He upbraided Fergusson primarily for overlooking the drawbacks too readily and for his failure to keep proper records.

Fergusson's disciples could be equally passionate. The surgeon, PC Price, writing in 1857, was so convinced of the efficacy of resection that he had this to say to the dissenters: (This patient) 'offers another valuable illustration of the advantages of the operation, and a testimony of the utter worthlessness

116 JFF West, Chronic Joint Inflammations, and their Treatment; *BMR*; 1882; pp.145–146.
117 JFF West, Excision of the Wrist Joint; *Medical Times and Gazette*; 1868; i: p.353.
118 T Holmes, Progress of Surgery during the Present Century; *BMJ*; 1864; ii: pp.156–160.

of the opinions of those who, from prejudice and ignorance, are willing to condemn a proceeding, the merits of which they are loath to believe and not sufficiently candid to admit.'[119] Price's expression of confidence in the procedure, it will be remembered, coincided in time with those of West's comrade, Mr Oliver Pemberton and others, who were alerting colleagues to the dangers of performing resections on growing limbs.

How many individuals lurched around on flailing legs or sported boots with tremendous heels to compensate for drastically shortened limbs it is impossible to say. Nor can we know how many were subjected to secondary amputation as a result of failed resections,. No doubt opinions differed as to what exactly constituted a successful outcome. The avoidance of secondary amputation or even survival itself would have been enough to constitute success for some.

If comments about one of his patients is anything to go by, the enthusiasm the surgeon Thomas Jones voiced in favour of resection may have been considered by some to be misplaced. In a paper published in 1883, Jones urges others to undertake the operation by citing the cases of two individuals under his own care. One did well, but the other could hardly have been cause for congratulation. When Jones wrote 'The convalescence of this patient has been exceedingly tedious, and even now his condition is a source of a good deal of anxiety' he was not describing what most people would think of as a successful outcome, but there is worse. 'It is not improbable' he writes 'that at last the limb will have to be sacrificed.'[120]

The Birmingham surgeon Ross Jordan (1832–1908), suffered a diseased knee joint himself. Jordan was West's contemporary and an ex-Queen's College student. He was the son of a Birmingham doctor and the brother of West's colleague, the surgeon Thomas Furneaux Jordan. The trouble started in 1877 when he was in his mid-forties. According to the account of his life in *Faces and Places*,[121] Jordan soldiered on in some considerable pain for three years and was compelled to relinquish his practice on account of its severity. As a doctor himself, Jordan would surely have been in the best possible position to choose between resection and amputation, but even with his own expertise to guide him and that of close relatives and colleagues, it was not an easy choice. Relief only came in 1880 when, acting on the advice of the distinguished surgeon, Sir James Paget and his brother, Jordan finally elected, not for resection but, for amputation.

---

[119] PC Price, Successful Case of Resection of the Knee Joint; *The Lancet*; 1857; i: p.84.
[120] T Jones, Cases of Resection of the Ankle-Joint for Injury and Disease; *BMJ*; 1883; ii: p.909.
[121] *Faces and Places*; 1893; pp.183–185. (BCL).

CANCER

Like many of his fellow surgeons, West made strenuous efforts to understand cancer and extirpate it from those who suffered its effects. Surgery was the preferred method of treatment although some surgeons used caustics. Given the difficulty in diagnosing some cancers at the time, it is likely that some patients were subjected to unnecessary surgery while others who should have had operations were not offered them. Biopsies were never mentioned in contemporary papers on cancer and most patients were treated only when the disease had reached an advanced stage. A few practitioners embraced a purely palliative approach to the treatment of cancer, seeking only to alleviate the symptoms of a doomed individual.

There were also quacks and charlatans who claimed they could cure cancer using a whole range of dubious remedies – therapies which were either bogus, unproven, unscientific, or even dangerous. One who enraged members of the medical profession in 1860 was The Reverend Hugh Reed. Reed was no medical man, but he did not let his lack of medical knowledge or qualifications stand in his way when curing diseases was at stake. So great was the indignation felt by professional medical men towards Reed, that the editor of *The Lancet* printed a denunciation of him in January, 1860 which occupied one and a half sides. Entitled, *Is Cancer Curable*, the article was designed to expose Reed's claims to be able to cure cancer in the first place. But cancer was only one of a number of diseases that Reed maintained he could cure, and *The Lancet*'s editor took delight in enunciating some of the others. 'He cures cholera, prevents small-pox without vaccination, cures phthisis,[122] ovarian dropsy, and "many other incurable diseases," not forgetting cancer.'[123]

For some practitioners, the outrage felt towards Reed and other quacks, was personal. John Goodchild MRCS wrote to *The Lancet* in March, 1860 [124] to acquaint readers with the plight of his patient – a man who was dying of cancer. Goodchild said his patient consulted him on account of a small epithelial cancer on the lower lip some two years earlier. He advised surgical removal of the growth but the man, frightened, no doubt, by pain and disfigurement, had refused. According to the account given, the sick man, then 'devoted his disease and his scanty purse to the attentions of various quack practitioners, male and female, the last being the now

[122] A term for Tuberculosis, now obsolete.
[123] *The Lancet*; 1860; i: p.41–42.
[124] John Goodchild, letter to *The Lancet*; 1860; i: p.286.

notorious Reed, who six or seven weeks ago undertook the case for £50, of which he has actually received £13.'[125]

Not all of those who sought to cure cancer without resorting to the knife were unqualified quacks. In another paper dating from 1860,[126] the surgeon, Thomas Hunt, cites two cases from among the many women for whom, he says, he has had good results in the non-surgical treatment of breast cancer. He fondly imagined that cradling a cancerous breast in a sling or resting it on thick cushion of wadding was, together with a good diet and the administration of iron and arsenic, sufficient. He does not say whether he ever performed an excision of the breast, and we do not know what his contemporaries thought about his ideas. Today, the paper comes across as somewhat cranky, and it is hard to take him seriously when he happily admits that he cannot even remember the name of a 'pathologist of repute' whose opinion on the inadvisability of applying warm coverings to a cancerous breast, he tells us, he does not share.

In the first half of the Victorian period death from post-operative infection or even chloroform was, in any case, enough to discourage some practitioners from backing surgery as the preferred treatment in cases of cancer. James Arnott cites both of these risks as a deterrent in 1860. He says that Mr Paget and others have shown that 10% of patients with cancer die as a result of the operations they have to cure the disease. Arnott says that some practitioners advocate subjecting cancerous sites to intense cold. He does not have great confidence in the idea himself, although he does think intense cold can ease what he describes as 'the dreadful and prostrating suffering'[127] caused by caustics.

Discussions on cancer were common at medical society meetings at both local and national level. West and his colleagues frequently turned up at meetings with cancerous specimens or live patients on whom they had operated for the disease. The growing use of the microscope in the second half of the nineteenth century made the identification of cancer cells less of an art and more of a science, but as we saw earlier, when medical practitioners met to discuss their findings and observations, they did not always agree.

Surgeons were generally agreed on one thing; namely, that excising a cancerous tumour was no guarantee that a patient would remain free of the disease. Many expressed the view that recurrence on the same site – that is

[125] Ibid., p.286.
[126] Thomas Hunt, *BMJ*; 1860; i: pp.47–48.
[127] James Arnott, On the Curability of Cancer; *The Lancet*; 1860; i: p.59.

on, or close to, the scar – was common. Comments on the invasion of the surrounding lymph vessels were frequently seen in papers on cancer and reports on secondary growths can be found dating back to the early 1860s.[128] A champion of the lessons that can be learnt from post-mortems, James West was among those who could produce concrete evidence of the dissemination of cancer and secondary growths in more distant parts. A clinical lecture on cancer of the tongue given by West to the students of Queen's College was reported in the *BMR* by West's former dresser, Mr W Wright Wilson in 1875. West speaks of the invasive nature of this type of cancer. He says, untreated, it progresses rapidly through fascia, muscle and even bone and that the invasion of the lymphatic glands is characteristic. But another feature mentioned by West is, in his own words 'its liability to appear in another place after the removal of the disease from its original site.'

A year later West wrote a paper [129] which includes a description of secondary cancers found post-mortem. From West's account, it is clear that his patient must have been doomed from the start. Admitted to Queen's Hospital on 18 November, 1875, with a diseased head, she was Emma F, a forty year old mother of nine who worked in a brickyard carrying bricks on her head. She was also regularly knocked about by a drunken husband. Emma F told West that she had been ill for four months and had, at the beginning, lost flesh and suffered weakness. She said she had been treated for three painful lumps on her head before she consulted West. One, opened by her medical attendant, had produced a large quantity of matter and had continued to discharge. She said fragments of dead bone had come away and West removed another piece of necrosed bone on 22 November. The bone taken away by West involved the entire thickness of the skull and was almost an inch square. Protruding through the cavity was what West describes as a globular, pulsating tumour the size of a walnut. By the time Emma F was in West's care she had regained the weight that she lost in what she considered to be the initial stages of her illness and, but for the occasional headache (moderate, but worse in the mornings) and failing eyesight, she described herself as quite well.

James West seems to have been puzzled by his patient's condition and put her under ether on the 29 November in the hope of gaining a better understanding. He made three exploratory radiating incisions through the

---

[128] Cunder Juler "Primary" and "Secondary" Cancer; *The Lancet*; 1863; ii: pp.713–714. Juler says that he believes cancer is always local in origin but that cancer cells can enter the lymphatic system and the blood and thus spread to other sites.

[129] J West, Case of Fungus of the Dura Mater; *The Lancet*; 1876; i: pp.457–458.

scalp in order to expose the bone adjacent to the tumour. West found the extent of necrosed bone greater than he had at first realised, and he also found one area which had given way altogether leaving another hole in the skull of about an inch square. A fungating tumour which he thought sprung from the dura mater protruded through the cavity. The dead bone was removed from Emma F's skull, and as soon as West deemed it safe to do so, he ordered moderate pressure to the tumour by means of a well padded mould of gutta percha. Emma F's wound healed well and the tumour succumbed to the pressure and protruded no more, but all was not well. No sooner did the wound appear to heal and the tumour disappear, than Emma F began to suffer occasional numbness in the extremities and loss of speech. This was quickly followed by a fit and loss of consciousness. More fits, first right-sided and then more general, followed and she died comatose on 2 January, 1876.

The post-mortem examination of Emma F's brain revealed to West a 'great congestion of the meninges and of the brain-substance. Three or four flat hard nodules in the dura mater covering the right hemisphere, about half an inch thick, flattening the convolutions beneath, and causing absorption of the bones of the skull on which they pressed….. On the internal surface of the right parietal bone, around the opening, the brain and thickened dura mater were incorporated together, and were adherent to the margin of the bone.'[130] West found the lungs, heart, uterus and kidneys free of disease but not so, the liver. There, he tells his readers 'Deep and disseminated in the substance of the liver, five or six round masses, as large as a walnut, were found, which, with those in the dura mater, presented all the microscopic characters of scirrhus.'[131]

West said in the paper that he was aware that pathologists and surgeons alike were not all agreed on how to categorise fungal tumours of the dura mater or about the seat from which the disease springs. He went on to cite what others had written on the subject. Some, he said, believed they were fibro-plastic rather than cancerous and also that while Louis [132] and Chelius [133] thought the disease sprang from the dura mater itself, Siebold [134]

---

[130] Ibid., p.458.

[131] Ibid., p.458.

[132] Possibly the physician Pierre Charles Alexander Louis (1787–1872) of Paris. Louis was a pioneer of clinical epidemiology.

[133] The German surgeon, Maximilian Chelius (1794–1876).

[134] The identity of Siebold cannot be verified. One possibility is Carl Theodor Ernst von Siebold (1804–85), a physiologist and zoologist although there were several other members of that eminent family who were medical men.

considered the seat to be the diploe. West also cited the conclusions drawn by two of his own Birmingham colleagues, Oliver Pemberton and Robert Lawson Tait. Pemberton, he pointed out, wrote a paper expressing his belief that in a case of his, the disease had originated in the compact tissue of the cranial bones. Lawson Tait, West said, gave a résumé of cases recorded by others and concluded that tumours of this sort originate in the osteal cells. Tait claimed, that the diseased cells should be classified as cancerous and, in that, West agreed.[135]

West said his case was unique in that it proved that malignant disease could be coexistent in another organ, but this claim is puzzling. It is not clear from the way West phrased this comment whether or not he believed the tumours found in the liver were what we would call secondaries. The word 'coexistent' could equally mean two unrelated seats of cancer existing at the same time in different parts of the body. Yet we know from the clinical lecture he gave a year earlier that he was aware, even if he had never found any himself, that the existence of secondaries had been reported already. In any case, the medical journals contained articles on the dissemination of cancer throughout West's career. One, written by Mr Weeden Cooke of the Cancer Hospital in the year of the election dispute, 1857, for instance,[136] speaks of a victim of breast cancer whose body at post-mortem revealed that the cancer was widely disseminated. It had not only spread into the ribs, lung and pleura costalis on the side afflicted but also the pericardium, liver and the pyloric orifice of the stomach.

Oral cancer – 'a capital new lip'
We tend to think nowadays that a growing awareness of the link between smoking and cancer began in the 1960s, and we have seen already that many Victorian doctors thought smoking quite harmless or even beneficial. The truth is that a number of medical practitioners suspected a connection between cancers of the mouth and smoking more than a hundred years before that. Some expressed their suspicions in papers and the cases they made were convincing enough to satisfy the editors of the medical journals to merit inclusion in their pages.

---

[135] Consultant neurologist, Dr Christopher Gardner-Thorpe FRCP FACP, has informed the author that neither fungus of the dura mater nor malignant tumours arising from the dura are recognised today. Gardner-Thorpe believes that Emma F may have had osteomyelitis of the skull arising from injuries to her head and a meningioma, which he says can become malignant.

[136] Weeden Cooke, Cancer of the Breast, extending to the Ribs and Neighbouring Tissues; Cancerous Deposits in the Lungs, Pleura, Pericardium, Liver and Stomach, with Thoracic Effusion and Cardiac Displacement; Renal Calculi; *The Lancet*; ii: p.83.

Under its heading 'The Foreign Department' *The Lancet* contained a short article entitled 'Smoking, the Exciting Cause of Cancer' in September, 1859.[137] M. Bouisson had, the report states published a paper in the *Montpellier Médical* in which he sought to prove that smoking could cause cancer of the tongue, lips, sides of the cheeks and the soft palate. 'M. Bouisson has' the reporter writes 'collected sixty-eight cases of cancer and cancroid of the lips, in which the habit of smoking was either carried to excess or was very inveterate. He considered that such morbid products had more frequently been seen since the custom of smoking had become general...He further stated, that labial cancer mostly attacked the lower lip, where the cigar or pipe rests; and that such cancer is rare with women and children.' Bouisson claimed that the more inveterate the habit, the greater the chance of contracting cancer. He also suggested that this was particularly true of those who smoked short pipes and used strong tobacco. While there is no evidence to suggest that the link between smoking and oral cancer was universally acknowledged from that time onwards, some surgeons did refer incidentally to a connection. In one paper, for instance, Augustin Pritchard of Bristol, says under the sub-heading 'Cancer of the Lip' 'GJ, aged 26, a weak subject, much accustomed to smoke, had a large ulcerating projection on the lower lip.'[138]

James West performed numerous operations on patients for cancer of the lip. In order to reduce the disfiguring consequences of the disease, he did what he could to re-build the lip that had been removed. In a meeting of the Birmingham and Midland Counties Branch of the BMA in December, 1868, he related a case of plastic operation for the restoration of the lower lip in a man of forty. West says he formed the lip after Syme's (1799–1870) method although he does not go into detail about the technique. The result, according to his own judgement 'having a tolerably natural appearance.'[139]

A few years later, West had the opportunity to learn about reconstruction of the lip first hand from German experts in plastic surgery. West spent what he described as a holiday of two months in Germany in 1874. Holiday or not, he could not resist the lure of their medical schools and hospitals. In a paper based on this trip, West made observations on eight of the institutions he visited as well as some thirteen practitioners associated with them. In relation to plastic surgery in particular, West said that Professor Simon of Heidleberg

[137] Smoking, the Exciting Cause of Cancer; Foreign Department report on M. Bouisson's paper: *The Lancet*; 1859; ii: p.240.

[138] Augustin Pritchard, Ten Years of Operative Surgery in the Provinces; *BMJ*; 1860; p.795.

[139] JFF West, Association Intelligence; *BMJ*; 1868, p.600.

(1824–76) was held in such high esteem that cases were sent to him from all over the continent. West described a number of plastic procedures he learnt about at the Heidleberg hospital under Simon, although not all were undertaken to disguise disfigurement caused by cancer. One which was, though, was the reconstruction of a lip which had been excised on account of cancer. West was much impressed. He says nothing of Simon's technique but states 'A capital new lip had also been formed, after removal of the old one for epithelioma, in a man æt. fifty-nine.'[140]

West gave a clinical lecture on epithelioma of the tongue to the students of Queen's College in 1875. Its survival in print [141] suggests West was sufficiently well pleased with it to submit it to the *BMR* for publication. Of the numerous clinical lectures he delivered during his career at Queen's Hospital, few now remain. Given the nature of the lecture, it contains graphic detail about the sort of operative treatment undertaken by West in cases of this sort. In the first place, West made sure his students were acquainted with the way in which cancerous tumours are categorised. He reminded them that there were three principle types – scirrhus, encephaloid and epithelioma – and described how they differed from one another. West defined the three types of cancerous tumours as follows in this lecture:

'In scirrhus the cells are found embedded in a fibrous stroma and very irregular; the cells are of all shapes and sizes. In encephaloid there is an absence of the fibrous stroma, or only a very fine delicate fibrous tissue is observed, but the cells are abundant. In epithelioma the fibrous stroma is present in a marked degree, surrounding a quantity of densely-packed cells resembling the cells of true epithelium, but arranged differently to the other forms of cancer. They occur in "concentric globes," or as they are more familiarly called, "Birds' nests." '[142]

West also reminded the students that while scirrhus and encephaloid cancers may, and do, invade any organ of the body, epithelioma had a predilection for the mucous and muco-cutaneous orifices such as the mouth and anus. He said that all tend to ulcerate and fungate if untreated, and that, although in epithelioma weight loss or cachexia is less marked than in the others, both pain and cachexia are usual.

Before going on to describe treatment, West gave an indication of how to identify epithelioma of the tongue and a warning about the importance

---

140 JFF West, Impressions of German Surgery; *BMR*; 1875; p.47.
141 JFF West, A Clinical Lecture on Epithelioma of the Tongue and its Operative Treatment; *BMR*; 1875; pp.191–197.
142 JFF West, A Clinical Lecture on Epithelioma of the Tongue and its Operative Treatment; *BMR*; 1875; p.191.

of thorough extirpation. He not only said 'The recurrence of a cancerous growth is a most formidable matter' but more specifically, that 'in the removal of the diseased portions of the tongue, it is imperatively necessary that none of the disease shall be left behind, therefore it is customary to take away a good margin of healthy along with the infiltrated tissue.'[143] West said that, untreated, patients with epithelioma of the tongue generally die in about two years. The students were told that, on the tongue, this type of cancer has the appearance of an ulcer with ragged, raised, everted edges and is surrounded by a ring of induration.

West explained to the students why he favoured total ablation of the diseased parts and the surrounding tissue using the knife or scissors, the galvano-cautery or the ecraseur. In his view, caustics made up of Vienna paste, chloride of zinc or nitrate of silver were the only alternative but could not be recommended. Not only did a much increased flow of saliva in the mouth dilute them and render them useless, but patients were at risk of being poisoned if they swallowed the chemicals used.

'It is the duty of a clinical teacher of surgery' stated West 'to bring forward all the ways and means employed in his art, to place them before his class, to explain the various uses and employments of those ways and means, without prejudice or bias. He should then detail his own experience, explaining his own favourite methods of operation and instruments, but not to the complete omission of any important or valuable agent, or to the casting aside of any method which he may not have himself considered or employed.' It is in this spirit that West described and rejected the methods of Professors Syme and Wood. He disliked Syme's method because it involved dividing the jaw using a saw, and that of Wood because of the way in which he sealed the arteries to prevent haemorrhage – a technique which involved picking up the vessels between the blades of a pair of forceps. West said that this was impossible because they simply break away. He also said that when Wood gave a clinical lecture on extirpation of the tongue to the students of King's College Hospital, he failed to mention the two most valuable methods for sealing the arteries; namely, the galvano cautery and the ecraseur.

The techniques used by four other surgeons were alluded to by West in his lecture. His colleague, Furneaux Jordan of Queen's, was one, but he also mentioned Dr Macleod of Glasgow, Mr Nunneley of Leeds and the Italian, Regnoli of Pavia. All used methods involving cutting cheek or throat to widen access, but West believed this was unnecessary and advocated instead using gags designed by either T Smith or Professor Wood to keep the mouth open

---

[143] Ibid., p.192.

wide. West described the galvano-cautery as 'an instrument having a platinum wire, which, by means of the galvanic current set up by the action of six or eight cells, is made white hot almost immediately after the poles of the battery are connected.'[144] He said it was used to remove large hæmorrhoids and diseased cervix uteri as well as the tongue.

The case described in West's lecture is that of William Davies, a man of seventy-two. West used two ecraseurs in parallel to remove Davies' tongue and attained a pleasing result. Davies made a quick recovery and was discharged after a stay of only fourteen days. West said that he could eat, drink and articulate 'fairly.' The lecture was concluded when the satisfied Davies was brought in for all to see. West's dresser then added his own observations in parenthesis. 'He (Davies) was requested to drink water, which was given him in a tumbler. Turning to the glass, he said, "Good health, gentlemen," very distinctly, and drank off the whole of the contents of the glass, only a few drops falling to the floor during deglutition. When spoken to he answered readily and without much difficulty.'[145]

Earlier on, West described the procedure he used to remove Davies' tongue in some detail. He told his students that he had used the ecraseur of Chassaignac. West's own description of the instrument is clear and concise. 'It is made of iron wire or steel chain, worked by means of a rack movement at the end of the handle. The loop of wire or chain is passed round or through the base of the portion to be removed, and the rack is worked at intervals of half a minute. The rack draws down the chain through the handle, and the loop being rendered smaller at each movement, crushes through the tissues and thus obliterates the vessels and prevents haemorrhage.'[146] How many assisted West in the operation is not known, but he cannot have done it single-handedly. He said the ecraseurs were held at right angles to each other and that the movements of the two racks were started simultaneously and continued every thirty seconds. One ecraseur was assigned to the separation of the base of the tongue from the floor of the mouth and that one did its work in seven minutes. The second – engaged in severing the dorsum of the tongue from its anchor – took marginally longer at nine minutes. No haemorrhaging occurred, recovery was swift and the aftercare minimal. While he remained in hospital, Davies' mouth was simply kept clean and free from odour by washing it out frequently with a mixture Condy's fluid and water.

---

[144] JFF West, A Clinical Lecture on Epithelioma of the Tongue and its Operative Treatment; *BMR*; 1875; p.194.

[145] Ibid., Words of Wright Wilson. p.196.

[146] Ibid., p.194.

Identifying and defining cancer

A lecture entitled 'On Innocent and Malignant Tumours' delivered by T
Spencer Wells (1818–97), surgeon to Her Majesty's Household in 1864,
highlighted the difficulties encountered by medical practitioners in making
accurate diagnoses. Wells said that claims made by practitioners about cases
of cancer that had been cured were sometimes based on diagnostic error.
Tumours extirpated as cancerous may have been entirely innocent all
along. Spencer Wells tried to simplify the distinctions between innocent
and malignant tumours by drawing up two tables – one designed to aid
diagnosis before surgery containing nine points, and the other to identify
cancer in specimens examined post-operatively with four points. The table
appears at the beginning of the paper, but he runs into trouble almost
straight away, having to use terms like 'generally,' 'seldom,' 'usually' and
'rarely.'[147] An expansion of what lies in the table follows, but again it is clear
that making a reliable diagnosis is fraught with difficulty. Spencer Wells
dealt first with each of the nine points in the first table and then with the
four he made in the second.

The first remark, for instance, elaborates upon his observation that
cancerous tumours are often multiple, occurring simultaneously in different
tissues or organs. Now he says 'Several innocent growths may be multiple; for
example, warts, encysted tumours, enchondroma, fatty tumours and fibroids.
Hence this character is only distinctive of malignancy when other characters
of innocent growths are wanting.'[148] Under number two, Spencer Wells
covered the existence of pain. He expanded what he said in the table by
adding 'Malignant tumours are usually painful at some stage of their growth'
but having said that, he cautioned against over reliance on the presence of
pain as a diagnostic tool with the words 'There are but few exceptions to this
rule, although encephaloid, melanosis, and colloid, sometimes attain a large
size before there is much pain.'[149] In number three, Spencer Wells
endeavoured to explain yet more apparent contradictions. Three concerned
speed of growth. Here he pointed out that 'Although malignant tumours, as
a rule, grow faster than others, yet there are many exceptions to this rule.'[150]

Spencer Wells' attempts to expand upon the remaining points proved
equally difficult. He had undertaken a formidable task, but far from
thinking he had got to the bottom of the problems involved in diagnosing

[147] T Spencer Wells, On Innocent and Malignant Tumours; *BMJ;* 1864; ii: p.685.
[148] Ibid., p.685.
[149] Ibid., p.685.
[150] Ibid., p.685.

cancer, he was acknowledging them. What Spencer Wells wanted to achieve in this paper was, not solely the opportunity to provide others with the benefit of his experience and his advice on diagnosis, but the chance of acquainting practitioners with the complexities and contradictions involved.

Defining and identifying cancer was no easier twenty years later. An entry on cancer taken from a dictionary of medicine compiled by Richard Quain [151] dating from 1883, the year of West's death, ends with these words:

'Our knowledge of the pathology of new growths is undergoing a process of rapid evolution. While, therefore, the writer has endeavoured in this article, and in that on Tumours, to represent the opinions most widely accepted at the present day, he is conscious that in a very short time these opinions may require considerable modification.'

Quain's section on cancer includes a set of sixteen diagrams illustrating tumours of the epithelial type drawn to a scale of X 87 diameters. Definitions, histological structures, clinical characters, recurrence, mode of growth and appearance to the naked eye are all included. RJ Godler, the expert responsible for these pages gives the following subdivisions of cancers:

Glandular Type:	**Epithelial and Epidermic Type:**
Hard cancer or Scirrhus	Cylindrical Epithelioma
Soft cancer or Encephaloid	Lobular Epithelioma
	Colloid

Godler says there are others, and that of these, some had been given names – melanotic, teliangiectasic and osteocancer being three. He left colloid cancer to the end saying that it may result from the degeneration of one of the other classes of cancer he had described above. He points out that this was something which was still being debated, but he did warn readers that its malignancy was great. The paragraph on prognosis in general is sobering and begins with the words, 'The prognosis is always bad, especially in encephaloid cancer, but least so in epithelioma.'[152] His contribution to the dictionary covered diagnosis, prognosis, course and treatment in general, but he also discussed specific types of cancer in more detail. Anyone hoping to find a foolproof aid to the early diagnosis

---

[151] Richard Quain MD FRS (editor), *Quain's Dictionary of Medicine*, (London: Longmans Green and Co., 1883), pp.203–206.

[152] Richard Quain MD FRS (editor), *Quain's Dictionary of Medicine*, (London: Longmans Green and Co., 1883), pp.204.

of cancer within the pages of the dictionary would have been disappointed almost immediately. Under the heading Diagnosis, Godler states 'That of an advanced case of cancer is generally easy; in the early stages it is mostly impossible.'[153]

In the section on specific types, Godler expanded what he said earlier and added comments on both the treatment and microscopical appearance of the disease. The constraints under which Godler laboured in covering cancer in the space allocated to the subject in a medical dictionary, meant he was compelled to gloss over certain aspects. He realised, for instance, that he could not do justice to the topic of treatment and said simply that, since early treatment could only be undertaken by the surgeon, the reader should refer to the relevant surgical textbooks. Godler did not express much support for the efforts of physicians and others in their attempts to alleviate the suffering of cancer patients in the later stages of the disease. Their endeavours were described as ineffective, if not harmful, irrespective of whether or not they were regular practitioners or quacks. The sections covering the appearance of cancer cells as seen under the microscope were more detailed and refer the reader to the appropriate illustration.

The systematic analysis of urine gained momentum in the 1850s, when West was a student at St Thomas' Hospital, London. A series of lectures given by Dr Lionel Beale [154] to the Pathological Laboratory in the session 1857/8, includes his own observations on the usefulness of this type of investigation in facilitating the detection of cancer of the bladder. In lecture X1, section 1V, he states that cancer cells had been found in the urine of patients suffering from cancer of the bladder. He also cites a case in which he was asked by the surgeon, Mr Fergusson, to analyse some gelatinous matter passed by a patient with a bladder affection. Beale explains that while before the specimen was examined under the microscope it excited some difference of opinion, a microscope with a power of two hundred diameters enabled him to identify, without difficulty 'loops of capillary vessels covered with a thick layer of cancer-cells. The specimen' he writes 'presented the usual appearances which distinguish a cancerous tumour which is rapidly growing into a hollow viscus, and was evidently one of the tongue-like or villous processes, broken off from the mass.... The diagnosis' he continues 'was confirmed by the subsequent examination of the parts.'[155]

---

[153] Ibid., p.204.
[154] Lionel Beale, A Course of Lectures on Urine, Urinary Deposits, and Calculi; delivered at the Pathological Laboratory during the session 1857–58. *BMJ*; December, 1860; pp.987–990.
[155] Ibid., p.989.

Like so many who came before and after him, Beale declares that cancer is not always easy to identify. He points out, for instance, that the epithelium of the ureter and some cells procured from certain parts of the mucus membrane of the bladder bear a striking similarity, in both form and appearance, to the cells of what he calls 'hard cancer.' Beale cautions that he has had urine specimens containing numerous well-defined but innocent spindle shaped cells resembling those of scirrhus which had derived from the ureter.

From time to time medical practitioners asked whether or not there had been an increase in the incidence of cancer. In a letter to the *BMJ* dated August, 1883,[156] Hugh Dunn called for a proper scientific inquiry into the matter. He suggested that a body such as the *Collective Investigation Committee* should conduct a study in order to establish if there had been an increase in the number of cases and also to find out whether, as some suspected, cancer was hereditary.

Dunn was not alone in expressing an interest in data on cancer, of course. Various practitioners had collected data on cancer throughout West's career. One was Septimus Sibley, whose paper '*A Contribution to the Statistics of Cancer, Collected from the Records of the Middlesex Hospital*'[157] was published by *The Lancet* in 1859 in one of its reports on *The Royal Medical and Chirurgical Society*. Some of those present at the meeting, and some who responded to the article later, thought Sibley's statistics were flawed, and debate followed their publication.

Mr Weeden Cooke [158] questioned, in particular, how Sibley could justify the figures he had published in relation to survival times. The difficulties inherent in the collection and analysis of statistical data are too numerous and complex to go into here, but the questioning approach and caution of Cooke and others reflects the growing sense of scientific discipline that was emerging at the time. To be fair, Sibley said that his life expectancy figures, which he based on how long patients lived after the disease had been discovered, caused difficulty. He realised, for instance, that some cancers were invisible to start with, and that those who submitted to an operation were, to a large extent, selected cases. He openly acknowledged that flaws and over simplification were a danger, and he was not trying to gloss over the shortcomings. He even began by saying that while the more recent

---

156 Hugh Dunn, letter to *BMJ*; 1883; ii: p.558.

157 Septimus Sibley, A Contribution to the Statistics of Cancer, Collected from the Records of the Middlesex Hospital; *The Lancet*; 1859; i: pp.291–292.

158 Weeden Cooke, letter on The Statistics of Cancer; *The Lancet*; 1859; i: pp.327–328.

cases were reported with uniformity, some of the earlier cases used were not as perfect.

Sibley reported that he had examined 519 cases of cancer altogether and looked at the records of 172 post-mortem examinations. He discovered that cancer in males accounted for just 103 of those cases. Only 305 patients were asked whether they knew of relations who had succumbed to cancer, and of those thirty-four answered in the affirmative. Sibley himself believed these figures to be unreliable, saying that patients' memories and even their awareness that a member of the family had suffered from cancer were not to be trusted. He did give a table to show the seat of the disease in each of the thirty-four cases though, and from that it emerged that seventeen concerned the breast. Sibley also established that out of the thirty-four, six had more than one relative who had suffered from cancer and that one individual had five cancerous relations. Those who contributed to the discussion on the occasion of the Royal Medical and Chirurgical Society meeting that day, talked for the most part of recurrence and life expectancy. Some told stories of long survival times, but the overall consensus was that dissemination was to be expected and that surgery could only provide a temporary solution. One, Dr Webster, told his colleagues that cancer was 'very fatal' and reported that the average number of deaths from cancer in England and Wales was approximately 6,000 per annum.

That cancer was the bane of many surgeons' lives in the second half of the nineteenth century is almost certainly true. After all, even with the superior knowledge and additional remedies available today, it is still notoriously difficult to cure the disease. Specialisation amongst surgeons was unusual during the days when West and his contemporaries practised and there were few specialist hospitals. James West and his colleagues had to tackle virtually all types of cancers and most of their patients applied for relief only when the disease was in an advanced state. For all that, patients did leave hospital cured of cancer in Victorian England, and even when that had not been possible, medical practitioners frequently had the satisfaction that comes from prolonging a person's life and alleviating suffering. Those who saw their patients gain flesh and return to their families must have enjoyed the gratification experienced when a job is well done.

CHAPTER FIVE

Marriage

James Fitzjames Fraser West was just as much a member of the community in which he lived as he was of the town's medical institutions. As we have seen, West resided at Queen's Hospital as one of its residential officers to begin with. This arrangement, by its nature was temporary. In common with many doctors before and after him, West sought accommodation in one of the streets favoured by members of the medical profession when he had to vacate his rooms in the hospital. Edgbaston prices were probably too high for West in the mid-1850s and he may not have been able to afford properties in other locations favoured by medical professionals – Temple Row or Old Square.

He moved, instead, to Newhall Street. Also favoured by medical men, Newhall Street was not as long established as Temple Row or Old Square. It was within easy reach of the town centre and its hospitals and it still had the attraction of being near to open countryside. The census of 1861 shows that West's mother, Mary, his grandmother, Mary Anna and his half-sister, Fanny de la Hunt, had all moved up to Birmingham and were living with him at number 95, Newhall Street by that date. It is possible that, like Joseph Sampson Gamgee, West sent word to his family in London and suggested that they keep house for him in Birmingham. With their help, West would have been able to economise on paid domestic help. The census of 1861, indeed, suggests that the Wests managed on minimal domestic assistance. One individual, by the name of Elizabeth Yates, is the only servant listed, and she may well have been their only employee.

Like his hospital colleagues, West had to build up a private practice during the course of his career. It will be remembered that, with the exception of residential hospital posts occupied at the beginning of their medical careers, doctors who worked for charitable hospitals held honorary positions. Income derived from the use of their professional skills came from private patients. James West would have had to work hard to build up a practice of his own in these years. The fact that he won the support of some of Birmingham's influential and affluent townsfolk during the election dispute may have been to his advantage in his efforts to build up a

Sarah Hammond West (née Sellers), 1844–1910, wife of James Fitzjames Fraser West ca.1864, the year of her marriage. Source: JFF West Archive.

private practice. Changing loyalties during that unhappy time undoubtedly brought benefits as well as injures in their wake. Patronage of the powerful or no, West enjoyed early success. By the time he married in 1864 at the age of thirty-one, he was able to move to a larger property in Acock's Green, a village four and a half miles south east of Birmingham, and, from there, to Edgbaston some ten years after that.

West was a married man for the last nineteen years of his life and had a family of eight by the time he died in 1883. Sarah Hammond Sellers, the woman who became his bride in 1864, was the daughter of a Yorkshire farmer. Sarah had moved to Darfield (population ca.750), five miles east of Barnsley with her widowed mother and spinster Aunt by the time she married, but she spent her childhood in nearby Great Houghton, a village with a population of just 300. Growing up in close proximity to the Yorkshire coalfields, she would have been no stranger to the effects of the extractive industries on the landscape, but an essentially rural region with scattered mines is very different from a large industrial town. It is not, therefore, unreasonable to suppose that it was Sarah's objections to the thought of living in Birmingham that lay behind the decision to live in a village within easy reach of Birmingham rather than in the town itself. In any case, the property, Carlton House in Sherbourne Road, Acock's Green, was in more in keeping with her husband's growing status than the terraced house he had occupied as a bachelor.

The marriage took place in Darfield Parish Church, Yorkshire, on Thursday 6 October, 1864. The couple married by licence in a service witnessed by the half-sister of James, Fanny de la Hunt, and someone called, James Scott. West announced the marriage in *The Lancet*, The *Doncaster, Nottingham and Lincoln Gazette*, the *Birmingham Daily Gazette* and in the *Birmingham Daily Post*. All but one state the bare facts only. The one which differs, is the one placed in the *Birmingham Daily Gazette* which ends with the words 'no cards.' There were no photographs to commemorate the event.

The summer of 1864 had been hot and dry, and whilst relief had come in September, October brought with it an Indian summer. Yorkshire farmers had brought their harvests in by 6 October that year, but the future looked worrying. No after-grass was sprouting in the fields following harvest, according to an article in the *Birmingham Daily Gazette*.[1] Readers were informed that, as a result of conditions in June, July and August, no amount of rain could make the sunburnt pastures recover in time. There were problems in Birmingham too. A report in *The Lancet* in 1864, states 'smallpox is unusually prevalent in Birmingham.'[2] And, at the time of West's wedding, one disgruntled visitor to the town wrote to the *Birmingham Daily Gazette* to complain about the offensive smell of human sewage which, according to custom, had been spread on the town's surrounding fields.[3] He was made aware of it, he explained, as he approached the town by train. The town's butchers, were probably disgruntled too. The meat inspectors had had to condemn 22,000 lbs, or nearly 10 tons of meat as unfit for human consumption, in the space of just one fortnight that summer. The 'putridity' apparently 'having been occasioned by the unusual high temperature of the season.'[4]

West remained as close to his own family after marriage as he had been before it. As a result, his new bride, Sarah, took on more than just a husband in 1864. Her mother in law, Mary, her husband's half-sister, Fanny, and his grandmother all had to be accommodated at Carlton House. The young wife, nineteen years of age at the time of her wedding, had much to occupy her in the early years of marriage. The couple's first son was born the year after they married and their second, two years later. In between, came the death from 'senile decay' of West's grandmother at the age of seventy-five years. Sarah Hammond probably always had more than the single servant recorded at her

[1]   Harvest in Yorkshire *Birmingham Daily Gazette*, 8 October, 1864. (BCL).
[2]   Smallpox at Birmingham, *The Lancet*; 1864; ii: p 684.
[3]   Letter by Henry Bird, *Birmingham Daily Gazette*. 8 October, 1864. (BCL).
[4]   Diseased meat; *The Lancet*; 1864; ii: p 685.

husband's former abode in 1861, but still it cannot have been an easy start. What we do know,[5] is that the family had three servants – a cook, a nurse and a housemaid – by the time she had been married seven years.

The family remained at Carlton House for ten years altogether. Two daughters, the couple's third and fourth children, were also born in Acock's Green. The house has not survived, but contemporary photographs of the part of the road where the house was located show it as a quiet and somewhat genteel place. The house was large and was set in just over one and a quarter acres of grounds.[6] Their neighbours were, for the most part, industrialists and merchants. West had been in practice for about seven years when he moved to Acock's Green and almost certainly owned his own transport, but even if this were not the case, he and his family were within five minutes walk from the railway station.

In 1883, nearly ten years after West moved to Edgbaston, the diary shows that West frequently returned to Acock's Green and its environs to treat patients. Travel in the opposite direction during the years he lived in Acock's Green must have been correspondingly high. West thought nothing of travelling considerable distances, but he was city born and bred and, as the diary reveals, very sociable. The hospital, medical societies and associations and various non-medical organisations West had connections with were all based in Birmingham. The advantages of living near to the centre of Birmingham may, in the end, have outweighed the pleasures of life in a semi-rural location like Acock's Green.

Incomes

If it were possible to compile data on the incomes of doctors and compare that with the incomes of other groups, we could measure how affluent medical practitioners were in the second half of the nineteenth century. It is not possible. Information on medical incomes for the period 1850 to 1900 is virtually non-existent. Historians have suggested a number of ways in which incomes could be calculated (patient fees, sale prices of practices,[7] public sector pay etc.), and they have drawn attention to reports and guides which were compiled for the purpose of enlightening the government or parents. All are flawed in one way or another.

---

[5] Census, 1871.

[6] *The Return of Landowners, England*, for the year 1873 shows the Acock's Green site in West's ownership and gives the acreage as 1 acre, 1 rood and 6 perches.

[7] Historians have calculated that it was usual for a practice to sell for 1–1½ times its annual income.

We have no way of knowing what West's annual income was. What James West earned from private practice is completely unknown. He invested money in stocks and shares, but there is no record of the income he derived from them either. The family's income would have been boosted after 1871 when Mrs West inherited land and property in Yorkshire. The extent of Sarah West's inheritance and, to some extent the income derived from it, were recorded but the surviving archive is patchy. James West's personal estate was complicated at the time of his death. Valued initially at £20,969/12/9d in August, 1883, it was re-sworn in February, 1888 when the figure was placed at £23,127/2/9d. What is known about Sarah West's inherited wealth and the family's lifestyle, would certainly suggest that they had a sizeable income by the standards of the time.

Medical historians can provide isolated examples of incomes which range from each of the two extremes. The colossal incomes made by men lucky enough to be in the right place at the right time are legendary, but there were also men who lived on a pittance or were forced to abandon the profession altogether. Ivan Waddington [8] cites Sir Astley Cooper (1768–1841) as an example of a high earner. His annual income was reported to have been in excess of £15,000 and it even reached a figure of £21,000 in 1815. Others came close, according to Waddington.

Examples of both types can be found in the Midlands. The nineteenth century physician, Henry Jephson (1798–1878) of Leamington Spa, for instance, was reputed to have earned more than £20,000 for several years in succession, and his income even went as high as £24,000 one year.[9] At the other end of the scale, Robert Coane Roberts Jordan (1825–90), the Birmingham physician, told the writer of his biography in *Edgbastonia*, that his earnings amounted to no more than £20 in his first year in general practice.[10] Thomas Heslop, also a physician, was another who suffered hardship at the commencement of his career. In an obituary dated 19 June, 1885, *The Birmingham Post* described Heslop's struggle to survive as a private practitioner after he resigned from Queen's Hospital following the election dispute in 1858. His failure to attract patients brought him close to leaving Birmingham to try his luck elsewhere, according to the newspaper account. Gilbert Barling

8   Ivan Waddington, *The Medical Profession in the Industrial Revolution*.
    (Dublin: Gill and Macmillian, 1984).
9   J Lane and R Bearman (eds), *Dr Jephson of Leamington Spa* (Warwick: Warwickshire Local History Society, 1980), p.32
10 *Edgbastonia*; 1885; V: p.66. (BCL).

(1855–1940),[11] later Sir Gilbert, and a man who would go on to become first, Dean of the Medical Faculty at the University of Birmingham and then its Vice Chancellor, endured a slow start too. He had to supplement his income with coaching work according to the author who wrote an account of his life in 1899.[12]

Edgbastonia's account on the life of Samuel Berry (1808–87), a man who later became a specialist in obstetric surgery at Queen's Hospital and The Women's Hospital, was written by him, and in describing his early career he wrote 'My progress was so slow that some of my friends advised me to remove to another sphere.'[13] The surgeon, William Henry Sprotson (1822–94), was another Birmingham practitioner who struggled to make a living. The son of a vicar, his apprenticeship fees were paid by the Governors of the Corporation from a charitable funding source for the sons of clergy.[14] Sprotson may have found it difficult to live within his means throughout his professional life. He was described in one obituary as very religious man who was a member of St Paul's Lodge of Freemasons.[15] West's diary reveals that he was indebted to him in 1883. Before he left for the continent, West decided to excuse Sprotson the last £5 of the loan he had made him of £100.[16]

Medical practitioners working in Birmingham probably fared better on average than their counterparts in some other parts of the country. According to Irvine Loudon, prospects were best in the towns and the cities; and the Midlands and the South were better than the North and Wales.[17] Real incomes in the middle of the nineteenth century were generally lower than those of men who had practised fifty years before that, but Loudon says that an income of at least £200 was necessary for the upkeep of a lifestyle which would have been appropriate for a middle class professional man.

---

[11] While working as a newly qualified doctor at The General Hospital, Barling seems to have assisted West in at least one of his operations. West recorded the fact that he was helped by Barling and Sims (probably Charles Sims, a practitioner West would have known on account of his involvement in the Dental Hospital) in a case of strangulated hernia in his diary on 10 February, 1883. (JFF West Archive).

[12] *Edgbastonia*; 1899; XIX: p.63. (BCL).

[13] *Edgbastonia*; 1881; i: p.59. (BCL).

[14] *Edgbastonia*; Obituary; 1894; XIV: p.82. (BCL).

[15] The obituary, in *The Lancet*, also said that the ill-fated Sprotson's life was an 'uneventful' one. *The Lancet*; 1894; i: pp.646–7.

[16] JFF West, Diary; 7 March, 1883. (JFF West Archive).

[17] I Loudon, *Medical Care and the General Practitioner 1750–1850*, (Oxford: Clarendon Press, 1986).

The 1885 edition of *Showell's Dictionary of Birmingham* contains an article entitled 'Birmingham Men of Worth' for the year 1878. An unidentified 'man of figures' was reported to have used income tax returns and other information (although we are not told what) as the basis for his calculations. According to the source, there were 800 people worth more than £5,000 each, 200 worth over £10,000, 50 worth over £20,000, 35 worth over £50,000, 26 worth over £100,000, 12 worth over £250,000, 5 worth over £500,000 and 2 worth over or near £1,000,000.

A year or two spent working as a residential medical officer in one of the town's hospitals could pave the way for a successful career. There, an unmarried junior doctor could cultivate personal contacts and gain expertise whilst in receipt of free board and lodging and a guaranteed a salary of around £60 per annum. Senior hospital doctors, on the other hand, held honorary positions and it was beholden upon them to live off incomes they could earn outside hospital. Some took on salaried posts in the public sector or worked for Sick Clubs or Friendly Societies, but for the majority, income was derived from teaching and private practice. Evidence on both incomes and wealth is patchy and circumstantial, but what there is strongly suggests that most Birmingham hospital doctors enjoyed a standard of living in keeping with that of other successful members of the professional middle classes. Providing they were not prevented from working through ill health or other misfortune, most could afford to mix on equal terms with the best society.

Although there is no way of knowing whether individuals took measures to pass on their wealth before death, wills can be a useful guide to affluence. Waddington [18] cites the estates of some 300 practitioners who died in 1858 as evidence of how well, or otherwise, doctors prospered. Three out of the sample left sums of more than £50,000, while seventeen left between £10,000 and £50,000. At the other extreme, more than one in nine died leaving less than £100.

Some, like West, refer to investments in property or stocks and shares in their wills and some state their intention of leaving specific sums of money or possessions to named individuals. The wills of both Robert Saundby and Oliver Pemberton (1825–97) show that they had properties in addition to the ones in which they resided, while those of Saundby and Dickenson Crompton show that they also had money in investments. The will of Edward Malins included specific bequests to a number of different individuals and to members of his extended family. With an estate worth

[18] Waddington, *The Medical Profession in the Industrial Revolution.*

£81,852/10/9d, he would have known he was in a position to make the generous bequests he specified in his will. Those made to family members alone consisted of £4,000 to each of his two grandchildren, £1,000 to each of his nieces, and a further £500 to each of his two nieces and his nephew. In examining wills themselves, it is important to remember that unlike Malins, some testators lacked the capital to fund the bequests of money and property alluded to in their wills. We should also bear in mind that the changing value of money over time makes the comparison of one individual with another problematic. Nevertheless, if we examine the value of doctors' estates after probate it is possible to get some idea of how successful Birmingham doctors were.

A sample of thirty Birmingham doctors who died between 1875 and 1933 shows that exactly half left estates valued at over £10,000. West was one. He was one of five who left estates of between £15,000 and £25,000. Just six exceeded this group – Sir Edward Malins who, as we have seen, left £81,852/10/9d; West's successor, George Jordan Lloyd (1854–1913) with £60,383/10/5d; Robert Jolly (1841–94) with £37,026/10/–; Sir James Sawyer with £41,310/13/10d; Thomas Savage (1839–1907) with £45,325/1/11d and Dickenson Crompton (1805–94) with £33,921/8/–. Eight out of the thirty left between £5,000 and £10,000, while seven left under £5,000. We have seen that Jordan Lloyd died a very wealthy man, but the same cannot be said for some of West's colleagues. Two who were rivals of West at the time of the election dispute serve as examples. Benjamin Hunt, for instance, left £7,662/5/4d when he died in 1883, and when Joseph Sampson Gamgee died three years later, he left an estate of only £817/14/6d. Two colleagues of West who fell outside the group of thirty, Edward Mackey and Charles R Suffield, were well below the average with estates of £155/14/9d in 1906 and £5/0/– in 1898 respectively.

Yorkshire land and property

West's fortunes were enhanced through his union with Sarah Hammond Sellers, although it is doubtful that he could have predicted the extent to which it would benefit him at the time of his marriage. Her father, John Taylor Sellers was a tenant farmer who died when his daughter was fifteen. Sarah's paternal grandfather, born in Ashton under Lyne, Lancashire, came to Yorkshire some time after his marriage in 1801. Her mother's family, on the other hand, had been resident in Yorkshire for generations and were descended from the Shaws and Hammonds. When Constance Margery Fryer (née West) died childless in 1991, her step-daughter, the author of this biography, was surprised to find a sizeable collection of documents relating to her grandmother's family amongst the deceased's effects. Although the majority span the period of one hundred and forty years starting from the early 1740s, the earliest dates back to the reign of Queen Elizabeth I.

The farm worked by Sarah's father was in Great Houghton, five miles east of Barnsley. The survival of a record documenting the personal effects of her father following his death in 1859, provides a fascinating insight into the family's standard of living and status. The farm, of 171½ acres, was what in agricultural terms was called a mixed farm. John Sellers grew cereals and animal fodder and kept some fields for grazing. He had livestock consisting of 184 sheep, 27 pigs (one, a sow in pig), 28 cattle (one, a cow in calf) and one calf plus 70 fowls and 12 geese to a total value of just over £691. The eight draught horses, one pony and four foals he kept to work his land and provide transportation for his family were valued at £213/16/-d. Apart from his beasts and the produce of the land he farmed, he also owned a significant quantity of agricultural machinery and equipment. His household furniture and effects were valued at £156/14/0d, of which £4/4/0d was for wines and spirits. This amounted to just 6% of the total.

The document, which provides a complete inventory of the furniture and household effects, gives a clear picture of the conditions in which the family lived. The house had two kitchens. One, the back kitchen, seems to have been used primarily for laundry and brewing although it did have a plank table and an old dresser. The other kitchen contained two deal tables, two windsor chairs, an oak chest and bookshelves, an arm chair and three oak chairs. It was probably where the family ate and relaxed on a day to day basis. The parlour, no doubt reserved for high days and holidays, was large enough to accommodate a mahogany dining table, six mahogany chairs, a sideboard and mahogany card table. There were four bedrooms with additional sleeping quarters for the labourers in the attics. The main bedroom was furnished with a mahogany bedstead with hangings, matching curtains, a feather bed and bedding, a mahogany wardrobe, chest of drawers, toilet glass, covered wash stand and requisites and an easy chair. The other bedrooms were a little more basic. There were numerous beds in the farmhouse, although six were described as 'camp beds.' Apart from this, there was a pantry, and there were passages and landing areas large enough to store household goods ranging from linen, clothes, silver, glass, cutlery and a dinner service to books.

The farm was passed on to John Sellers, Sarah's older half brother. The acreage of the farm had increased to 218 by 1881 according to the census of that year. John Sellers junior was recorded as having had four servants. Three were men, and they were identified as 'farm servants.' It was much the same set up as his father had had before him. The census of 1851 shows that the Sellers had four live-in servants – two female and two male. Given the nature of the agricultural calendar in the days of labour intensive farming, John Sellers and his son probably employed casual workers in addition to the regular live-in workers from time to time. The census also shows that Sarah's widowed mother had moved to live with her unmarried sister in the nearby village of Darfield by 1861. Directories of this part of Yorkshire show that it was not unusual for farmers' widows to continue running farms after their husbands had died. Sarah Sellers certainly looked upon herself as a farmer and not just a farmer's wife if the census is anything to go by. She may have farmed the Great Houghton lands for a short time after her husband died or simply have been his helpmate, but whatever her exact role, she identified herself in the census of 1861 as a 'farmer.' Her sister, Ann Shaw, described herself as a landed proprietress in the same census. The two women employed three servants in 1861, one a groom and gardener and the others, both females, were general servants.

West's future wife, Sarah, was not recorded as living in Darfield with her mother and aunt on the census of 1861. She attended a local school, Highfield House, Wath upon Dearne, which is described in both the directories and the census as a boarding school, but she is not listed among the pupils there on the night of the census either. Sarah probably attended school from an early age. We know from the inventory that her parents had books at the Great Houghton farm during her childhood, and she was described as a scholar in the census of 1851 when she was just six. The survival of two book prizes proves that Sarah attended Highfield House for at least four years. In 1855, shortly before her eleventh birthday, Sarah was awarded first prize for reading. Four years later, she won second prize for history and general improvement.[19] Wath upon Dearne was only one and a half miles from Great Houghton and just three quarters of a mile from Darfield, and although this makes the supposition that she attended Highfield House as a boarder unlikely, it cannot be ruled out. There is no

---

[19] The first was a copy of the *Memoir of Old Humphrey*, by the author George Mogridge, a highly religious man who produced quantities of children's literature. The second, *Cowper's Poetical Works*, and awarded to Sarah when she was nearly fifteen, was a book aimed at an adult readership. Both would have provided the young Sarah with copious amounts of moral advice and guidance. (JFF West Archive).

doubt that Sarah received an adequate education. Evidence from James West's diary points to the fact that Sarah was a competent pianist, and surviving letters of reply to letters she had written, show that she wrote intelligently to both friends and professionals alike. In any case, it is unlikely that James West would have considered her a suitable match if she had not been both intelligent and educated.

Sarah – 'free from control of husband'

Sarah found herself the beneficiary of the wills of both her maiden aunt, Ann Shaw, and her mother, Sarah, in 1870 when she was just twenty-five. Sarah Sellers died first at the age of 63 in April, 1870. She decreed in her will that money on bond due to her by her deceased husband's son should be cancelled. Then she went on to bequeath her furniture to her sister, Ann, and make provision for the appointed trustees of her personal and real estate to invest the residue to pay rents for her sister for life. Following the death of Ann, the same was to go to her daughter, Sarah Hammond, wife of JFF West. It was to be a legacy which, in the words of the will itself should be 'free from control of husband.' Sarah Sellers wanted to ensure that her daughter would be spared from marital interference although she did permit her to appoint rents etc to her husband for his life only. She also decreed that the inheritance was to pass on to her daughter's issue after her daughter's death. Sarah and James West had started their family by the time the wills were made but, nevertheless, Sarah's mother made provision for the possibility that her daughter might die without issue, by devising her trust estates to Miss Elizabeth Lorraine,[20] her heirs, executors and administrators should that be the case.

Ann Shaw survived her sister by just over seven weeks. Her will [21] closely resembles that of her late sister. She had given her trustees the power to invest monies from her real and personal estate for the benefit of her sister, Sarah Sellers, and then to pay the same to her niece, Sarah Hammond, wife of JFF West, free from marital control. Like her sister she devised the same to Elizabeth Lorraine should her niece die without issue.

What followed turned out to be anything but straight forward. Sarah West (née Sellers) was probably only too grateful for her husband's interference during the decade following her mother's death. Her

---

[20] Elizabeth Lorraine was very close to Sarah and James West. The author has not been able to establish the exact nature of the relationship, but Sarah Sellers was a witness at the marriage of the parents of Elizabeth Lorraine in 1840. Their daughter Elizabeth Silverwood was the only girl in a family of four. One brother, William James became a Wakefield surgeon.

[21] Both wills are dated 6 December, 1867.

mother's effects were valued at under £5,000 at probate and consisted mostly of mineral rich land and property. Another legacy, devised by the will of Elizabeth Hammond, and which was both long forgotten and unpaid, surfaced in the late 1870s. It dated back to 1813. Elizabeth Hammond, third wife of the maternal grandfather of Sarah Sellers and Ann Shaw had bequeathed £500 to one James Green who apparently left England in her lifetime. The £500 had been invested wisely and amounted to over £4,000 by the late 1870s. This episode involved the Wests and their Yorkshire solicitors, Nicholson, Saunders and Nicholson of Wath upon Dearne near Rotherham, in trying to trace the descendants of James Green and in trying to establish whether or not there were other claimants. It transpired, eventually, that Mrs West was one of eighteen claimants and that her entitlement would be either an eighth or ninth of that legacy.

The legacy involved Sarah West because both her mother and her aunt had been beneficiaries of the will of their brother, George Hammond, who had been the chief beneficiary of Elizabeth Hammond's will in 1813. Sarah Sellers' will was impounded eventually and the necessary adjustments made but it was not until January, 1882 that the administration with will was finally passed at the Principle Registry.

The real estate inherited by Sarah Sellers and her sister, Ann, had come to them courtesy of their bachelor brother, William, who died intestate in 1848. It was the property that had once belonged to him that was in time passed down to Sarah, wife of James West.

Income from rents and coal

During the 1870s, James West became deeply involved in Sarah's inheritance of land and property back in Yorkshire and in the complications caused by the non-payment of James Green's legacy. Apart from managing her household budget, it is unlikely that West's wife, Sarah, had had much experience of financial affairs at the time. James West, on the other hand, had managed his own private medical practice for some years and had been one of five individuals on the Finance Committee of Queen's Hospital in 1865.[22] This no doubt gave him the confidence to tackle the task which lay ahead in 1870. Thirty-one letters written between 30 July, 1870 and 3 May, 1877, have survived and are in the JFF West archive. The letters show that West was obliged to travel up to Yorkshire on numerous occasions. Nineteen letters are from the solicitors Nicholson, Saunders and Nicholson. West instructed them to keep him informed even when he was away from home. He received a letter

---

[22] Annual Reports 21–28, 1861–1868. (BCL).

from them at a hotel in Penzance when he was on holiday with his family on 4 April, 1876. A few days later West wrote to the solicitors from Penzance [23] to say that he could be reached again via the post office in Torquay. In the event, it was not even necessary for West to go to the post office – the letter [24] when it came was addressed to the Victoria and Albert Hotel, Torquay.

There is also a private letter in the archive from Elizabeth Lorraine in Wakefield to Sarah West,[25] which indicates that both the Wests and Miss Lorraine thought the solicitors had been dragging their heels over the legacies. Her letter starts affectionately with the words 'My dear Sarah' and contains gossip about the family and about the proposed move of the surgeon, Robert Lawson Tait and his wife, to Birmingham, but she also expressed her relief that James West had pushed the solicitors into action. She said 'I am exceedingly obliged to Mr West and you, to have Miss Shaw's request so promptly fulfilled, perhaps after all Nicholsons have not been so bad as we all imagined but I certainly think Mr West rounded them up when he was in Yorkshire.'

West was well aware of the financial potential of the estates bequeathed to his wife and went to a great deal of trouble to ensure the income derived from them was maximised. Only a few of the surviving letters were written by West himself. He wrote notes and comments in the margins or on the back of some of the letters he was sent and kept copies of some he had written, but even when we do not know exactly what he said in reply to the solicitors' letters, it is clear that he was not to be trifled with in matters of business. Some letters from the solicitors suggest he may, in the early days, have thrown caution aside in his haste to get matters underway. On 4 June, 1873 for instance, Nicholson, Saunders and Nicholson wrote to West warning him against negotiating with individuals directly himself. 'Dear Sir' the letter begins 'Negotiations for the sale of coal require very careful management and we should therefore strongly recommend you not to correspond with Mr Higson but to leave it to Mr Hedley.' They added a postscript, saying 'PS. We have known many chancery suits arise from coal negotiations hence our caution.'[26]

Identifying the property and land inherited by Sarah Hammond West has been facilitated by virtue of the fact that Nicholson, Saunders and Nicholson summarised the extent of the estate on Sarah Hammond West's death in 1910.[27] The inheritance included a farm of fifty acres with a three

[23] Letter dated 7 April, 1876. (JFF West Archive).
[24] Letter dated 13 April, 1876. (JFF West Archive).
[25] Letter dated 23 July, 1871. (JFF West Archive).
[26] (JFF West Archive).
[27] *Sellers & Shaw's Trust. Mrs SH West deceased. Particulars of Estate. 1910.* (JFF West Archive).

bedroomed dwelling house known as Jump Old Hall Farm along with its stables and outbuildings and two cottages at Jump, Nether Hoyland, three and a half miles south east of Barnsley *(See illustration p.235)*. Mrs West also inherited two separate plots of land at Thurnscoe, eight miles east of Barnsley – a messuage with farm buildings and several closes of land, amounting to a further 96 acres, and a close of land called the Dam Bank which consisted of nearly five acres. In addition to that she owned ten garden allotments at Jump. Had Sarah West's land been suitable only for agricultural use, her income would have been quite modest, but these lands were rich in minerals.

Jump farm and its lands were literally on top of coal. Right up to the time of her death, Mrs West received rental from a series of tenant farmers [28] who lived in the farmhouse and worked the land, but James West demanded, and got, much higher returns from the coal mining company who worked the coal seams underground. With the help of the Yorkshire solicitors he negotiated high rents from the coal company for the privilege of using way-leave over his wife's land, and he secured a sizeable income from the lease of the coal seams. He also bargained hard over the size of the royalties due to them from the coal extracted by the coal company.

Sarah West and her husband, James, lived at the right time to capitalise on the minerals under Mrs West's Yorkshire lands. Carol Jones,[29] economic historian, says that the period between 1830 and 1870 was one of rapid growth in the coal industry. Her table on regional coal output for 1830–1913 [30] shows that the coalfields of Yorkshire produced just under 15 million tons per annum in the 1870s which was 11.03% of the national output. The 1880s brought a small increase in production with a tonnage of just over 20 million – 11.92% of the national output. Jones says that demand fell after the 1870s because the iron and steel industries developed new production methods which were more fuel efficient. It meant that in some coal mining areas unworked seams lying at greater depths had to be exploited, and this resulted in higher costs for coal companies and increased danger to the workforce. David Hey also talks of the exploitation of deeper seams in the Yorkshire pits after 1870 as well as providing a chilling insight into the human cost of this trend in his book on the county.[31]

---

[28] Thomas Lodge, for instance, was paying Mrs West an annual rental of £65/0/0d for Jump Farm at the time of her death in 1910.

[29] Rex Pope, Editor. *Atlas of British Social and Economic History since c.1700*. (New York: Macmillan Publishing Company, 1989) Chapter on Coal, Gas and Electricity, pp.68–95.

[30] Ibid., p 71.

[31] David Hey, Yorkshire From AD 1000. (London and New York: Longman, 1986) pp.277–285.

The farm at Jump already had a tenant farmer when Sarah West inherited it, but letters from Nicholson, Saunders and Nicholson dating from the final months of 1872 and early 1873 reveal that there was a change of tenant around about that time. The Wests were offered a rental of £105 per annum with the tenant taking responsibility for putting the cottages and outbuildings in good repair in November, 1872. James West wrote to the solicitors suggesting instead, an annual rental of £120 with the landlord undertaking repairs. The Wests finally seem to have settled for the former, though with a different tenant. On top of that, The Hoyland Silkstone Coal and Coke Company took a lease for forty-five years on a strip of Sarah's land which they wanted to use for a colliery tramway from 1 January, 1874 at an annual rental of £60. This was a rate nearly as high as that for the whole farm in 1910. The document detailing the extent of Mrs West's estate and made by the solicitors on her death in 1910, said that this particular strip of land was expected to revert to agricultural use at a rental of less than £1, when its lease expired in 1919. Through the solicitors West also succeeded in securing £400 per annum for the lease of the underground coal seams by the Hoyland Silkstone Company. A few days after that was settled, West got the coal company to agree to royalties of £60 per foot on the valuable Silkstone seam and £30 for the other seams.

Mining the Silkstone seam in Hoyland was a new enterprise. The coal was of high quality but it lay under the partially worked Barnsley seam. West used the services of a mineral surveyor to assess the quality of the coal and the feasibility of extracting it before terms agreeable to both parties were finally agreed. It resulted in the sinking of a new pit, one of six that opened in the vicinity during the 1870s. The Silkstone seam was one of two coal mining enterprises that occupied James West during the last ten years of his life. In early October, 1873 the solicitors alerted the Wests to the fact that a proposed new stretch of railway would make mining the coal seams under their lands at Thurnscoe more cost effective.

Small parcels of Sarah's lands were sold off over the decades that followed. The first was to the trustees of a religious body called the Methodist New Connection.[32] It consisted of just 298 superficial square yards of land at Jump and was bought by the church trustees for the building of a new chapel. Another plot of land, also at Jump, was sold by the Wests in 1875.[33] This time it amounted to 755 superficial square yards. It was sold to John Duke, farmer, and the contract contained a restrictive

[32] West Yorkshire Archive Service, Registry of Deeds, Wakefield. Volume 666, no. 483, p.415.

[33] West Yorkshire Archive Service, Registry of Deeds, Wakefield. Volume 735, no. 633, p.567.

covenant to ensure that Duke forfeited any right to coal lying underneath the land. In 1877 James and Sarah West sold a further 605 superficial square yards of the Jump estates [34] and in 1883, the day James West began his last diary, the Wests sold property in Doncaster,[35] about fourteen miles east of Barnsley. There is no reference to this property prior to this transaction but since Henry Shaw lived in Doncaster before buying the farm at Jump, it is no surprise. The property was number 3, Oxford Place and it consisted of a dwelling house with yard, outbuildings and appurtenances. The fact that the West's were busy with the sale of number 3, Oxford Place probably explains why West did not start the diary on 1 January.

Sarah West sold another small plot five months after her husband died. This pocket of land was at Jump and consisted of 474 square yards of superficial land on one edge of her Jump estate.[36] The Thurnscoe lands, which it will be remembered consisted of a ninety-six acre plot and another of about five acres, were broken up in two separate transactions. The first was the sale of the five acre close of land known as Dam Bank. This plot was sold to The District Council of Doncaster on 20 November, 1897 [37] for £298/2/6d, fourteen years after the death of James West. The remaining Thurnscoe estate consisting of lands, farm buildings and the underlying minerals were sold off in their entirety for £10,500 in 1900.[38] They were sold to the Reverend TT Taylor, who paid £7,000 for the surface lands and £3,500 for the minerals.

The contacts West made in Yorkshire – the solicitors, coal companies, surveyors and tenants – continued to demand his attention right up to the end of his life. The diary reveals that he wrote to Nicholson, Saunders and Nicholson enclosing Mr Povey Harper's statement of the coal he had got for 31 December, 1882 and that he sent a cheque to Mr J Povey Harper for a survey he had carried out on the coal seam at Hoyland on 6 February, 1883.

Income derived from private practice, teaching, investments, rentals and the sale of lands all helped James West and his family to maintain a high standard of living. A letter, which had contained a cheque for £11/1/9d to cover the interest owed to him on a South Yorkshire Railway bond,[39] is positive proof of the fact that West was investing his capital in the early 1870s, but he had almost certainly been doing so for some time. The way in which

---

[34] West Yorkshire Archive Service, Registry of Deeds, Wakefield. Volume 779, no. 76, p.61.
[35] West Yorkshire Archive Service, Registry of Deeds, Wakefield. Volume 888, no. 244, p.184.
[36] West Yorkshire Archive Service, Registry of Deeds, Wakefield. Volume 904, no. 246, p.184.
[37] West Yorkshire Archive Service, Registry of Deeds, Wakefield. Volume 4, p.1.
[38] West Yorkshire Archive Service, Registry of Deeds, Wakefield. Volume 9, p.208.
[39] Letter from Nicholson, Saunders and Nicholson, 5 July, 1873. (JFF West Archive).

he managed Sarah's land and property and the extent to which he referred to his investments in his last diary and in his will suggest that West was astute when it came to business. Both diary and will show that he had a portfolio of invested capital and that he was actively involved in its management himself. The diary, for instance, reveals that he had shares in Birmingham Bank, the Eastern Extension Telegraph Company and the Pref. Grand Trunk Railway of Canada. There are several entries relating to shares during the first half of February. The first is noted down on the 1st of the month. Four days later, on 5 February, he reports having sold seventy-six of his Birmingham Banking Shares and on 14th, he said he received £1,218/10/– for them, fifty-six at £16 and twenty at £16/2/6d. West records that he dined with one of Birmingham's long established men of business, Mr Holliday, on 15 February and was advised by him to offer £1,500 to the Metrop. Wagon Company at 4%. A few days later, on the 19th, West says he paid the secretary of the Metrop. Wagon Company the sum of £1,500 on debenture for three years at 4%.

Sarah was not the only woman close to West who relied on him to manage her investments either. He followed the entry made on 19 February with these words, 'and also got him to take £100 from F De La Hunt at the same rate. This ought to be a safe investment at any rate!' Elizabeth Lorraine received help from West in managing her investments too. On 28 January, West records 'I sent Lizzie Lorraine 5 new shares in Eastern Extension Telegraph Co at £11 for the investment of the £50 I hold of hers.'

West continued to juggle his finances around before leaving England for his month-long trip to the Continent on 10 March, 1883. Illness and death brought West's dealings on the stock market to an end shortly after he returned home, but he still managed one final set of adjustments to his portfolio. On Tuesday 17 April, the last entry in the diary, West says he dined at the Liberal Club with Mr Sutton of the Lancashire Ass Company. He says he paid into the Birmingham Bank Company the following coupons – Perry and Company, £7/10/–; Cape of Good Hope, £11/5/– and New Zealand, £6/5/– to a total of £25/0/–. These are not his final words, but they are the penultimate ones.

Social standing

There is no doubt that the income on which the Wests relied was more than adequate. It not only covered their routine expenses and made it possible for them to indulge in luxuries like foreign travel, but it provided a surplus. This, as we have seen, was wisely invested. In Victorian England, just as today, it

House of James Fitzjames Fraser West & his wife, Sarah, on the Hagley Road, Edgbaston, Birmingham. It was numbered 117 in his lifetime but was re-numbered 247 shortly after he died in 1883. Source: JFF West Archive.

was important to show one's contemporaries some tangible evidence of one's success. An impressive house in one of the town's most desirable districts was the most sought after way of securing respect and admiration, but West, like so many before and after him, achieved that prestige stage by stage.

The house in Newhall Street was in a terrace and had a modest garden, but the one in Acock's Green, it will be remembered, was set in its own grounds. Their next house, and James West's last, was a large, double fronted early Victorian house on the north side of the Hagley Road in Edgbaston. The property, number 117, Hagley Road, had a rateable value of £102 and an estimated annual rental of £120.[40] It occupied a plot of one rood and nine perches. If we use J Redfern's study of the elites of Edgbaston society as a guide, the house West and his wife, Sarah, occupied was likely to have been in the mid-range of Edgbaston properties.[41] Hagley Road marked the northern boundary of the Edgbaston lands owned by the Lords Calthorpe from that of other landowners. The Calthorpes allowed the building of houses on their Edgbaston estates from 1786 onwards but only on strict conditions. With the help of their agent, they maintained tight control over the new development by leasing rather than selling the plots, and by imposing a stringent restrictive covenant on developers and

---

[40] Rate Book for 117, Hagley Road, 1876. (BCA).

[41] J Redfern, 'Elite Suburbians: Early Victorian Edgbaston', *The Local Historian*; 1982–3; 15: pp.259–271. Redfern discovered in his study of Edgbaston elites, the mean rateable value for an Edgbaston property in 1851 was around £35.

Sarah Hammond West with three of her children ca.1881.
Source: JFF West Archive.

leaseholders alike. Edgbaston streets were wide and tree-lined and the houses built were elegant. It was, as David Cannadine [42] and others have described it, the Belgravia of Birmingham.

Cannadine's book contains the most exhaustive study of Edgbaston society to date although if writers of fiction are taken into account, the late Francis Brett Young who resided in Edgbaston as a medical student, comes a close second. Cannadine points out that even within its boundaries, Edgbastonians were zoned according to their status and affluence. By and large, the town's most affluent occupied the area in the middle. They were cushioned by the upper middle classes who lived in the next zone moving out from centre and they were shielded from the lower classes by the lower middle and middle middle classes on the periphery. The peripheries identified by Cannadine and occupied by those of lower social status did not include either the Bristol Road or the Hagley Road in West's day. These roads, Cannadine tells us, formed a 'broad crescent of middle-middle-class houses ...prosperous and comfortable, belonging to successful professionals – doctors, lawyers, solicitors and accountants – with large gardens, three servants and perhaps even a cook or a nanny.'[43]

---

[42] David Cannadine, *Lords and Landlords: The Aristocracy and the Towns. 1774–1967.* (England: Leicester University Press, 1980).

[43] Ibid., p 201.

   As Cannadine puts it, there were at one extreme, the brewers, chocolate makers, and screw manufactures who owned houses frequently costing in excess of £2,000 and set in several acres, and at the other, clerks, business men, shopkeepers and skilled labourers. Joseph Gillott, the pen manufacturer and millionaire, was one of Edgbaston's affluent elite. When he died in 1872 he not only left a fortune in real estate, but also a personal estate which included 140 musical instruments including seven Stradivarius violins and a choice collection of paintings. The paintings alone realised £170,000 and included thirteen Gainsboroughs, nine Constables, twenty-five Turners, seven Landseers and three Reynolds.

   To ensure that Edgbaston was peopled with professionals and others of similar status, the Calthorpes forbade the construction of any houses below the value of £400. Buildings given over to industrial use were strictly prohibited. When the landowners who owned the estates on the northern side of Hagley Road decided to develop their lands, they too, envisaged elegant middle class housing of a similar style to those on the Calthorpe estates. They developed their plots according to that principle initially but, unlike the Calthorpes, they failed to impose covenants. This oversight resulted in the construction of housing aimed at the artisan market and once that began in the late 1880s, the difference between the north and south sides of the Hagley Road became more pronounced. Those which do

The marker shows the location of West's house on the Hagley Road, Edgbaston in 1923. Source: By kind permission Birmingham Central Library.

remain have suffered the indignity of being converted into offices with only their Georgian frontages intact or of being multi-occupied.

Servants and other living expenses

Apart from buying and maintaining costly houses, the day to day expenses incurred by West and his colleagues were considerable. West, who had fathered eight children by the time he died in 1883, was obliged to clothe, feed and school his family according to their status. He also had to dress himself and his wife in a style which would reflect their standing in Edgbaston society. Servants were another expense. The census shows that by 1881 West employed three female living-in servants [44] but the diary proves he employed male servants too. These men may have worked as grooms, coachmen or footmen and lived in the coach house but if they did, the enumerators failed to record the fact. West almost certainly employed non-resident gardeners too. He gave one male employee, William Swinbourne, a fortnight's notice to leave on 27 January, 1883 and according to the diary 'engaged Daniel Hermisan, an old man of 60 who had been 18 years with Mr J Steed (?)'[45] in his place. Horses and carriages and the men who cared for, drove and adorned them, were a constant drain on the purses of medical men like West. The medical historian, Irvine Loudon [46] and others, have pointed out that no self-respecting medical man would have been without his own transport. The diary proves that West had at least two carriages – one open and one closed. The will confirms this and points to the fact that he owned more than one horse too.[47]

But for the survival of West's last diary, it would have been impossible to identify any of the men employed by him. With the exception of a few isolated examples, the same is true of the male servants employed by his colleagues. This is puzzling. The men who tended the gardens of Edgbaston probably did live elsewhere, but coachmen, footmen and grooms frequently lived in coach houses or stables on the premises. According to the instructions given out to enumerators, they should have appeared in their own right as householders in the census. In the event, they were often overlooked.

For all its shortcomings, the census of 1881, reveals that at least three of Oliver Pemberton's [48] eight servants were male. Two, the butler and

---

[44] Fewer than three would have been shameful.

[45] JFF West, Diary; 27 January, 1883, (JFF West Archive).

[46] I Loudon, Doctors and Their Transport, 1750–1914; *Medical History*; 2001; 45: No. 2.

[47] He used the plural when referring to his horses and carriages in his will.

[48] Oliver Pemberton (1825–97) was a surgeon at The General Hospital and was the city's coroner from 1891 until his death.

footman, probably lived in the house with the family and female servants but the other one, a coachman, could easily have resided in the coach house. The three listed in the census return might not have been his sole male employees. Pemberton lived near to West on the Hagley Road in 1881, and would have had a sizeable garden. He would probably have employed a gardener or two as well. The census also reveals that the surgeon John Archer (1809–57) also had a footman, while James Hickenbotham (1840–84), physician, employed a coachman.

Robert Saundby, Thomas Heslop and James Gibbs Blake (1833–1900), the homœopathic practitioner mentioned earlier, all identified male employees in their wills. When he died in 1918, Saundby bequeathed £100 to his chauffeur, Joseph William Oliver, on condition that he was still in his service at the time of his death. Heslop's will [49] indicates that he was in the habit of employing more than one male servant. In it, he devised one month's wages free of all duty to each of the male servants still in his employment at the time of his death. Blake was also generous to a male servant. He left £50 to his coachman in recognition of the faithful service he had given him.[50]

In his book, *The Rise of Professional Society*, Harold Perkin asserts that, by around 1900, middle class incomes ranged from between £1,000 to £10,000.[51] In discussing how adequate these incomes were, he cited a series of articles published in Cornhill Magazine in 1901 on how to live on different incomes. The lowest, between £150 and £200, was probably exceeded by West and most of his colleagues once they had become established. Next came an income of £800. Out of this, a man and his wife could have expected to rent a house in a fashionable street for £130 per annum and employ two servants and a cook at £20 per annum each and a house parlour maid at £18. Other annual expenses would have included £208 on food and washing, £30 on alcohol and tobacco, £70 on the husband's club and pocket money, £40 on his clothes, £50 on clothes for the wife and £20 for her pocket money and £75 on holidays, travel and entertaining. On an income of £1,800 a middle class man should have been able to afford three or four servants, especially if the fourth was a lady's maid who could save the family money by making clothes. The author of the Cornhill articles believed that, with the exception of those living in the country, an income in this range would have been insufficient to cover the cost of a pony, a carriage or a groom.[52] If this is true, doctors must

---

[49]   Thomas Pretious Heslop – Will 1885. (BCA).
[50]   James Gibbs Blake – Will 1900. (BCA)
[51]   Harold Perkins, *The Rise of Professional Society. England Since 1880* (London: Routledge, 1989), p.92.
[52]   Harold Perkins, *The Rise of Professional Society. England Since 1880*. (London: Routledge, 1989), pp.93–95.

have been the exception to the rule. Loudon's research into the transport used by members of the medical profession [53] has convinced him that horse transport was indispensable to doctors and that for anyone but the most lowly to be without it, would have been unthinkable.

Transport
Loudon gives numerous examples of the extent to which medical men would go to secure the most flamboyant carriages and equip both horses and footmen with eye catching apparel. He cites a contemporary observation of an incident which took place in 1825 when there was a vacancy for a post at the Worcester Infirmary. The three aspiring applicants 'made a grand exhibition of gigs and highly decorated horses and footmen, driven with such rapidity through the streets that "merciless death was never before so closely pursued." '[54] According to Loudon, one of the three was the young Chas Hastings, the man who would go on to found the *British Medical Journal*. There is no record of whether West or his rivals in the election for the surgeoncy at Queen's Hospital in 1857 drew attention to themselves by appearing in magnificent carriages, but there is one account of a similar scenario, albeit less extravagant, involving a colleague, in *Edgbastonia*. Alfred Baker who, it will be remembered, was victim to the poison pen of Thomas Gutteridge, is reported as having shared the expense of a gig with a fellow candidate when he was canvassing for the post at The General Hospital in 1848.[55]

Horses and carriages, together with the grooms and liveried footmen who looked after them, were very costly. Loudon [56] says that when cars first became established as viable alternatives, the cost of a car was much the same as two horses and a carriage but was much cheaper to run. He points out that in the transitional period between horse transport and car, one doctor put the price of a horse, carriage and harness at between £135 and £165. Loudon also records the observations made by doctors on the running costs of horse drawn transport. One reckoned that the cost of fodder, a coachman and stabling came to £2/8/– per week, while another claimed that running horse-drawn transport amounted to £98/5/– per annum. Loudon's research suggests that the carriages most

[53] I Loudon, Doctors and Their Transport, 1750–1914; *Medical History*; April, 2001; 45: No. 2.
[54] I Loudon, *Medical Care and the General Practitioner 1750–1850* (Oxford: Clarendon Press, 1986) p.123. Loudon is quoting from *Gazette of Health*; 1825; 10: p.338.
[55] *Edgbastonia*; 1891; X1: p 68. (BCL).
[56] I Loudon, Doctors and Their Transport, 1750–1914, *Medical History*; 2001; 45: pp.185–206.

likely to have been owned by West would have been a Victoria and a Brougham.[57] Both have a separate seat up front for a coachman. The Brougham was closed in and would have been suitable for use on cold or rainy days, but West was a devotee of fresh air and the diary proves that he was not averse to using the open carriage in February. On the occasion referred to, West may have regretted the decision he made that day. He wrote 'Drove over to Acock's Green in the open carriage with Tadie (Sarah).[58] ....A very cold ride back in the evening.'[59]

There was nothing unusual in owning more than one horse or more than one carriage amongst West's circle. Broughams and Victorias were, in any case, designed for the use of two horses. Like West before them, Oliver Pemberton (d.1897), James Sawyer (d.1919) and Dickenson Crompton (d.1894) all refer to horses and carriages in the plural in their wills. Loudon says that doctors embraced the motor car readily. It is no surprise, therefore, to find that the advantages of the motor car were being extolled by the magazine, *Edgbastonia*, as early as April, 1896. Described initially as a 'horseless carriage,' an illustration of the vehicle accompanied the text. Its very resemblance to the familiar horse-drawn carriage prompted the writer to say 'one might have imagined that it was an ordinary carriage from which the horse had bolted – with the shafts.'[60] Interestingly, none of the three seated in the car is facing the road ahead. In December of the same year, a second article featuring the car appeared in the magazine. Referred to now as a 'motor car,' the car is seen carrying two people – one, a woman, clutches the steering wheel and faces the road ahead while the other, her male companion, holds the brake and faces the opposite direction.

Those colleagues who outlived West by thirty-five years or more would nearly all have become car owners. Advertisements, like the one placed in *The Midland Medical Journal* in March, 1902 by Dr Young of Whitfield, were becoming common in the early years of the twentieth century. It appeared in the journal's Sale or Exchange column and read as follows: 'For Sale, single Brougham by Windover, London; nearly new dark green, red lines, rubber tyres, ventilator, electric bell; overhauled and re-varnished last summer; buying motor.'[61]

---

[57] Ibid. p.190. Loudon says that the Brougham (a closed carriage) and the Victoria (an open carriage) were used by consultant physicians and by the more prosperous general practitioners.

[58] Author's bracket.

[59] JFF West, Diary; 13 February, 1883. (JFF West Archive).

[60] *Edgbastonia*; 1996; XVI: p.96. (BCL)

[61] *The Midland Medical Journal*; March, 1902. p.84.

Civic Gospel

As we have seen, social responsibility mattered to many who belonged to the professional classes of Victorian England. In Birmingham and elsewhere enlightened reformers fought for better educational provision, habitable housing, greater social justice and other causes. Many professionals like James West gave their time freely or dug into their pockets in support of the less fortunate and many left legacies to charitable institutions such as Queen's Hospital.

For an industrial town, the social composition of Birmingham in the latter half of the nineteenth century was a little out of the ordinary. Mention has already been made of the nature of its industries and its traditional tolerance of dissenters. The former favoured small workshops in which, the social gap between master and labourer was often small. The latter fostered the growth of the 'civic gospel' by allowing great men from the non-conformist churches to lead the townsfolk in philanthropic enterprise.

Histories of Birmingham almost invariably contain sections on the 'civic gospel' and the 'caucus' which grew out of the Birmingham Liberal Association. Victor Skipp [62] devoted six out of a total of 182 pages to the 'civic gospel' in his book, *Victorian Birmingham* while Asa Briggs [63] focused exclusively on the phenomenon in his chapter on Birmingham's history in *Victorian Cities*. Birmingham Liberal Association worked closely with the Reformers' Union, and it served as a mechanism whereby voting would be manipulated in favour of the reformers during the 1860s and 70s. It paved the way to power and influence for a number of Birmingham reformers – Joseph Chamberlain [64] being the chief among them.

The emergence of the 'civic gospel' goes back to the arrival in Birmingham of the non-conformist minister, George Dawson (1821–76). Dawson took up his first post at the *Mount Zion Baptist Chapel* in 1844, ten years before the arrival of James West. Within three years he had opened his own church, *The Church of the Saviour*. From there, this inspired and intelligent man could address the people of Birmingham without constraint. His congregation consisted of many who were, or who would become, the most influential in the civic life of the town. As a practising Anglican,[65] West

---

[62] *The Midland Medical Journal*; March, 1902. p.84.

[63] Asa Briggs, *Victorian Cities*. The chapter is entitled, Birmingham: The Making of a Civic Gospel. pp.184–240.

[64] Joseph Chamberlain held office as Birmingham's mayor three times (1873 to 1875 inclusive). He went on to hold office in the Cabinet, and was the father of Prime Minister, Neville Chamberlain.

[65] If the diary is any guide to West's behaviour in other years, his regular church seems to have been St Augustine's Church, Edgbaston.

was unlikely to have been in Dawson's regular congregation, but he may have gone along to some of his services out of curiosity or out of admiration for this highly respected man. In Dawson's own words the 'gospel' was pledged to ' "the authority of the conscience" ' and its aim was ' "to clothe the naked, to feed the hungry, and to instruct the ignorant." '[66] One of Dawson's most memorable addresses was at the opening of the Free Reference Library in 1866. In his view, the public library movement was ' "the largest and widest Church ever established." ' He went on to say ' "we have made provision of God's greatest and best gifts unto men." '[67] Briggs believes that the 'civic gospel' was indeed, a true gospel. He states that 'The ideals which lay behind it were greater than the men who brought it into being.'[68]

Birmingham could boast other outstanding nonconformists. Those who worked for reform alongside George Dawson included his successor at the *Mount Zion Chapel*, Charles Vince. HW Crosskey, who was minister at the *Unitarian Church of the Messiah* and Robert William Dale, pastor of *Carr's Lane Congregational Church* from 1854 to 1895, also deserve mention. Unitarianism was the religion of Birmingham's most influential families, and it was Crosskey who inspired in them a new sense of social duty. Robert Dale loved Birmingham according to Skipp. As Dale himself once eulogised 'There is nothing in this magnificent view (Lucerne, Switzerland) which makes me feel half the thrill I have sometimes felt when I have looked down on the smoky streets of Birmingham from the railway as I have returned to work from a holiday.'[69] From 1867, Dale was actively calling for the greater participation in local government of Birmingham's Christians. Christians should, he said 'give their time as well as their money to whatever improvements are intended to develop the intelligence of the community.' They should ' "see to it that the towns and parishes in which they live are well drained, well lighted, and well paved; that there are good schools for every class of the population....that all parochial and municipal affairs are conducted honourably and equitably." '[70]

Joseph Chamberlain, who undertook his first service to the community as a teacher of Sunday and evening school classes at the Church of the Messiah, heeded Dale's words. In his years as Birmingham's mayor, Chamberlain undertook the reform of its services and its facilities and swept away many of the town's slums. He was one of the founder members of the town's school

---

[66] A Briggs, *Victorian Cities*. p.196.
[67] Ibid., p.197.
[68] Ibid., p.197.
[69] Ibid., p.199.
[70] Ibid., p 200.

board together with Dr Dale, George Dawson, and two other illustrious townsmen and served as its chairman for almost three years. It will be remembered that it was Chamberlain who tried to persuade Queen's College to admit female medical students in the mid-1870s. He was also the main driving force behind the foundation of a university in Birmingham. Proposals that Birmingham's Mason College should join a federation based on Victoria University in Manchester or one based on a Birmingham, Bristol and Nottingham alliance were rejected by Chamberlain who insisted, instead, upon the establishment of a self-contained university. When the University of Birmingham opened in 1901, he was its first Chancellor.

Philip Elliott [71] tells us that while professionals like West could depend on their social status as an indication of their worth in the first half of the nineteenth century, they had to rely on their occupational expertise to attract the same kudos in the second half. In Birmingham, respect for expertise certainly accounted for an increase in status for the town's professionals, manufacturers and merchants, but whether non-conformist or not, they could not easily have ignored the sentiments the town's great social reformers. They had to earn their elevated positions in society both through their professional knowledge and through altruistic endeavour.

Most worked hard at making themselves the stalwarts of middle class respectable society through duty to the public. They knew what was expected of them, and the majority of them lived up to those expectations. Most felt proud of Birmingham and many held positions of influence, not only over its medical institutions, but over the town's day to day administration. Margaret Homes [72] says that, in Birmingham between between the late 1870s and 1911, most of the professionals who occupied a place on the council were doctors. Some of West's closest colleagues were politically active and undertook work as Justices of the Peace,[73] and some became involved in national politics. A few were rewarded for their efforts with knighthoods.

West's name does not appear in the local membership lists of either the Liberal or the Conservative Club, although entries in the diary indicate that he dined at the clubhouses of both with friends in the final months of his life. There is nothing in the diary to suggest that this was unusual. As an Edgbastonian, West lived among the town's mayors and its councillors as

[71] P. Elliott, *The Sociology of the Professions*. (London: Macmillan, 1972), p.32.
[72] Brian Hall (editor), *Aspects of Birmingham*. Chapter by Margaret Holmes; Fit and Proper Councillors? (England: Wharncliffe, 2001), p.77.
[73] A typical list of Birmingham's JPs contained the names of about four doctors. Four out of 37 in 1877 and four out of 51 in 1881 were doctors, for instance.

well as others who were among the politically active elite for the last nine years of his life. In this climate, he could hardly avoid political influences even if he chose not become involved himself directly.

In any case, West was not immune to the politics of medicine. The diary provides us with some examples. In January, 1883, for instance, he says he attended a meeting at the Birmingham and Midlands Counties branch of the BMA for a discussion on the alteration of its constitution. West does not give his own views of the proposals in the diary, but says that Gamgee and Sawyer were the 'principal reformers.'[74] Gamgee and Sawyer were indeed energetic reformers, but so were some of West's other colleagues.

After his death in 1885, Thomas Heslop was remembered for his 'unwearied exertions on behalf of the welfare of others.'[75] Heslop worked as a JP, was a governor to King Edward's School, and chairman of Mason's Science College, but he was also involved in the founding of a hospital for children and a skin and lock hospital in the town, as well as taking an active role in the success of the Women's Hospital. It is hardly surprising then, that when West and one of his sons called on Heslop on his way back from the Botanical Gardens one Sunday in January, 1883, West wrote 'we had three hours gossip together about Hospital reform – general politics and almost every thing under the sun.'[76]

Joseph Sampson Gamgee's efforts on behalf of the town's hospitals have already been mentioned. Like Heslop and many of his other contemporaries, Gamgee never received any formal recognition for his services to medicine or anything else. Some of West's other colleagues did win awards from high places for the duties they undertook, though. In most cases, the awards had little or no connection with their services to medicine, but were rather to do with perceived or real distinction in the world of politics. The account given in *Edgbastonia* of James Sawyer's knighthood, indicates that the honour he received was because he had exceptional qualities as a physician. Its reporter said he received the knighthood 'in recognition of his distinguished position in the medical profession, and his long and valuable service to the Queen's Hospital.'[77] Some of Sawyer's contemporaries would have challenged these sentiments. Following its report [78] of the banquet held for Sawyer at the time of his award, some readers of the *Birmingham Post* wrote in to say precisely the opposite.

---

[74] JFF West, Diary; Thursday 11 January, 1883. (JFF West Archive).

[75] *Edgbastonia*; 1885; V: pp.97–101. (BCL)

[76] JFF West, Diary; Sunday 14 January, 1883. (JFF West Archive).

[77] *Edgbastonia*; 1890; X: p.82 (BCL).

[78] *Birmingham Post*, 24 December, 1885. (BCL).

Many Birmingham doctors – James West amongst them – gave money to medical causes both during and after their lifetimes. Wives, children and widows also made donations to medical institutions and some left money in their wills. It will be remembered that Sarah West and the West's first-born son, Walter, are recorded in the Queen's Hospital Annual report of 1875 [79] as two of the fifty-eight individuals who contributed to a relief fund to help poor patients on their discharge from hospital. Walter was a boy of eleven at the time of their first donation. Each gave a nominal 5/–, but with the exception of two individuals who gave 10/–, it was the norm. Twelve of the subscribers were women that year, but Walter West was the only child. His parents were obviously eager to instil a sense of social duty at an early age. Both subscribed again in 1876 and 1877. West's daughter, Gertrude, born in 1872, was only eleven when her father died, but she retained a sense of duty towards Queen's Hospital right up to the time of her death in 1951 when she bequeathed £100/0/– to her father's old hospital.

As we have seen, West contributed £20 to funds for the new extension at Queen's Hospital in the early 1870s. A few years later, in February, 1875, he donated £21 to the building fund for the newly established Birmingham Medical Institute, and on his death, he bequeathed £100/0/– to Queen's Hospital. We also know that he organised a relief fund for the family of Charles Davenport, Medical Officer of Health of Bromsgrove, who died in 1875 leaving a widow and eleven children. West's appeal first appeared in *The Lancet* on 30 January, 1875. He pointed out that his colleagues Dr Heslop and Mr Oliver Pemberton had already donated five and two guineas respectively and said that he was willing to take responsibility for the collection of further contributions. By 6 February another twenty-one individuals had come forward. This included ten more from among West's Birmingham colleagues. West himself gave two guineas, as did another Birmingham doctor, Mr J Archer. Six, including WH Sprotson and JS Gamgee, gave one guinea and the remaining two gave ten shillings and sixpence each. It cannot have been enough to sustain the family, but it was a help and, as we shall see later, the family did receive further relief from the Birmingham Medical Benevolent Society.

On his death in 1885, Thomas Heslop's estate was valued at £10,492/4/9d. Heslop, who died a bachelor, chose to leave some of his money to medical causes. Queen's Hospital received £100, as did the Children's Hospital, while Mason Science College was given £100 in addition to the £500 which he had already promised. He had already given

[79] Queen's Hospital, Birmingham. *Annual Reports 29–39*, pp.35–36. (BCL).

a substantial number of books to Mason College, which it will be remembered, was the forerunner of the University of Birmingham. The collection has survived to this day and is preserved in the Heslop Room in the library of the university. James Gibbs Blake gave generously to the University of Birmingham too. He devised £900 to the university, which he said was to be in addition to the £100 he had already given. Robert Saundby left all of his medical books to the Birmingham Medical Institute when he died in 1918, but stipulated that they were to go to the university if they were not wanted by the former. Edwin Rickards (1841–1908), also left money to medical institutions. In this case it was The General Hospital and Birmingham Medical Institute who profited, with a legacy of £100 each.

Another man who showed generosity to medical causes in his will was William Sands Cox, founder of both Queen's College and Queen's Hospital. When he died in 1875, he not only gave consolidations amounting to thousands of pounds which were to be shared between numerous named hospitals but consols worth tens of thousands of pounds towards the foundation of others. He also made provision for medical scholarships at King Edward's School, Birmingham. Never one to relinquish control readily, Cox even stipulated that any residue of his estate which remained after the death of his widow should be shared out between the Cottage Hospital at Moreton-in-the-Marsh and the five dispensaries alluded to in his will. Neither Queen's College, nor its hospital, were given a bequest. Doubtless bitter at the way in which he had parted company with Queen's, Cox probably seized the opportunity to indulge in a little revenge. Still, he was not without sentiment for the old institution. He stated in the will that it was his wish to be carried to the grave by six old medical students of Queen's College, to whom each would be presented with a gold ring to the value of five guineas.[80]

Clubs and Societies

West's membership of clubs and societies deserves special mention. Like many professional men of his time he belonged to several. Many were inextricably connected with his role as a medical professional, but some reflected other interests and concerns. His membership of the Birmingham Medical Institute, the Midland Medical Society, the Pathological Society of London, the British Medical Association Pathological Section and its Birmingham and Midland Counties Branch have already been alluded to,

---

[80] Bequests to Medical Charities. Article on the bequests of the late Mr William Sands Cox. *Medical Times and Gazette;* 1876; i: p.312.

but West was also a freemason and belonged to the Birmingham Dramatic and Literary Club. He invariably held office on the committees of these institutions and took his turn as vice-president and president of most. Society and club minute books which record attendance of their officers show that West was an active member in all of them.

Birmingham Medical Benevolent Society

Founded in 1821, the Birmingham Medical Benevolent Society was established to provide financial help to subscribers and their dependants if they were unfortunate enough to fall on hard times. A few suffered hardship as a result of poor money management skills, but the majority were victims of bad luck. Those who had been unable to save as a result of inadequate incomes and those who were unable to work through infirmity or long-term ill health were the society's chief beneficiaries. Apart from subscriptions, the society was funded by revenue from ground rents, dividends, donations, investments and the occasional legacy. Arthur Burdett left the society £2,000 in 1910 but when a Dr Sharples of Lincoln, left them £250 in 1895 he said was acting out a promise he made earlier to repay the money he had been granted by them during his lifetime. He had written to the society in 1892 to say that their assistance was enabling him to continue his payments to a life insurance company and that he would instruct his executors to use the cover to repay the Medical Benevolent Society on his demise.

The society was run by a board of directors who met quarterly to consider cases and authorise relief. West's name appears as one of the society's directors in the minute books from 1878 through to the end of 1882. While membership lists for the years during which West was involved have not survived, there are a few from the last decade of the nineteenth and first of the twentieth century. In this period membership numbers seem to have ranged between about ninety and one hundred and fifty.

We have seen how some medical practitioners endured privation during their early careers but without governmental welfare schemes or professional pensions it is easy to understand that even well established doctors and their families were vulnerable. When adversity struck practitioners or their dependants and they found themselves having to make a claim, many expressed their sense of shame.

West was not a director when the needs of Charles Davenport's widow and her large family were assessed in 1875, but his appeal in *The Lancet* for donations to help the family following Davenport's death proves he was sympathetic to the needs of his less fortunate colleagues before he took on an official role with the Birmingham Medical Benevolent Society. When Mrs Davenport first wrote to the society, the sale of her husband's practice, horse, carriage, drugs and surgery fittings had already been agreed. She explained that the sale would amount to £800, but said the money would be paid in three instalments. Mrs Davenport also had £400 from a policy her husband had paid into, but said that that was the only real provision she had. The directors considered Mrs Davenport's case 'urgent and pressing' and granted her £20 payable half yearly. In the end Mrs Davenport received aid amounting to £340 between 1875 and 1884 with the society awarding a further grant of £15 to her remaining dependants in 1885.

Joseph Taylor, Mary Wood and Mary Ann Smith, who asked for relief in the years 1857, 1860 and 1878 respectively, all made applications which they described as 'painful.' In 1888, the latter said that while she had been able to relinquish the aid granted to her when her husband died four and a half years earlier, she was suffering difficulties again. She said she had taken in boarders to make ends meet, but that due to failing sight in her only surviving eye, she had been reduced to living off the interest on a legacy which amounted to just £25 a year. She finished off her letter with the words 'It is a painful necessity to me. I have tried so hard to do without help.' In the end, the society paid Mary Smith £998 between 1878 and 1921 with a gap of four years from 1883 to 1887.

Not all claimants cost the society dear. Some recipients of aid only received one or two payments. Sarah Catherine Johnson left with seven children in 1871, was taken off the society's books after just three payments of £15, when she wrote to say she had received a legacy from her mother and that money from her late husband's estate had been made available to her. Others turned out to be more of burden on the society. Fanny Dixon Edwards, widowed at thirty-nine, cost the society £819 between 1876 and her death in 1902, while Elizabeth Edmonds and Ellen Hickenbotham who claimed for thirty-five years and twenty-five years respectively were both granted aid totalling over £1,000. Mary Simons, who lived for a further thirty years after she made her first claim in 1857, received a total of £837/10/– in the end. She had supplemented her income for many years through income derived from running a school and by letting part of her house but, by the age of eighty-three, was entirely dependant on the pay outs from the society and reduced to living as a lodger herself.

The plight of one individual evoked much compassion in the final years of her life. Harriet Gutteridge, the unmarried sister of the infamous Thomas Gutteridge, was left in abject poverty after her bachelor brother died in 1880. A court of directors which met to discuss the needs of Miss Gutteridge on 27 July, 1887, considered her case urgent. It was said that 'since Thomas Gutteridge suffered towards the close of his life great privations and poverty without applying for or receiving any benefit whatsoever from the funds of the society, a grant of £20 be made to his sister, the only surviving member of his family, who is 80 years of age, bedridden and entirely destitute of all means of support.'[81]

Society minutes record a document headed 'A Case of Distress' which relates how friends agreed to club together to subscribe funds to 'keep Miss Gutteridge from starvation' after her brother's death. It was signed by some of the Birmingham's most illustrious townsfolk – Thomas Avery JP (1813–1914), a man whose name is linked with scales to this day; HB Bowlby, Rector of St Philip's; Edward Gem JP and William Wilkinson, Rector of St Martins. The four who signed the document went on to say that the subscriptions had been 'greatly reduced' due to deaths and withdrawals and that Miss Gutteridge 'is now nearly blind, very infirm and entirely confined to her bed. We believe' they went on 'that if these circumstances were made known many others might be willing to save Miss Gutteridge from ending her days in a workhouse, and laying aside all recollections of bygone days, would think only of the blindness of this aged and forlorn woman...'[82] Their plea was heeded. A special appeal to raise money for the impoverished Miss Gutteridge brought £65/11/9d in that year while the annual subscriptions and donations amounted to a further £80/1/6d. Forty-nine people subscribed to the special fund. Donations ranged from the £10 given by the Bishop of Worcester to 1/6d donated by L Miller. Thirteen of the donors were women and another eleven were anonymous. The names of the distinguished and affluent of the town can be found in the list of regular subscribers. They include George Dixon; Joseph Chamberlain; Lord Calthorpe; JD Goodman, a man who had grown wealthy through the gun trade and a good friend of West, William Holliday as well as two medical colleagues, Robert Lawson Tait and Thomas Hiron Bartleet.

Bowlby also wrote his own letter on 25 July. He wrote 'Harriet Gutteridge... is in a state of destitution which it is most painful to

---

[81] *Birmingham Medical Benevolent Society Recipients' Case Book.* Directors' Court 27 July, 1887.
      (B Med I).
[82] Ibid.

contemplate in the case of she who had formerly lived in comfort..... Harriet Gutteridge had once a good fortune of her own, and spent it entirely in helping her brother during his lifetime.'[83] These were powerful words and not easy to ignore. The Birmingham Medical Benevolent Society granted £40 per annum in aid to Miss Gutteridge between 1887 and 1889. She followed her brother to the grave at the beginning of 1890 and had the dubious distinction of being the last to be interred in the catacombs of Birmingham's Christchurch, now demolished.

That Harriet's brother, Thomas Gutteridge, was self-important is irrefutable. He even assumed the surname of the distinguished British surgeon, William Cheselden (1688–1752) [84] in his latter years on the grounds that he believed his reputation in the practice of lithotomy matched that of Cheselden, a man renowned as one of the great pioneers of successful lithotomy. The last will and testament of Harriet Gutteridge, made on 6 February, 1881, with its codicil of 26 February, 1881, is a sad testimony to the fact that she seems to have harboured a few delusions of her own. In the first place, she instructs her executors to 'expend a sum not exceeding sixty pounds in the erection of a tablet to the memory of my late parents and brother and myself in Christ Church Birmingham.' She also directs them 'to present (her) late brother's surgical instruments and works to some public institution in London to be exhibited to the public with his name thereon.' By 26 February the former project had become more ambitious. In the codicil of that date, she states that recent circumstances have led her to believe that her residuary estate is to be increased to the value of £200 and adds that she is now able to direct her executors to erect a tablet to the value of £200 instead of one of £60 as stipulated earlier.

James West knew many of those who became recipients of aid personally. Some, like George Beauchamp Knowles claimed during West's own lifetime. Knowles, who it will be remembered held the post of surgeon at Queen's Hospital before West was elected in his place, was compelled through hardship to apply for aid in 1864 by which time he was an eighty year old widower. His application is unusual in that he is one of the few who believes that he is fully justified in expecting a hand-out and his letter expresses no shame. After explaining that he is no longer capable of work he stated 'and will see no objection to my partaking of the benefit arising

---

[83] HB Bowlby, Rector of St Philip's, Letter dated, 25 July, 1887. Recipients' Case Book from 1857. (B Med I).

[84] Cheselden held three positions of 'first lithotomist' during his lifetime – at St Thomas', Westminster Hospital and St George's. The operation involves the removal of stones from the bladder.

Surgeon-Major George Yates (1824–1907). Friend and colleague of JFF West. Source: By kind permission Special Collections, University of Birmingham.

from an institution to which I have contributed for so many years.'[85] Knowles died two years later after having received just £125.

The widows of two others close to West also applied to the society for aid though after West's own lifetime. Marion Gamgee, widow of Joseph Sampson Gamgee, West's rival in the election dispute, had to apply for assistance straight after her husband's death in 1886. Gamgee's reputation for living beyond his means was legendary and has been commented upon by biographers. Marion Gamgee was granted an immediate award of £40 as well as continuing support over an extended period. In July, 1895 Mrs Gamgee wrote to thank the society for the support they had given her and explained that since her son was at last in a position to assist her, she could manage on half the amount granted. Aid was discontinued in 1899 after another letter from Marion Gamgee saying that by then her son was able to give 'substantial assistance.'

One of West's closest friends was the surgeon, George Yates (1824–1907). In 1904 at the age of eighty, widower Yates must have caused a few raised eyebrows when he married a woman of twenty-three years. He became a member of the society in 1869 and had already been reduced to asking for relief by 1897. Aid was discontinued in 1903 when his financial circumstances improved, but Yates's death in May, 1907 meant he left a widow who was still

---

[85] Letter from GB Knowles, 1 July, 1864; Recipients' Case Book from 1857. (B Med I).

in her mid-twenties. That in itself, must have been enough to make the society reluctant to acquiesce with the claim she made for support shortly after her husband's demise. Her request met with a resolve by the directors to obtain further information and to reconsider the application at the next meeting initially, but on hearing the results of their enquires at the next meeting, the directors decided to reject the claims of Mrs Yates.

British Medical Association

The local branch of the BMA had a membership of 352 in 1883,[86] the year West died. At least 171 were from Birmingham and many of those were residents of Edgbaston. West was personally acquainted with a surprisingly large number of these individuals.

Annual Meetings of the BMA would have facilitated opportunities for coming into contact with, and befriending, practitioners from other parts of the country, and for catching up with acquaintances and old friends. One BMA Visitor Book for the Annual Meeting which was held in Birmingham in 1872 has survived. Assuming the number of signatories is a true reflection of those who were present, the meeting was attended by some 534 practitioners. One hundred and three came from Birmingham and what would now be regarded as its suburbs, while fifty-nine came from London. The rest came from other towns and cities of the United Kingdom or from overseas. The few who came from abroad came from both far-off countries like the USA, Jamaica and India and from England's European neighbours such as The Netherlands, Switzerland, Poland and France.

The Visitors' Book is particularly interesting because those attending were required to give their own residential addresses and say where they were staying during the time they spent in Birmingham. Although some 229 omitted to comply with this requirement,[87] what remains gives a fascinating insight into how participants were accommodated. The town's hotels certainly benefited from the event, with *Queen's Hotel* proving the most popular with visitors. Sixty-five medical men stayed there, but *The Great Western* was not very far behind with forty-four. Other hotels used by visiting practitioners were *The Hen and Chickens* (25), *The Stork* (12), *The Swan* (10), *The Royal Hotel* (4), *Woolpack House* (3), *The Union Hotel* (2), *The Plough and Harrow Hotel* (2) and *The Warwick Arms* with just one.

---

[86] *BMJ*; 29 December, 1883; ii: pp.v–vii.

[87] Most of those who failed to give their addresses were Birmingham men and must have assumed that it was unnecessary, but some members seem to have omitted to fill it in simply because the person whose name came immediately above had failed to fill in theirs. This tendency resulted in clusters of blanks.

A surprisingly large number of visitors stayed with local men. Those who offered overnight accommodation included several men who held office in the local medical societies and it is possible that the organisers asked local practitioners to accommodate colleagues from further afield. For the most part, though, those accommodated in private houses were probably friends, friends of friends or former colleagues. When the BMA Annual Meeting of 1872 took place, West was living temporarily at 18, Broad Street, Bingley House, the building in which Joseph Sampson Gamgee resided. That did not stop him from giving hospitality to Mr William Adams (1827–92) from Henrietta Street in London. Adams had been a demonstrator in morbid anatomy at St Thomas' Hospital when West was a student at the medical school and had been one of West's referees in 1854 when West sought and gained the post of residential medical officer at Queen's Hospital, Birmingham. He went to the Royal Orthopædic Hospital, London, as an assistant surgeon when he left St Thomas' and from there to the National Orthopædic Hospital, Great Portland Street, London. West was doubtless indebted to Adams for his interest and expertise in diseases of the joints. Gamgee, for his part, gave accommodation to R Barnes from London.

Some foreign visitors left no indication of where they stayed. Two Swiss visitors, a Pole, an Irishman and a Frenchman left no clue as to the type of accommodation they used, but the visitors' book shows that some foreign colleagues were given hospitality by Birmingham men. Three French visitors, including M. Demarquay, were given accommodation in the home of John Birt Davies at 280, Hagley Road, Edgbaston, while William Stevenson of Jamaica and JB King, army surgeon from Bengal, stayed at number 11½, Hagley Road.

Robert Lawson Tait provided a bed for Edinburgh's Alexander Simpson (d.1916) as well as Stanley Haynes of Malvern and an unidentifiable practitioner [88] from Ossett, West Yorkshire. The surgeon, Oliver Pemberton, and Dr Balthazar Foster (1840–1913) also gave accommodation to three colleagues from outside Birmingham, but the hospitality provided by Alfred Baker, president of the local branch in 1872, and James Harmar surpassed even that. Harmar accommodated four visitors while Baker had five in his house, one of whom included Sir William Fergusson.

One visitor who came up from London for the Annual Meeting of the BMA in 1872 and was one of the forty-four accommodated in *The Great Western* was William MacCormac (1836–1901). James West had known

---

[88] The name is illegible.

MacCormac for some years before he died in 1883, although how and when they met is not known. MacCormac was an early devotee of Lister's antiseptic treatment of wounds [89] and Lindsay Patricia Granshaw [90] believes that McCormac may have invited West to publish a paper on the subject in the *St Thomas' Hospital Reports* in 1879 in the hope of convincing the hospital's sceptics of its efficacy. While this does not prove that the two men were known to each other personally even then, West acknowledged the various 'professional friends'[91] who had helped him by giving him introductions to his German brethren when he visited that country in 1875, and William MacCormac's name was among them.

MacCormac came to St Thomas' Hospital, London from Belfast in 1871, and already had a Harley Street address by the time he attended the BMA Annual Meeting the next year. It was not long before he could boast a knighthood. He was six feet three inches tall and had a larger than life personality to match, according to the account given by EM McInnes in *St Thomas' Hospital*.[92] McInnes says he was given to driving up to the hospital in a red-wheeled Brougham drawn by a pair of choice black horses. James West had put his name forward for the post at St Thomas' in 1871, but those responsible for making the appointment no doubt recognised the stature and qualities possessed by MacCormac outshone those of his rivals, West included. The prestige and stature of Sir William was so great by 1881 that he was seen as the natural organiser for the seventh International Medical Congress of that year.

International Medical Congress, London, 1881

The prestige and stature of medical practitioners in general was nowhere better demonstrated than by the events of the International Medical Congress which was held in London in 1881. West was one of 3,181 delegates at this, the seventh International Medical Congress. Alex Sakula describes the occasion as 'arguably the greatest and most historic medical congress ever held.'[93] It began on Tuesday 2 August, and lasted a week. In between the social functions, festivities, outings, dinners and the informal

[89] William MacCormac had written a paper on the subject as early as 1869. William MacCormac, On the Antiseptic Treatment of Wounds, *Dublin Quarterly Journal*; 1869. pp.52–62.
[90] Lindsay Patricia Granshaw, *St Thomas' Hospital, London. 1850–1900*. pp.247–248.
[91] JFF West, Impressions of German Surgery; *BMR*; 1875; p.42 (B Med I).
[92] EM McInnes, *St Thomas' Hospital*, (London; Special Trustees for St Thomas' Hospital, London, 1990) p.134.
[93] Alex Sakula, Baroness Burdett-Coutts' Garden Party: The International Medical Congress, London, 1881; *Medical History*; 1982; 26: pp.183–190.

sharing of expertise, 450 members read papers and 858 gave speeches in the discussion time that followed. James West did neither. The majority of the participants (2,085) came from the United Kingdom which, of course, then included the whole of Ireland. After that, medical men from Continental Europe were the most numerous. Two hundred and three delegates came from Germany, a figure that was nearly matched by France with 201. Italy came next with seventy-three participants while The Netherlands, Belgium and Switzerland followed with seventy-three, sixty-one, fifty-five and thirty-six respectively. The English Colonies accounted for a further sixty-two members, but they were not the only ones to come from far afield. Two hundred and twenty came from the USA, and there were representatives from China, Argentina and other Latin American countries.

Not surprisingly, the majority of the delegates were medical men, but those working in the related sciences were also represented. Louis Pasteur, for instance, spoke on the topic immunisation against chicken cholera and anthrax and Paul Koch demonstrated his new bacteriological techniques using solid media. Thomas Henry Huxley (1825–95), for his part, gave an address on 'The Connection of the Biological Sciences with Medicine.' Sakula says that the congress marked a landmark in the acceptance of bacteriology in medicine, surgery and public health.[94]

The status that scientists like Pasteur and Koch had attained within medical circles was demonstrated in concrete terms by Pasteur's inclusion in the group of some ninety-two distinguished visitors who received invitations to a garden party at the Highgate home of one of the greatest philanthropic socialites of her time, Baroness Burdett-Coutts. The occasion was commemorated in a painting by AP Tilt, now hanging in The Wellcome Institute for the History of Medicine. There is no key to aid the identification of those present. Eighteen of the guests were female and are assumed to be wives, but of the remaining seventy-four male figures, Pasteur is one of only thirty-six who have been positively identified.

As someone who has seen several photographs of James West, the author is fairly confident that he was not among the guests at Baroness Burdett-Coutts' garden party. There is no evidence to suggest that any of his Birmingham colleagues were either. Wounded pride apart, it would hardly have mattered to them. West and his colleagues would have had numerous opportunities to participate in the other festivities, dinners and outings on offer. Not only was the Baroness' party one of many organised

[94] Alex Sakula, Baroness Burdett-Coutts' Garden Party: The International Medical Congress, London, 1881; *Medical History*; 1982; 26: p.184.

events which took place during the week-long congress, it was not even the only one of its type. Private receptions and garden parties were also given at the homes of Sir James Paget of Hanover Square; Sir Thomas Spencer of Hampstead; Mr and Mrs Spencer Wells of Golder's Hill, Hampstead; Sir Joseph Hooker at Kew; Mr and Mrs Saunders at Wimbledon; Dr Wood at the Priory, Roehampton; Dr Langdon Down of Hampton as well as at the homes of Mr Alfred de Rothschild; Sir Trevor Lawrence; Lord Granville, the Foreign Minister and the Duke of Wellington.[95]

The congress was launched at the Royal College of Physicians and the first general meeting was held in St James' Hall on 3 August at 11am. His Royal Highness The Prince of Wales, His Royal Highness, the Crown Prince of Germany and Prussia plus the Archbishop of York, Cardinal Archbishop of Westminster and the Bishop of London were all present. The occasion was described by the BMJ as a conversazione which was organised by the English for the entertainment of their foreign counterparts.[96] Given at the South Kensington Museum, it outshone any previous events at the same venue by virtue of the fact that its quadrangle was lit up by electric lighting. The museum's quadrangle was not the only conference venue lit up by electricity that week. Also illuminated by electric light was the Guildhall which the Lord Mayor and the Corporation used for their Grand Reception for participants on Friday 5 August and the Museum of the Royal College of Surgeons at the Conversazione given by its president and vice president.

Few delegates would have missed the inaugural address given by Sir James Paget or papers given by some of the other eminent figures, and many, who like West were not specialists, probably listened to papers on a wide range of topics by lesser mortals. Organised trips were as varied as the papers. For those who shared West's fascination for hospitals in other parts of the country or, indeed, the world, there were two organised trips. One was to the Bethlem Convalescent Hospital at Witley in Surrey. The other was to see the new wing of the aptly named hospital, The Royal Sea-bathing Infirmary, at Margate.

The Royal Sea-bathing Infirmary was the sort of institution much admired by West and it is tempting to think that he would have gone along to take a look. Its facilities were the product of a highly ambitious scheme, as the article in the BMJ shows. The new wing consisted of 'a large tepid sea-water swimming bath; four large wards, each provided

---

[95] The Festivities of the Congress, *BMJ*; 1881; ii: p.303.
[96] Ibid., pp.303–304.

with its own separate rooms for the nurse, and lavatory; and two day rooms.' The article's author went on to describe how the new day rooms would, with the original building, form a quadrangle which was to be laid out as a garden. Attention to the prevention of hospital infection was extended to the very surfaces of the inner walls and ceilings. Constructed out of 'fire-bricks with a porcelain surface, so that every part of the internal surface, with the exception of the floor, presents a smooth face of porcelain, incapable of absorbing impurities' their magnificence must have been apparent to all. The floors were of the 'hardest teak.' Machinery for raising, heating and distributing sea-water was housed in the basement. 'The cloisters' according to the author's account were 'intended to enable the patients to take exercise and breathe the open air, protected from the wind and rain; and the roof of the four wards (was) laid out as a terrace, upwards of 200 feet in length, for the purposes of exercise, and from it a magnificent view of the sea (could) be enjoyed; the south end of the building being almost surrounded by the sea at high-water'[97] The Victorian conviction that an individual's health and well-being was not solely physiological was also reflected in the hospital's design. A chapel, spacious enough to hold 300 people, was testimony to the fact that the spiritual needs of patients had not been overlooked.

Another outing was to the famous 460 acre sewage farm at Croydon and the Beddington Female Orphan Asylum. Little was said about the latter in the *BMJ*, but when the 120 participants who accompanied Dr Alfred Carpenter moved on to the sewage farm later that day, they were given a banquet at the Old Hall, Beddington which consisted of produce from the manure-rich soils of the former.

On Saturday 6 August, about 150 delegates, accompanied by some thirty to forty ladies, witnessed the unveiling of the statue of the English physician responsible for discovering the circulation of the blood, William Harvey (1578–1657). The statue, seen by delegates at the conversazione at South Kensington days earlier, was being erected at the end of Castle Hill Avenue on the Leas in the seaside resort of Folkstone on the south coast. Sir Edward Watkin (1819–1901), railway entrepreneur, provided free transport for conference members by hiring a special train for the occasion. According to a separate article, the group was conveyed to the site by forty or fifty carriages after their arrival at Shorncliffe station. It was a 'fine, breezy and fresh' day and the procession travelled to the Leas 'amidst flags,

---

97 The Festivities of the Congress, *BMJ*; 1881; ii: p.303.

Statue of William Harvey, Folkstone. Author's photograph 2005.

decorations, and every sign of rejoicing.'[98] Some, perhaps tired of serious professional business, probably forfeited the free train ride back to London and stayed on in Folkstone instead.

Others who sought diversion from medicine or health had the option of joining a party that visited the Siemens, Brothers and Co. telegraph works at Woolwich. One hundred and fifty availed themselves of this opportunity. The group were taken initially to the cable laying ship which was due to set sail across the Atlantic some nine or ten days later. After, members of the group were conducted around the works themselves – a visit which lasted a full two hours. Once that was over, they were taken to inspect another department. There, the group saw the manufacture of electric lamps and the cables which were used to convey electricity to buildings and streets.

Another picture to commemorate the congress was a group photograph of 684 delegates. The backcloth suggests it was taken in St James' Hall on 3 August. This picture does have a key, so it is possible to say with certainty that James West was among those photographed. He is not seen standing amidst his Birmingham colleagues, but with a group of men who practised in London, Dublin and Paris. His immediate neighbours were Professor

98 Unveiling of the Statue of Harvey, at Folkstone; *BMJ*; 1881; ii: p.304.

A group photograph taken at the International Medical Congress, London,
1881. West's head is encircled. Source: Wellcome Library, London.

Quinlan of Dublin, Dr J Marion Sims (1813–83) who was resident in Paris
at the time and Dr J Scott and FT Taylor esquire of London. Professor E
Ray-Lankester, JJ Halford and NC Macnamara esquire of London were
also in close proximity to West. The survival to this day of his own copy of
a key to the photograph, suggests that West was proud to have been
photographed alongside so many distinguished members of his profession
in 1881. West was one of a contingent of thirty-five delegates from
Birmingham and its surrounding districts. The Birmingham group
included men he would have known either as neighbours or through the
various local medical societies and through his work in the town's hospitals.
Like West, they were men who held office in the town's medical societies
and who saw themselves as both active researchers and innovators. Six of
West's colleagues read papers at the conference.

Robert Saundby, a man who already had a string of publications to his
name by 1881, gave a paper on the *Histology of Granular Kidney*. Robert
Lawson Tait (1845–99), another much given to publishing, read a paper on
Recent Advances in Abdominal Surgery. Another colleague, Thomas Savage,

gave a paper on *Ophorectomy*. Savage had the misfortune to die twenty-six years later in an earthquake [99] in Kingston, Jamaica, but not before he had been President of both the Birmingham Medical Benevolent Society and the Midland Medical Society and Vice-President of the Birmingham Medical Institute. Priestley Smith (1845–1933), then ophthalmic surgeon at Queen's Hospital, read a paper entitled *On the Pathology of Glaucoma*, a subject on which he had taken the Jacksonian Prize in 1879. David Charles Lloyd Owen, (1845–1926) of The General Hospital, gave a paper on *A Case of Nystagmus* [100] *with Family History over Four Generations*. Joseph Sampson Gamgee spoke on wounds, a subject close to his heart. The subject matter of his paper, *On the Primary Union of Wounds,* had the advantage of affording him the opportunity to show the assembled company his latest gauze dressings.

Papers like these must have resulted from industry over and above the duties of hospital and private practice, but the diversions organised by the various congress committees were probably welcomed by the industrious and their less active colleagues alike. According to Sakula, it was a hot summer with a high of 97°F (36°C) having being recorded in July, but it rained on the afternoon of the Baroness's party. It was probably of little consequence. Set in twenty-one acres, the house had a substantial conservatory. Its doors stand open in the painting suggesting that visitors were free to wander in and out as they wished. Two large horse chestnut trees in full leaf would have provided additional shelter.

The reception at the Royal College of Physicians has been mentioned, as has the conversazione at The Royal College of Surgeons but there was also a dinner at the Worshipful Society of Apothecaries. A banquet was also given by the Lord Mayor at the Mansion House and there was a soirée at the Albert Hall. Special services were held at St Paul's Cathedral and in Westminster Abbey and the Crystal Palace was the venue for the final dinner of the congress. That, by itself, must have been a quite a spectacle, but there was more. The evening culminated with a fountain and fireworks display with portraits in fire of the Englishman, Sir James Paget, the French neurologist, Jean-Martin Charcot (1825–93) and the German, Professor Bernard von Langenbeck (1810–87). It was, perhaps, as much a gesture to the three official languages used in the congress – English, French and German – as it was to the eminence of the three individuals involved.

[99] It was not Thomas Savage's first trip to the West Indies according to the obituary in *The Lancet*. He was killed along with his companions, a nephew and a female friend of the family. *The Lancet*; 1907; i: 261.
[100] A disorder of the eyes involving rapid eye movements.

The programme of social events alone, would have sapped the energy of most delegates. Some of Baroness Burdett-Coutts' guests, for instance, would have squeezed her party in between a morning boat trip along the Thames and the dinner at the Worshipful Society of Apothecaries which, in turn, was followed at 9pm by the soirée at the Albert Hall. Sakula points out that the congress ended the day before the Annual Meeting of the BMA which took place in the Isle of Wight that year. If the visitors' book of that event has survived it probably contains the names of numerous men who had gone on to it directly from the congress in London.

West and his circle

James West belonged to a circle which would be considered gigantic by today's standards. His medical colleagues alone amounted to over a hundred individuals and there were non-medical friends, patients and neighbours on top of that. As a member of the town's elite, he came into close contact with Birmingham's most influential men. Individuals like George Dawson, Robert Dale, HW Crosskey, George Dixon and Joseph Chamberlain were present at dinners West attended and held positions on boards of governors of institutions with which he was involved.

He met scores of fellow practitioners through his membership of medical societies and the town's hospitals and formed close links with dozens of these men. His involvement in local societies like the Birmingham and Midlands Counties Branch of the BMA, the Midland Medical Society, The Birmingham Medical Institute and The Birmingham Medical Benevolent Society brought him into contact with numerous professional colleagues from the town and its outlying districts. Many of the key figures in the town's societies overlapped but even when this is taken into account, the number of associates West came into regular contact with through his participation in the work of these institutions was formidable.

Professional circles

The earliest records of West's membership of a medical society are in relation to the Midland Medical Society. New members were proposed by existing members and the election of West was completed on 14 October, 1868 along with that of fellow-practitioner, Dr George Fowler Boddington (1830–1902). They joined the society at a time when its officers were on the brink of making a decision on the advisability of amalgamating with the local branch of the BMA. West's integration into the affairs of the society was rapid.

The society's membership stood at sixty-nine in 1868. October 14 marked the date of the Annual Meeting and the election of new officers. West almost certainly knew most of these men already. Alfred Baker was elected to the position of president that year. As we have seen in relation to the charges brought against him by Thomas Gutteridge in the early 1850s, Baker was a surgeon at The General Hospital. Oliver Pemberton, another surgeon from The General Hospital, and Mr Samuel Alan Bindley (1809–1876) were made Baker's vice-presidents while the roles of treasurer, honorary secretaries and librarian went to Mr J Harmar (1814–90), Dr Balthazar Foster (1840–1913), Mr John St Swithin Wilders (1837–1907) and Dr Edward Mackey (1842–1906) respectively. Other members of Council consisted of Dr Willoughby Wade (1827–1906), Dr James Russell, Mr Charles J Bracey (1838–87), Mr Thomas Swain (d.1874) and Dr J Lumley Earle (1841–71). Fellows and rank and file members for that year included many men with whom West had had close connections by the time he died in 1883 – George Yates, Thomas Pretious Heslop, WH Sprotson, Joseph Sampson Gamgee and James Sawyer to name a few.

West's diary of 1883 has shed light on his relationships with professional friends in a way no other source could. He mentions numerous people by name and, of these, at least thirty-two are local medical practitioners. Even though some of the Midland Medical Society's membership of 1869/70 died before he did, sixteen of those who were West's contemporaries in 1869/70 were mentioned by him in the diary. A further three, one member of the Underhill family, Mr RC Suffield (1832–1898) and John St Swithin Wilders, (1837–1907) were close enough to West to attend his funeral.

The Midland Medical Society may have come close to an amalgamation with the local branch of the BMA in 1868, but the proposal was defeated as a result of last minute doubts. It was not long before West became directly involved in the affair. At a meeting on 23 December, 1868, Gamgee moved and Dr Johnston seconded a motion that it was not expedient to proceed further with the treaty of amalgamation. A decision was made to refer the proposal to the membership and take a vote on the issue, but the result when it came was inconclusive. The society's chairman felt he could not accept the responsibility of making a casting vote on a matter of such importance and it was left to members to decide for themselves whether or not the society should have an independent future.

Gamgee moved and Mr Yates seconded a resolve to appoint a sub-committee to consider by what means the objects for which the society

The survival of this ticket for the George Dawson Public Memorial Ceremony in 1881 strongly suggests that the Wests were amongst those gathered to remember this remarkable man. Source: JFF West Archive.

exists could best be met in future. Mr Gamgee then moved and Dr Nelson seconded a motion that the sub-committee should consist of Dr Marshall, Dr Johnston, Mr West, Mr Jordan, Mr Yates, Mr Wilders and Mr Gamgee. When they reported back on 6 January, 1869, West was their chairman. They identified the society's two main objects – to share expertise by means of papers and the exhibition of pathological specimens and to provide a well supplied reading room. The sub-committee made various recommendations. One was to buy a high quality microscope to facilitate the further study of pathological specimens and another was a resolve to appoint sub-committees to investigate specimens of particular interest. With his keen interest in pathology, these two proposals would have had great appeal to West. It is probably not fanciful to suggest that he may well have been responsible for the inclusion of this clause.

The society met fortnightly in the Birmingham Midland Institute in the late 1860s with meetings alternating between three o'clock in the afternoon and eight in the evening. West's support for the society was reflected in his regular attendance at meetings and it was not long before he was elected onto the council. The Annual Meeting of 6 October, 1869 saw Mr SA Bindley as chairman, with Mr Harmar as treasurer and Mr Wilders and Mr William Slingsby Mann (1842–1912) as honorary secretaries. Dr Mackey held office as librarian. Mann was one individual who may have been close to West already by 1869. It is known for certain that by the time West died in 1883, Mann had been his partner in private practice for many years. Alongside West, Drs Russell, JL Earle, Wade, Sawyer, Thomas Bell Elcock Fletcher, JW Keyworth, Boddington senior and Gamgee occupied seats on the newly elected council of that year.

West's first year on the council was an active one. He read two papers and exhibited four specimens. His attendance rate was high and he was one of eighty-four professionals to attend the society's inaugural lecture which was given by Dr BR Richardson at the Great Western Hotel on 21 October of that year. In common with other members, West had the right to introduce new members and propose existing members for election to the fellowship. By the end of the year, membership was up nineteen from the previous year and stood at 107. Mr John White Keyworth (d.1898/9) took the chair as president for the year 1870/1, but it was West himself who occupied it the following year. In the year of West's presidency, several office holders from his earliest days on the council remained. Harmar was West's treasurer and Mann and Sawyer were his honorary secretaries while Mackey acted as librarian. Two new members, John Bassett (1826–1892) and Ross Jordan worked alongside three colleagues from his earliest days on the council – Willoughby Wade, JW Keyworth and Bell Fletcher. The inaugural lecture of West's year in office as president – referred to as a 'conversazione' in the press – was held in the Royal Hotel, Temple Row,[101] and was given by Dr Lionel Beale FRS. Beale spoke about contagious disease germs – their nature and origin.

Following his year as the society's president, West remained an active member and held office on its council on numerous occasions. The session 1871/2 had been the first to have its annual report printed out. It is a proud document, charting the society's achievements and posting details of the next inaugural address. Fellows and members went up to 114 again during West's term as president. In 1875 West became involved in another medical society. It was a new society which was being founded thanks to the generosity of one of the town's well-known doctors, the late Dr George Fabian-Evans (1807–73). Evans had wanted to found a medical institution for the purpose of providing the town's medical professionals with a library and had entrusted his trustees to realise this dream. The funds originally amounted to £1,000 but further donations, some large, brought the project to fruition.

---

[101] The press reported that the conversazione was held in The Lovegrove Hotel.

Birmingham Medical Institute

The seven trustees of Dr Evan's will were joined by a further six medical practitioners for the purpose of bringing his vision to fruition, and it was these men who formed the original members of the committee. Most were leading figures in the Midland Medical Society. Bell Fletcher was made chairman at the first meeting on 4 February and George Harrison Evans honorary secretary. Other committee members included Alfred Baker, Samuel Berry, Samuel Bindley, Dickenson Webster Crompton, Thomas David Fabian Evans, Alexander Fleming, Thomas Heslop, Furneaux Jordan, Richard Middlemore, James Russell, and Willoughby Francis Wade. James West was one of forty-five individuals on the first list of donors [102] who contributed towards a building fund to house the newly founded Institute. Donations ranged from £1/1/– to £100. The twelve individuals who gave donations of £100, were all well-known local medical practitioners. They include John Birt Davies, Bell Fletcher, Thomas Heslop, John Archer, Alfred Baker, Samuel Berry, Dickenson Crompton, Thomas Chavasse, James Russell and Willoughby Wade. Seven, including Furneaux Jordan, Oliver Pemberton, Samuel Bindley, George Harrison Evans, TDF Evans and Richard Middlemore donated £50 or just over. James West, Robert Lawson Tait, Dr James Johnston, and Charles J Bracey all gave £21 while Joseph Sampson Gamgee, Samuel H Agar (b.1830),[103] Dr Thomas Savage and Dr Edwin Rickards gave 10 guineas. The total collected from the forty-five donors amounted to £1,938/3/–

West was directly involved in the fledgling institute right from the start. He attended the first meeting on 4 February, 1875 as well as the second a day later. With twenty-one others he was placed on a special committee to admit the first members of the Institute. Not surprisingly, the thirteen committee men together with the twenty-one additional committee members were comprised, for the most part, of men whose names were already familiar in the town's institutions.

What should have been a time of satisfaction and harmony for the Institute's founding fathers, soon descended into discord. A furore erupted when the town's homœopathic practitioners, and in particular, Dr Gibbs Blake, donated money to the building fund and would, it was assumed, demand membership of the new Institute. By 15 February, the contentious issue of whether or not to admit them was brought into the public domain by Oliver Pemberton, whose objection to the idea was

[102] *Midland Counties Herald*, Thursday 10 February, 1875. (BCL).
[103] Samuel H Agar was head of Burman House Asylum, Wooton Wawen, Warwickshire.

expressed in an angry letter to *The Lancet*.[104] The journal supported Pemberton, as did many of his medical brethren. The Institute's chairman, Bell Fletcher and George H Evans, honorary secretary, defended the committee's acceptance of the donations and made a case for admitting the town's homœopaths into the Institute. In their letter to *The Lancet* [105] they pointed out that the individuals concerned were all medically qualified and argued that, that on those grounds alone, their exclusion could not be justified. Pemberton was quick to retaliate [106] and set about winning support from professional colleagues by calling a meeting and insisting on a vote.

The meeting took place on 31 March. It attracted ninety-one members and was widely reported in the local press. Three apologies were sent in. One, sent by Dr James Johnston, asked for his vote supporting the inclusion of homœopaths to be registered. He said 'the honest scepticism so frequently engendered by the earnest study of our – as yet undefined – art is the blossom which develops into the full fruit of toleration in others of that from which we entirely disagree.'[107] Johnston's view was almost certainly in accordance with the majority. He did not agree with the ideology or methods advocated by homœopaths but that was no justification for denying them membership.

It was an episode that must have made many very uncomfortable. Pemberton was a surgeon at The General Hospital at the time, but he also had connections with Queen's College. Like West, he lived in Edgbaston on the Hagley Road, and he mixed in the same circles. West was among the ninety-one individuals who attended the meeting that day, and although he did interject on two occasions, he seems to have been content to leave the debate to others.

Pemberton claimed the committee had allowed homœopaths to think they could enjoy membership thanks to the donations they had given, without having first consulted their professional brethren, and he insisted that he had found considerable support for barring their admission amongst his colleagues. He said that he thought the committee had acted wrongly, although he made a point of saying that he did not question their honour or integrity. Pemberton made the supposition that the committee had acted as a body in accepting the donation of Dr Blake and others, but

---

[104] Letter from Oliver Pemberton, *The Lancet;* 15 February, 1875; i: pp.3–4.
[105] Letter from Bell Fletcher and George Harrison Evans, *The Lancet;* 24 February, 1875; i: pp.5–6.
[106] Letter from Oliver Pemberton, *The Lancet;* 1 March, 1875; i: pp.6–7.
[107] *The Birmingham Daily Gazette*, 1 April, 1878. (BCL).

this was shown to be wrong minutes later, when Thomas Heslop claimed sole responsibility for having asked Dr Blake for a contribution.

One of the remarks made by James West indicates that he was at least prepared to be open-minded. His comment, recorded for posterity by the press, raised a laugh among the assembled company.[108] 'Mr West' it reported 'was quite certain that if the homœopathists did not do so much good as they (regular practitioners) did, they did not do so much harm.' Pemberton's chief opponents that day were Alfred Baker, Thomas Heslop and Josiah Clarkson (1818–78). Baker summed up his words by saying 'Upon their judgement that day depended the question, whether Birmingham should lean upon generous, free-handed, and free-hearted liberality – (hear, hear) – or whether it should be governed by the narrow views of a party and a factious clique – (loud and prolonged applause).' Clarkson said that he had been in accord with Pemberton initially but that on mature reflection had come to realise that the only acceptable course of action was to deplore restrictions on the grounds that to do otherwise would mean that 'they would simply be the disciples of bigotry and intolerance.'[109] His remarks too were met with calls of 'hear, hear.'

Thomas Heslop opened his remarks by alluding to a claim made by Pemberton to the effect that he, Pemberton, was not in the habit of changing his long-held convictions. Pemberton had backed up his assertion that his views were steadfast by describing an incident which had occurred some twenty years ago at The General Hospital. He had asserted that he had been instrumental in ejecting his own uncle and Mr John Cadbury from the hospital board on account of their suggestion that a number of hospital beds should be allocated to the homœopathists. He pointed out that he had not spoken to his uncle since that day.

Heslop, on the other hand, set out to emphasise the extent to which his own views had changed over time. He said that he had been told by 'one of the most eminent, one of the most able, and one of the most charitable men' he would come to regret the first letter he ever wrote to the press. It had been a letter denouncing his homœopathic brethren. Heslop went on to say that he was glad to have the opportunity of refuting his earlier prejudices. 'He was not responsible' he said 'for the thoughts that he had when fresh from the benches of prejudiced leaders hounding down gentlemen who differed from them.' One of Heslop's concluding remarks referred to Pemberton's reluctance to allow the town's homœopaths access

---

[108] *The Birmingham Daily Gazette*, 1 April, 1878. (BCL).
[109] Ibid.

to the Institute's library. 'Mr Pemberton' he declared 'had never imagined the overwhelming ridicule which would attach to a person who should dare to close a library against people holding different opinions.'[110]

Ultimately, Birmingham's homœopaths were allowed to take up membership of the Birmingham Medical Institute and the matter was laid to rest. Pemberton, himself, was elected to a committee of twenty-five officers of the Institute at its second Annual Meeting on 30 March, 1876, alongside Heslop, Baker, Johnston and others who had opposed his views on homœopaths. He had originally donated £52/10/0d to the Institute's building fund and there is no evidence to suggest that he demanded, or got, a refund. It is not acknowledged in the hand written lists, but the scribe also failed to mention West's original donation. The omission of Pemberton's name is just as likely to be an indication that the source is flawed. In any case, the hand written records of 1881 show that Pemberton did make a gift of £21 in that year.

One year on from its inception, the Institute was not only viable, but had a membership of 172, with twenty-four applications for membership awaiting consideration. For Oliver Pemberton a family tragedy lay just a few years ahead. In 1879, the newspapers reported the suicide of his second son, Thomas, at the age of twenty-three.[111] A young man destined for his father's profession, Thomas Pemberton shot himself shortly before completing his finals. He left a note saying that he feared that he would not be able to fulfil his promise – a sentiment which had no justification according to his tutors.

A male member of the medical profession wrote in 1880 of the scandalous exclusion of women from the forthcoming International Medical Congress which, as we have seen, took place in London in 1881.[112] The two female doctors who applied for membership of the Birmingham Medical Institute in 1880 faced no such prejudice. The Institute's officers[113] together with the twenty committee members voted their applications through without debate. The two women, Ann Elizabeth Clarke and Annie Reay Barker, the officers agreed, were fully qualified members of the profession and therefore entitled to the same rights as their male colleagues.

---

[110] Ibid.

[111] *Birmingham Post*, 12 May, 1879. (BCL).

[112] The article, though written by a French medical practitioner, is anonymous and finishes with the words – Le Progrès Médical. *BMR;* 1880; 9: Page following 383.

[113] Mr John Archer was the Institute's president for the year 1879–80 with Dr James Russell and Mr JV Solomon acting as vice-presidents. Archer's successor was Mr Crompton who had Drs Wade and T Underhill as his vice-presidents.

*The Birmingham Medical Institute in the 1960s. Reproduced by the kind
permission of the General Committee of the Birmingham Medical Institute.*

No doubt the irony of denying women membership when it had been
offered to their medically qualified homœopathic brethren would have been
in the minds of all involved.

The admission of women was not the only significant act of 1880. It was
also the year in which the new building was opened. The occasion, which
took place on 17 December, was marked by an address by Sir Risdon
Bennett (1809–81), President of the Royal College of Physicians,[114] and the
task of declaring the building open fell to Alderman Richard Chamberlain,
the town's mayor. More than seventy members, West included, joined the
dignitaries and eminent men and women of Birmingham for a celebratory
dinner at the Grand Hotel in the evening.

By the time the Institute had reached its second anniversary it could
boast a membership of 188 and a library of 6,826 volumes, 1,365 of which
were duplicates. Before West died in May, 1883, he instructed his executors
to give fifty medical books from his own library to the Birmingham Medical
Institute. In the event they took thirty-eight. Gifts and bequests of books
helped to keep the bookshelves of the Institute's library well stacked, but its

---

[114] James Risdon Bennett was responsible for Jacob and Ann Wards at St Thomas' Hospital when
West was a student at St Thomas' Medical School. That he knew West personally is certain. He was
one of the staff at the hospital who wrote a reference for West when he sought the post at Queen's
Hospital. The reference has survived to this day.

librarians also bought newly published books and journals. In the year of West's death, the library had 10,176 books, of which 2,126 were duplicates. By the 1890s it also had a comprehensive list of surgical instruments which could be loaned by members for a modest fee. West did not live long enough to reap the benefits of reading the Institute's books and journals under electric light, but many of his contemporaries did after an electrical supply was installed at a cost of £58/8/6d in 1895.

The Institute continued to flourish and has survived to this day albeit with a somewhat different purpose and in a different building. West was on the council in 1876 and again in 1881 and was elected to the position of vice-president on 29 March, 1883, a little under eight weeks before his death. The election took place while West was still in Italy. West was not the only one who died in office. Joseph Sampson Gamgee, who died in 1886, occupied the chair as president of the Institute in 1885–6.

Non-medical societies and festivals

As we have seen, West belonged to two non-medical societies – the Birmingham Dramatic and Literary Club and the Society of Freemasons. He was admitted as a freemason to Lodge 482 in 1867, which met at St James' Chapter in Handsworth, a suburb of Birmingham.

Freemasons played a major role when the foundation stone for the new wing of Queen's Hospital, Birmingham, was laid on 4 December, 1871. Secret society or no, their presence was anything but secret. A procession of over 400 freemasons representing numerous lodges made the journey from Athol Lodge in Severn Street, Birmingham, to the site adjoining the existing hospital in Bath Row. As Provincial Grand Master of the Freemasons of Warwickshire, Lord Leigh, a man with a long standing if not always happy attachment to Queen's, performed the ceremony albeit rather later than expected. He was also the guest of honour at a luncheon for VIPs afterwards. One newspaper report on the event named twenty-three individuals before its final etceteras.[115] Apart from the Chairman, Lord Leigh, and the man behind the funding of the new extension, Joseph Sampson Gamgee, the party included the surgeons James West and Furneaux Jordan; the industrialists GF Muntz (also a Mason) and Mr T Avery; the pioneers of education in Birmingham, Mr George Dixon MP and Mr Charles Vince; the Bishop of the diocese, The Reverend Canon Wilkinson; the leading figures of the town's Civic Gospel, Mr RW Dale, Mr George Dawson and HW Crosskey as well as other members of the clergy and a number of military men.

---

[115] *Daily Post*. 5 December, 1871. (BCL).

The event was covered by all of the town's newspapers, most in considerable detail. Long speeches were quoted in full, and *The Daily Gazette* even the quoted West's words when he proposed a toast to the Chairman, Lord Leigh. The paper also gave the names of various other medical professionals present. Its report, for instance, shows that Drs Fleming, Fletcher and Langford, and Mssrs WS Mann and H Sprotson were also at the luncheon. *The Daily Gazette* put the number present at between three and four hundred individuals, and indicated that the party included both ladies and gentlemen.

West's Freemason's certificate has survived but, apart from a couple of clues in the diary, little is known about his involvement with the society. One entry in the diary indicates that he lent money to the surgeon Henry Sprotson, a man who was described in both *Edgbastonia* and his obituary in *The Lancet* as a Mason, and another records his promise of 'a guinea for the Masonic pupils' aid fund.'[116] It is but little, but it does show that he maintained his affiliation with the Masons right through to the end of his life.

THE ARTS

Birmingham's middle classes could indulge their taste in the arts not only in the town's theatres and its concert hall, but through membership of the town's literary clubs. Where a club's archive has survived, we can both identify its members and find out the extent of their interest and involvement. From *Edgbastonia* and *Faces and Places,* the magazines which documented the lives of the town's illustrious inhabitants, we may learn of one person's collection of paintings or his artistic abilities or of another's library or literary tastes.

Music

West participated in informal musical making with friends, went to concerts, sought out and appreciated the visual arts and enjoyed reading. All four interests are alluded to in the diary. He may have left piano playing to his wife, Sarah, but, as the following entry in the diary shows, he was willing to sing even when the conditions were far from perfect. 'The duet from Verdi's Macbeth and the song of Noel (Dvorák) was sung' he wrote 'and then I being asked to sing gave There You'll Remember Me to the accompaniment of Cap. P d'Amore who tried his best to keep to my tune but was very far from it all the time.'[117] West made sixteen references to

---

[116] JFF West, Diary; 24 January, 1883. (JFF West Archive).
[117] Ibid., 29 March, 1883. Written in Castellammare, Italy.

music altogether in his final diary. Some, like the one above, relate to amateur music making while others refer to concerts and the opera.

The best known series of concerts hosted by Birmingham were those which comprised the Triennial Music Festival programmes. From their inception in 1768 until their demise in 1912, they were fund-raising concerts in aid of the General Hospital. Two composers, George Frederick Handel and Felix Mendelssohn, dominated the programmes during West's time in Birmingham. The programme included works by Handel from the onset. Sung at every festival, the Messiah was firm favourite, but the programmes frequently included one of Handel's other oratorios or cantatas as well. Mendelssohn was himself, a great admirer of Handel. From 1837 until his death in 1847, Mendelssohn both composed for, and conducted concerts at the Triennial Festivals, but it was his oratorio, Elijah, premiered in August, 1846 which attained the greatest acclaim. Like Messiah, it became one of the annual staples. That said, the festival organisers did not neglect the works of other celebrated composers. Thanks to the festival and, of course, other series like it, the people of Birmingham had access to performances of the greatest musical works ever written and the opportunity to listen to outstanding performers. There were ten Triennial Festivals during West's time in Birmingham. For a man with a proven interest in music, it is inconceivable that he did not take advantage of them.

Eighteen eighty-three was not one of Birmingham's renowned Triennial Music Festival years, but there were numerous concerts nonetheless. The diary proves that West and his family went to the series of concerts organised by Percy Harrison as well as those given by the Festival Choral Society and The Birmingham Amateur Harmonic Association. Any Birmingham music lover who went to those, would almost certainly have gone to the concerts which made up the programme for Birmingham's Triennial Music Festivals as well. West says he went to a Festival Choral Society performance of Faust by Hector Berlioz in The Town Hall on Thursday 1 February, 1883.[118] Cast and orchestra were conducted by Mr Stockley. Miss Mary Davies sang the role of Margaret and Mr Edward Lloyd sang Faust while Mssrs Ludwig and Lander sang the parts of Mephistopheles and Brander respectively.

Described as a quasi private subscription series, the Birmingham Amateur Harmonic Association offered subscribers attractions over and above its regular series of concerts. One was an annual excursion. It is

---

[118] Ibid., 1 February, 1883.

reasonable to suggest that since West and his family attended the concert series they probably also availed themselves of the Association's annual excursions. They were lavish occasions if the local press reports are anything to go by. In 1884, for instance, the outing involved a day's sightseeing tour of the Peak District. For the price of 12/6d per head, subscribers and their families travelled by a special train to Rowsley some two and a half miles south east of Bakewell. From there they were first transferred by a series of carriages to the nearby Haddon Hall and from there to Bakewell for lunch at one or other of two hotels – The Castle or The Royal Oak. Once lunch was over, participants were driven over to visit one of the country's finest stately homes, that of the Dukes of Devonshire at Chatsworth. After that, the group was conveyed by carriage to Matlock Bath, a village a mile south of Matlock itself, in order to dine at the Royal Hotel. All that remained to round off the day's activities was the trip back to Birmingham through pleasant countryside which again, was by special train.

West had tickets for one of the Birmingham Amateur Harmonic Association concerts on Thursday 1 March, 1883, but noted in the diary that he was too tired to go to it.[119] He had intended taking his wife, Sarah, and daughter, Marion Lucy, then aged fourteen, but he sent their tickets along with his own on to friends instead. His unwritten assumption that wife and daughter should sacrifice their tickets on his account and their presumed acceptance of that assumption, probably means they also missed the Birmingham Amateur Harmonic Association outing to the Peak District later that year because of mourning his loss some weeks earlier.

Fatigue did not interfere with West's plans to attend the last of Harrison's series of concerts on Thursday 6 March. The concert took place in Birmingham's Town Hall, a fine building designed to resemble a Greek Temple. Ticket prices ranged from 3/6d to 7/6d for reserved seats according to *The Birmingham Post*, while unreserved seats were priced at 1/– or 2/6d. The advertisement suggests that the artists were not the only attraction. Those who attended the concert that evening would have experienced the novelty of seeing the Town Hall illuminated by electric light. West took his sister, Fanny, with him to the concert that evening. The orchestral parts were performed by the seventy-one strong Manchester orchestra, the Hallé, known at the time simply as Halle's band. Its conductor, the great Charles Hallé, presided over an orchestra comprised of some of the best musicians from across Europe. By

---

[119] JFF West, Diary; 1 March, 1883. (JFF West Archive).

recruiting musicians from Germany, France and Italy – a contingent which made up just over a third of its otherwise British forces – Hallé had created an orchestra that was already renowned in 1883. The concert was not purely an orchestral one, though. Instrumental solos were performed by Charles Hallé, himself, who played the piano and the woman who became his second wife, the famous violinist, Mme Norman-Neruda. The equally well known baritone, Mr Charles Santley and Miss Orridge sang works by Schubert, Pepusch and Handel. When West wrote up his diary on his return home that evening, he recorded that it was 'a good affair'[120] thanks to the soloists Madam Norman-Neruda, Mr Santley and Miss Orridge. *The Birmingham Post*'s critic thought it was a good affair too, although he claimed that Hallé had not stretched his audience as much as he usually did.

West also sought out opportunities to listen to music when he went to the Continent for a month on 9 March, 1883 with Sarah. Not content to settle down in their London hotel for an early night in readiness for their

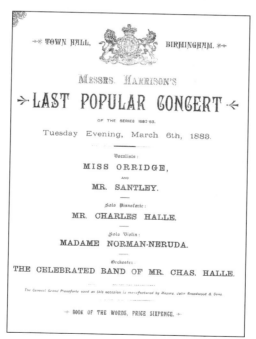

Programme for the concert attended by West on 6 March, 1883. Source: By kind permission Birmingham Central Library.

---

[120] Ibid., 6 March, 1883.

journey to Paris the next day, West and his wife met up with a good friend, the novelist Frederick William Robinson and his wife, to go to a performance of Gilbert and Sullivan's opera, *Iolanthe*. It was, he reported 'a poor affair.'[121] Fortunately, West and Sarah fared better the following day in Paris. They did not even arrive at their hotel until 6.30pm but, after a hearty meal, they had sufficient energy left to go to the Grand Opera and see what West considered to be a fine performance of *William Tell* by Rossini.[122] Most of the remaining music they listened to on their Continental trip was either informal or heard by chance, but the sung mass they heard in the Vatican on Easter Sunday 25 March, was probably by design.[123]

John Charles Huxley (1852–1926), one of the town's homœopathic practitioners, was also a music lover,[124] as was Alfred Carter (1849–1918), who started the College Vocal and Instrumental Society in his years at University College, London.[125] Gilbert Barling (1855–1940) who, as we have seen, assisted West in an operation for strangulated hernia on 10 February, 1883, and who went on to become Sir Gilbert as well as Dean of Medicine and Vice-Chancellor at the University of Birmingham, was another enthusiastic amateur musician. Barling was a musician and a singer of distinction according to *Edgbastonia*.[126] He took a leading part in *The Sorcerer* by Gilbert and Sullivan in 1885 and was instrumental in both organising and participating in concerts for hospital patients and staff.

Visual arts

There is no way of knowing how discriminating West was when it came to the visual arts, but the diary proves that he appreciated both paintings and sculpture and knew what he liked. On 6 February West took a look at Jaffray's new picture by Hall [127] at the Joint Stock Bank. His remark 'it makes those by Munro [?] look ridiculous'[128] leaves us in no doubt that he approved of what he saw. His interest in the art he saw in Italy was not restricted to the great works of the Renaissance either. The pages of the

---

[121] JFF West, Diary; 9 March, 1883. (JFF West Archive).

[122] Ibid., 10 March, 1883.

[123] Ibid., 25 March, 1883. West recorded that although the singing was good, the organ was poor. The author assumes it was the playing that was poor, rather than the instrument.

[124] *Edgbastonia*; 1900; XX: p 164. (BCL).

[125] Ibid., 1899; X1X: p 182.

[126] Ibid., p 65.

[127] Probably a portrait by Sydney Prior Hall (1842–1922) of the Scottish newspaper proprietor, John Jaffray (b.1819) who lived in a Park Grove, a mansion on the Bristol Road, Edgbaston.

[128] JFF West, Diary; 6 February, 1883. (JFF West Archive).

diary abound with references to art and architecture, both ancient and modern. West and Sarah met up with the distinguished English-born Dominican priest, Peter Paul Mackey OP SMT [129] (1851–1935), during their visit to Rome in 1883. The brother of West's former colleague, Edward Mackey,[130] Peter Paul became an expert on Roman History during the fifty-five years he spent in Italy. He had been summoned to Rome to work in the preparation of the Leonine definitive works of St Thomas Aquinas in the first place, but his interest in archæology resulted in his elevation to a Chair of Archæology at the Pontifical University of St Thomas in Rome. As West says in the diary (1 April) 'Father Mackey joined us and he kindly acted as our cicerone during the day. We visited the Forum and the palace of the Cæsars and by his knowledge we got a much better idea of the various wealths than when going with an ordinary guide.'

The trip to Italy provided West and his wife with the opportunity to see numerous art treasures and they embraced the chance with enthusiasm. They were rather disappointed in Guido's Beatrice and Raphael's Fornarina in the Palace Barberini in Rome (21 March), but marvelled at the collection of statues, bronzes and pictures in the collection housed in the Museo Borbonico in Naples. West said that the Toro Farnese found at Rome and the Hercules were the finest he had ever seen (26 March). Raphael and Titian, West wrote were 'splendidly represented' in Florence (3 April) and he said that the Lateran Museum in Rome contained 'fine sculptures and exquisite mosaics but nothing great re. pictures' (22 March). West viewed Michelangelo's statue of Moses in St Pietro in Vincoli, with a surgeon's eye for detail and declared it 'a grand piece of artistic anatomy' (25 March).

West pronounced the architectural merits of St Croce in Florence unequal to those of London's Westminster Abbey when he saw it on 3 April, but was in awe of St Peter's, Rome when he visited it on 19 March. 'Went to St Peter's… and was much delighted with the beauty of its proportions and the lightness and elegance of the internal decorations. Its size from the outside does not appear very great but within you realise how large it is. It

---

[129] The OP refers to the Order of Preachers and denotes a member of the Dominican Order. SMT stands for Sacred Master in Theology and was the highest award given by the Dominicans. Mackey gained the award in 1892, nine years after West met him in Rome. Mackey was also a keen amateur photographer. Many of his photographs can still be seen on The British School at Rome website.

[130] West's former colleague, the surgeon Edward Mackey, was the brother of Peter Paul. There is no way of knowing for certain that the brother referred to here is Edward or another brother who had remained in Birmingham. Edward had moved to Brighton by the time West went to Italy in 1883 but he was almost certainly in regular contact with Birmingham relatives and colleagues.

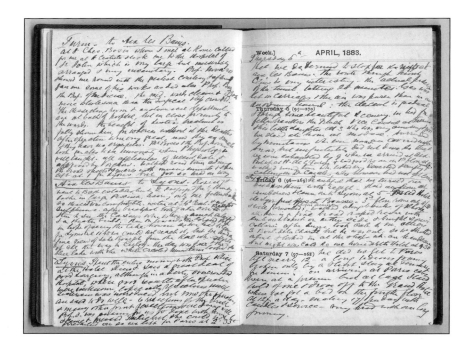

Page from the diary of James Fitzjames Fraser West, April, 1883.
Source: JFF West Archive.

took Tadie 80 seconds to walk round one of the pillars which support the dome. The colossal monuments strike one with wonder and yet they are quite in character with the building.' Robert William Edginton (1850–1935), who would have known West while a student at Queen's College, had more than a passing appreciation of architecture. The account given on his life in *Edgbastonia* says that initially Edginton's inclinations were divided between architecture and medicine and that he was even involved in the restoration of Worcester Cathedral.[131] Edginton was not the only colleague with artistic talent. Alfred Baker, a man West knew through a number of different channels, put his gifts to use as a surgeon when he executed pathological drawings for Joseph Hodgson of The General Hospital. Baker's talent had been recognised by his teachers at King Edward's School, Birmingham. He had been encouraged by them to pursue a career as an artist, but faced with parental disapproval, he became a surgeon instead.[132]

---

[131] *Edgbastonia*; 1897; XVII: p 238. (BCL).
[132] *Birmingham Faces and Places*; 1893: p.163 (BCL).

Languages, ancient and modern

Given the emphasis placed on classical education in nineteenth century England, it is probably true to say that all of West's medical brethren were conversant with Latin and Ancient Greek. In addition, most would have studied at least one modern language. French was the language of choice at most schools. Joseph Sampson Gamgee spoke several European languages and was fluent in both Italian, which he was said to have spoken like a native, and French,[133] while *Edgbastonia* claimed, for West, complete mastery of Latin and several foreign languages. West said in his paper on German surgery that, while his knowledge of German was limited, he did speak French. His deficiency in German did not stop him from translating Langenbeck's monograph on gun-shot wounds of the hip-joint. The obituaries which appeared on West's death in both the *BMJ* and *The Lancet* said this was an able translation, and one which had been 'executed much to the satisfaction of the eminent German surgeon.'[134]

Only two of the medical textbooks given to the Birmingham Medical Institute by West's widow, Sarah, have survived to this day, but the full list, recorded in the Institute's minute books, shows that of those selected by the librarian seven were French and one was in German. West would have used his proficiency in French and German not only to read books and papers in those languages, but to converse with his foreign colleagues during his many trips abroad. He also used his knowledge of languages in purely social situations, as the diary shows. 'We were...too tightly packed to be very comfortable' West wrote of a journey he made with Sarah between San Remo and Pisa 'However all our fellow travellers fortunately were very agreeable and chatted in French all the way.'[135]

West and his colleagues would also have been well-drilled in the study of Classical Literature during their school days. Some maintained a strong interest in the classics and were renowned for their libraries as well as their expertise in these subjects. Thomas Heslop, still remembered in the University of Birmingham on account of the gift he made to them of 11,000 books from his own personal library, had a keen interest in Classical Studies. Oliver Pemberton's principle tastes during his schooldays at King Edward's School lent towards Literary Studies and Classical Literature. It was an interest he continued to foster. The account of his life which appeared in *Edgbastonia* alludes to his collection of rare books and his

[133] Obituary, *BMJ;* 1886; ii: p.604.
[134] Obituary, *BMJ;* 1883; i: p.1097.
[135] JFF West, Diary; 1883. Train journey from San Remo to Pisa. 16 March, 1883. (JFF West Archive).

loaded bookshelves and goes on to say that Pemberton even had libraries in more than one house.[136]

Literature

The surgeon, William Bates (1820–84), whose career in medicine did not even commence until he reached the age of fifty-four, was hailed by *Edgbastonia* as 'essentially a scholarly man' with 'unquestionably, a larger knowledge of English literature than most living men ....Shakespear (sic) was as well known to him as the alphabet.'[137] His scholarship in French was said to be so extensive that 'he was often consulted by natives of France as to the meaning of French words and the grammatical construction of French sentences.'[138] The extravagance of *Edgbastonia's* homage to Bates' abilities in French and English literature is matched by their effusive account of his knowledge of the Classics. Exaggerated though these claims may have been, Bates was indeed an authority on the arts and his first appointment was as a Professor of Classics at Sydenham College. It is no exaggeration to say that if Bates is remembered today it is through his role as an author in the periodical, *Notes and Queries*. The author of the article on Bates in *Edgbastonia* devoted just a small fraction of the six pages he wrote on him to an account of his career in medicine.

James West almost certainly knew William Bates. Bates lectured at Queen's College after its amalgamation with its rival college, Sydenham, before he entered the medical profession in 1874. The two men shared an interest in the arts and, for the last nine years of West's life, a profession. Bates was one of the Edgbaston set, and both West and Bates belonged to the Birmingham Medical Institute and the Midland Medical Society in the 1870s and early 80s. Bates' work for *Notes and Queries* would have brought him into intimate contact with the literary circle of James Fraser, father of James Fitzjames Fraser West. *Edgbastonia's* account of Bates states that his contributions to that particular periodical would, if brought together, amount to several large volumes. In 1874, Bates edited the quarto edition of the *Maclise Portrait Gallery of Illustrious Literary Characters*, based on a series of loosely caricatural portraits of eminent men and women who lived and worked in the first half of the nineteenth century. Bates was also responsible for an extended edition of the 'Portrait Gallery' which was published in 1883. The original portraits appeared in *'Fraser's Magazine'* in

---

[136] *Edgbastonia*; 1889; 1X: pp.4–5. (BCL).

[137] Ibid., 1884; 1V: pp.145–6.

[138] Ibid., p.145.

the second half of the 1830s, during the time when it was edited by West's father, James Fraser. Most of the original eighty-one sketches were executed by the artist, Daniel Maclise.

Bates' involvement with the project would have started well after the death of James Fraser but one picture he would go on to reproduce was *The Fraserians* which, as we have seen in Chapter One, included a portrait of West's father. Seated in the foreground and in profile, Fraser surreptitiously reveals the artist's name which he has been concealing in his coat tails. Fraser's group consisted of twenty-eight members of the intelligentsia. Most, but not all, were well-known literati. Thomas Carlyle (1795–1881), Samuel Taylor Coleridge (1772–1834) and William Makepeace Thackery (1811–63) were perhaps the most renowned writers who belonged to the Fraserians, but the circle also included William Maginn (1793–1842) – poet, journalist and writer who was also co-founder of *Fraser's Magazine*, Sir David Brewster (1781–1868) Scottish physicist, William Dunlop (1792–1848) army surgeon and writer, and Robert Macnish (1802–37), physician and author. It is doubtful that Bates knew West was Fraser's son, but West did, and he must have known of Bates' involvement with the enterprise. If he had not heard about it through any other channels, *Edgbastonia* itself, published an article on the work Bates was doing in The Portrait Gallery in February, 1883.[139] It included the picture alluded to above.

All of this must have made West, his mother, and his half-sister, Fanny de la Hunt, decidedly tense. West had lied about his paternity when he married Sarah Hammond Sellers by modifying his father's name to James Fraser West, and his avoidance of the 'Fitzjames Fraser' component of his name after his move to Birmingham, indicates that his abandonment of it was deliberate. One thing is certain, is that as far as Sarah was concerned, James West got away with the deception during his own lifetime.

James Fraser, himself, had exercised discretion in his acknowledgement of the son he had fathered as we saw in Chapter One and, by dying in 1841 at the age of thirty-seven, when his son was just eight, took the secret to an early grave. The Fraser family were just as eager as James West and his mother, Mary, to avoid revelations about any Fraser offspring born out of wedlock. James West, his mother and Fanny also took the secret to the grave, but it was probably evidence which had lain hidden amongst their effects that aroused Sarah's doubts and led her to track down James Fraser's surviving kin for confirmation of her suspicions. The survival of

---

[139] Ibid., 1883; pp.18–19.

letters written by John Fraser, brother of James, to Sarah dating from 1889 and 1890, prove that she did ultimately discover the truth. John Fraser was somewhat evasive to start with, but when he was made aware that Sarah could only be satisfied by a clear admission he finally confessed to his knowledge of the affair. In his final letter his words are unequivocal. 'I believe' he writes 'Mr James Fraser left a son, named after his mother James —— West. Yours truly, J Fraser.'[140]

Like his father, West was very partial to literature. He was an active member of the *Birmingham Dramatic Club* and he referred to books he was reading in his diary. One entry refers to Frederick William Robinson's new book, *Women are Strange and other Stories*,[141] which he says he read from 4 till 7am on Tuesday 13 February.[142] Robinson sent West a copy of the book on 2 February. West describes the book as being a collection of short stories of which *Women are Strange* is the chief. He must have dipped into it immediately, because he goes on to say 'full of humour and with a keen insight into human nature.'[143]

Frederick Robinson lived in Lambeth, London, with his wife and ten children. He described himself on the 1881 census as a 'literature novelist.' There was nothing fanciful about the claim. The British Library has some forty-seven volumes of novels by Frederick Robinson and there are allusions to two more. One, *Female Life in Prison. By a Prison Matron (ie. FW Robinson)* had such popular appeal that it went into four editions. It was not the only book to run to more than one edition. There were others that went into three editions and several had 'by the author of......' on the title page. Less sensational than *Female Life in Prison*, *Women are Strange* was also intended for the mass market. It was one of many. Other titles include such gems as *Owen a Waif*, *Grandmother's Money*, *Her Face was her Fortune*, *The Wrong that was Done* and *Memoirs of Jane Cameron. Female Convict by a Prison Matron (ie. FW Robinson)*.

Robinson was active as a writer between 1862 and 1898. Still, it must have been difficult for him to clothe, feed and educate his children out of the proceeds of his books alone. He had just two servants in 1881, which suggests that he was not an affluent man, but he did have sufficient reserves to leave an estate worth £2,840/6/9d when he died in 1901. Robinson was a personal friend of the Wests. He acted as a witness when Sarah registered the deeds

---

[140] 24, November, 1890. (JFF West Archive).
[141] FW Robinson, *Women are Strange and Other Stories*. (London: Chatto and Windus, 1883).
[142] JFF West, Diary; Monday 12 February, 1883. (JFF West Archive).
[143] Ibid., Friday 2 February, 1883.

Jump Farm. Source: By kind permission Barnsley Archives.
Copyright of Arthur Clayton.

for Jump Farm in 1875 and, as we have seen, both she and James met up with him and his wife in London en route to the Continent on 9 March, 1883. Robinson's name even shares the distinction with that of John Kershaw of being in the very last sentence of James West's diary. His parting words 'Received letters from Fred Robinson and J Kershaw declining to my regret invitation to the Shakespeare Festival'[144] were words of disappointment.

Birmingham Dramatic Club

West's involvement with the *Birmingham Dramatic Club* was considerable. Some *Birmingham Dramatic Club* archive has survived, although it is flawed and lacks detail. Nevertheless, it does provide information about when and where members met and what went on at meetings as well as giving some indication as to who its members were. It is not clear when West took up membership, although his first paper, *Life and Works of Abraham Cowley* is recorded as having been delivered on 15 November, 1873. Two years later, as Vice-President, West gave a paper entitled *Life and some of the Plays of Ben Jonson*. The archive shows that West also read papers on the plays of J Thomson (1877) and on *Erasmus in Praise of Folly* (1883). The latter has survived in manuscript and is the JFF West archive, and a further paper which went unrecorded in the official club records has been preserved through publication. This paper, *Shakespeare from a Surgeon's Point of View*, was delivered to club members at the annual celebration of Shakespeare's birthday in the spring of 1881, the year when West held office as president.

---

[144] Ibid., 17 April, 1883.

The solicitor, Samuel Dinsdale Balden (b.1865) photographed in 1895 during his time in office as a councillor. Born in Acock's Green in the same year as West's firstborn son, he was later prosecuted for fraud. Source: By kind permission Birmingham Central Library.

The rules of 1877, state that exclusive of honorary members, membership should be restricted to no more than thirty. Meetings took place on the second Saturday in each month from September to May inclusive at 6pm with one additional gathering in the summer. Members ate together before papers were read for a cost of not in excess of 3/6d. The club had no fixed venue and incidental expenses were covered by an annual subscription of 2/6d. Although it was an exclusively male membership in West's day, members came from all walks of life. West was not the only medical man, but they were in the minority. Robert Lawson Tait was Vice-President in 1874–5 and President in 1875–6, the year West was Vice-President. Other medical colleagues included David Charles Lloyd Owen, Thomas Savage, James Hickenbotham, Francis W Underhill and Ross Jordan. All held positions as either vice-president or president in their turn. Even though his knowledge and interest in both literature and drama were legendary, William Bates, it seems, was not a member.

Non-medical members included Major TH Gem, solicitor; RH Burman, reflector manufacturer; Edward W Badger, newspaper proprietor; Charles John Baptiste Duchemin, professor of music; Arthur W Adams, school master; Alfred Gosling, auctioneer and James Rodgers, pearl button maker. Another was Samuel Dinsdale Balden (b.1865), solicitor, who was later prosecuted for fraud. West and his wife were close to Balden. An exact contemporary of West's son Walter he, too, was born in Acock's Green. James and Sarah christened their fourth son Arthur Balden, and their children used Balden's services as a solicitor in the years to come. Samuel Dinsdale Balden, it later transpired, was not what he had seemed. Using his position as a respected solicitor and his place in Edgbaston society as cover, Balden was busy siphoning money into his own pocket rather than protecting the assets of his clients. By the time he was arrested on charges of fraud, the sum he was accused of embezzling stood at over £10,000. A newspaper clipping referring to the case has survived in the JFF West archive and is testimony to the family's sense of betrayal.

The club remembered the anniversary of Shakespeare's birth each year, as we have seen. A newspaper cutting of the anniversary dinner which took place at the Midland Hotel in 1881, the year of his presidency, was kept by West and has survived to this day. Originally stuck in West's diary, it has survived only because Sarah or her children cut newspaper articles of sentimental value out of his earlier diaries. This and other articles about the annual dinners show that the gathering attracted between forty and fifty members and friends. Frederick Robinson and John Kershaw may have declined West's invitation to the Shakespeare dinner in 1883, but they were both there in 1881. The Wests were close to the Kershaw family. A letter addressed to James West at Park House, Willesden Lane, London, the home of John Kershaw, in 1873, indicates that he stayed there on at least one occasion. Kershaw was an East India Broker and was of a similar age to West. His wife, Louisa, had borne him seven children by 1881. The Wests also chose the name Kershaw as the middle name for their second son, Conrad.[145] West eulogised about the genius of Shakespeare at the anniversary dinner, as we might expect, and toasts to various aspects of that literary giant's talents were made by West's friend Robinson and others. The evening concluded with songs and recitations, according to the article in the press.

West's paper, *Shakespeare from a Surgeon's Point of View* had been printed by late summer, 1881 – an accomplishment that did not escape the notice of the editorial staff of *Edgbastonia* who alerted readers to its existence in the August issue.[146] Papers on Shakespeare were not read every year, but he was one of

---

[145] Conrad's first name, it will be remembered, was the same as that of Conrad Pinches, head of West's school in Kennington, London.

[146] *Edgbastonia*; 1881; i: p.69. (BCL).

*Charles Green (1844–1906), manufacturer of jewellery, friend and executor
of JFF West. Source: JFF West Archive.*

the most popular subjects chosen by members. West was one of two who gave
papers on Shakespeare in 1881–2,[147] but there were five in the year 1865–6.
This was the year of J Langford's Vice-Presidency. He gave two papers on
Shakespeare – one on how the bard was seen by his contemporaries and one
on Shakespeare's views on plays, players and playing. James Sunderland
spoke on Shakespeare as a word-painter and Gem on Shakespeare as a
sportsman;[148] while the surgeon, Samuel William Langston Parker,[149] gave a
paper entitled *On the Psychology of Shakespeare as illustrated in the characters of
Hamlet, Ophelia, and Lear*. Other papers on Shakespeare ranged from
Shakespeare's Sonnets and *The Divinity of Shakespeare* read by West's close friend
and executor, Charles Green (1844–1906), during the years he occupied the
chair as Vice-President and President to *Jealousy as Depicted by Shakespeare* (W.
Ross Jordan in 1888–9) and *On Shakespearean Music* (Thomas Anderton in
1866–7). One of the most controversial, must have been a paper read by J.
Suffield junior who, on 10 October, 1874, spoke on doubts concerning the
identity of the author of 'Shakespeare's historical plays.'[150]

---

[147] West's paper on Shakespeare went unrecorded in the club's official record. The records do show,
however, that the surgeon, W Ross Jordan, gave a paper on the *Merchant of Venice*.

[148] Slater says that Major TH Gem was a particularly active sportsman himself. Apart from
participating in athletics, horse-riding, cricket and tennis, he ran the twenty one miles from
Birmingham to Warwick in just over three hours at the age of forty three. Terry Slater. *Edgbaston.
A History;* (England: Phillimore, 2002), p 118.

[149] Samuel William Langston Parker (1802–71), was one of the original surgeons to take up an
appointment at Queen's Hospital when it opened in 1841.

[150] J Suffield, *That Shakespeare was not the Author of the series of Historical Plays bearing his name.* Read
before the *Birmingham Dramatic Club*, 10 October, 1874. (BCL).

Embracing an aspect of Shakespeare's writing that corresponded to the speaker's professional interest was popular among members, and while the bard's writing lent itself admirably to analysis by those representing certain callings, connections were made by the skilful lateral thinker from the most unlikely professions. William Thomas Bennett, for example, was a master builder who was employing sixty men by the time the 1881 census was taken. His paper *Shakespeare from a Builder's point of view* shows that Shakespeare's works even provide sufficient material on his area of expertise. West and his Birmingham colleagues were not the only medical practitioners to write on Shakespeare's understanding of medical issues either, as a glance through the lists of published papers in The Wellcome Institute for the History of Medicine shows.

West's paper on Shakespeare is twenty-four pages long and contains numerous quotations.[151] The extent of Shakespeare's observations and knowledge of the human body and its afflictions struck West as being marked. West concluded that without the benefit of the medical advances of his own time, Shakespeare had demonstrated an understanding of psychology, materia medica, infectious illness and wound management. "Does not every physician recognise the fact that 'Care's an enemy to life'" (*Twelfth Night*, act i., sc. iii), and that 'Short time seems long in sorrow's sharp sustaining' (*Lucrece*); while on the other hand daily experience shows us that 'A light heart lives long' (*Love's Labour Lost*, act v., sc. ii.) and that,

'our remedies oft in ourselves do lie
Which we ascribe to Heaven.' *All's Well that Ends Well*, act i., sc. i.[152]

West quoted extensively in relation to Shakespeare's knowledge of the efficacy of plants used for medicinal purposes.

' "What rhubarb, senna, or what purgative drug
Would scour these English hence?" ' act v, sc.iii.

is one of three he quotes from Macbeth.[153] He also drew attention to references made to the properties of henbane and hemlock in Shakespeare's plays.

---

[151] JFF West, William Shakespeare from a Surgeon's Point of View, An Address delivered to the Members of the Birmingham Dramatic Club, at the Annual Celebration of Shakespeare's Birthday, *BMR*; 1881; pp.3–24. The paper contains sixty-five quotations altogether. (B Med I).

[152] Ibid., p 14.

[153] Ibid., p.19.

As we have seen, the effective treatment of wounds was close to West's heart. It was a subject which, West tells us, Shakespeare dealt with 'not infrequently with great judgement. "Your plantain leaf is excellent for a broken shin" – *Romeo and Juliet*, act i., sc. ii'[154] reflects on sound practice, while,

> ' "It will but skin and film the ulcerous place,
> Whiles rank corruption, running all within, infests unseen." ' *Hamlet*,
> act iii., sc. iv.[155]

shows what can happen in cases which are mismanaged. Furthermore, West says 'Who but a surgeon would be aware that new life follows the throwing off of dead tissue in severe injuries or burns? Probably no pathological process was ever so succinctly or beautifully described as in the following lines:

> ' "The organs though defunct and dead before
> Break up the drowsy grave, and newly move
> With casted slough and fresh legerety." ' *Henry V.*, act iv., sc. i.[156]

West found Shakespeare's observations on death both poignant and plausible, but he was also amused by the employment of a little black humour as used by Shakespeare in *Romeo and Juliet* when Mercutio gave the following facetious reply in response to Romeo's enquiry as to the gravity of the sword wound he had suffered. ' "No" remarked Mercutio "tis not so deep as a well, nor so wide as a church door; but 'tis enough: 'twill serve: ask for me tomorrow and you will find me a *grave* man." ' (act iii, sc., i).[157] Also appreciative of wit directed at his own profession, West says that Shakespeare 'wisely reminds us that though,

> "By medicine life may be prolonged, yet death
> Will seize the doctor too." ' *Cymbeline*, act v., sc., iv.[158]

---

[154] JFF West, William Shakespeare from a Surgeon's Point of View, An Address delivered to the Members of the Birmingham Dramatic Club, at the Annual Celebration of Shakespeare's Birthday, *BMR*; 1881; p 14.. The paper contains sixty-five quotations altogether. (B Med I).

[155] Ibid., p.17.

[156] Ibid., p.15.

[157] Ibid., p.23.

[158] Ibid., p.24.

James Fitzjames Fraser West ca.1880. Source: By kind permission Special Collections, University of Birmingham.

Death overcame West himself two years after quoting Cymbeline's words from act five, scene four of Shakespeare's play of that name. How did he spend these last two years of his life and what does it tell us about him?

"By medicine life may be prolonged"

James Fitzjames Fraser West died at his house 117, Hagley Road, Edgbaston, on 24 May, 1883. He was buried at The Church of the Ascension in Hall Green, now a Birmingham suburb close to Acock's Green on 29 May. The service was attended by some forty-seven named mourners. The *Birmingham Daily Post* report on the funeral gave the chief mourners as his three sons Walter Sellers then aged seventeen, Conrad Kershaw, fifteen, and John Frederick, a mere boy of nine. West had five other children, three girls and two more sons. Two of the girls, Marion Lucy and Gertrude, were older than John Frederick, but in accordance with the customs of the day, neither they nor their mother, grandmother or Aunt Fanny attended the funeral. West's three youngest children, Amy Valentine, Arthur Balden and Bertram Evelyn were young children of seven, four and two respectively and are not mentioned either.

West's close friend from London, the novelist, Frederick W Robinson, was the first listed after family. His name was followed by other close friends, John Kershaw, Samuel Balden, George Yates, JW Daniell, JC

MR. WALTER N. FISHER.

Walter Newton Fisher, (b.1844), friend and executor of James Fitzjames Fraser West. Source: By kind permission University of Birmingham Library.

Onions, ET Grimley, T Webley and Charles Green and Walter Newton Fisher, executors. Henry Sprotson, Dr Robert Jolly, John St Swithin Wilders, Dr Suffield and Mr J Leah also followed the cortège on its journey from Edgbaston to Hall Green as did his partner in private practice, William Slingsby Mann, and his successor to the hospital post, George Jordan Lloyd. Drs Alfred Carter, JH Palmer of Solihull, Underhill [159] and Robert William Edington and Messrs Joseph Sampson Gamgee, F Nelson, T Webber, TH Smith of Alcester, and John Garner were also present, as was the man whose firm organised the funeral, West's friend William Holliday.

It was a stylish send-off in keeping with West's status in the community and with his status as a professional medical man. Like most of those present that day, the two executors were Edgbaston men of standing. Living in one of Edgbaston's grandest houses, Lawnfield on Church Road and, Sir Walter, by the time he died, Walter Newton Fisher (1844–1932) was a highly successful Chartered Accountant and esteemed philanthropist. He would leave a grand total of £80,128/19/2 when he died in 1932. West's other executor, Charles Green, was recorded by the enumerator of the 1881 census as a manufacturer of jewellery who employed twenty-one men, five boys and four girls. He was living at Ashmead, an elegant early Victorian house in Carpenter Road at the time of West's death.

The cortège left the Wests' house at about 11.45am, according to the press, and arrived at its destination some four miles away, at approximately

---

[159] Without an initial, it is impossible to say for certain which member of this prodigious family this was.

1.30pm. It was en route, but nevertheless fitting, that the final journey of James West took him past Queen's Hospital. The service was conducted by the Reverend JC Blissard, incumbent of West's local church, St Augustine's Church, Edgbaston, and the Reverend R Jones of The Church of the Ascension, Hall Green. Fraser, the name which linked West to his father was not recorded on the inscription which adorned the coffin. It read simply 'James Fitzjames West, died May 24, 1883, aged 49.' The funeral arrangements were, as we have seen, carried out by a family well-known by, and friends of, West, Messrs Holliday, Son and Co. of Warwick House in New Street.

West's death was certified by his partner, William Slingsby Mann MRCS. The certificate states that West suffered rheumatic fever for a duration of thirty-five days along with pneumonia for twenty-two days and œdema of the lungs for twenty-four hours. The diary had ended, then, just two days before the full-blown onset of the disease responsible for his death. Those called in to attend to West in his final illness, his partner WS Mann and colleagues George Jordan Lloyd and Dr James Sawyer and the London physician, Sir William Jenner (1815–98), would have made every effort to ensure that 'by medicine life may be prolonged.'

Anyone reading West's diary would be forgiven for thinking that, but for a fleeting cold and sore throat, West was in excellent health during the early months of 1883. This was not the case. Fortunately for us today, curiosity about the causes of death in nineteenth century medical circles was so marked that detailed obituaries frequently appeared in the medical journals. West, no doubt, read with fascination of the final illnesses of numerous colleagues who pre-deceased him. So it is, with the benefit of the medical perspective, that more is revealed courtesy of *The Lancet* and the *BMJ*. 'For some months before his death, Mr West had been in failing health, which rest from work and a trip to Italy did not suffice to remedy.' we are told. 'For the last few weeks of his life he was confined to his house with irregular articular rheumatism, which was complicated by evidences of cardiac failure, renal inadequacy, and pulmonary embarrassment.' It goes on 'During the last few days general dropsy supervened, and the end came quietly at last from œdema of the lungs.'[160] The Lancet added that the rheumatism had been acute and severe and that it had been complicated by old cardiac lesions. It also said that he was 'fully conscious of his approaching end.'[161]

---

[160] *BMJ*; 1883; i: p.1097.
[161] *The Lancet*; 1883; i: p.1024.

At what point West became aware of his approaching end is not clear. There is nothing to suggest that an autopsy was performed, so he and his physicians presumably knew of the defect or illness – an earlier bout of rheumatic fever, perhaps – which caused the 'old cardiac lesions.' The diary reads as a testimony to someone who was living life to the full and at full speed, rather than the reverse. As we have seen, West was tied up with business relating to Sarah's land and property in Yorkshire during the early days of 1883. That probably accounts for the fact that West's first entry is for the eleventh day of January rather than the first. The diary is not an appointment diary. Rather, it is a diary of comment and reflection. It is a record of what has taken place and it tells us much about West and his family, as well as shedding light on his colleagues and friends. Patients, who are spoken of on numerous occasions, come across as friends as much as patients. The diary helps us to fill in the details of West's life in the last months of his life in a way that medical society, club and association records do not.

Medical and other society records and the newspaper reports of their activities can, if used together with the diary, give us a good idea of what West's day to day life was like. It is fair to assume that the diary is representative of his earlier diaries. If West went with his friends and family to concerts and the opera in the first months of 1883, it can only be assumed that he did so with as much enthusiasm in earlier years. If he enjoyed reading fiction in 1883, we can be fairly sure that he read for pleasure throughout his adult life. It is also reasonable to surmise that he socialised to the same extent in the years that led up to 1883 as he did during the final months of his life. The diary also records West's last two holidays; the first a short break to that most fashionable of Welsh resorts, Llandudno, and the month long trip to Italy. This, too, was nothing new. West was, as we have seen, renowned for his predilection to travel. West's involvement with clubs and societies is also alluded to in the diary.

The survival of club and society archive, especially when it contains records of attendance, allows us to gauge an individual's commitment to the organisation. It will not come as a surprise to find that West's involvement in them seems to have remained considerable up until the end of his life. On 29 March, 1883, West was elected in absentia to the position of vice-president of the Birmingham Medical Institute. He only attended one of their meetings after that. It took place the day after he returned from his trip to the continent, on 10 April, but he made no

mention of it in the diary. He preferred instead, to grumble about a dis-
satisfied patient. West must have been tired after his trip but he seems to
have made no objection when those present voted that he should form a
House Sub-committee along with Thomas Hiron Bartleet (1837–91),
Dickenson Webster Crompton, Joseph Sampson Gamgee, James Vose
Solomon (1817–99), Joseph Priestley Smith (1845–1933),William Gammon
Archer (1848–90), Arthur Oakes (1830–1925) and James Russell. West
even went to a medical society meeting on the 18 April, the day after the
diary ends. It was a Midland Medical Society meeting, and it was here that
the last recorded words of James Fitzjames Fraser West were noted down
for posterity.

West's address on Shakespeare from a surgeon's point of view took
place two years before that meeting. Eighteen eighty-one was a busy year
for West. His eighth child, Bertram Evelyn, was born on 17 January, and
he was both president of the *Birmingham Dramatic Club* and the *Pathological
Section* of the *BMA Birmingham and Midland Counties Branch*. Apart from the
list of papers and the names of those who gave them, there is no record of
attendance at the Birmingham Dramatic Club meetings. If his conduct
when he occupied similar positions in medical societies is anything to go by,
West was probably at the six ordinary meetings held during his year in the
chair as well as the anniversary dinner. If this is the case, he would have
attended meetings on 10 September, 8 October, 12 November, and 10
December during 1881 and on 14 January and 12 February in 1882.

He was elected to the *Chair of the Pathological Section* on 25 August, 1881
and missed just one out of the six meetings which took place during his
time as its president. Apart from one minute book dating from 1882 to
1890, records relating to the *Pathological Section* of the *BMA Birmingham
and Midland Counties Branch* have not survived. Loss though that is,
meetings were reported in brief in the Association's journal the *BMJ*. The
reports are brief, but they do tell us who chaired the meetings and they
record the names of the practitioners who brought exhibits along and say
what they consisted of. West, as chairman, attended meetings on 25
November in 1881 and on 27 January, 24 February, 31 March and 28
April in 1882. He exhibited on three occasions – one fewer than Gilbert
Barling (1855–1940) who exhibited four times. Robert Saundby, Robert
Michael Simon (1850–1914) and George Jordan Lloyd (1854–1913) all
exhibited on two occasions. Seven other colleagues brought exhibits along
in that year.

Apart from the fulfilment of his duties to these two very different societies, West had obligations to Queen's Hospital, family, patients and friends. All were competing for his attention, and they were not the only demands on his time either. So what else did West do in 1881? We know already about the *International Medical Congress* in August, an event of several days duration. It was probably the highlight of the year although there was a Mayor's Fancy Dress Ball in the Council House, Birmingham, the same year. If the ball did come second it was probably a close second. There is no proof that West and his wife, Sarah, attended the Mayor's ball, but there are clues to suggest they probably did. The family not only kept a newspaper report of the occasion but, significantly, it was pinned to a page cut from a diary identical in design to West's final diary of 1883. Sarah and James would have been one of seven hundred guests if they did go. Many, but not all, rose to the occasion and sported fancy dress. Apart from listing the most distinguished guests, the report dwells primarily on those who were attired in the most interesting or most exotic costumes. No expense was spared, or so it seemed from the description, in the adornment of the Council House. Magnificent plants and flowers from far away places and drapes of the finest fabrics were in great abundance for all to enjoy.

Records show that West attended no meetings of the Birmingham Medical Institute in 1881. He attended a meeting at the Midland Medical Society on 30 June and was elected onto its council on 5 October, 1881. It meant that West was serving as a member of council or president on three societies concurrently. Eighteen eighty-two was another busy year. With the exception of December, he had meetings at one or other society every month. The meetings which took place at the *Pathological Section* of the BMA's local branch in 1882 have already mentioned, but West also attended two of the regular branch meetings of the BMA and the Annual meeting on 20 June – an occasion which culminated in a dinner at the Grand Hotel – as well as four meetings at the Midland Medical Society, three at the Birmingham Medical Institute and two at the Birmingham Benevolent Medical Society. On 15 February the Midland Medical Society and the Birmingham Medical Institute both held meetings on the same day. West attended both. The paper he gave on Rapid Lithotrity [162] at the final meeting of his local branch of the BMA on 9 November, 1882, was not West's last paper, but it was to be the last he ever read to Association members of that organisation.

[162] JFF West, Case of Rapid Lithotrity, with Remarks on Bigelow's Operation; *BMR*; 1883; 13: pp.14–21.

West also attended two meetings at the Dental Hospital in the last two years of his life. He had been elected consulting surgeon to the hospital in 1871 along with Willoughby Wade, in the same year that Lloyd Owen was appointed chloroformist. We do not know what professional duties West carried out at the Dental Hospital as a surgeon at any stage, but he did attend Surgical Committee meetings from time to time. One was on 20 January, 1882. There was no significant business and West may well have regretted his decision to go along that day. This meeting was followed some three months later by a special meeting, convened by their president Mr Charles Sims (b.1840) for the purpose of discussing student attendance and punctuality.[163] It was proposed by Sims, seconded by West and resolved that no action would be taken against students who failed to arrive on time up to 1 May, 1882, but that thereafter those who arrived after 9.15am would not have their attendance recognised. West and Sims were joined on that occasion by dental surgeons Frederick Robert Batchelor, WH Breward Neale and Francis E Huxley.

The last four months

When West started his new diary in January, 1883, thoughts of his own demise were unlikely to have been at the forefront of his mind. One obituary states that although West had been ill for some time, its nature was such that 'until within a recent period a fatal termination was not anticipated.'[164] If we consider what we know of West's involvement with societies and hospitals from other sources and examine the correspondence he had with the professionals who administered Sarah's land and property in Yorkshire we can see that West was a busy man. Add to that the demands of his private patients, his family and friends and we see a man with little time to spare. What the diary tells us is that West found a hectic lifestyle irresistible. It confirms how devoted he was to his family and how close he was to a significant number of friends and colleagues. His social calendar was always full. It is virtually inconceivable that the diary is not representative of other years.

West speaks of patients frequently in his diary. He describes the medical conditions with which they were afflicted and comments on the effect that these had upon their lives. He also comments on their personalities and how their characters impinged on his relationships with them. West, like many of

---

[163] *Dental Hospital Minute Book. March 19, 1880 – August, 16, 1887. Surgical Committee.* Meeting 28 April, 1882. (Ronald Cohen Dental Library, Birmingham Dental Hospital).
[164] The Late Mr JF West, *Birmingham Daily Post*; Friday 25 May, 1883. (BCL).

his generation, was as much friend as doctor to many of his patients and many of his friendships probably stemmed from doctor/patient beginnings. An appreciable number of colleagues were also close friends. When it came to getting the best outcome for a patient, he did not hesitate to consult colleagues, and the fact that he took the surgeon George Yates and others with him to visit patients on a number of occasions in the early months of 1883, suggests that this was, for him, common practice.[165] Yates, with five consultations, was the man most sought after when he wanted direction, reassurance, confirmation of a diagnosis or just an extra pair of hands, but West also consulted Dr Russell twice regarding his patient, Mrs Hornsby,[166] as well as Mr Sutton [?] with regard to Mrs Talbot.[167]

In nineteenth century England the sick and injured who could afford to do so were attended at home by the family doctor. Even complaints which required surgery were generally dealt with in the family home. Kitchen tables were used as makeshift operating tables and a rag drenched in ether or chloroform sufficed as a means of administering an anæsthetic. Equipped with an MRCS and a LSA, a hospital doctor like West could deal with almost any eventuality. With a ready supply of colleagues who could provide assistance, administer an anæsthetic or be consulted in difficult cases, his services would have been in demand. He also had the advantage of having access to the hospital's facilities if it should prove necessary.

In any case, levels of hospital infection, though much reduced compared to those of earlier times, was still a risk to the lives of those who were treated in hospital. As Robert Lawson Tait was able to show, even highly dangerous procedures such as abdominal surgery, could be more safely carried out in patients' own homes than in hospital. He discovered that whilst mortality rates of 55% were suffered by women who had ovariotomies in hospital, the figure for private patients was only 28%.[168] Tait, as we have seen, was opposed to Lister's methods, but he did uphold the belief that operations should be performed under scrupulously clean conditions. Whether West used Lister's methods in the surgical treatment of private patients is unknown, but we do know that like Tait, he would have taken the necessary precautions to eliminate the risk of infection.

---

[165] A surviving letter addressed to George Yates and written by Gamgee, proves that West was not alone in making use of Yates' services. It reads, My dear Yates, Can you be at no. 13 Reservoir Road 10am. tomorrow to assist me in a Lithotomy case? Answer this evg (sic) will oblige. Yours vy (sic) faithfully S Gamgee. 24 June, 1865. (On loan from Dr A Llewellyn Lloyd of Birmingham).

[166] Probably the wife of the Reverend John Hornsby of Broad Lane, Acock's Green.

[167] Probably Mrs Talbot of Greenfield Crescent, Edgbaston.

[168] Tait, Robert Lawson; Fifty Cases of Ovariotomy; *BMR*; 1878. (B Med I).

Neither Tait nor West would have worn surgical gloves or masks. First to become common place was the surgical glove. It received its patent in England in 1878, although it did not become routine until well after Dr William S Halstead (1825–1922) of Baltimore pioneered its use in operations in 1890.[169] The Polish surgeon, Johannes von Mikulicz-Radecki (1850–1905) was reputedly the first to use a face-mask during an operation in the year 1897.[170]

It was noted earlier that references written for West in 1857 allude to his kindness and compassion. Much of what West recorded in his diary of 1883 reflects these qualities. A firm believer in the power of the positive and the optimistic, West did what he could to restore the spirits of those afflicted by sickness and infirmity. On 15 January for instance, he combined his duties as a professional with those of benevolent fellowship by taking a house-bound patient on his rounds with him. 'Drove over to Acock's Green and took poor young Bikker who has been 3 months in the house from the railway accident with me. The sun shone brightly and he thoroughly enjoyed the ride,...'[171] The journey took its toll on Bikker though, and West says that he had to be revived on his arrival by Mrs Atkins, the patient he had gone to visit, with a glass of champagne.

West also saw Mrs Atkins [172] on 19 January and again on 23 of the month and Bikker two days after that. He said he took George Yates with him on the second visit of the year to Bikker as he did on the one after that. 'Called for George Yates and took him to see Arthur Bikker who is now much better'[173] West reported cheerfully. Bikker may have been much better but his convalescence was not over by any means. West consulted Yates on Bikker once more on 19 February and wrote this time that his patient was 'slowly improving.' It is impossible to say how many times West visited Mrs Atkins altogether in the early months of 1883 because in some entries he simply recorded 'Went to AG in the afternoon.' We do know, though, that he went to see her again on 7 March. Finding her better, West asked her to settle her account. The request, he tells us, fell on deaf ears.[174] Non payment of fees was the 'bête noir' of general practitioners.

---

[169] Hæger, Kurt, *The Illustrated History of Surgery* (England: Harold Starke Publishers, 2000), p 214.
[170] Ibid., p 214.
[171] The individual referred to may have been Arthur Wellesley Bikker, son of Charles Hay Traise Bikker of 53 Charlotte Road, Edgbaston. Diary, Monday 15 January, 1883. (JFF West Archive).
[172] Mrs Atkins could have been a member of the Atkins' family who, according to the 1881 census, lived in Shirley Road, Acock's Green.
[173] Monday 5 February, 1883; Diary. (JFF West Archive).
[174] Ibid., Wednesday 7 March, 1883.

Waddington, in citing evidence garnered by FB Smith,[175] says that doctors working in poor districts suffered most. Mrs Atkins was unlikely to have been poor, but practitioners working in the meaner parts of London and Manchester could expect to receive only about one third of their fees, according to Waddington.

Other patients mentioned by West in the diary include the servant girl admitted to Queen's Hospital with gun-shot wounds and the boy with a ruptured kidney alluded to earlier, as well as a child suffering from croup, a drunken Mrs Hopwood,[176] Frank Holliday and the Hallidays. Frank Holliday's plight amused West. 'Had to go to Chester Road' wrote West on 9 February 'to see Frank Holliday who had ricked his back by lifting his bedstead with his wife in it! too much conjugal affection!' West was a close friend of the Holliday family. He went to dinner with one member of the family (probably Frank's father, William) at Warwick House in February, and it was their firm that undertook the funeral arrangements when West died in May, 1883.

William Holliday lived near the Wests in Augustus Road, Edgbaston. He was a man who seems to have been unwilling to leave anything to chance. When he died in 1898, he left a grand total of £76,224/2/6d, but not before he had written a will of twenty-eight pages with seven codicils to authorise the distribution of his fortune.[177] William Holliday was determined to be scrupulously fair to his family by apportioning more money to those members who had received less financial assistance during his lifetime, but he also left money to the Church of England, four hospitals including Queen's and to the two institutions who provided care and education for the blind and the deaf and dumb.

West must have treated the servants, grooms and gardeners of his friends and patients on numerous occasions. Without the benefit of a ledger we have no way of knowing for certain who bore the cost of these visits or of the treatment that resulted from them. Historians agree, though, that Victorian society was still very much attached to the concept of paternalism, so it is fairly safe to assume that employers paid in most cases. Just as in the days before the hospitals became free, many employers provided employees with tickets for admission to the hospital for use in times of need, many called their own doctors out to their homes on account of sick servants.

---

[175] FB Smith, *The People's Health 1830–1910* (London, 1979) p.41. Cited by Waddington, *The Medical Profession in the Industrial Revolution*, p.34.

[176] Probably of the Hopwood family who lived in nearby Portland Road, Edgbaston.

[177] Will of William Holliday, 1898, pp.498–526. (BCA).

When West was called out on Saturday 10 February, it was to the gardener of Mr Holliday rather than Mr Holliday himself. 'Sent for at 6' wrote West 'to go to Mr Holliday to see poor old John Oxford who has been his gardener for 35 years. Found him suffering from strangulated hernia so I operated with the assistance of Dr Barling and Mr Sims.' Barling was a newly qualified surgeon at the time and Sims was a colleague West would have known through his involvement with the Dental hospital and as a neighbouring practitioner in Union Passage, the street where West's own surgery was located. As West's report shows, the operation proved difficult. 'The dread and excitement caused his poor old wife to have an apoplectic seizure. I did the operation all right but under great difficulties.'[178]

The story unfolds unhappily over the next few days. On Sunday 11 February, West says he walked round to see 'poor old John' with his son Conrad. He reports that he had been as well as could have been expected until his 'poor old wife died, whence he succumbed to be prostrated.'[179] A day later and 'poor old John' was dead. West says he died from 'exhaustion.' 'He had had no sickness after the operation' West wrote 'and seemed easier from pain.'[180] That the death of Holliday's gardener, John, and his wife, moved West and was a cause for regret is apparent from the words he chose to use in describing the incident in his diary and adds weight to the accolade he won for compassion in his testimonials.

Unlike some of his modern counterparts in General Practice, West thought nothing of working on Sundays. So unusual was it for West to have a Sunday free of commitments to patients that he commented on the fact when it happened. Apart from those occasions when he was out of town, what happened on the second Sunday of January was unusual. 'For the first time for many weeks' West wrote 'had not a single patient to see so took Daisy (Amy Valentine, then nearly six) and Arthur (then four) to Mr Platten's chapel where we heard a capital sermon on the efficacy of earnest prayer to God.'

West attended church every Sunday irrespective of whether he was away from home or not. He was discerning and quick to criticise poor sermons and second rate music. The week after he heard the capital sermon on the efficacy of prayer at Mr Platten's chapel, West, Fanny, his mother and various members of his young family were in the fashionable Welsh seaside resort of Llandudno. They went to the church of St George which he described as a large cold building. If that was not enough, the

---

[178] JFF West, Diary; Saturday 10 February, 1883. (JFF West Archive).
[179] Ibid., Sunday 11 February, 1883.
[180] Ibid., Monday 12 February, 1883.

sermon, too, left much to be desired. 'Heard a young clergyman read himself in with a sermon from the first lines of Genesis' which was in West's opinion 'mediocre in a high degree.'[181]

A week later and he was back in his home territory at St Augustine's Church, Edgbaston, with his daughter, Gertrude, where he heard 'a good sermon from Dr Blissard.'[182] St Augustine's Church did not always deliver to West's satisfaction, though. On Sunday 4 February, West had to sit through another sermon that fell below his expectations. 'Went to St Augustine's at night and heard an indifferent school-masterly sermon from Rev Ogle.' Mr Irwin, also of St Augustine's, had the distinction of being unpredictable. The sermon he gave on Sunday 11 February was described as 'very good' but when he preached a week later, Irwin's sermon was 'poor.' On another occasion his sermon is described as 'long' (presumably too long), but at least Mr Woodward played the organ 'very well' on 25 February.

While West recorded names of family members who accompanied him to church on Sundays and frequently referred to activities they did en famille, he does not always make clear whether or not his wife was present or involved. We know, for instance, that Fanny and his mother went to Llandudno with him on 19 January, 1883, and by inference 'all up to see me on my return with open arms'[183] that his wife and some of the children stayed at home. We know that Walter returned on 14 February and that his mother and Fanny returned sixteen days later with some of his sons. Conrad, John and Arthur are obvious possibilities but there is no way of knowing for certain. West simply records their return with the words 'Ma and Fan and the little boys returned from Llandudno and seemed very much benefited by the change.'[184]

Llandudno was considered so desirable in late Victorian times that prizes were awarded for articles on its merits by the magazine *Edgbastonia* in 1892. Miss ME Todd of Blythewood, Edgbaston and Mrs Thomas of Newtown, Wales, were joint winners and shared the premium of two guineas between them.[185] The title given to competitors was *'Llandudno in the Season'* and much of what they say reflects on the attractions the resort had to offer in summertime. The bands, donkey rides, Punch and Judy shows and other entertainments they spoke of would undoubtedly have been unavailable to the West family in the early months of 1883, but West nevertheless revelled in the seaside and all it had to offer. There was 'a tremendous gale with rain

---

[181] JFF West, Diary; Sunday 21 January, 1883. (JFF West Archive).
[182] Ibid., Sunday 28 January, 1883. (JFF West Archive).
[183] Ibid., Monday 22 January, 1883.
[184] Ibid., Friday 2 March, 1883.
[185] *Edgbastonia*; 1892; XII: pp.137–140. (BCL).

blowing' when they arrived 'and the sea looked fierce.'[186] A calm descended
that evening according to West and it was followed the next day by 'a lovely
bright Summerlike day and Fan Jack and I walked round the Orme's Head
enjoying the scene with its brilliant sea and sunshine and with that calm wh.
only hard toilers in town can really experience after dinner took another
walk for the evening.' Astonishingly West follows this by saying 'Jack and I
had a last sea bathe followed by a cold shower.'[187]

Son, husband and father
The obituary written up by *Edgbastonia* speaks of West as being a devoted
son. Evidence taken from the diary supports this statement. By Sunday 21
January, West had not only arranged for a local doctor to take a look at his
mother during her stay in Llandudno, but was able to report that his
mother's health was already benefiting from the change.

West's relationships and involvement with the various members of his
family would have remained obscure but for the survival of his last diary.
Sarah, who is referred to affectionately as 'Tadie' by West is mentioned
eleven times by name in the diary although there are many more
references by implication. When West says things like 'Left at 7 and got to
Pisa at 9'[188] we know that he meant that he left with Sarah. He was, after
all, accompanied by Sarah on this trip. He also uses 'we' and 'our'
throughout the entries on his excursion to Italy. His closeness to Fanny is
also reflected in the diary. With fourteen references, Fanny outdid her
mother who was named on nine separate occasions. With the exception of
Bertram Evelyn who was only two years of age in January in 1883, West
mentioned every one of his children in the diary. The author is fortunate
to have known West's granddaughter well and to have been made aware of
the various nicknames and diminutives used by the Wests. Jack, West's son,
John Frederick, was referred to eight times altogether, but it was Walter
who clocked up the greatest number with ten.

Amy Valentine, known affectionately as Daisy, is spoken of twice, once
in relation to her birthday on 14 February and again a month later. She
almost certainly enjoyed her birthday. As West says 'Daisy was 6 years old
today and she had all the little Greens to spend the day with her and
Tadie and I saw them home in the evening.'[189] The Wests were close to

---

186 JFF West, Diary; Friday 19 January, 1883. (JFF West Archive).
187 Ibid., Saturday 20 January, 1883.
188 Ibid., Friday 16 March, 1883.
189 Ibid., Wednesday 14 February, 1883.

the Green family. The diary shows that they saw them on a regular basis and Charles Green was one of James West's executors. Daisy was the only child mentioned by West during his trip to Italy. A chance meeting with the husband of someone known to the Wests in San Remo led to an invitation to the home of Mr Squire and West's encounter with their little daughter. 'He invited us to his house and we saw his wife, a charming young woman and his little girl aged 7 who was just as roguish and funny as Daisy.'[190]

West enjoyed the company of his children to such an extent that he thought nothing of taking them on his rounds at weekends. On one Sunday in late January, West says he walked to Mr Webley's with 'the boys.'[191] He was probably referring to Walter (17), Conrad (15) and John Frederick (8). The following week West was more specific, saying 'Walked with Conrad and Gerty (Gertrude, then 11 years) to Oldbury as it was a fine bright morning.'[192] Conrad went to Chester Road with West the following Sunday as we have seen, but the week after that it was Gerty's turn to accompany her father. The next entry to fall on a Sunday was West's last before he left for Italy. He seems to have made a point of calling on as many patients as possible before his departure but he did so in the comfort of his carriage and in the company of Walter. He recorded the occasion with the words 'Long round with Walter in the carriage in the morning.'[193]

Walter Sellers West

Walter seems to have enjoyed a special relationship with his father. Apart from accompanying West on his rounds, he seems to have been blessed with other privileges. It was Walter who admired orchids at the Botanical Gardens with his father on 14 January, and it was Walter who visited the new King Edward's School at Five Ways on 3 February with his father. And when West needed some clerical assistance during the evening of 25 January, Walter provided it. 'I spent the evening at home' wrote West 'and sent off some of my pamphlets on Bigelow's [194] operation which Walter directed for me.'[195] It was unlikely to have been the first time Walter was called upon to assist in this way. West's paper *Erasmus in Praise of Folly* has

---

[190] JFF West, Diary; Thursday 15 March, 1883. (JFF West Archive).
[191] Ibid., Diary; Sunday 28 January, 1883. (JFF West Archive).
[192] Ibid., Sunday 4 February, 1883.
[193] Ibid., Sunday 25 February, 1883.
[194] HJ Bigelow, (d.1890).
[195] Diary; Thursday 25 January, 1883. (JFF West Archive).

survived in manuscript and all of the quotations are written out complete with spelling errors in the hand of a child or youngster. Most of the twenty or so youngsters who attended the children's party given by the Wests on 12 January were, in West's words 'mostly Walter's and Lucy's.'

As we shall see in the epilogue, Walter and Marion Lucy both died young and within months of each other in 1895. Both had suffered mental illness. There is no hint of their mental health problems in the diary of 1883. Records which relate to the life of Marion Lucy are minimal, but her will suggests she was a sensitive girl with a social conscience.

Later documents show that Walter succumbed to some degree of mental illness before his father died. He had been the victim of an accident during his schooldays at Derby School four years earlier and was blind in one eye – an episode which was said to have triggered changes to his personality. Sarah and James West must have been horrified when they received a telegram from the headmaster of Derby School on 26 January, 1879 to say that their son, Walter, had suffered an injury to the eye. Two letters relating to the incident have survived. One was from the headmaster, Walter Clark. 'I can unhesitatingly say' he stressed 'that the accident, to which I referred (in the telegram), is probably quite unprecedented.' He went on to say that he was much distressed by what he called 'this most exceptional accident.'[196] Clark expressed the hope that the damage to the eye was temporary. It was not. A testimony given in 1895 by Walter's mother, Sarah, at the time of his death, declares that Walter's eye suffered irreparable damage and was totally destroyed as a result of the incident.

The other letter is more poignant. It was written by Conrad who was just eleven at the time. The writing is impeccable and the letter appears excessively formal by modern standards but it still reveals much about the family dynamic. Conrad's letter to his father is dated 26 January, 1878 (sic) and is worth quoting in full.

'My dear Papa,

I hope you are quite well. A boy let cap off by the gass (sic) this morning and it flew back and hit Walter in the eye, the doctor has been to see him this afternoon, his name is Mr Copesteak (sic) he asked your address and I think he is going to write to you. I should have put this letter with Walter's only he had cealed (sic) it up when the accident was done. I thought I

---

[196] Letter from Walter Clark, head of Derby School, to JFF West, dated 26 January, 1879. (JFF West Archive).

better write to tell you about it as you told me never to keep anything away from you.
I must now conclude
with love to all your affectionate son CK West'[197]

Clark said nothing about the discipline issues which no doubt lay behind the incident, and, as we have seen, emphasised the fact that accidents of that sort were hitherto unheard-of in school. He told the Wests he realised at once that the injury was serious, and that he had responded by calling in first one medical practitioner, Mr Copestake, and then a second, Mr Gisborne. He thanked West for his telegram and said, though it is unlikely to have been true, that he was pleased to hear that he was coming up to Derby the following day.

Conrad's letter reads as though he is not sure the head of the school will even bother to notify his father. The gravity of its content must have been a terrible burden to the young Conrad, but he knew it came into the category of matters which should be reported to his father and he acted accordingly. One of the most moving features of the letter is its innocence. His grasp of spelling was still a little shaky and he even talked of a missed opportunity to economise on the stamp. There is no doubt, though, that Conrad perceived the impact the letter would have on his father. The formula he had been taught on how to begin and end his letters must have seemed formal and inappropriate in the circumstances. Nevertheless, and regardless of his immaturity, he faced up to his responsibilities and put pen to paper. He did it in spite of his own anxiety and in the knowledge that what he said was going to bring pain to his father and probably make him angry.

What happened after the accident is unknown. The 1881 census shows that Conrad remained at the school, although none of the younger boys was sent to Derby School. Any decision to send other sons to the school would, in any case, have been made by West's widow, Sarah. No reference to the incident has been found in either the school's own records or in the local press. The Trustee's Minute Book for 1865–79 is devoid of any reference to the accident as is the relevant section of the Headmaster's Report. The latter document contains quite a detailed account of school affairs and the absence of comment is surprising if not suspicious.

West's affection for, and his attachment to, his family is evident from letters and the diary. He gave them love and practical help, but his

---

[197] Letter from Conrad Kershaw West to his father, dated 26 January, 1878. (JFF West Archive).

Roseneath, Reservoir Road, Ladywood, home of Mary West and
Fanny de la Hunt. Photographed by the author in 2002.

commitment to them was reciprocated. Fanny and his mother may have enjoyed the opportunity to take a holiday in Llandudno, but they had some of James and Sarah's children with them. So too, when Sarah joined her husband, James, on his final trip to the Continent in early 1883, she left her home and children in the care of Fanny and her mother-in-law. As we have seen, the youngest member of the family was just two at the time and all eight were still minors. Even with the help of servants, Fanny and her mother, Mary, would have been kept busy.

Friends

West's diary has fifteen blank days in it altogether, but in those that remain and cover time spent in Birmingham rather than Llandudno (19–22 January) or the Continent (10 March – 9 April), when he would of necessity dined out, West ate out a total of nineteen times before the diary ends on 17 April. The diary begins and ends with entries which record dinner parties. In the first he wrote 'Dined at Dr Foster's with a lot of medicos'[198] and in the last he dined at the Liberal Club with Mr Sutton of the Lancashire Association company.[199] Two meals were taken in the company of friend and colleague, George Yates – one, described by West as 'a capital feed' was at The Stork Hotel [200] and the other was at The Hen and Chickens.[201]

West said he 'supped' with his mother on two occasions and there were meals taken at the clubs of friends or his own club, The Birmingham

---

[198] JFF West, Diary; 11 January, 1883. (JFF West Archive).
[199] Ibid., 17 April, 1883.
[200] Ibid., 19 February, 1883.
[201] Ibid., 16 April, 1883.

Dramatic Club. The rest were taken with friends or colleagues or both when the two circles coincided. West generally remarked on the success or otherwise of the dinner parties he attended, saying who was there and whether or not company and food were up to scratch. At least two dinner parties culminated in a game of rubber. One was at Dr Foster's dinner party on the 11 January. West said he stayed on after dinner to play a rubber with Foster – a move which meant he had 'not to sit more than an hour waiting for Walter to come from his first evening party at Shepherd's.'[202] The other was at Mr Archer's medical party fifteen days later. West clearly enjoyed the evening saying he had 'much pleasant chat after dinner and then a rubber which lasted till the small hours.'[203]

On one occasion West expressed his regret that he had sacrificed one dinner party in order to go to another. The Wests enjoyed excellent food when they dined at the home of Mr T Barney in the middle of January but the evening was dull. On returning home later that evening, he recorded 'It was a gorgeous feed but a very slow affair and I would rather have been at Fisher's who were also giving a dinner party that evening to wh. we were invited.'[204] Barney's party was not the only one to be condemned by West for being slow. The party given by Dr Russell for twenty guests on 20 February prompted West to write 'As usual with medical parties it was slow so slept at 10.'[205] West may have been critical of what he dubbed a 'slow' evening, but he was not averse to one which was quiet. The dinner party given by the Colls in early February was both quiet and agreeable.[206] The Wests returned to Birmingham the following day with the Farndales and Mr Colls after having stayed overnight with their hosts.

The last medical party West attended was one given by Oliver Pemberton on 8 March, the day before he left Birmingham for the Continent. He said he was last to arrive on account of the fact that he had spent the day clearing up as much work as possible before his departure. He was almost certainly glad that he had made the effort to go to the Pemberton's party since, as he later recorded 'I sat between Dr Mc Veagh of Coventry and Mr Baker and we got on well together.'[207]

---

[202] JFF West, Diary; 11 January, 1883. (JFF West Archive).

[203] Ibid., 26 January, 1883.

[204] Ibid., 18 January, 1883. West presumably meant Walter Newton Fisher, friend and executor of his will.

[205] JFF West, Diary; 20 February, 1883. (JFF West Archive).

[206] Ibid., 8 February, 1883.

[207] Ibid., 8 March, 1883.

The diary shows that West called on numerous friends in the early months of 1883. While in many cases the object of these visits was simply to chat, he also took the opportunity to play cards, billiards or tennis whenever he could. He mentioned playing a rubber four times altogether although he did not say which game they referred to. He lost 27/6d when he played a rubber at the Branson's house in the company of Haynes and Balden on 9 February and was disturbed three times when he played with them again on 23 February. West's partiality to billiards is evident in four entries, but one game in particular seems to have both surprised and satisfied him against his expectations. The day before the diary ends, West wrote 'In evening played 3 games of billiards with Councillor Jas Baldwin. He gave me 40 in 100 and strange to say I beat him.'[208] Two days before that, West recorded playing tennis [209] with Charles Green, one of the two executors of his will.

James and Sarah West saw the Greens on a regular basis and it was at Charles Green's house that West played what was almost certainly his last game of lawn tennis on the afternoon of Saturday 14 April. West's first mention of the Green family in the diary of 1883 was on 12 January when he listed Green children among the guests at the children's party they gave on that date. Charles Green was probably at the meeting of the Birmingham Dramatic Club on 13 February when West gave his paper on *Erasmus in Praise of Folly*. Even if he was not, he probably saw Charles Green again when the 'little Greens' were at the West's house for Daisy's birthday celebrations on 14 February. Green's wife, Katharina, spent two evenings with the West's in early 1883. The first was on 4 March and the second was on 11 April two days after the Wests returned from their trip to the Continent.

Displeasure

The Wests brought a number of presents back with them from their trip to the Continent in April, 1883. One was a rosary which had been blessed by the Pope for a Mr Richards. West said Richards seemed pleased with the gift which he said was 'just the thing he wanted.'[210] The Greens were more difficult to please. When Mrs Green came round on the evening of 11 April, West recorded 'I gave her some photos of pictures we had bought wh. with

---

[208] JFF West, Diary; 16 April, 1883. (JFF West Archive).

[209] The game of lawn tennis was devised by Major TH Gem and JBA Perera of Firelight, Ampton Road, Edgbaston. Slater says that no respectable home in Edgbaston was without a tennis court by the 1890s. Terry Slater, *Edgbaston. A History*, (England: Phillimore, 2002), p.118.

[210] JFF West, Diary; 13 April, 1883. (JFF West Archive).

Mrs Katarina Green in 1886. Source: JFF West Archive.

the red stockings from Sorrento and a vol. of Tennyson for Charles we thought a nice little present. I doubt however if one or other of our gifts was much appreciated.'[211] The reference to the game of tennis alluded to above was just three days after Mrs Green was given the presents brought back by the Wests. In it, West indicates that the Greens continued to vex him. 'Spent afternoon at Chas. Green's playing lawn tennis. He and his wife have both turned abstainers and it did not seem to have improved his temper.'[212]

Charles and Katarina Green were not the only people who displeased James West. He gave his employee, William Swinbourne, two weeks notice to leave in late January, 1883. West did not say why he was dismissing Swinbourne in the diary, but it cannot have been anything to do with the man's lack of physical strength. He went on to say that he had engaged 'an old man of 60' in Swinbourne's place.[213] Whatever Swinbourne's fault, as a servant he would have been at West's mercy and would have had little alternative but to accept his fate and go quietly.

The same would not have been true when West found himself among his equals. When he attended a meeting of the Birmingham and District

[211] JFF West, Diary; 11 April, 1883. (JFF West Archive).
[212] Ibid., 14 April, 1883.
[213] Ibid., 27 January, 1883.

Land Company in late February, West said that the meeting was stormy and that he had a row with a Mr Pollach.[214] West did not elaborate on the details, but one thing is clear, West was no bystander. Hospital affairs also caused him frustration from time to time. He was one of forty-four committee members appointed to vote for a new House Surgeon at the Children's Hospital in early February, 1883. There were six candidates altogether. One, Miss Shore, was West's favourite, while the person he placed second was C Grinling. The two were in competition with J Allman Powell, F Sturges, ED Vinrace and WF Law. As his words in the diary reveal, West's preference was thwarted 'Voted at election for HS of Children's Hospital for Miss Shore from Birmingham and afterwards for Grinling but Dr Powell was elected. Again on the losing side.'[215] His words suggest something more than mere resignation. In the event, as the minutes show, J Allman Powell, the successful candidate, received twenty-three votes, while Grinling was given eighteen.[216]

Miss Shore seems to have abandoned Birmingham after she failed to secure the post at the Children's Hospital. Medical Directories list her practising first as a Female Medical Officer for the General Post Office, London, and then as a Residential Medical Officer at the New Hospital for Women in London. Whether West actively championed women's causes is impossible to say, but if he did, he would have been out of step with many of his contemporaries. In December of the same year, the Children's Hospital sought to make further appointments. One successful candidate for the job was the female practitioner, Annie Clark. To the surprise of some, she was appointed alongside Drs Richard Drury, and Thomas Richards. Annie Clark's success could have provided *The Lancet* – the supposed defender of the underdog – with the perfect opportunity to uphold its principles and endorse the appointment. No such endorsement was given. Instead, the journal's Birmingham correspondent wrote 'The appointment of a lady to this post is an experiment which time will prove the value of, but according to the experience of the same institution with regard to house-surgeons, the plan cannot be said to have worked well for the interests of the hospital or the comfort of the residents of the opposite sex.'[217] Luckily Annie Clark [218] did prove an asset to the hospital and she continued to serve there until 1910.

[214] JFF West, Diary; 27 February, 1883. (JFF West Archive).
[215] JFF West, Diary; 5 February, 1883. (JFF West Archive).
[216] *Children's Hospital Reports 20–24, 1880–84*: Committee of Election meeting 5 February, 1883.
[217] *The Lancet*, 1883; ii: p.1066.
[218] *The Lancet* made amends on the occasion of Clark's death. Her obituary comes complete with a photograph and amounts to more than one and a half columns. *The Lancet*; 1924; i: p.571.

The diary indicates that West also suffered minor irritations and frustrations from time to time on his last trip to the Continent. He recorded, for instance, that they both caught bad colds as a result of one woman's refusal to allow him to close the windows on the train on their journey from Paris to Avignon. West described her as 'a regular caution.'[219] He was equally aggrieved by what he considered to be exorbitant rates at the Hotel Splendid in Cannes the following day. The Wests did not arrive there until 10pm by which time it was probably too late to do anything about it. As he put it they 'got taken in literally at H Splendid cheap being 12f for the night.' Still, there were compensating factors and West had to admit that accommodation and facilities were acceptable. 'However' he conceded 'we were opposite the sea and had a good chintz covered room on the third floor to which we were taken by a lift.'[220] It would seem that there was nothing to cancel out the overcharging practised by the Hotel de Louvine [?] in Rome a few days later. West's booking of the hotel of his choice by telegraph seems to have failed so that he not only found himself in the wrong hotel, but to put it in his own words was 'swindled.'[221]

Sarah – wife

West's affection for his wife, Sarah, is demonstrated more than once in the diary. As we have seen, he times her as she goes round one of the columns in St Peter's, Rome, but he also talks of the day they 'fooled around in a boat for two hours looking into various grottoes.'[222] When they left Rome on 2 April, he says 'we left it with great regret' suggesting that they had been happy there. He also makes comments that suggest that Sarah was both independent and stubborn at times. West says he met Sarah at St Peter's, after he had finished touring the medical school and hospitals of San Spirito and St Carlo in Rome. There is no mention of Sarah's having a companion with her. Likewise, he refers to her taking a walk alone during their stay in Castellammare 'Tadie had a walk from 5 till 6.30 and watched the sun set over the island of Ischia.' Interestingly, he goes on to describe the sunset as though he was there too, but perhaps he saw it from the hotel or some other place. If West had cause to be frustrated or even angry with Sarah, he does not give it expression in the diary. The frustration he must have felt when, on one occasion, Sarah refused an invitation to dinner with

---

[219] JFF West, Diary; 12 March, 1883. (JFF West Archive).
[220] Ibid., 13 March, 1883.
[221] Ibid., 17 March, 1883.
[222] Ibid., 30 March, 1883.

a medical colleague in Lyons is recorded simply as 'Prof. — was anxious for us to dine with him and came round and pressed Tadie but she would not be prevailed on so we left for Paris at 2.33.'[223]

The diary entry for Wednesday 28 March, reads as though it was written by West, but is not in his hand. The scribe was almost certainly Sarah. She was there, and the handwriting is the same as that found in two hand written recipe books which belonged to her. James' third night in Naples was a bad one and he discovered he had a temperature of 101°F in the morning. A physician was called. He advised his patient to stay quiet and remain in situ, but on finding the landlord would not allow them to change their room for one with sunshine and a sea view, the Wests instead left for Castellammare. The journey was by train. It would not be unreasonable to think that, once there, James West would have settled himself into bed in their hotel, the Hotel Royal. He did not. Dinner, writes the scribe on his behalf, set him up so much that he spent the evening in the hotel's club enjoying music, songs and billiards. It is not clear from the diary whether or not West was joined by Sarah that evening. The word 'club' alone might have indicated to a Victorian reader a domain for the exclusive use of men. Whatever the case, Sarah obliged her husband by taking on the role of amanuensis on his return to their room that night.

West, as we know, succumbed to illness and death shortly after he returned to Birmingham. Sarah was just thirty-eight years old and a mother of eight when her husband died. Two of her children were under the age of five and all were under twenty. James' passing was marked with a fine funeral, as we have seen. There were flattering obituaries in the medical journals, *Edgbastonia* and the press and, no doubt, numerous letters of condolence. One letter came from the officers of the *Birmingham Medical Institute*. It was an address of condolence emblazoned on vellum and bound in silver and black, according to *Edgbastonia*. West may have got off to a difficult start in 1857, but by the time he died he was a well respected and much-liked man. He had been, in the words of *Birmingham Medical Review*, one of the 'oldest and most constant contributors' to its journal. It said 'the surgical profession of this town (has lost) one of its leaders.'[224] Altogether, it was an accolade that should have been good enough for anyone.

---

[223] JFF West, Diary; 7 April, 1883. (JFF West Archive).
[224] Obituary; *BMR;* 1883; 14: p.47 (B Med I).

EPILOGUE

Sarah Hammond West was left with eight children when James Fitzjames died on 24 May, 1883. She was thirty-eight, and her first-born son only seventeen. The youngest child, Bertram Evelyn was, as we have seen, just two years of age. Sarah's own parents were deceased and, if *Edgbastonia* is to be trusted, her mother-in-law in poor health. It is also possible that Fanny de la Hunt's health was failing by that time too. Sarah and James Fitzjames had accumulated a substantial amount of capital between them by 1883, but it was now up to Sarah to safeguard it with the help of James' executors, Walter Newton Fisher and Charles Green. Fisher, a chartered accountant and philanthropist and Green, a jewellery manufacturer, were trusted friends of the Wests. Both had considerable business experience.

Executors

James West left few clues as to how close he was to Walter Newton Fisher. He mentions him just once in the diary,[1] when he expresses his frustration at having turned down the Fisher's invitation to dinner in favour of one given by the Barneys. The only observations of his character and achievements we have are those made by others. Fortunately Walter Newton Fisher was the subject of a six page eulogy in *Edgbastonia*[2] and one of four pages in *Birmingham Faces and Places*.[3] Described as a strong churchman whose sympathies extended to other denominations, the author of the article in *Faces and Places* states 'The work he has done for the Church in Birmingham can scarcely be over-rated.'[4] Fisher had the distinction of founding the St Barnabas' Mutual Improvement Society along with the Reverend SW Winter. It was a society founded to provide lectures, readings and classes for the working people. Many Birmingham men, we are told 'look back with pleasure upon the days when they attended probably the largest reading, writing and arithmetic classes ever held, and received the rudiments of education from... Mr Fisher.'[5] He was

---

[1]   JFF West, Diary; 18 January, 1883. (JFF West Archive).
[2]   *Edgbastonia*; 1888; VIII: pp.129–135. (BCL).
[3]   *Birmingham Faces and Places*. Date unknown pp.165–169. (BCL).
[4]   Ibid., p.165.
[5]   Ibid., p.166.

almost certainly a lively and entertaining teacher. He had the first prerequisite, a clear voice, but it was probably his ability to mimic which earned him most praise. Like Charles Dickens, himself, Fisher delighted audiences when he read selected passages from the novels of that larger than life novelist. He was renowned for the way in which he read sections of *A Christmas Carol*, to schools and institutions in and around Birmingham. His portrayal of the guests at Bob Sawyer's supper, and for his impersonation of Sergeant Buzfuz, in particular, he won great acclaim.

Trinity Church, Birchfield, near Handsworth, Birmingham, was the first to benefit from Fisher's work as church warden, but he later became warden of The Church of St John, Ladywood, and the parish church of Edgbaston, St George's. Fisher is described in *Faces and Places* as a man of great integrity. He eschewed office in both the local council and parliament, but he worked tirelessly for the town's institutions. He had a long-standing commitment to Sampson Gamgee's Hospital Saturday, was Chairman of the Royal Institution for the Deaf and Dumb, a member of the Council of the College for Girls, a Treasurer of the Children's Hospital, Honorary Secretary to the General Hospital and the Jubilee Committee amongst other things. He is quoted as saying 'To begin life with egotisms and self-sufficiency is fatal to all success' as well as 'To every man belongs his fair share of toil and duty' in *Faces and Places*.[6]

The Wests' first-born, Walter, was born when Fisher was just twenty-one years of age and James thirty-two, so it is a little unlikely that the boy was named after Walter Fisher or that he was his godson. It is possible that West's relationship with Fisher was largely professional, but by agreeing to act as West's executor, Fisher undertook the task of managing the affairs not only of the deceased but also those of his family. If the speed with which he administered one task is anything to go by – namely, donating a number of West's books to the Birmingham and Medical Institute, he was a good choice. West died on 24 May, 1883. The transaction had been completed and was recorded in the institution's minute book on 3 July of the same year.

James West's other executor, Charles Green, clearly was a close friend of the family. Green was ten years younger than West, and if all his offspring were at home on the night of the census, his wife, Katharina, had borne him six children by 1881. Green was described in the census as a 'master jeweller' who employed thirty-four people. The Greens seem to have started their married life in the village of Moseley, now a suburb of Birmingham, but they had moved from there to Olton, near Acock's Green

---

6   Ibid., p.167.

Elizabeth (Lizzie) Silverwood Lorraine. Source: JFF West Archive.

by 1873. From Olton the family moved to nearby Solihull and from there
to Edgbaston sometime between 1877 and 1880. James and Sarah could
have become friends with the Greens in any of those places although Olton
and Solihull are immediate neighbours of Acock's Green, the place where
the Wests first took up residence.

The two families saw each other frequently. Their children played
together, and the adults joined forces to play cards and tennis. As we have
seen, the relationship was not without friction. West was certainly feeling
somewhat impatient with them in the final weeks of his life. He reported in
the diary that their abstinence from alcohol had done nothing for their
sense of humour and he was convinced that the presents he brought back
for them from Italy were unappreciated. Still, the Greens almost certainly
supported and comforted Sarah in her bereavement.

Other friends and family
Sarah was on close terms with many of James' colleagues and their wives as
well as with individuals like Frank Holliday, Frederick Robinson and John

The West family help out with hay-making in Yorkshire, ca.1900.
Source: JFF West Archive.

Kershaw, but she also had her own friends and relatives. One, mentioned earlier, was Elizabeth Silverwood Lorraine of Wakefield, Yorkshire. Otherwise known as 'Lizzie,' she seems to have been particularly close to Sarah. The fact that Sarah's mother, Sarah Sellers (née Shaw), and maiden aunt, Ann Shaw, both wanted Elizabeth Lorraine to inherit their estates should their daughter pre-decease them and have no offspring, and the fact that Sarah Sellers was a witness at the wedding of Lizzie Lorraine's parents suggests that they may have been related. Lizzie Lorraine was not Sarah's only remaining connection with Yorkshire. Her half-brother, John (1833–1909) and his wife, Ann, continued to farm in Great Houghton. The couple were childless, so Sarah had no nieces or nephews and her children no cousins in Yorkshire. Nevertheless, surviving photographs of the West youngsters helping out with hay making, suggest that the family did go up to Yorkshire from time to time.

Bereavement

The only other close relative Sarah had was James's young cousin, Edward John Hunwick. The son of Mary West's sister, Harriet, and her husband,

The West family in the company of friends and relatives in the eighteen nineties.
Sarah, widow of James Fitzjames Fraser West is seated just to the left of centre with
most of her own family to her right. Source: JFF West Archive.

Elijah Hunwick, Edward John was twenty-two years James West's junior.
Harriet married comparatively late, at the age of thirty-five, and bore just
one child in 1855. This meant that although Edward was neither close in
age to his cousin, James Fitzjames, nor his cousin's children, the age gap
was smaller between himself and his cousin's first-born than it was between
himself and his cousin. The Hunwicks maintained close links with the
Wests during their lifetimes. Harriet died in Brixton in 1876, but Elijah
died at 71, Reservoir Road, Edgbaston, home of Mary West and her
daughter, Fanny, in 1877, and it was James West who had signed his death
certificate. Cousin Edward remained close to the Wests after his parents
died and with Sarah and her children up until the end of his own life.

Sarah suffered another bereavement in 1885 with the death of Fanny
de la Hunt at the age of fifty-five. The death certificate indicates that
Fanny died as the result of apoplexy or a stroke. Sarah was present at the
death and it was Sarah who registered it. Like her half-brother, James,
before her, Fanny was buried in the family grave at the Church of the
Ascension in Hall Green.

We know from the diary and *Edgbastonia* that Mary West's health was below par in 1883. The article in *Edgbastonia* goes as far as describing her as an invalid and says that her son seldom missed a day without visiting his mother. He 'tended her in her ailments with affectionate solicitude' we are told.[7] Presumably, then, when Mary followed her daughter to the grave in 1887, her death was not unexpected. She died as a result of gout and paralysis according to the death certificate which, in this case, was signed by her son's old partner in private practice, William Slingsby Mann. The paralysis was doubtless the result of a stroke, but at least it was of only six days duration. How infirm Mary became in old age can only be guessed at, but she would almost certainly have had to rely on her daughter-in-law, Sarah, to support her to some extent in her final years. She was also interred in the family grave at the Church of the Ascension in Hall Green.

With ailing in-laws, a family of eight to feed, clothe and educate and property in Yorkshire to manage, Sarah West would have been busy in the early years of her widowhood. Conrad, her second-born son remained at Derby School, but Walter who, it will be remembered, had suffered serious injury to the eye as a result of an accident at the school in January, 1879, seems to have left. He was neither at home nor at Derby School on the night of the 1881 census when he would have been fifteen. A nation wide search of the census has failed to reveal convincing evidence as to his whereabouts. A boy by the name of Walter West was a pupil at the Blind School, Hampstead, London, in 1881, but this boy's age is recorded as thirteen and the enumerator failed to record his place of birth. Though hardly plausible, it is not impossible.

Walter Sellers West committed suicide in 1895 when he was twenty-nine years of age. When the family's doctor William Slingsby Mann (who, it will be remembered was West's old partner) wrote to the coroner, Oliver Pemberton,[8] he described the incident as Mrs West's 'crowning misfortune.' It was not. Walter was the first of three of her children to follow their father to their graves in the graveyard of the Church of the Ascension in Hall Green in a period of just four months and one day. The letter to the coroner also states that Walter had been of unsound mind since his father died in 1883. The statement given by Sarah, on the other hand, suggests that Walter's disturbed mental state dated back to the time of the accident.

---

7   *Edgbastonia*; 1883; iii: p.98.
8   Inquest on Walter Sellers West, 31 May, 1895. (BCA).

It is inconceivable that Sarah was indifferent to Walter and his troubles. His unhappiness and strange behaviour must have affected the whole household. They probably felt a sense of helplessness and may well have been ashamed. He even spent the years 1887 to 1892 confined in a private Lunatic Asylum in Edinburgh. They must have seemed five long years for all concerned. Sarah may have been advised to send Walter to an asylum in Edinburgh on account of its reputation, but the decision could equally have been based on a desire to hide him away from prying eyes or even banish him. The stigma of mental illness has not, after all, been entirely eradicated today and it is significant that the author, though close to Constance Margery Fryer (née West), granddaughter of James and Sarah West, had never heard of Walter until she conducted her own research following the death of Constance in 1991.

Walter died on 29 May, 1895. He was found seated upright on the seat of the water closet in the yard shortly after 5pm by one of the family's servants, Carrie Tarrant.[9] Walter had given his mother no particular reason for concern, never mind alarm, that day. He went out during the morning but returned home shortly after mid-day. He refused food at lunch time, but appeared cheerful. Sarah heard him leave home again at about 2.30pm, but presumably thought nothing of it. Walter went straight to Bellamy and Wakefield, registered chemists in Easy Row, Paradise Corner, after leaving home. In his statement, John Wakefield says that initially Walter asked his assistant, Henry Cullwick, to sell him some Prussic Acid. Cullwick was uneasy about the request. Being out of the ordinary and one which involved the sale of a highly dangerous poison, Cullwick decided to hand over responsibility to John Wakefield himself. Wakefield says that Walter had been a customer of his for several years and his response suggests that he was fearful of Walter's intentions. He says he asked Walter to justify the purchase with the words 'What do you want Prussic Acid for? You're not going to kill yourself.' Walter's answer was an emphatic 'not hardly.' He then explained that it was simply to poison a cat and it was on hearing this that Wakefield directed his assistant to go ahead with the transaction.

Wakefield was not alone in fearing that Walter might harm, or even kill, himself. His mother, Sarah, said in her statement that he had threatened to kill himself on numerous occasions. He had, she said, even expressed the wish that he had the courage to take Prussic Acid. James West's former

9   The statement made to the coroner's court by Carrie Tarrant. What follows is based on the statements of Sarah Hammond West, John Wakefield and Police Constable, Elem Brain.

Bertram Evelyn West (1881–95), son of James Fitzjames Fraser West.
Source: JFF West Archive.

partner, William Slingsby Mann, was the family doctor and was the first professional on the scene. As his words indicate, he too, had been apprehensive lest Walter should take his own life. On seeing Walter's dead body, he declared 'just what I expected.' Mann's words at the scene and those found in the letter he sent to the town's coroner, Oliver Pemberton, suggest that he was somewhat impatient and out of sympathy with Walter. After pointing out that the unfortunate Walter had been of unsound mind for some time, Mann damns Walter in a stroke with the declaration 'he was a masturbater.' Mann was no more likely to have thought that the act of masturbation could lead to madness or that an individual would have to be mad to do it than his contemporaries, but if a myth is repeated often enough, it can still be powerful. Both Mann and Pemberton lived on the Hagley Road and were neighbours of the Wests at the time. Pemberton, as we know, lost one of his own sons in similar circumstances in 1879, and was likely to have been particularly receptive to the need to protect the bereaved family from the attention of the press. Mann's letter is marked

'Private.' He ends by saying 'Poor Mrs West is of course greatly distressed at this, her crowning misfortune, and she trusts that it may be in your power to kindly consider her, and if possible keep the report of the inquest out of the papers.'

The unhappy Sarah West suffered another loss just two months later. Bertram Evelyn, her last-born son, died from diphtheria on 28 July, 1895, at the age of fourteen. The death occasioned much bitterness in the family. West's granddaughter, Constance, spoke of it as an avoidable death throughout her life. This may have been unfair. It is true that diphtheria, though dangerous, was not always fatal. The medical journals of the period do contain papers on saving lives endangered by constriction of the throat due to diphtheria through the use of tracheotomy and there were, of course, some who recovered spontaneously. Even a timely tracheotomy – a procedure not without risk – was no guarantee against loss of life through diphtheria though. The bacterium which causes the disease releases a toxin as it multiplies and when this enters the bloodstream, it can cause irreparable damage to the nerves and heart. The death certificate does indeed indicate that Bertram's heart had been affected. Born before both immunisation and antibiotics, Bertram would have had little other than his own body's immune system to fight off the disease.

Bertram began his education at Edgbaston Preparatory School (Hallfield), but was a pupil of King Edward's School, Birmingham, at the time of his death. The survival of his final report which remained unfinished forever, is one of the most poignant documents in the JFF West Archive. A single letter of condolence sent by AWW Dale, one of the school's maths masters, has also survived. It is two and a half sides long and comes complete with black borders. Dale explains that days earlier some of Bertram's work passed through his hands and he goes on to say he gave it his 'special attention.' Its survival undoubtedly means that the letter was a comfort to the once-more bereaved Sarah.

Calamity struck again on 27 September with the death of Marion Lucy West. It cannot have been expected. The death strikes the author as somewhat suspicious for two reasons. One relates to the cause of death and the other to the fact that, like the death of Walter Sellers, this one was never mentioned by West's granddaughter either. Marion Lucy, the Wests' first-born daughter, died at the age of twenty-five. The death certificate was signed by CC Purslow MD and gives Acute Mania followed by collapse and coma as the cause of death. It was either the fifth attack in forty-eight hours or the fifth attack, the duration of which was forty-eight hours. The words on the death certificate 'Acute Mania (5th Attack) 48 hours Collapse – Coma' do not make it clear. Quain's Dictionary, like others of its day and type, defines mania as a mental condition and there is nothing in them to suggest that it could result in death per se. Although there is always the chance that Marion Lucy's condition was mis-diagnosed, and that she died as a result of a physical malady, it is hard to ignore the possibility that she too may have committed suicide.

Photographs of Marion Lucy suggest she was an imaginative young woman who liked to adorn herself in fancy or exotic dress. Unlike Walter, she left a will. Walter Sellers and Bertram Evelyn, both of whom, as we know, pre-deceased her, were remembered in her will. It had been her intention to leave her youngest brother, Bertram, £200 and her oldest brother, Walter, £100. Gertrude, Amy Valentine and Conrad Kershaw were also bequeathed the sum of £100 while her younger brothers, John Frederick, and Arthur Balden were given £200 each. Marion left all her jewellery to her sisters, Gertrude and Amy Valentine in equal shares. Also remembered in the will were two servants. Fanny Dodd who, she states, was in her mother's service for many years, was given £20, as was Harry Tarrant who was still at the time of writing in her mother's service. Tarrant, we can only assume, must have been a gardener, coachman, stable boy or groom and was probably related to Carrie Tarrant, abovementioned. Any residue was to be divided between her brothers and sisters in equal amounts.

The only other source which sheds light on the character of Marion Lucy is to be found in an album containing poems and Christmas cards. A poem written by her father's cousin, Edward John Hunwick, at Christmas 1885, and entitled 'To Lucy' starts affectionately 'Ma petite cousine' and goes on to tease her on account of the fact that she dislikes being kissed. Marion Lucy was sixteen years of age at the time. She was not the only 'cousin' to receive a personal poem. Edward also addressed poems to Gertrude (Gertie) then thirteen; John Frederick (Jack), eleven; Amy Valentine (Daisy), eight; Arthur Balden, six and Bertram Evelyn (Bertie) four years. The poems are carefully presented and the script legible and attractive. They are, without doubt, a labour of love. Cousin Gertie is promised a kiss but only 'if Mama will allow it,' Jack is alerted to the fact that his name appears in the poem with the words 'Can you your name see in these lines?' Arthur is encouraged to enjoy his plum pudding and to 'emulate Arthur of old' while 'dear little Bertie' is urged to enjoy his turkey and mince pies in order to remain strong.

The poems say as much about Edward Hunwick as they do about the recipients. He had married the previous year and was living in London, but he still found time to compose a set of six verses designed to bring cheer to his little cousins. They did not arrive in the post. Either Edward suggested it himself or someone asked him to write them directly in an established album and he had obliged with what can only be described as devotion.

Today, Sarah and James West have no descendants. Sarah herself died in 1910 at the age of sixty-five. She maintained her involvement in the property and land she had inherited in Yorkshire. As a letter from John Kershaw shows, she also lent money on mortgage to at least one of James' friends. Kershaw, the individual concerned, complained bitterly to Sarah about the way he had been treated by her solicitor who, in turn was acting on behalf of the trustees of James's estate, over a mortgage for £1,000 on Hope Lodge in London. John Kershaw himself, lived at Park House, Willesden Lane, London, a place James had stayed in on at least one occasion. Unfortunately the letter is undated. After detailing the exact nature of his grievance, Kershaw declares 'I feel altogether that I have been badly used in this affair.' He goes on to say that he considers, above all, that such heavy-handedness is unacceptable between friends. Kershaw says he wants the matter discussed 'in a friendly way, and not with sharp practice.' He asks Sarah not to show his letter to her solicitors and instructs her to reply to his business address in order to avoid worrying his wife. Whether this affair was resolved happily is unknown, but if Sarah valued the friendship she certainly had some bridge building to do to maintain it.

Sarah's long standing friend, Lizzie Lorraine, died in 1901 at the age of fifty-seven. No doubt the two women saw a lot of each other in the years between the death of James and Lizzie's death, but there is not a shred of evidence to support the supposition. Apart from Lizzie Lorraine, Sarah's personal friends and associates are unknown. Sarah was unlikely to have been a personal friend of Birmingham's most generous female philanthropist, Miss Louisa Ryland (1814–89), although she is listed amongst the hundreds of mourners at her funeral. Miss Ryland was born at The Laurels in Edgbaston (later home to John Birt Davies and afterwards to Edgbaston High School for Girls) and owned estates in and around Birmingham as well as land elsewhere. She moved as a child to Warwick Priory initially and then to Barford Hill, near Warwick where she remained for the rest of her life, but the scale of her beneficence towards Birmingham and its needy was unparalleled.

Sarah was more likely to have attended Miss Ryland's funeral out of respect for this inspirational woman than because she knew her personally. Miss Ryland gave to charities and other causes throughout her adult life and she did not disappoint on her death. The General Hospital was to be rebuilt largely thanks to a legacy of £25,000 from Miss Ryland, but countless other institutions benefited too, including Queen's Hospital which received the sum of £1,000. Not that Miss Ryland forsook her friends and family. One, the wife of Dr Thomas F Chavasse and second cousin to Miss Ryland, received a legacy of a staggering £40,000.[10] It was a good time to have had connections with the great lady.

Issue

All of Sarah's remaining children outlived her, though only two married. Arthur Balden remained a bachelor and died in Coton Hill Hospital, Stafford at the age of seventy-nine in 1949. In common with Walter Sellers and Marion Lucy, neither Arthur's history nor even his existence were ever mentioned by Constance Fryer, West's last descendant. It was, therefore, sad though not entirely surprising, to discover that Coton Hill Hospital was a lunatic asylum. The death certificate gives us a clue as to Arthur's occupation as well as the cause of death which was put down to cardio vascular degeneration. Arthur, it seems, had worked as a clerk at Selly Oak Hospital. The precise wording raises questions though. Instead of simply writing 'clerk' or even 'clerk at Selly Oak Hospital' it says 'of Selly Oak Hospital Birmingham CB a clerk.' What this implies is likely to remain a mystery, though it does at least suggest that Arthur was able to work at some stage of his life.

Coton Hill opened in 1854. It was originally built as an extension to the County Asylum at a cost of £42, 000 to house private patients of the middle and upper classes. Set in park lands, with fine views over the nearby countryside, the hospital could boast amongst its facilities a large recreation room which was used for dances, a cinema and theatre and a chapel. The chapel is now all that remains. The asylum itself closed down in 1979 and was demolished a year later although the site it occupied has become Stafford District General Hospital. It is painful to consider Arthur's plight,

[10] *Birmingham Faces and Places*; 1889: p.170. (BCL).

the more so because one suspects that he may have been effectively abandoned by his family.

Amy Valentine

The remaining children went on to occupy a number of different roles. Amy Valentine, or Daisy as she was known, married Charles Frederick Redfern in 1902 when she was twenty-five years of age. Redfern was an auctioneer and surveyor from a long established, well-known and respected Birmingham family. If hints dropped by Constance Fryer are anything to go by, it was not a happy alliance. A codicil to the will of Daisy's older sister Gertrude adds credence to this supposition. When Gertrude originally wrote her will in 1909, she chose Daisy's husband as one of two executors and trustees. Three years later she rescinded the decision and wrote the following 'I hereby revoke the appointment of Charles Frederick Redfern as one of the executors and trustees of my will and I revoke the legacy of forty pounds bequeathed by my said will to the said Charles Frederick Redfern as an

Amy Valentine Redfern (née West); 1877–1937 in 1906.
Source: JFF West Archive.

Barbara Joyce Redfern (seated) and Constance Margery West with their grandmother's maid in 1907. Source: JFF West Archive.

executor and trustee thereof and I hereby appoint my sister Amy Valentine Redfern....in the place of ...Charles Frederick Redfern.'

Amy bore just one child, a girl. The child, Barbara Joyce, but known as Joyce, was born in 1906 and was looked upon by her cousin Constance as a sister. The two cousins remained close right up until the time of Joyce's demise in 1983. Numerous photographs have survived of both Daisy and her daughter, Joyce, and of the houses they occupied. When Joyce married in 1932 at the age of twenty-six her cousin Constance was one of her bridesmaids. The couple remained childless. Amy herself had no occupation save for the time she worked as a nurse in the Voluntary Aid Detachment during the First World War. There is no record of her work, but since she had a young child at the time, she is unlikely to have been posted abroad.

John Frederick

John Frederick West, otherwise known as 'Jack,' attended Birmingham's most prestigious school, King Edward's School. He was the first member of the

John Frederick West with Conrad Kershaw West's widow Ellen, in the 1930s.
Source: JFF West Archive.

family to go to there. Founded in the sixteenth century, the school underwent a radical change to its outdated curriculum in the second half of the nineteenth century thanks to the influence of the town's close-knit and socially aware elite. John Frederick applied himself to the study of medicine on leaving school, as we have seen, but gave it up in favour of law and became a solicitor rather than a medical man. John never married himself, but he was very close to Conrad and his family. He is even recorded as living with them at 1 Reservoir Road, Edgbaston, in a will he made in the year 1911. After Conrad's death in 1930, John Frederick maintained close ties with Conrad's widow and daughter and Conrad's widow, Ellen, was the beneficiary of his will. John Frederick died in 1936 at the age of sixty-one in Henley in Arden, a picturesque village some fifteen miles south east of Birmingham.

Gertrude

The West's second daughter, Gertrude, was also very close to Conrad and his family. Like her sister, Marion Lucy, she was educated at the recently founded Edgbaston High School for Girls, a school which from its

Gertrude West (1872–1951) ca.1918. Source: JFF West Archive.

foundation in 1876 provided first class education for daughters of the town's elite. The institution, still flourishing today, owes its existence to that champion of educational reform, the illustrious Edgbastonian, George Dixon. With three daughters of his own and no suitable school available, Dixon masterminded a scheme to establish a school which could compete with rival institutions for the opposite sex. The combined forces of 243 shareholders, each worth £10, and an advance of £2,000 from Josiah Mason meant Dixon's dream soon materialised. Dixon himself was the first chairman of its governing body – a body made up of both men and women. By including science in the curriculum, the ethos of the school was to foster and celebrate equality of the sexes from the start.

Gertrude West is remembered today as a painter of miniatures. She went on to study art in London and Paris and, with the exception of a period during the First World War, was able to devote her life to her art. She never married. From October, 1918 until she was demobilised from the Postal Censorship services in June, 1919, Gertrude occupied the role of Examiner in the Postal Censorship. Her punctuality and conduct were excellent according to the Certificate of Service in Civil Appointment she received on the completion of her duties.[11] She had, it was stated, worked in a steady and methodical manner and had a good knowledge of German.

Biographical accounts of Gertrude West in reference books on art are brief. She must have been among the last of the miniaturists, but her paintings sold and she was able to support herself on the proceeds. Much to the delight of her niece, Constance, who received regular invitations to stay with her glamourous aunt, she lived and worked in Hampstead, London. Monday 24 April, 1922 saw the launch of her first exhibition at the Grieves Art Gallery in Old Bond Street, London. As the press notices declare 'Yesterday, two hours after the opening there were already half a dozen pictures bearing the red badge which denoted "sold." '[12] The prices were modest, the highest at that point being £7/17/6d but that was, after all, day one of an exhibition which was of a week's duration. The notices suggest that Gertrude did not paint miniatures exclusively although virtually all the surviving examples of her work known to the author are miniatures.

The press notices mentioned above are not the only mementos of Gertrude's life as an artist to have survived in the JFF West Archive. A set of four letters regarding the possibility of putting one of her miniatures in Queen Mary's dolls' house, together with a triumphant telegram on a related matter sent by Gertrude to her niece, Constance, have been carefully preserved for posterity. The first three letters are from Mabel Hawkes, lady in waiting to Princess Marie Louise.[13] It appears from the first letter, that Gertrude had written to the Princess and sent her a sample of her work. The letter insists that the Princess was delighted by the painting Gertrude had sent, but says that she should write again on the subject in two months time, by which time, she believed, Sir Edwin Lutyens, the designer and co-ordinator, would have returned to England. As a word of warning from the lady in waiting suggests 'only as I told you everything has to be very tiny,'[14] Gertrude's painting was too large.

---

[11] Gertrude West's certificate and two letters sent to her by the War Office thanking her for her contribution to the war effort have survived. (JFF West Archive).

[12] Press cutting, *The Nottingham Evening News*. Tuesday 25 April, 1922. The archive also contains cuttings from newspapers as far afield as Belfast, Ipswich, Dublin and Sheffield. (JFF West Archive).

[13] Princess Marie Louise, granddaughter of Queen Victoria had seized upon the idea of indulging Queen Mary's penchant for miniature objet d'art by commissioning the country's leading architect, Sir Edwin Lutyens to design a dolls' house for the Queen. Lutyens designed a Palladian house which was perfect in every detail. The contents had to be made to a uniform scale of 1.12. The Queen appointed the Princess her liaison officer.

[14] Letter dated December, 1922. (JFF West Archive).

A painting small enough to satisfy the requirements for the dolls' house never materialised and Gertrude lost out to her competitors. Still, as a letter from Mabel Hawkes shows,[15] when Gertrude offered her painting to the Princess Marie Louise as a gift, it was accepted. Gertrude received another letter a few days later in which she was again thanked for one of her paintings. It is not clear whether this was a second painting. The picture had, as the lady in waiting was quick to emphasise 'delighted' the Princess.[16] Gertrude was told that a letter from her Highness would follow shortly. It did.

Gertrude received a letter from Princess Marie Louise in early February, 1923.[17] The Princess expressed her gratitude for the painting Gertrude had sent, and although she explained that she would leave the final decision to Sir Edwin Lutyens, she felt sure they would be able to place it somewhere in the Queen's Dolls' House. This was not the end of it. On 21 February, 1925, Gertrude sent her niece, Constance, a telegraph which must have made the chests of sender and recipient alike swell with pride. Like most telegraphs it was brief and to the point, but the words, simply stated, speak volumes 'Princess Mary purchased other miniature Gertrude.'[18]

'Aunty Gerty' cropped up in numerous conversations between the author and her late step-mother, Constance. The author heard about school holidays spent with Gertrude in London and of the many trips they made to the theatre and the city's well-known teashops. Gertrude also sent Constance innumerable postcards over the years which the recipient kept until the end of her life. They were of sentimental value only and have been destroyed, but they did show how close the relationship between them was. Gertrude returned to Birmingham at the end of her life and died in 1951 at the age of seventy-nine. She lived with Constance and her mother for some years and with Constance alone after the latter's death in 1945 but her death took place nearby, in an Edgbaston nursing home.

Conrad Kershaw

The Wests' second-born son, Conrad Kershaw, had what his daughter described as a 'weak heart.' Still, Conrad was more fortunate than some. He lived until the age of sixty-two at a time when treatment was limited and prognosis poor. He was certainly regarded by his wife, Ellen, and his

---

[15] Ibid., Letter dated January, 1923.
[16] Ibid., Letter dated January, 1923.
[17] Ibid., February, 1923.
[18] Telegraph, 21 February, 1925. (JFF West Archive).

Conrad Kershaw West ca.1900. Source: JFF West Archive.

only daughter as an invalid who required a quiet life and restorative trips to the seaside. As a very young man he had been sent off to Switzerland for the benefit of his health and there is a letter in the archive which alludes to another rejuvenating trip abroad. Ultimately, though, the diseased state of his heart and cardio-vascular system were responsible for his death. The death certificate states that he was afflicted with aortic valvular disease of the heart and that he died comatose having suffered a cerebral thrombosis.

Conrad trained initially as a land surveyor and worked as a surveyor, valuer and estate agent. He married Ellen Ward in 1904 and became a father for the first and only time later the same year. If the first hand accounts of him given by Constance are reliable, he must have been a much loved man. Judging from the various documents relating to his life that have survived, he seems to have been a popular and dutiful friend and colleague too. One, a letter from Alfred Boggust, written to Conrad when he tendered his resignation from office as Honorary Treasurer of the Central Edgbaston Bowling Club gives us an idea of how non-family members saw him. 'May I add a personal note to say how exceedingly sorry

I am that our labours together are to be ended. To me it has been a real pleasure to work with you and such a contrast to the Hon. Treasurers of the past. I shall miss you dear boy more than you think.'[19]

Constance Margery

The Wests' last descendant, Constance, died in 1991 at the age of eighty-seven. In common with most of her family, she was not known by the name on her birth certificate. She was known instead by her second name, Margery. Margery enjoyed good health until the last few weeks of her life and never spent a single day of her long life in hospital. She went to Edgbaston Church of England College for Girls (founded in 1886) – a school which held, for her, the happiest of memories. On completing her schooldays there, she remained at the school to avail herself of a Froebel teacher training qualification. It was a sought after qualification by those who wanted to pursue a thoroughly modern approach to teaching. After a

Constance Margery with her father, Conrad Kershaw West in 1911.
Source: JFF West Archive.

---

[19] Letter dated September, 1917. (JFF West Archive).

Constance Margery West, affectionately known as 'Margery' all of her life in the 1940s. Source: JFF West Archive.

few years teaching infants, Margery took up a post at Wellesbourne School in Acock's Green, Birmingham. Wellesbourne School was an independent school which catered for boys between the ages of four and eighteen. She taught boys of nine, ten and eleven. The author's father, Cyril Fryer (1909–80), taught maths, physics and chemistry to the older boys at the same school and it was there that they met and fell in love.

The two married in 1961 when Margery was fifty-six years of age. Margery retired from teaching in 1968 having spent the last two years working at Hallfield School, Edgbaston – a move she made on account of the closure of Wellesbourne School. Her marriage took place sixteen years after her mother's death. She mentioned a boyfriend in her diary at one stage but nothing came of their relationship. In any case, it may have been anathema to Margery to sacrifice the place she held in her mother's heart for that of another. She was the product of a happy childhood and

Church of the Ascension, Hall Green, Birmingham – burial place of James Fitzjames Fraser West and most of his family. Photographed by the author in 1999.

remained devoted to her mother until the latter's death in 1945. Her mother was regarded by her as her best friend. They walked together, visited friends and family together and went to the cinema and theatre together. Fortunately, her marriage to the author's father gave her nearly twenty years more of happiness which was terminated only on the death of Cyril at the age of seventy in 1980.

Like her paternal grandfather, Margery kept a diary. She destroyed all the diaries up to 1929, but those written between 1930 and 1991 have survived. Margery had been actively involved in the church of St Germain's on City Road, Birmingham. When she died in 1991, the funeral was attended by many local mourners as well as friends and family. For the conversations about her family and the sense of duty which prompted her to safeguard the family archive, the author is truly grateful.

James West never became a grandfather, unless an individual can be said to occupy the role posthumously. Sarah Hammond, on the other hand, met both of her grandchildren. She died in 1910 at the age of sixty-five. The death certificate cites Diabetes, a disease for which there was then no effective treatment, as the cause of her death. It was a condition that had been diagnosed twelve years earlier, so it is fair to assume that she suffered from increasingly poor health from that time onwards. She remained in Edgbaston until her death.

One hundred and seventeen, Hagley Road was subject to re-numbering along with its neighbours in 1884 when it became number 247. Sarah and her family stayed there until 1901. In that year they moved a little further out of town along the same road to number 232. It was not her last move. In 1908, just two years before she died, she moved into number 11, Manor Road, a road which stands at right angles to the Hagley Road. Number 232 Hagley Road is the only one of her marital homes to have survived. The sites of both Carlton House in Acock's Green and 117, Hagley Road are now occupied by flats and 11, Manor Road was flattened by German bombers in the Second World War. Sarah's daughter in law, Ellen, and granddaughter, Margery, spent many a night in the bomb shelter in the garden of their house, number 1, Reservoir Road, during the Second World War and doubtless heard the sound of the German bombers and the bombs they dropped on Sarah West's old house.

Sarah was buried with James and the children who had pre-deceased her in the churchyard of the Church of the Ascension in Hall Green. With five surviving offspring and two grandchildren under the age of six, it is unlikely that Sarah Hammond West died fearing that her family was close to extinction. Doubtless she assumed the number of grandchildren would swell over the coming years. It was not to be. Were it not for Constance (Margery) West, granddaughter, the task of tracing Sarah's roots and gaining an insight into her character would have been formidable. Unlike her husband, James, whose personality and professional life have been exposed in a number of sources, the diary and his publications chief among them, Sarah left no written word except for a book containing her favourite recipes and another comprising a selection of poems. What inspired Sarah's forebears to safeguard some of their family documents for hundreds of years is unknown, but the fact that Constance continued to preserve them along with material relating to her grandfather, facilitated the author's efforts in writing this book and has galvanised her intention of saving the archive for posterity. It is hoped that readers have gained an insight not only into the professional life of James Fitzjames Fraser West, but also the man.

DIARY OF JAMES FITZJAMES
FRASER WEST,
JANUARY, 1883 – APRIL, 1883

[Some additional punctuation has been inserted by the author. Square brackets are editorial].

Thursday 11 January
Discussion at BMA on alteration of constitution of Com. of Council. Gamgee and Sawyer the principle reformers. Dined at Dr Fosters with a lot of medicos. Sat between Russell and Boddington. Dr Joy Dr Mackenzie of Rugby, Foster and I afterwards played a rubber so that I had not to sit more than an hour waiting for Walter to come from his first evening party at Shepherds[?]

Friday 12 January
Gave a children's party to about 20 youngsters, mostly Walter's and Lucy's friends. W and S Balden, A and W Daniell, WJ Clarke, E Garman. J Warey, S Colls, C Green, and A Feeney and misses Restall, Feeney, Green, Hopwood and Pl.....[?]. Daniell, Swinden and Mrs Lee all seemed to enjoy the dancing for wh. Tadie did most of the playing.

Saturday 13 January
Read a paper on Erasmus in Praise of Folly prefacing with a short account of his life. It occupied nearly an hour and was I suppose acceptable, as the discussion lasted till 10 when it was too late for any music. Only 7 present. I lent the Praise of Folly to Oliver Suffield and the Colloquies to Ross Jordan, the president. 3 new members were elected.

Sunday 14 January
For the first time for many weeks had not a single patient to see so took Daisy and Arthur to Mr Platten's chapel * where we heard a capital sermon

---

* The Reverend Plattern was the incumbent at The Baptist Church of the Redeemer on the Hagley Road.

on the efficacy of earnest prayer to God. In the afternoon Walter and I went to the Botanical Gardens and admired the orchids. Coming back called on Dr Heslop and we had three hours gossip together about Hospital reform – general politics and almost every thing under the sun. I supped at my mother's and arranged for her to go to Llandudno on Friday and for myself to go with her if possible.

Monday 15 January
Drove over to Acock's Green and took poor young Bikker who has been 3 months in the house from the Ry [railway] accident with me. The sun shone brightly and he thoroughly enjoyed the ride, but was so faint that Mrs Atkins gave him some champagne to revive him. Called to see Mrs Hornsby who had a sort of epileptic attack wh. frightened her family very much.

Tuesday 16 January
Met Dr Russell about Mrs Hornsby.

Wednesday 17 January
[Blank].

Thursday 18 January
Dined at Mr T Barneys with Will. and Walter Warden, Round, Brace, Mitchell and their wives. It was a gorgeous feed but a very slow affair and I would rather have been at Fisher's who were also giving a dinner party that evening to wh. we were invited.

Friday 19 January
Met Dr Russell at Mrs Hornsby's then rushed to the G* to see Mrs Atkins [?] and back in time to leave by the 1.40 train with mother, Fanny and Jack for Llandudno wh. we reached about 7. A tremendous gale with rain was blowing when we got there and the sea looked fierce. However it became calm later on and the moon lit up the sea like a sheet of silver. Played a game of billiards at the.....[?] with W R Allen.

Saturday 20 January
A lovely bright Summerlike day and Fan Jack and I walked round the Orme's head enjoying the scene with its brilliant sea and sunshine and with

---

* Acock's Green.

that calm wh. only hard worked toilers in town can really experience. After dinner took another walk for the evening. Jack and I had a last sea bathe followed by a cold shower. The Hollingsworths * who had kindly taken rooms at.....[?] House for us asked us to play a rubber in their rooms.

Sunday 21 January
Fanny, Jack and I went to St George's Church Llandudno – a large cold building and heard a young clergyman read himself in with a sermon from the first lines in Genesis, mediocre in a high degree. After dinner Jack and I went to Mr Roland alluis [?] a pretty house in a nook close by the little Orme's head, where we were kindly received as friends of Mr Hollingsworth. We met Dr Bold Williams and the apt [?] Ragwood. In the evening Dr Dalton came to feed and spent an hour pleasantly chatting with us and offering to give a look at Ma during her stay at Llandudno. Mr and Mrs Hollingsworth also spent an hour with us and after they had gone I read the evening service to our party. Ma seems already improved by the change.

Monday 22 January
Llandudno Fan and Jack and I with Puck the pug dog set off for a church up the signal post on the top of the Orme's head. It was a lovely morning, not too hot and yet warm enough to be pleasant. We climbed and walked for 2 hours getting fine glimpses first of the Colwyn side and then of the Conwy but could not reach our destination as our time was too short, so we descended into Mostyn and looked at the pictures in Woodcock's gallery and so back to dinner at 1 and then after a hurried goodbye to Ma to the station, Mr and Mrs H as well as Jack and Fan accompanying me to see me off by the 1.45 train. Long, cold, ride to B'ham which we arrived at 7. Found message from T Webley so went to the Conservative Club to see him – all up to see me on my return with open arms. Clarke had done my work at least what little there was, as I had arranged to give him a minimum of it.

Tuesday 23 January
A very busy day as everyone had to be seen. Mrs Atkins taking up some time by the journey to Acock's Green. Asked Clarke to lunch with me but he was engaged.

---

* Mr Samuel Henry Hollingsworth was proprietor of John Hollingsworth Ltd, tobacconists, New Street, Birmingham. When he died at the age of ninety in 1941, West's granddaughter, Constance Margery, wrote the following on the newspaper obituary 'Grandfather brought his daughter into the world.'

Wednesday 24 January

Leigh Lodge – Young Mr Swinden made WM. Large muster of Phils.*
Handsome banquet at wh. I sat between Howkins and Tom Smith.
Promised the price of a guinea for the Masonic pupils' aid fund so sent it
through F G Swinden. Rather a long sitting.

Thursday 25 January

Went with G Yates to see W Bikker and afterwards to the market to buy
some flower pots. Lunched at Warwick House with Mr Diamo [?] of
Kidderminster and Mr Browning. Mrs H still very ill under Dr Jordan's
care. I spent evening at home and sent off some of my pamphlets on
Bigelow's operation which Walter directed for me.

Friday 26 January

Mr Archer's medical party where I met Mr Howard Marsh of St Bart's – a
pleasant gentleman. Drs Russell, Sawyer, Carter and Messrs Pemberton,
Jordan, Solomon, Jolly and W Thomas. Much pleasant chat after dinner
and then a rubber which lasted till the small hours. Path and Clin. Branch
of BMA. Manby, in chair, brought forward a case of secondary papilloma of
arm removed that day from Mr Monk, a butcher. Several very interesting
specimens, but few members to see them.

Saturday 27 January

Very wet and stormy. Gave William Swinbourne notice to leave this day
fortnight and engaged Daniel Hermisan an old man of 60 who had been
18 years with Mr J Steed of Northfield. Went to A G [Acocks Green] in the
morning. Home to dine and in the afternoon to Solihull to see Miss
Dickens who has returned from the asylum but little improved and then on
to WW Richards, Olton, where I spent the eve. He much worried with
Fraser coal troubles though still buying Bretts and Holls!

Sunday 28 January

Walked with the boys in the morning round Harborne to Mr Webley's.
Walter so tired that he turned back. Went to St Augustine's at night with
Gerty and had a good sermon from Dr Blissard. I sent Lizzie Lorraine 5
new shares in Eastern Extension Australian Teleg Co at £11 for the
investment of the £50 I hold of hers. Wrote also to Nicholson enclosing Mr
Povey Harper's statement of coal got to Dec 31st 1882.

---

* Philalethes: association of Freemasons who seek light and have light to impart.

Monday 29 January
[Blank].

Tuesday 30 January
Q H [Queen's Hospital] Committee 4.30pm [and back to?] nurses' school as I did not approve of, I sent their 3 tickets for Festival Choral Soc and 2 for Harrison's concert.

Wednesday 31 January
Read up Billroth on Classification of Tumours for clin. lecture on case of Resection of upper jaw for round celled sarcoma. Patient seemed quite recovered.

Thursday 1 February
Festival Choral Soc 'Faust'. Handed to Mr Leah and son 18 B Bk [Birmingham Bank] shares which they had sold at £16.2.6 per share for 14 Inst. – they have bought for me £500. 3d Pref. Grand Trunk Ry of Canada at £62½. 1st lecture since xmas.... only one student present. Operated for Fissure of anus. Children went to party at Hopwoods.

Friday 2 February
Miss Con [?] of Saltburn came and spent the day with us. She is as young and bright as ever although she has a niece to keep. Fred Robinson sent me his last account – a collection of short stories 'Women are Strange' being the chief: full of humour and with a keen insight into human nature.

Saturday 3 February
Walked with Walter to see the school at five ways acquired recently by the grammar school under the guidance of Mr Beuttler one of the masters. Everything is in excellent order. Played a game of billiards with Mr and Mrs Warden and Branson at the house of the former. He has some fine Sea..........[?] and other good pictures.

Sunday 4 February
Walked with Conrad and Gerty to Oldbury as it was a fine bright morning – we called at Mr Torbitt's and had a rest and then returned. Went to St Augustine's at night and heard an indifferent school-masterly sermon from Rev Ogle. Supped with the Hopwoods.

Monday 5 February

Birmingham Joint Stock Bank meeting. Called for George Yates and took him to see Arthur Bikker who is now much better. Engaged [?] young Ben Beasley of Hall Green for assurance [?]. Harrison's concert – my tickets from the Q H nurses. Voted at election for HS of Children's Hospital for Miss Shore from B'ham and afterwards for Grinling but Dr Powell was elected – again on the losing side. Agreed to sell Bullen for some client of his 56 Bm [Birmingham] Banking Co. shares at £16 – he selling them for £16.2.6 for Mr Thomas Mills of 57, Villa Road, Handsworth, Stafford.

Tuesday 6 February

Long round – went to see Jaffray's picture by Hall at the Joint Stock Bank. It makes those by Munro [?] look ridiculous. Went to AG in the afternoon. Sent off cheque to J Povey Harper for £10.10.0 for surveying the Hoyland Colliery. Wrote letters which were somewhat in arrears.

Wednesday 7 February

[Blank].

Thursday 8 February

Colls' Dinner party. Mr and Mrs Farndale, Mr and Mrs Prosser, Mr Gales and Mrs Whittaker formed the party and a very agreeable quiet evening was spent. We stayed the night and the Farndales also.

Friday 9 February

Came back by the 9 train with Mr Farndale and Mr Colls. Had to go to Chester Rd. to see Frank Holliday who had ricked his back by lifting his bedstead with his wife in it! Too much conjugal affection! Spent evening at Branson's and played rubber with him, Balden and Haynes when I had bad luck and lost 27/6.

Saturday 10 February

Sent for at 6 to go to Mr Holliday to see poor old John Oxford who has been his gardener for 35 years. Found him suffering from strangulated hernia so I operated with the assistance of Dr Barling and Mr Sims. The dread and excitement caused his poor old wife to have an apoplectic seizure. I did the operation all right but under great difficulties.

Sunday 11 February

Conrad walked round with me in the morning to see poor old John who was as well as could be expected, until his poor old wife died, whence he seemed to be prostrated. Went to St Augustine's in the evening and heard a very good sermon from Mr Irwin.

Monday 12 February

Poor old John Oxford died during the day from exhaustion. He had had no sickness after the operation and seemed easier from pain. Went round the Hospital. Read Fred Robinson's new novel *Women are Strange* from 4 till 7am and got very much interested by it so that sleep deserted my cases.

Tuesday 13 February

Drove over to Acock's Green and Solihull in the open carriage with Tadie to call on Capt. and Mrs Wiley. They have a very pretty little place at Blossomfield, near Shirley and seem as happy as two turtle doves. A very cold ride back in the evening.

Wednesday 14 February

Walter returned from Llandudno having enjoyed his little holiday very much. Daisy was 6 years old today and she had all the little Greens to spend the day with her and Tadie and I saw them home in the evening. Rec.d £1,218.10.0 for 76 B – Banking Co. Shares from Mr A [?] Bullen for his clients Mr Mills (56) and Mr Vincent Taylor (20). Sold the 56 at £16 and the 20 at £16.2.6 nos 1796 to 1854, 17936 to 17952 both inclusive. I paid the money into the Bm Bank Co.

Thursday 15 February

Went to Hospital at 9.30 and found only 2 students waiting for Clinical Instruction, so I gave up the idea of a regular lecture. Dined with Mr Holliday at Warwick House and he advised my offering the £1,500 to the Metrop. Wagon Co. at 4 pc. On my way home called on Beresford and Dr Suffield and at Roseneath where I found Fanny's legacy from Mrs Davies £89.8.8 and her gold watch and chain awaiting her, so sent the receipt for her to sign at home. Reading and writing all evening.

Friday 16 February

[Blank].

Saturday 17 February
[Blank]

Sunday 18 February
St Augustine's in the evening with poor sermon from Mr Irwin. Walked with Gerty to Webley's in the morning.

Monday 19 February
Consultation with Mr G Yates re Bikker who is slowly improving and we afterwards dined together at the Stork Hotel and had a capital feed. In the evening wrote paper on Chronic Joint Inflammation for Mid Med Soc. Paid to Mr FS Taylor sect. of Metrop. Wagon Co Ltd sum £1,500 on debentures for 3 years at 4 pc and also got him to take £100 from F De La Hunt at same rate. This ought to be a safe investment at any rate!

Tuesday 20 February
Dinner party at Dr Russell's. 20 present. Sat on right of Mrs R and next to Dr Richards. As usual with medical parties it was slow so slept at 10.

Wednesday 21 February
Read paper on Chronic Joint Inflammation and their Treatment at Mid Med Soc. Dr Malins pres. T Chavasse, Warden and many spoke and the thing went off fairly well only there was but a small meeting probably owing to Ophthalmic paper by Priestley Smith coming first.

Thursday 22 February
Hospital work light. Only 3 students, so no lecture. Called on George Yates who gave me some pictures for the children and promised me a cup and saucer for my wife's drawing room. Drove over to see Mrs Owens, Tysley.

Friday 23 February
Went to a rubber at Haynes to meet Balden, Woodward and Brandon but disturbed 3 times: to Hopwoods – Mrs in state of alcoholic excitement, Hornsby's ch.ds croup and lastly to Hospital to a case of pistol shot wound of girl at 18 just over pubes. The result of accident at Mr Parton's, Kingswood: tried to find bullet but without success. To bed at 2am.

Saturday 24 February
Amputated hand for cancer at Hospital in woman at 52. Gun shot case doing fairly well. No wound of bladder. Dined at club and afterwards went with Onions [?] to see his wife – a beautiful day. In evening called out to see Hornsby's chd and Mrs Grimly [?] so went to bed at midnight very tired.

Sunday 25 February
Long round with Walter in the carriage in the morning. In evening went to St Augustine's. Mr Irwin preached and Mr Woodward played the organ very well.

Monday 26 February
Met Mr Sutton in consultation over Mrs Talbot. Went round Hospital feeling poorly with sore throat and asked Mr Lloyd to do my work for a few days. Breast case doing well but gunshot girl evidently dying with peritonitis. Dined at club..... Gave Mr Rein [?] character of Mr Swinbourne. In evening worked at paper on chronic joint disease for Bm Med. Review.

Tuesday 27 February
E Handley's dinner party 6.30. Large party. Miss E and Mr T Grimley [?], Arnold, H and G Payton. Harrison and their ladies made up the party which was well done but slow. Attended meeting of Birmingham District Land Co which was stormy and I had a row with Mr Pollach – attended QH Committee where we appointed both HS and Grinling obstetric surgeon.

Wednesday 28 February
Long round – made arrangements as to tour with Cook's representative – sent Fanny £7 to pay the scores at Llandudno before leaving. Paid call [?] of £55 to Eastern Australian and China Teleg Co. Lim for 5 new shares of £11 each for Bm Bk Co.

Thursday 1 March
Amateur Harmonic concert in Town Hall 7.30 but I got home so tired that I could not take Tadie and Lucy so we sent the tickets on to the Walford's.

Friday 2 March

Ma and Fan and the little boys returned from Llandudno and seemed very much benefited by the change.

Saturday 3 March

Performed nephrectomy on boy at 15 who was admitted with rupture of kidney on Nov 5. It was a difficult operation but was well seconded by my colleagues. Went down to town at 6 to see the insurance case by appointment and then spent an hour at the club.

Sunday 4 March

Conrad walked round with me to see my patients. To St Augustine's in the evening: long sermon about healing Jairus' daughter. Mrs Green spent the evening with us.

Monday 5 March

Amateur Dramatic at Royal Hotel 7pm to which Fan and the boys went. My case of nephrectomy doing well. Met George Yates in consultation. Took Mr and Mrs Grubb, his nephew and his niece for a ride to see the Calthorpe and Cannon Hill Parks and the Botanical Gardens; brought home some bronzes of Rubens and Rembrandt from Mr Brown [?] which I took in payment of his acc. £3.5.0.

Tuesday 6 March

Harrison's last concert to which Fan and I went. Halle's band with Mad. Norman-Neruda and Miss Orridge made it a good affair. Supped with Mrs Hopwood after taking her home.

Wednesday 7 March

Nephrectomy case going on well so I wrote annotation for the Lancet and sent it on to Dr Wakely. Went to Acock's Green and finding Mrs Atkins better asked for my acc. but without avail. Mr Herbert and Mr Wm Leah came to dinner. We had a pleasant evening. Strangely enough Mr L is going also to Rome at Easter. Sprotson paid £5 on acc. and I gave him up his IOU for £100. Although he has only paid in all £95 – still I did not like to leave lest that should be brought up against him, if anything happened to me. I drew £10 47825–6–789 from the B Bk Co to take with us.

Thursday 8 March

Mr O Pemberton's dinner 6.30 at wh. I was last to arrive, having had a very busy day so as to clear up work before leaving. I sat between Dr Mc Veagh of Coventry and Mr Baker and we got on well together. My case of nephrectomy wh. is still talked about as the last new thing exciting some attention. Walked home with Lloyd Owen. Snow on ground and a very hard frost.

Friday 9 March

Sold 25.... [?] Bank Shares to N Lea and son before leaving and drew £120 on acc. £50 I took with me, making a 2nd £50 and £70. I paid into Bm Bank Co.4. Paid Cook and Son £37/4/6 for travelling tickets for Tadie and me to Naples and back. Cleared up all patients I could and then left with Tadie at 2 for London. Fanny seeing us off: arrived at 5 and went to Charing Cross Hotel in evening with Fred Robinson and his wife to see Iolanthe – a poor affair.

Saturday 10 March

London to Paris Left London at 9.15 and crossed by boat to Boulogne. The day bright and sunny but the wind bitterly cold. We both kept the upper deck and so avoided the sea sickness. Arrived at Paris at 6.30 and then drove to the H de St Petersburg where we dined with great zest being almost famished. Went to Grand Opera afterwards and saw William Tell finely done Salomon and Melchesden [?] in principal parts... it is a magnificent concert house.

Sunday 11 March

Paris Got up late feeling very full of cold as well as very tired. Called on Dr Miller at 1 and by his advice went to see Panorama of Battle of Champigny by De Neuville and Detaille. Wonderfully realistic. In the afternoon walked down Champs Elyses to Hotel de Ville where we were turned back because the mounted Gendarmes were preventing anyone from assembling there and they looked bent on mischief. Selected us a cab and went to dinner at 7.30 at Dr Miller's. Wrote to Fanny and told her to write to me at Rome. Gave Miller a tortoiseshell cigar case.

Monday 12 March

Paris to Avignon Left H. St Petersburg at 8.15 for Gare de Lyon. Bright frosty morning so that roads were very slippery. Travelled all day with an old gentleman from Liverpool and his wife: (a regular Caution) she would have the window open and would not let me smoke so we both got bad colds. Snow covered the country all the way and made it look very wintery. We got to Avignon at 10pm and went to H d. Europe – the streets were quite deserted and the town looked empty and ancient. We breakfasted at Tonerre and dined at Dijon, but did not fare sumptuously. We were cold enough at our journey's end, but had a fire to warm us and nothing but some cognac and eau de vie before going to bed.

Tuesday 13 March

Avignon to Cannes turned out early for a walk before breakfast to see the Palace of the Popes – a gloomy old fortress now used as a barrack; the cells in wh. the cardinals were confined during the election of the pope, the chapel of the inquisition and other interesting objects shown: after breakfast saw the castle again and admired the view from Les Rochers, a garden just beyond the cathedral whence there is a fine view up and down the Rhone for miles. Also visited the Roman Bridge of wh. only part remains but wh. is a marvel of lightness and strength. Later in the musée wh. contains Horace Vernet's mazeppo. A. is his native place. Also a fine carved ivory Christ on the cross, done by a prisoner of the inquisition. T & I froze in all the streets and squares and the thermometer stood at 2° cent. so it was too cold to enjoy it much. Left A at 12 and travelled by Marseilles where we dined and had Bouillabaise. To Cannes which we reached at 10pm. Got taken in literally at H Spendide. Cheap being 12f for the night. However we were opposite the sea and had a good chintz covered room on the 3rd floor to which we were taken by a lift.

Wednesday 14 March

Cannes to Monte Carlo A lovely morning though snow had fallen and the mountains at the rear of the town even snow covered. Walked to the top of the castle hill before breakfast and also to the end of the pier and enjoyed the fine views there to be seen. After breakfast by the little steamer to Theoule a lovely sail of two hours across the mediterranean. The blue waters of which literally sparkled and danced in the sunlight. Fine view of the Isles of St Marguerite and St Honorat and of Cannes harbour [?]. We left Cannes at 1 and went to Monte Carlo for 4 hours without however risking a 5 franc piece for the place is lovely 'but man alone is vile' including women of which sex the majority of the gamblers consisted.

Dined at H. de Paris very well and then caught 7.30 train to San Remo where we put up at H.Victoria one of Cook's Hotels, pleasantly situate at .....[?] east of town.

Thursday 15 March
San Remo Spent a very bright and happy day. Comfortably lodged and well fed and amused ourselves with the company first of Mr Myers [?] who was staying at the same hotel and who took a long walk with us through the town and then over a hill whence there were exquisite views of the Iigurian Sea. Secondly of Dr Barman [?] whom we met at Monte Carlo and who has a villa here. He brought out some good Ca....[?] and was very hospitable and thirdly with Mr Squire, an English clinician on whom I called by chance to get some quince and sorrel for my cough and who turned out to be the husband of Miss Blake, Mrs Davis's protege. He invited us to his house and we saw his wife, a charming young woman, and his little girl aged 7 who was just as roguish and funny as Daisy. We then met a Mr J.... llnworth [?] of Lincoln who had a manufactory at Vienna. In the afternoon we took a 2 horse carriage and had a beautiful drive to Madonna della Guardia, a church on top of a high hill overlooking S Remo and the Med. coast for miles. Olive gardens reach up the hillsides in every direction till the snow line is met and below lemons, oranges. Palino, aloes and cacti grow in profusion, so that S Remo is one of the most lovely spots on this coast; it is however greatly spoiled by their railway running as at Dawlish along the sea shore and so preventing any promenade in front of the sea.

Friday 16 March
San Remo to Pisa Left at 7 and got to Pisa at 9 going though a succession of tunnels for the greater part of the way between wh. there were lovely glimpses every now and again of the coast. We were 8 in the carriage and too tightly packed to be very comfortable. However all our fellow travellers, foreigners, were very agreeable and chatted in French all the way. Snow was to be seen on the Appenines for some sheltered spots along the fields. Dined at Genoa in the restaurant but did not stay long. After dinner at H. de Londres turned out with 2 English gentlemen to see the leaning tower and other sites by moonlight. The tower looked very quaint [?] and ghost like and its 14 [?] feet of lop-sidedness showed with painful......[?]

Saturday 17 March

Pisa to Rome Went to PO to see for letters but found none. Walked about the streets of Pisa and along Arno admiring church of Madona della Spina. A little gem; the cathedral a notable building with mosaics by Giotto and madonna by A del Sarto. The baptistry and the leaning tower which seems as though it must topple soon and the Caccis Campo Santo with its frescoes. We had only half an hour to spare and it was much too short a time to even notice slightly all there was to be seen. Bought photos. Left Pisa at 12 and got to Rome at 10 a very tedious journey with only a short stoppage at Orbietello for dinner. The eternal city looked brilliant in the moonlight as we entered. Although we telegraphed to H.......[?] we were sent to H. de Livourne and swindled.

Sunday 18 March

Rome of which we had a good view from the roof terrace out of our bedroom on the fifth floor, embracing Pincian Gardens, Barberini Palace and not liking our room or the price (30/– for the night and breakfast) we went to H Minerva at back of Pantheon and in centre of city. Called on Father Mackey and gave up his brother's treasures. Then saw interior of Pantheon where Raphael is buried; a fine relic of old Rome with no side lights but only a round opening in centre of roof through wh. rain and sun shine equally fall. Attended English church outside P[iazza] del Popolo. Well attended. Good sermon. Staid * for sacrament. After lunch took a drive in Borghese gardens and on Pincio. Bright sunny and picturesque. Band playing. Rich and poor from the Queen of Italy downwards enjoying the sunshine and the music. The carriages are as fine as those in Hyde Park and the Italian officers are fine handsome [?]. After a very good dinner at our hotel, went to a cafe and where was a respectable company and smoked a cigar.

Monday 19 March

Rome Went to St Peter's the first thing and was much delighted with the beauty of its proportions and the lightness and elegance of the internal decorations. Its size from the outside does not appear very great but within you realize how large it is. It took Tadie 80 seconds to walk round one of the pillars which support the dome. The colossal monuments strike one with wonder and yet they are quite in character with the building. There is no stained glass but the colour of the various marbles

---

*   archaic spelling for stayed.

supplies all want of coloured light. After lunch in the P[iazza]. S Pietro went by omnibus to St John Lateran, the second finest church in Rome and the former house of the Pope from the porch of which he used to pronounce the benediction. 12 marble statues of the apostles of colossal size surround the nave. The chapel of the Corsini is very handsome and beneath it is a vault in which is a beautiful marble pieta by Bernini. Walked home by way of the Coliseum which is of wonderful size and must have been a grand place when covered with marble and adorned with statues. Thence our way lay along the Forum which is full of remains of Roman arches of Constantine Titus and Sep[timius] Severus being almost as perfect as when first erected.

Tuesday 20 March

Rome Spent the morning in the Vatican museum and although we took 4 hours to it only saw about a quarter of it. The pictures and sculptures are wonderful and would take a lifetime to master. What struck me most was the transfiguration of Raphael, the decoration of the Sistine Chapel and the Borgia Rooms in which are the Laocoon, the Apollo Belvedere and the athlete of Canova; the pope was holding a reception and from the Loggia Raphael we saw number of cardinals entering and leaving in fine carriages with black tunics. After lunch took a carriage and drove to St Maria Maggiore, another fine church St Croce where is the tomb of Helena to which no woman is admitted and the handsome church beyond the walls of recent date dedicated to St Paul and built on the spot where he was beheaded. It was a beautiful drive and we finished up with the church of St Peter in Montonio where the apostle was crucified. There is a full view of Rome from the porch of the church.

Wednesday 21 March

Rome Visited first Trajan's forum and column. Then the Palazzo Rospigiosi where is seen the lovely ceiling picture of Aurora by Guido – a thorough gem and the face by Domenichino then the Pal Quirinale where we were shown the state room of the palace of the king of Italy, the state room and dining room very handsomely filled. Pal. Barberini celebrated for Guido's Beatrice Cenci and Raphael's Fornarina both of which are rather disappointing. Andrea del Sarto's holy family and Domenichino's Adam and Eve were grand pictures the [?]... ....[?] of the .....[?] and Diana.....[?] very fine sculptures. Thermae of Diocletian and

St Maria del angeli with tomb of Salvatore Rosa. Pal. Doria is a fine palace but the pictures are not of first quality. After lunch called on Prof. Mazzoni and then down by Porta San Sebastian to Baths of Caracalla, vast ruin which shows what luxury and taste the old Romans possessed and then to the catacombs of St Calixtus along the via Appia on which are numerous sepulchral monuments.The catacombs are terrible and contain numerous sarcophagi and drawings done by the ancient christians who used them as a refuge. Spent evening with Chev. * Boses of Turin an agreeable Italian which I met.

Thursday 22 March, Rome

I spent the morning at the Hospital of St John and St James in company with Dr Polensky and Dr Mazzoni, the aids of Prof. Mazzoni who were very courteous and showed me the whole of these institutions and also the details of their surgical practice which from that Italian [?] is quite up to the mark. Lister's treatment assiduously adopted and as a result only one case of erysipelas. Although hosp. is old and its hygiene arrangements are far from perfect. After leaving there visited the House of Deputies which is a well arranged and handsomely fitted building. The chair of Garibaldi is taken away and a golden wreath of laurel occupies its place. So that no one shall ever sit there again. Had another look at the Pantheon and saw the monuments of Raphael and Victor Emanuel. The sun shining through the open centre of the roof gave the church a warm and pleasant appearance. After lunch Tadie found me and we went to the Pal. Colonna whi. contains some good portraits by Holbein, Paolo Veronese and Titian but not much else. Took carriage to Lateran museum whi. contains some fine sculptures and exquisite mosaics but nothing great re. pictures. 2nd visit to St John's church and then home by colosseum wh. satisfactory and looks grander on acquaintance and then to the palace of the caesars wh. impressed me more than anything yet seen with the magnificence of the Roman emperors in their grandeur. There are several of the old buildings of the Republic then of Augustus and Sept – Severus and other of the emperors. The Stadium basilica and house of Livia are very disturbing and also the corridor paved with exquisite mosaic in wh. Caligula was assassinated. On the way home called at church of Ara Coeli, the Tarpeian Rock wh. does not now seem very high and the church of the Jesu in which the Tenebrae was being given. Heard *Stabat Mater* at Cafe Venezia.

---

* Chevalier. Fr. Literally a knight of industry. One who lives by his wits and his savoir faire.

Friday 23 March, Rome

I spent the morning visiting the medical school and the hospitals of San Spirito and St Carlo. The former is the medical department of the university and the latter is a military hospital. Wards badly constructed – ill-ventilated and much too full. The pathological and anatomical collections far from first rate. Courteously treated by the inspector and one of the assistant physicians who showed me over the whole establishment. Met Tadie at St Peters and again admired its sculptures and magnificent proportions: heard some good music.

In the afternoon paid a visit to the museum of the Capitol where are some splendid pieces of sculpture. The Venus of the capital and Dying Gladiator being the most remarkable. Visited church of St Martino (ai Monti) where is fine recumbent bust of the saint by Bernini and in the crypt are some of the old columns of the Forum.* Walked through the Forum and wondered at its many historical arches and ruins wh. culminate in the colosseum. Afterwards had a drive in the Pincian gardens which were very empty as the evening was cold. Terrible storm at night.

Saturday 24 March, Rome Tivoli

Took bus from P. Venezia to railway station and walked thence to station of tramway beyond porta San Lorenzo The day was fine and we had an agreeable company in a Scotchman named Park: we passed a circular tomb like that of Cecilia Metella and the acqua Albrida [?] on [?] sulphur springs which are evidently strongly sulphurous. Then up a steep ascent to Tivoli which is prettily situate among the hills. From the Garden of the Sibeyella Hotel, which contains the circular temple of the Sibyl there is a fine view of the falls which are partly natural and partly artificial: The Anio forming cascades of great beauty and the water also coming through an artificial tunnel in the mountain and falling in a straight line 320 feet. Visited Neptune and the Siren's cave under the guidance of the raggedest and most cheerful cicerone I have met with. He would not be got rid of though three of the guides kicked him and tried to drive him away. Park and I walked down the hill to Adrian's villa and spent an hour exploring, but we only got a mere impression of it as it is a vast ruin and would have taken a day. At night we saw the Coliseum illuminated by the full moon and...[?]

Exchanged 2nd £10 note to pay bill at H. Minerva wh. absorbed 210 lira.

---

* actually of Baths of Trajan if the identity of the church is correct.

Sunday 25 March, Rome Tivoli

Spent the morning at St Peter's and heard High Mass by Cardinal Howard.* The singing was good but the organ poor and the procession not very grand. By chance in the crowd we met Mr H Leah who was on the look-out for us, though among ten thousand people it was little likely we should meet. Took carriage and drove to St Pietro in Vincoli to see M. Angelo's fine statue of Moses, a grand piece of artistic anatomy. Lunched at Nazzari P.di Spagna: there walked to P. del Popolo and went by train to Pavioli monte where is a fine view of Tiber and St Peter's. Saw the Sunday holiday manners [?] of the natives wh. are simple and.... Walked in the Pincian gardens and heard a good band discourse sweet music. The drapes of the ladies and of the officers very fine. On our way back to Hotel where Leah dined, called at St Trinita del Monte and Minerva.

Monday 26 March

Rome to Naples Left R at 7.40 and arrived Naples at 2 as good a bit of Ry** travelling (163 miles) as I have ever had in Italy. The line first traverses the Campagna. Then rides through the Albean mountains passing Cariali [?] and nearly all the way is through hilly country. On one elevated point is Monte Cassino Monastery, the head quarters of the Dominicans. Then through Caserta till the neighbourhood of Naples was reached wh. we knew by the smoke issuing from Mount Vesuvius wh. seems to overhang Naples. Drove in open carriage in most reckless fashion to H Nobili in best part of N near Chiaia and after lunch, walked down to the margin of the lovely bay which here has gardens, statues and a tomb of Virgil to add to the natural beauty. The enormous size of the bay with the islands of Capri and Ischia to the south and with Vesuvius to the north while the Castle of Sant' Elmo overlooks the city, form a view wh. can scarcely be surpassed. Walked around the castle of Oro as far as the king's palace and San Carlo Theatro and then returned to Hotel and dinner and staid in all evening.

Tuesday 27 March, Naples

Had a restless night so got up late and took carriage to Museo Bordonico where is a wonderful collection of statues, bronzes, pictures etc., re the Toro Farnese found at Rome and the Hercules are the finest examples I

---

* Edward Henry Howard (1829–92) was born in Nottingham. He was elevated to Cardinal in 1877.
** railway

ever saw. The remains found at Pompeii are remarkable and embrace every kind of machine and instrument in daily use. The collection of surgical instruments including specula and in rotas (uteri) struck me as very curious. Went to see the cathedral of St Jarmainus where is fine monument of St Restilucula by Canova and a special chapel in wh. the cheat of the liquefaction of the blood is carried out 3 times a year. Called on Prof. Palasciani who explained the Neopolitan operation of Lithotomy then drove in carriage to Reclusorio * past docks through heart of city, wh. is very close and dirty and on the way home fell very cold and chilly, so stayed at home all evening and took care of myself.

Wednesday 28 March, Naples – Castellammare
Passed bad night and in morning found my temp. 101. Great lassitude so lay in bed all morning and took quince but no food. Rec'd Phys, Dr Lyle, who persuaded me to stay here quietly, but as landlord would not change my room, which was on the ground floor, with a building approach to it, so that there was neither view nor sunshine, I decided to leave and go to Castellammare. Mr Leah was to have found us, so left word for him and caught 4.30 train for C. The route round the bay by Portier Rezina – Ercolaneum (the buried) torre del Greco destroyed in last eruption of 1872. Torre Annunciata and close under Mount Vesuvius is very interesting. It was blowing a gale when we got to Castellammare so we scudded as fast as the porter could carry our luggage to Hotel Royal – a large old palace of wh. we were the sole occupant. The waiter was most civil and gave us a good dinner which set me up so much that I went to the club held in the other side of the Hotel and had a genial reception from Dr Gentile, Cap P. d'Amore, the French consul and several others. We had songs and music, billiards and they stood Coffee and B. and S for me till 10[?] o'clock.

Thursday 29 March, Pompeii – Castellammare
This was by far the most notable day so far. Excursion and gave us material for much sad and mournful consideration. The day was fine, but the wind (*tramontana*) blew from the snow covered mountains at the back of C till it almost froze you to the core while the sun was very hot. A carriage and pair drove us in style to Pompeii through a well cultivated country and we arrived about 10 and spent at least two hours in exploring this buried city. The amphitheatre, tragic and comic theatres, baths, basilica, temples of

---

*   poorhouse

Jupiter, Isis and Venus with the shops, villas, houses and tombs just stand as they did in AD 79 when the flood of ashes (a sort of pumice stone) buried it. The frescoes and mosaics are some of them as clear and bright as though they had only just been painted. The bakers' ovens, the mill stone and even the lupanar * are there to testify to the customs of the ancient Romans. The houses of Meleager Glaucus, Pansa and Diomedes are the handsomest and show what luxury and taste the people of that time enjoyed. In the museum are casts of people of all ages whose bodies have been found showing the very form in which they lay when blinded and overcome by the fiery and blinding rain of ashes.

Castellammare

Returned to the H Royal to lunch. Then went with Dr Gentile to see mineral Bath Establishment which contains sulphur, iron, magnesia and acid.....[?] springs [?] in all 8. The establishment is small and out of order but the springs are rich and ought to be better known. Dr G. gave me his book and promised to write an article on C in the Lancet. Tadie had a walk from 5 till 6.30 and watched the sun set over the island of Ischia – it was a lovely sight – the clouds golden, red and purple. The Mediterranean in front of the islands showing a molten sea of gold. After dinner again joined the C. club and again rec'd much courtesy. The duet from Verdi's Macbeth and the song of Noel (Dvorák) was sung and then I being asked to sing gave There you'll Remember Me to the accompaniment of Cap. P d'Amore who tried his best to keep to my tune but was very far from it all the time. Finished up with billiards.

Friday 30 March, Castellammare Sorrento – Naples

Left C at 9 after trying in vain at 2 bankers to get a £10 note changed so losing an hour. The same carriage as yesterday but now with 3 horses drove us to Sorrento – all along the line of the lovely blue Mediterranean wh. in the sunshine looked calm and peaceful. The road resembling the Riviera and is now a very difficult road. Vines and olives are featured along the road. We arrived at Sorrento just too late for the boat for Capri so we spent the day at S buying curiosities of one sort or another under the guidance of an old man of 70 who took to us as we entered the place saying that he had acted as guide to all the kings of Europe and then we could not get rid of him. Lunched at H Mardi on a rock over looking the med. sea but 200 feet above it and where we looked right across the bay

---

* brothel

to Naples. Explored a large vineyard. Fooled around in a boat for 2 hours looking into various grottoes and finally left at 4 and steamed across to Naples. The view of the city and of Vesuvius grand. Went to Pension d'Orient.

30th Changed 3rd £10 note at Sorrento – first from Tadie's store to pay carriage to Sorrento only for 250 lira return.

Saturday 31 March, Naples

Comfortable pension with room overlooking the bay just at beginning of Chiaia. Rose at 8 and took train to Pasillipo [sic]. There walked to grotto wh. is another evidence of the clever workmanship of the Romans. It is a quarter of a mile long and leads to city of P. wh. was once home of Virgil and had its theatre and amphitheatre. Remains are still to be seen on emerging from the grotto. Here also are in sight the island of Nasida (to wh. Brutus retired) which is now a... station [?] there the bay and town of Pozzuoli – then Baiae. Cape museum and beyond the islands of *Prócida* and Ischia – a landscape of wonderful beauty and to me surpassing Sorrento. Drove back to Naples and got letters from home wh. rejoiced us. Then saw the kings palace in wh. are some handsome rooms and theatre and some good pictures. From the terrace, a grand promenade, the town and bay of N are well seen.

Left N at 2.30 for Rome and arrived at H. Minerva at 9 evening. Travelled pleasantly with Mr and Mrs Newberry.

Sunday 1 April, Rome

After a delightful warm bath, went to the English church (Trinity) service. Cold and sermon poor. Called at PO but no letters. Ate lunch at our Hotel Minerva. Father Mackey joined us and he kindly acted as our cicerone during the day. We visited the Forum and the palace of the Caesars and by his knowledge we got a much better idea of the various wealths than when going with an ordinary guide. When almost at the summit of Caesar's palace whence is a fine view of Rome and the Campagna a gentleman from below said, I think you are Dr West of B'ham. It turned out to be Dr Sleete [?] who was formerly sub editor of the Lancet and he asked me to call on him at 504 Corso wh. I did in the evening and had a pleasant chat about medical matters in Rome. Padre Mackey took us to see St Agnes a church of the Basilica type, wh. you enter by going down 20 or 30 steps and from which you enter the catacombs. The bodies are there in situ and the place but little altered in 1,500 years. On our way back to the hotel we visited church of St Maria

Maggiore wh. is also fine and has a fine chapel of all kinds of marble to the memory of the Borghese family. Wrote to Fred Robinson and Con.

Monday 2nd April, Rome to Florence

A long day in a Ry. Carriage entirely in company of Italians. It was fine on starting from H Minerva where we have been very comfortable and Rome looked brighter and cleaner than ever so that we left it with great regret..... Spent half an hour again visiting St Maria del Angeli wh. is constructed out of the baths of Diocletian. Some of the columns of a dark coloured marble now supporting the transept: left Rome at 10.30 and got to Florence at about 7 and put up at H. Caesar in centre of city through which we had a walk at night seeing the place of the Legionary where Savonarola was burned and the Uffizi Palace and also going across the Ponte Vecchio and looking down on the Arno, the sides of wh. brilliantly illuminated by a vista of gas lamps looked very pretty. Bought chocolate and had a cocktail.

Tuesday 3 April, Florence

Rose early and went to Duomo and Baptistry. Latter open but Forum closed – admired the lightness and........[?] of Giotto's campanile. Had the morning in Uffizi and Royal palaces – most in the Tribune wh. contains some of the finest paintings and sculptures. The Venus de Medici – apollo wrestlers and Sarmatian sharpening his sword. Raphael and Titian are splendidly represented. The madonna della Sedia. The Magdalen of Correggio are lovely pictures. Among the newest pictures are those of Watts, Millais and Leighton all well executed by themselves. After lunch went to Lorenzo to see the Medici chapel with its fine marbles and mosaics and above all the celebrated 'night and morning' with Cosimo de Medici of M.angelo. Drove for 2 hours in suburbs as far as San Miniato which is lovely view of F and the Val d'Arno with Fiesole on the opposite hill and the Appenines north – their snowy crests in the distance. On our way back looked in at St Croce and saw monuments of Dante, Alfiere, Machiavelli and Michelangelo – all handsome, though church is plain and not equal to our Westminster Abbey work. Left H Caesar in time for 7.40 train for Milan and travelled all night stopping 1/2 way at Bologna for a wretched lunch and getting to M at 7pm.

Wednesday 4 April, Milan and Turin

Walked through Milan in early morning and looked at Cavour and Dante monuments. La Scala – the V. Emmanuel arcade where all the shops were closed so that had to go to a small cafe in a back street and get breakfast of coffee, bread and milk for the modest sum of 1 lira. Walked through and round the lovely cathedral, the roof of wh. in the sunshine looked like a fine piece of lace. While we were there a funeral procession with candles lighted. Priest covered by a baldacchino and children singing and in the afternoon we saw another much grander at Turin. Some festival wh. was attended by 1,000 officers and soldiers and a military band. Left Milan 9 and arrived at Turin at 1. Hotel Central where Chev. Bosio, Mrs Brownly and Lady Oakes called on us, in return for our calls on them. Visited the Royal Palace wh. contains some good pictures. The armoury with Prince Eagens [?] sword and the Picture Gallery in wh. are a very few good works. Most of the rest being vile copies. Drove round town and saw public gardens. The river Po here spanned by 3 bridges. The city has broad streets with trees on each side and many fine monuments to Cavour Charles Albert. Then went to Café Romano and heard some singing.

4th Turin – changed 4th £10 note and recd. 10 napoleons and 50 lira: – 2nd from Tadie's store.

Turin to Aix les Bains At 8 Chev. Bosio whom I met at Rome called for me at H Centrale and took me to the Hospital of St John which is very large but miserably arranged and very insanitary. Prof Movaro [?] showed me round with the greatest courtesy and after gave me some of his works as did also Prof Bozzoli [?] the Prof of Medicine. The med. wards cleaner and more wholesome than the surgical and less crowded. The dissecting room and anatomical department are at the back of hospital, but in close proximity to the wards. The benefit of Lister's treatment is fully shown here for whereas without it the deaths after operation were very great now they are small and they have no erisypilas. Mr Bosio and the Prof Bozzoli [?] took me also to see University where Physiology is well taught. All appliances of recent date and approved by Virchow. Walked round town admiring its broad streets and squares with many monuments and then left at 1 for Lyons but got so bored on way that we determined to stop for the night at Aix les Bains. The route through Mount Cenis is very interesting – the actual passage of the tunnel taking 28 minutes. Gas was lit in carriages and the air was purer than in an ordinary tunnel. The descent is gradual and through some beautiful scenery. We had for fellow travellers the French Vice Consul at Turin and his little daughter at 3 who was very amusing and good. We staid after hour at Modane surrounded by mountains wh. even now are covered with snow, but unfortunately did not dine, so that we were exhausted by 9 when we arrived at Aix. Put up at H. de l' Europe and had a good room on 1st floor at 8 fr.. Walked round town wh. looked deserted and empty, calling on Dr Cazales, who unfortunately had not yet come.

Aix les Bains to Lyons Rose at 7 and went to Bath establishment and enjoyed for 1/2 hour a bathe in large piscina having only one fellow-bather so that it was comfortable water at 34 Cent. and not too sulphurous. After breakfast took Tadie out to baths too and then to see the casino wh. is being much enlarged and a theatre built. Then on towards the Grand Port in hope of seeing the lake. However as we had to leave for Lyons at 11.48 we could not reach it, but we had a fine view of Lake Boarget from the train wh. skirts it all the way to Culoz. The day was fine and the blue lake with the white crested mountains looked so beautiful that we turned our backs on them with regret. Staid an hour at Amberieu and came on to Lyons at 5. Grand Hotel de Lyon just off Place de la Bourse. 3rd floor room only 4 francs 50 and well furnished.

Before dinner walked along banks of Rhone wh. there is a fine broad rapid river with embankment on either side and bought some collars: after dinner took cab to M Olliers 3 Boul. de la Charite but he was out so we strolled about and looked in at the shops wh. are handsome but night was cold so we returned to Hotel at 9.30.

Lyons Spent the entire morning with Prof. Ollier at the Hotel Dieu and saw a great deal of good surgery, although in a dirty overcrowded Hospital where good results after operations were unknown before Listerism was introduced but now the operations are said to do well. 6 resections of the wrist and many other joint resections were doing well. Prof. O was anxious for us to dine with him and came and pressed Tadie but she could not be prevailed on so we left for Paris at 2.33. We did not get to Paris till nearly 12 – a long tedious journey broken only by a short stay at Tonnerre for dinner. On arriving at Paris cabs were at a premium but at last I laid hold of one and drove off to the Grand Hotel where we got a bed on the fourth floor at 12 fr. a day making 17 a day with candles and service – very tired with our long journey.

Sunday 8 April, Paris

Went to the English church to morning service. Called on Dr Miller but he and his family were in the country. Lunched at Cafe Valois in Palais Royal and then took steam boat to Suresnes and on landing saw one of the Eales

[?] of Longchamps. It was a bright cold day. Came back to Paris by train by way of Courbevoie and the avenue Neuilly. Dined at Duval's very well for 4 f. and then went to Grand Hotel and packed up and drove off to Gare du Nord in time to catch the express train for London. Arrived at Calais at 1.30 and at Dover at 4. The journey across was fine and very few were ill. Train got us to London at 6 and we had breakfast at Charing Cross Station. Then went to see marks of dynamite explosion at Local Government Board Offices and then to Westminster Abbey where early morning service was being read to the Westminster boys who most of them came trooping in very late. Got to Euston at 9.30 and down to B'ham at 12.20 Very glad once there to get back to Bh. [Birmingham].

Monday 9 April, London – Birmingham
Mr Leah met me at the station and I had a settlement with him receiving [?] £6 and giving him ten guineas with wh. he seemed quite satisfied. Called on J Grimley and saw other patients and all seemed glad to see me. All had colds and ma had been ill while we were away but is now better.

Tues 10 April
Lunched at Warwick House. Mr Heath severe on me for going away especially as Charlie had been so bad that Lloyd Owen had thought it right to extirpate the eye on wh. Chessire * had operated for cataract. One cannot please everyone, and selfishness seems the prevailing spirit that rules the world, of Bham at any rate. I got grumbled at today in every direction.

Wednesday 11 April
Ma and Fanny went home. Mrs Green spent the evening with us and I gave her some photos of pictures we had bought, the red stockings from Sorrento and a vol. of Tennyson for Charles wh. we thought a nice little present. I doubt however if one or other of our gifts was much appreciated. Mary has given notice to leave.

Thursday 12 April
Went round hospital with Jordan Lloyd and a few students and told them some of my Italian experiences. Called on Mrs Fisher and got a very cool reception, she having called on Mr T Bartleet.**

---

* Edwin Chessire 1819–1903.
** Thomas Hiron Bartleet 1837–91.

Friday 13 April

Drove to Solihull calling at Miss Dickins, Mrs Onions and Mr Richards. The latter seemed pleased with the Rosary blessed by the Pope wh. I bought him and which he said was just the thing he wanted.

Saturday 14 April

Mr Richards sent me Rosminian's philosophy with a very nice letter thanking me for my trifling present. Spent afternoon at Chas Green's playing lawn tennis. He and his wife have both turned abstainers and it did not seem to have improved his temper. Consultation with G Yates re Mrs Cooke.

Sunday 15 April

Had a long walk round Warley with Walter in the morning. Mr Walter Myers whom we met in San Remo, called and I went to his brother's to smoke a cigar after dinner. Dr Suffield and his daughter spent the evening with us.

Mon 16 April

Went round Hospital and then had a consultation with G Yates re case haemorrhoids. We dined at the Hen and Chickens. In evening played 3 games of billiards with councillor Jas Baldwin. He gave me 40 in 100 and strange to say I beat him. Wrote to Dr Miller. At home in evening reading and writing.

Tues 17 April

Dined at Liberal Club with Mr Sutton of the Lancash. Ass Co. Paid into B. Bk Co.

Perry and Co	£7/10
the following coupons:	
Cape of Good Hope	£11/5
New Zealand	£6/5
	£25/0

Received letters from Fred Robinson * and J Kershaw declining to my regret invitation to the Shakespeare festival.

---

* This was presumably a letter in response to the one West says that he sent him from Rome on 1 April, 1883.

APPENDIX

William Sands Cox (1801–75) FRCS, FRS, DL

Much has been written about William Sands Cox in the text of the biography. What follows is a summary for reference purposes. Born in Birmingham, the son of Edward Townsend Cox, surgeon, Cox was a pupil of King Edward's School, Birmingham. At eighteen, he became articled to his father and commenced study at The General Hospital. He subsequently studied at Guy's and St Thomas' Hospitals, London, and later in Paris under Laennec, Lisfranc, Larrey and Dupuytren, the surgeon remembered today chiefly for an operation to relieve the fibrous condition of the hand known as Dupuytren's Contracture. In 1825, at the age of just twenty four, Cox began a series of lectures in Anatomy at his father's house in Temple Row, Birmingham and it was from these beginnings that the town's school of medicine, Birmingham, Royal School of Medicine and Surgery (1836) later known as Queen's College (1843), sprung. Cox first hoped to arrange clinical instruction for his students at The General Hospital, but on finding his ambition thwarted, he founded his own hospital in 1840. The hospital opened in 1841 and was the first provincial teaching hospital in the country. Cox left Birmingham for Leamington in 1863, by which time his relationship with both college and hospital had largely broken down. On his death, Cox chose to make The Cottage Hospital, Moreton in the Marsh, Worcestershire and other existing and proposed medical institutions the beneficiaries of his will rather than the Birmingham institutions of Queen's Hospital and Queen's College. Cox's role in the election contest of 1857 can be found in the biography.

Chief sources: William Sands Cox and The Birmingham Medical School [Morrison, JTJ]; The History of the Birmingham School of Medicine [ed. Barling, Mackey and Morrison et al]; obituaries [press, medical journals].

John Birt Davies (1799–1878) MD

John Birt Davies was born in Hampshire, the son of a Welsh clergyman. He studied medicine at Edinburgh and graduated MD in 1822. He spent a year as house physician at the Edinburgh Royal Infirmary before moving to Birmingham. Once there, he was appointed to the General Dispensary. He was largely responsible for the foundation of an isolated fever hospital although it did not endure beyond a few years. Davies was an active Liberal and was one of the first magistrates appointed to the newly incorporated town council in 1838. He was made Coroner of the Borough a year later – a position he occupied for thirty-six years. Davies never elected a deputy, conducted every inquest himself, and never took a holiday throughout his time in office. He was a member of the forerunner of the British Medical Association from its foundation in 1832 and chaired the meeting at which the local branch was founded. William Sands Cox appointed Davies lecturer in Forensic medicine at his medical college in 1830 and to the post of physician to Queen's Hospital in 1841. Like Cox, Davies's part in the election dispute has been discussed in detail in the biography. *Edgbastonia* describes Davies as a man who was punctilious and attended to his duties with scrupulous care, but also as one with an irascible temper who never tolerated the slightest frivolity. In an article on Birmingham's prominent people in *The Birmingham Mail* dated, 8 July, 1899, Davies is reported to have learned shorthand in his 70th year. The whole court was said to tremble at times and if one incident typified the proceedings it is hardly surprising. A journalist was thrown to the floor along with sundry articles after a table which doubled as a seat over-balanced when one of their number stood up and left the court. Davies flew into a paralytic rage. 'This is an outrage which I as Her Majesty's representative must visit with proper punishment' he roared. 'I commit you to the gaol of this borough for fourteen days. Remove him, Freeth.' Davies did, at least, relent on discovering that the floored journalist was innocent. He lived at The Laurels, Edgbaston, birthplace of the well-known Birmingham benefactress, Miss Louisa Ryland. The house was a large red-bricked Georgian building with fourteen windows and a porch at the front. It became Edgbaston High School for Girls under Miss AJ Cooper following the death of Davies. Though elderly and frail, he nevertheless died somewhat unexpectedly while seated in his library.

Chief sources: William Sands Cox and The Birmingham Medical School [Morrison, JTJ]; The History of the Birmingham School of Medicine [ed. Barling, Mackey and Morrison et al]; obituaries [press, medical journals]; Edgbastonia; Queen's Medical Magazine (1961).

Joseph Sampson Gamgee (1828–86) MRCS, FRS Ed.

Joseph Sampson Gamgee was the son of Joseph Gamgee, a well-known English veterinary surgeon from Essex. Joseph Sampson was born in Florence during one of his family's visits to Italy. He, too, studied veterinary science initially but went on to complete his medical training at University College, London. Further study was undertaken in Paris, Pavia and Florence. He worked as a surgeon at Queen's Hospital, Birmingham, from 1857 until 1881 when ill health (probably Bright's Disease) forced him to relinquish his position and become consultant surgeon instead. The part Gamgee played in the election dispute has been covered in the biography. He is remembered today for the surgical dressings synonymous with his name, but he also founded Hospital Saturday, a workers' fund-raising project still extant as a workers' health insurance scheme and was responsible for the fund-raising efforts which led to the building of the detached fever wing of Queen's Hospital. Gamgee fathered a medical son, Leonard, who was a surgeon at The General Hospital, Birmingham, for many years. Sampson Gamgee died in Birmingham as a result of a fractured femur sustained in a fall whilst on holiday in Dartmouth, Devon. He returned to Birmingham in the care of his sons, but died some two and a half weeks later.

Chief sources: The Remarkable Gamgees A Story of Achievement [D'Arcy Thompson]; William Sands Cox and The Birmingham Medical School [Morrison, JTJ]; The History of the Birmingham School of Medicine [ed. Barling, Mackey and Morrison et al]; obituaries [press, medical journals].

Thomas Pretious Heslop (1823–85) FRCP, MD, JP

Thomas Heslop was born in the West Indies to an Irish mother and a Scottish artillery officer. He was first articled to a medical uncle, Thomas Underhill, in Staffordshire, but completed his medical education in Dublin and then Edinburgh. Heslop took a post at The General Hospital, Birmingham, before joining the team at Queen's Hospital in 1853. Disgusted by the conduct of Sands Cox and his supporters over the disputed election of West, he resigned his post at Queen's although he did resume work there in 1870. He worked alongside West at Queen's for many years and was a close personal friend and neighbour. Birmingham's Children's Hospital and the Skin Hospital both owe their existence to the efforts of Heslop, but he was also a key figure in the foundation of the Birmingham Medical Institute and the Women's Hospital. When Heslop died as a result of Angina Pectoris on holiday in Braemar, Scotland, he was Chairman of Mason College, forerunner of the University of Birmingham, and it was that institution to which he earlier gave some 11,000 books. Heslop was in the company of medical friends from Birmingham (John Carter and Robert Saundby) on the fatal day, but joined his companions when they got out of the carriage to spare the horse on its assent of a steep incline. He died within minutes of returning to the carriage. Thomas Heslop died a bachelor and was buried in Dublin alongside his mother.

Chief sources: William Sands Cox and The Birmingham Medical School [Morrison, JTJ]; The History of the Birmingham School of Medicine [ed. Barling, Mackey and Morrison et al]; obituaries [press, medical journals]; Lives of the Fellows of the Royal College of Physicians [Munk]; Edgbastonia; Children in Hospital. A Hundred Years of Child Care in Birmingham [Waterhouse, R].

Oliver Pemberton (1825–97) JP, FRCS Eng. and Edin.
A descendant of a prominent Birmingham family, Oliver Pemberton was educated at King Edward's School, Birmingham. He was an articled pupil of the surgeon, Dickenson Webster Crompton, during which time he attended lectures at Queen's College, Birmingham. Pemberton also studied at the University of London and St Bartholomew's Hospital. He returned to Birmingham in 1847 to take up a post at The General Hospital where he remained until he became the city coroner in 1891. Pemberton had given medical evidence at many trials, including that of the infamous Rugeley physician turned murderer, William Palmer, in 1856 on account of his expertise in medico-legal work. He was on the town council for over a decade and had a close association with the library. Pemberton lived for many years on the Hagley Road, Edgbaston, close to James West and his family. He had a strong interest in literature and had a substantial library. Death came at the age of seventy-two. Pemberton was still holding office as a coroner at the time and his illness surprised all. His condition came to the notice of the press on 5 March; death followed on the 8 March. Pemberton, a man who had written several papers on cancer himself, died from inoperable cancer without having suspected any such thing. Pemberton's widow died within days of her husband. They left three daughters and two sons although they had already lost one son, Thomas, who committed suicide in 1879 while a medical student.

Chief sources: Edgbastonia; Birmingham Faces and Places; Obituaries [press, medical journals].

George Jordan Lloyd (1854–1913), MRCS, LSA, FRCS, MD, Ch B, MSc, JP
The son of John Lloyd, teacher of anatomy, George Jordan Lloyd was educated at King Edward's School and at Queen's College Birmingham. He was appointed House Surgeon to Queen's Hospital in 1881 and became Honorary Surgeon there following the death of James Fitzjames Fraser West. Lloyd undertook further study in London and Durham as a young man, and at the University of Birmingham shortly after its foundation in 1900. Obituaries eulogise about Lloyd's gifts as a teacher and surgeon. He is remembered primarily for his contribution to kidney and gall-bladder surgery – a speciality he may have been drawn to early in 1883 as a result of West's nephrectomy operation and its aftermath. Jordan Lloyd wrote little. He has been described as a much-loved man who retained his boyish enthusiasm for life to the end. Matron ACG expressed the view of many when she wrote 'There was nothing small about him' and when she said he 'had the courage of his opinions' in *Edgbastonia*. That she held Lloyd in great esteem is clear although she excused his impatience on account of his 'artistic' temperament. Lloyd died at his home in Edgbaston as a result of a heart attack shortly after returning from a morning in theatre at Queen's Hospital. It had been an arduous morning. He had performed four or five operations and had had to perform artificial respiration on one of the patients, a child, who had stopped breathing. The physical effort demanded of him that morning may have cost him his life although he left the hospital knowing he had saved the life of his little patient.

Chief sources: The History of the Birmingham School of Medicine [ed. Barling, Mackey and Morrison et al]; obituaries [press, medical journals]; Edgbastonia; Æsculapius; Lives of the Fellows of the Royal College of Surgeons [Plarr].

Robert Lawson Tait (1845–99), MRCS, FRCS, LRCP, LRCS Edin.
Robert Lawson Tait was born and bred in Edinburgh. He attended Heriot's Hospital School. Tait began an Arts course at the University but abandoned it after a year. He was apprenticed instead to Alexander McKenzie Edwards and worked as his assistant for a further six years following qualification. He was favoured by both James Syme and William Fergusson during his time as a student. Tait worked for three years in Wakefield, Yorkshire, before coming to Birmingham in 1870. An application to The General Hospital in 1870 failed, but he was appointed

to the newly established Women's Hospital a year later. More has been written about Tait than any other Birmingham based contemporary of James West. All agree that Tait was an outstanding surgeon who pioneered numerous abdominal procedures and perfected others. His contribution to the reduction in mortality during and following ovariotomies is legendary but he was also first to surgically remove gall-stones, to operate for ectopic pregnancy, to remove hydatid cysts and the first to remove the uterine appendages for inflammatory disease. Tait won great acclaim in both Britain and America and was showered with distinctions. At the height of his fame and fortune, he enjoyed celebrity status. Following a visit to America and Canada in 1884, Tait was inundated with visitors from across the Atlantic to such an extent that he imposed restrictions to limit the obligation and turn it into financial gain. Visitors, he insisted, were only welcome if they would undertake a six-month pupillage for a fee of £100. Most accounts allude to his massive ego, to his outspoken outbursts and the troubles which befell him. He did not suffer fools gladly, had poor bed-side manner, was passionately opposed to vivisection and Listerism and was apt to become enraged over trivial matters. Lawson Tait's young colleague, Christopher Martin, likened Tait's temper to that of a 'raging bull' when he recounted how his superior tore a telephone [20] from the wall and dashed it to pieces on the floor following a frustrated encounter with a telephone operator. Tait fell from grace in the last seven years of his life. Unafraid of criticism or controversy, Tait had enemies. In 1892, Dr Denholm of Manchester sued him for libel and a paternity suit was served on him by one of the nurses at the hospital. Defamatory statements and rumours spread quickly and Tait was virtually ostracised by Dr Ernest Hart, editor of the BMJ. His reputation suffered a further blow the following year when his predilection for 'spaying' women was exposed. Tait had thought nothing of removing the healthy ovaries of the insane and the not-so-insane to combat melancholy, hysteria and mania. Whether Tait's actions were inspired by a genuine desire to alleviate suffering or by eugenics is unknown but they were thought unacceptable by most. Tait died from uræmia in his house in Llandudno, north Wales, after having informed the assembled company that he had just smoked his last cigar. His body was cremated at Liverpool – a decision no doubt at odds with the majority and certainly at odds with Catholicism, the religion he had been

---

[20] Tait is on record as having used a telephone as early as 1884. By 1886 he was one of four doctors out of twenty-seven private individuals listed in the National Telephone Company's List of Subscribers for Birmingham.

born into and brought up to endorse. Tait had, in any case, turned his back on religious doctrine years earlier.

Chief sources: Lives of the Fellows of the Royal College of Surgeons [Plarr]; Lawson Tait. The Rebellious Surgeon [John Shepherd]; Lawson Tait. His Life and Work with Personal Reminiscences [Christopher Martin]; Obituaries [medical journals, press]; Æsculapius.

BIBLIOGRAPHY

PRIMARY SOURCES
Miscellaneous
Case Book of Jordan Lloyd for 1893 [ms. 1510/1] (BCA)
Census for 1851, 1861, 1871, 1881, 1891 and 1901
Contemporary maps from *Plans of Birmingham and Vicinity.
Ancient and Modern*
Coroners' Inquest Files. 2/187D/197; 2/1876A/58; 2/1876A/88;
2/1876C/140. (BCA)
Parish records [various]
Privately owned archive of JFF West
Wills [various]

SECONDARY SOURCES
The references of some source material will be identified as follows:
Birmingham City Archives (BCA); The Birmingham Medical Institute
(BMed.I); and the Barnes Medical Library, University of
Birmingham (Barnes Library)
The JFF West Archive is in the private ownership of G.M. Goodman.
Some sources (eg. parish records and wills) have come from record
offices in various parts of the country and are not listed separately.
The remainder, unless stated otherwise, are available in
Birmingham Central Library

Magazines and Newspapers
Æsculapius The University of Birmingham Medical and Dental Graduates
Society Journal, 1981, 1982, 1986, 1991 (Barnes)
Argus [various]
Aris's Gazette, [various]
Birmingham Daily Post [various]
Birmingham Faces and Places 1889–93
Birmingham Gazette [various]
The Daily Mail [various]
Edgbastonia 1881–1921

Medical Journals and Directories
Birmingham Medical Institute Reports [various] (B.Med.I)
British Medical Journal – assorted 1850–1935
Birmingham Medical Review. 1872–83 (B.Med.I)
General Medical Council Register [various]
Index Medicus 1879–83 (Barnes)
Medical Directories [various]
Medical Times and Gazette [various] (Barnes)
The Dublin Quarterly Journal of Medical Science [various] (Wellcome Library)
The Lancet 1850–1935

Directories
Bisset's Magnificent Guide or Grand Copperplate Directory for the Town of
    Birmingham 1808
Edgbaston Directory 1853
Hulley's [various]
Kelly's [various]
Post Office [various]

Society Records
Birmingham Dramatic and Literary Club 1877–1905
Birmingham Medical Benevolent Society 1821–1900 (B. Med. I.)
Birmingham Medical Institute 1875–96 (B. Med. I.)
Midland Medical Society 1863–1900 (B. Med. I.)

Hospital Records
Queen's Hospital Records: M.S 1942 (BCA)
General Committee Book: January, 1873 – July, 1876; April, 1876 – April,
    1880; June, 1870 – February, 1872; May, 1880 – February, 1886;
    March, 1896 – March, 1907
House Committee Report Book: 1869–1871; 1866–1869;
    February 1883 – August, 1887; April, 1879 – February 1883
The General Hospital Records: MS 1921 (BCA)
General Hospital Board Minute Book, 1842–62
Medical Board Committee; 1855–67
Weekly Board Minute Book, 1870–78
House Committee Minute Book, 1885–89
Medical Patient Book, 1876–86;

Surgical Inpatient Book, 1862–79
Medical Inpatients, 1876–86
St Thomas' Hospital Reports: (St Thomas' Medical School Library)
St Thomas' Hospital Reports edited by Dr R. Cory and Mr F. Mason. Volume
    10 1879
The Children's Hospital Reports: 1/4/3 (BCA)
Medical Committee Minute Book, September, 1877 – January, 1893
Dental Hospital Records: (Birmingham Dental Hospital Library)
Dental Hospital Minute Book, 19 March, 1880 – 16 August, 1887
    Surgical Committee

BARNSBY GJ *Social Conditions in the Black Country 1800–1900,*
    (Wolverhampton: Integrated Publishing Services, 1980)
BRIGGS, A *Victorian Cities* (London: Penguin, 1963)
BROWN, GH (compiler): Munk*: Lives of the Fellows of the Royal
    College of Physicians of London, 1826–1925.*
    (London: The College, 1955)
BUNCE, JT *History of the Corporation of Birmingham, Vol 2*
    (Birmingham: Cornish Brothers, 1885)
CANNADINE, D *Lords and Landlords. The Aristocracy and the Towns.
    1774–1967* (England: Leicester University Press, 1980)
CARR-SAUNDERS, AM AND WILSON, PA *The Professions*
    (Oxford: GB, 1933)
CHEESEWRIGHT, M *Mirror to a Mermaid. Pictorial reminiscences of
    Mason College and the University of Birmingham 1875–1975*
    (Birmingham: University of Birmingham, 1975)
CHERRY, GE *Birmingham: A Study in Geography, History and Planning*
    (Chichester, England: John Wiley & Sons, 1994)
COHEN, RA *The History of the Dental Hospital and Dental School 1858–1958*
    (Birmingham: Board of Governors of the United Birmingham
    Hospitals, 1958)
COPEMAN, WCS *The Worshipful Society of Apothecaries of London.
    A History 1617–1967* (London, 1967)
D'ARCY, THOMPSON *The Remarkable Gamgees. A Story of Achievement*
    (Edinburgh: Ramsey Head Press, 1974)
D'ARCY POWER; Revised Plarr: *Lives of the Fellows of the Royal College of
    Surgeons. of England.* (published by the Royal College of Surgeons in
    two volumes, 1930)

DAVIDOFF, LEONORE AND HALL, CATHERINE *Family Fortunes. Men and Women of the English Middle Class 1780–1850* (London: Routledge, 1988)

DINGWALL, R AND LEWIS, P *The Sociology of the Professions. Lawyers, Doctors and Others* (London: Macmillan, 1983)

ELLIOT, BRIAN *The Making of Barnsley* (Barnsley, South Yorkshire: Wharncliffe Publishing Limited, 1988)

ELLIOTT, P *The Sociology of the Professions* (London: Macmillan, 1972)

ELLIS, H *Bailey and Bishop's Notable Names in Medicine and Surgery* [4th, edition – revised version] (London: Lewis, 1983)

ELLIS, HAROLD *Operations that made History* (Great Britain: Greenwich Medical Media, 1996)

ELLIS, HAROLD *Surgical Case – Histories from the Past* (London: Royal Society of Medicine Press, 1994)

GOURVISH, JR AND O'DAY, A (editors) *Later Victorian Britain 1867–1900* (Basingstoke: Macmillan Educational, 1988)

GRANSHAW, LINDSAY PATRICIA *St Thomas' Hospital, London. 1850–1900* [facsimile copy of PhD] (USA: University Microfilms International, Ann Arbor, Michigan, 1981)

GRAY, ERNEST A *By Candlelight. The Life of Dr Arthur Hill Hassall, 1817–94* (London: Robert Hale, 1983)

HÆGER, KNUT *The Illustrated History of Surgery* (Sweden: Harold Starke Publishers Ltd., 1988)

HALL, BRIAN *Aspects of Birmingham*, (England: Wharncliffe Books, 2001)

HAMPSON, MARTIN *Images of England, Edgbaston*, (England: Tempus Publishing Ltd., 1999)

HANDFORD, MARGARET *Sounds Unlikely. Six Hundred Years of Music in Birmingham, 1392–1992* (Worcestershire, England: Droitwich Print, 1992)

HAWKINS, CLIFFORD *Mishap or Malpractice?* (London: Blackwell, 1985)

HEY, DAVID *Yorkshire from AD 1000* (London: Longman, 1986)

JACKSON, LEE & NATHAN ERIC *The Victorian Dictionary. The Social History of Victorian London* (London: New Holland, 2004)

JOHNSON, TJ *Professions and Power* (London: Macmillan,1972)

LANE, J AND BEARMAN, R (editors) *Dr Jephson of Leamington Spa*. by Baxter, E.G. (Warwickshire: Warwickshire Local History Society, 47, Newbold Terrace, Leamington Spa. 1980)

LAZZETTI, GIOVANNI AND RIGUTTI, ENRICO (collaborators), *Atlas of Human Anatomy* (Surrey: TAJ Books Ltd., 2002)

LOUDON, I *Medical Care and the General Practitioner 1750–1850* (New York: OUP, 1986)

MCINNES, EM *St Thomas' Hospital* (Great Britain: Special Trustees for St Thomas' Hospital, 1990)

MCLACHLAN, GORDON & MCKEOWN, THOMAS (editors) *Medical History and Medical Care. A Symposium of Perspectives* (London: OUP, 1971)

MARLAND, H *Medicine and Society in Wakefield and Huddersfield 1780–1870* (Cambridge: C.U.P., 1987)

MOORE, RICHARD *Leeches to Lasers Sketches of a Medical Family.* (Ireland: Morrigan, 2002)

MORRISON, JTJ *William Sands Cox and The Birmingham Medical School* (Birmingham: Birmingham Cornish Brothers, 1926)

MURPHY, J KEOGH *The Practitioner's Encyclopædia of Medicine and Surgery in all their branches* (London: Henry Frowde OUP Hodder and Stoughton, 1913 second edition)

PARSONS, FG *The History of St Thomas' Hospital, from 1800–1900. Vol 3* (London: Methuen and Co. Ltd., 1936)

PERKIN, H *The Rise of Professional Society. England since 1880* (London: Routledge, 1989)

PETERSON, MJ *The Medical Profession in Mid-Victorian London.* (Berkeley: California, 1978)

PICKSTONE, JV *Medicine and Industrial Society. A History of Hospital Development in Manchester and its region 1752–1946* (London: Routledge, 1985)

POPE, REX (editor), *Atlas of British Social and Economic History since c. 1700* (New York: Macmillan Publishing Company, 1989)

PORTER, ROY *The Greatest Benefit to Mankind. A Medical History of Humanity from Antiquity to the Present* (London: Harper Collins, 1997)

QUAIN RICHARD (editor) *Quain's Dictionary of Medicine*: (London: Longmans, Green and Co., 1883)

READER, WJ *Professional Men – The Rise of the Professional Classes in Nineteenth Century England* (London: Weidenfeld and Nicolson, 1966)

REID, R *Microbes and Men* (London: BBC, 1974)

RUTKOW, IRA M Surgery. *An Illustrated History* (USA: Mosby Year Book Incorporated, 1993)

SHEPHERD, JAMES *Lawson Tait. The Rebellious Surgeon. 1845–1899* (USA: Coronado Press, 1980)

SKIPP, VICTOR *The Making of Birmingham* (Birmingham: published by the author, 1983)

SLATER, TERRY *Edgbaston A History* (England: Phillimore & Co. Ltd, 2002)

SOURNIA, JEAN CHARLES *The Illustrated History of Medicine* (England: Harold Starke Publishers Ltd., 1992)

STEVENSON, JUNE; STANLEY, CHRISTINE & FELL, SUSAN for Federation of Women's Institutes *The South and West Yorkshire Village Book* (England: Printed by JW Arrowsmith Ltd., Bristol, 1991)

TAYLOR, WARWICK *South Yorkshire Pits*, (England: Wharncliffe Books, 2001)

THOMPSON, FML *The Rise of Respectable Society* (Glasgow: Fontana Press, 1988)

TRAINOR, R *Black Country Elites. The Exercise of Authority in an Industrialised Area. 1830–1900* (USA: OUP, 1993)

VINCE, CA *History of the Corporation of Birmingham, Vol 3* (Birmingham: Cornish Brothers, 1902)

WADDINGTON, I *The Medical Profession in the Industrial Revolution* (Dublin: Gill and Macmillian, 1984)

WADE, OL *The Romance of Remedies* (Durham: Durham Academic Press, 1996)

WALLACE, ANTONY F *The Progress of Plastic Surgery, An Introductory History* (Oxford: Willem A Meeuws, 1982)

WATERHOUSE, RACHEL *Children in Hospital. A Hundred Years of Child Care in Birmingham* (London: Hutchinson, 1962)

WEAR, A AND FRENCH, R (editors) *British Medicine in the Age of Reform* (London: Routledge, 1991)

WOMEN'S INSTITUTE COMPILATION of notes on South and West Yorkshire, *The South and West Yorkshire Village Book* (Newbury, Berkshire: Countryside Books, Newbury, the SYFWI, Doncaster and WYFWI, Leeds, 1991)

WISE, SARAH *The Italian Boy. Murder and Grave-Robbery in 1830s London* (London: Jonathan Cape, 2004)

ARTICLES

ANON, (Copy of article on the removal of St Thomas' Hospital to its new site taken from the Illustrated News of 27 December, 1862) *St Thomas' Hospital Gazette; Spring 1982.* pp.14–15

ANON, Medical Students at Work. Sketches at St Thomas' Hospital; (article from *The Graphic*, 2 October, 1886); *St Thomas' Hospital Gazette; Summer 1985.* pp.76–83

CROFT, DESMOND A Family Perspective Part II 1850–1994; *St Thomas' Hospital Gazette; Summer 1995.* pp.17–19

DAVIS, BT John Birt Davies. First Coroner for Birmingham; *Queen's Medical Magazine*; 1961; Volume 53: pp 179–182

FORD, JOHN A District General Hospital; *St Thomas' Hospital Gazette; Winter 1981.* pp.102–106

FORD, JOHN Lord Lister at St Thomas'; *St Thomas' Hospital Gazette; Summer 1983.* pp.59–62

JOINT COMMITTEE OF THE MEDICAL FACULTY OF THE UNIVERSITY OF BIRMINGHAM AND THE BIRMINGHAM MEDICAL REVIEW, *The History of the Birmingham School of Medicine. A Special Number of The Birmingham Medical Review 1825–1925* (Birmingham, Cornish Brothers Limited. 1925)

LOUDON, I Doctors and Their Transport, 1750–1914; *Medical History*; 2001; 45: pp.185–206

LOUDON, I Two Thousand Medical Men in 1847; *Bulletin of the Society for the Social History of Medicine*; 1983; 33: pp.4–8

MARTIN, CHRISTOPHER; Lawson Tait. His Life and Work with Personal Reminiscences; Reprinted from *Journal of Obstetrics and Gynæcology of the British Empire*; 1921; Spring: pp. 2–7

MARTIN, CHRISTOPHER Some Reminiscences of Lawson Tait; Birmingham Medical Review; 1931; Volume 6: pp.137–142

PENNINGTON, TH Listerism, its Decline and its Persistence: the Introduction of aseptic surgical Techniques in three British Teaching Hospitals, 1890–99. *Medical History.* pp.35–60

PITHER, CHARLES Anæsthesia at St Thomas'. The Early Days 1848–1878; *St Thomas' Hospital Gazette, Winter and Summer* No. 85, 1987

REDFERN, JB Elite Suburbians: Early Victorian Edgbaston; *The Local Historian*; 1982–3; 15.

STONE, AFM AND STONE, WD Lady Mary Wortley Montagu: medical
    and religious controversy following her introduction of smallpox
    inoculation; *Journal of Medical Biography; November, 2002; Vol 10:* pp
    232–236.
WHARTON, THOMAS Sir Astley Cooper and the Resurrectionists; *St
    Thomas' Hospital Gazette, Winter 1986.* pp.38–40
WILLIAMS, TIM Sir Astley Cooper (1768–1841); *St Thomas' Hospital
    Gazette; Summer 1986.* pp.7–8